The U.S. Merchant Marine

The U.S. Merchant Marine

IN SEARCH OF AN ENDURING MARITIME POLICY

By Clinton H. Whitehurst, Jr.

NAVAL INSTITUTE PRESS
Annapolis, Maryland

Copyright © 1983
by the United States Naval Institute
Annapolis, Maryland

Library of Congress Cataloging in Publication Data

Whitehurst, Clinton H., 1927–
  The U.S. merchant marine.

  Bibliography: p.
  Includes index.
  1. Merchant marine—United States—Addresses, essays,
lectures. 2. Shipping—United States—Addresses,
essays, lectures. I. Title. II. Title: US merchant
marine. III. Title: United States merchant marine.
HE745.W495   1983   387.5′068   83-13467
ISBN 0-87021-737-2

To the merchant seamen
who served in
World War II

Lest We Forget

Sometimes when the bands are playing
    And the uniforms march by
You will find a seaman watching
    With a wistful-looking eye,
And you know just what he's thinking
    As he hears the cheering crowd
As the soldiers and the sailors
    Swing along, erect and proud.

He is thinking that his country
    Saves its honors once again
For the uniforms, forgetting
    All the seas' forgotten men.
He is thinking of the armies
    And the food and fighting tanks
That for every safe arrival
    To the seamen owe their thanks.

He is thinking of those buddies
    Who have paid the final score,
Not in khaki or in navy
    But the working clothes they wore;
And we'd like to tell him something
    That we think he may not know
A reminder he can stow away
    Wherever he may go.

All your countrymen are proud of you
    And though there's no brass band
Not a bugle or a banner
    When the merchant seamen land,
We know just the job you're doing
    In your worn-out, working clothes
On the seas where death is lurking
    And a fellow's courage shows.

So be sure to keep your chin up
    When the uniforms parade
What a man wears doesn't matter
    It's the stuff of which he's made!

Author Unknown

Contents

Preface

In 1980 an old friend who has represented U.S. shipping interests in Washington for longer than either of us cares to remember wrote asking where he might obtain a "broad-gauged textbook on the merchant marine." He was planning to hire two new employees, neither of whom had any knowledge of ocean shipping, its history, or the economic, political, and legal environment in which it operated.

Since 1954, when Carl E. McDowell and Helen M. Gibbs wrote the classic *Ocean Transportation*, many authors have written excellent books on the ocean shipping industry. The bibliography in this volume lists many of them. But each of these books has dealt with a specific area—operations, government policy, subsidies, national defense, and shipping economics, to name but a few. While several of these could provide a reading list more than sufficient for a graduate course in ocean transportation, no single book has comprehensively examined the industry and the environment in which the industry will be operating in the 1980s and beyond. This book intends to do so, and to be a "broad-gauged textbook" for students of the merchant marine both inside and outside of the classroom.

In 1954 the active U.S. merchant fleet stood at 1,123 vessels, of which 709 were employed in foreign trade. In numbers of merchant ships, including government-owned ships, the United States ranked first in the world. U.S.-flag ships lifted a respectable 27 percent of total tons of cargo carried in U.S. foreign trade, while the United States' share of cargo moving in its liner trades was almost 40 percent. Moreover, in 1954 the recent passage of a comprehensive cargo preference bill (legislation mandating that a fixed percentage of U.S. government–paid for cargoes would move in U.S.-flag ships) seemed to insure a permanent and significant American presence on the world's trade routes. Flag-of-convenience registry was not perceived to be a threat to the industry in the early

1950s nor was the size of the federal budget and federal deficits a major political issue.

Under such conditions, it is not surprising that the McDowell and Gibbs text devoted much space to the history and process of shipping, including such topics as vessel operations, traffic management, firm organization, marine insurance, and admiralty law.

However, the shipping world of the 1980s is quite different. U.S.-flag vessels move less than 4 percent of the country's oceanborne commerce in terms of total tons, while the United States' liner share is less than 28 percent. In late 1982 the active, privately owned fleet totalled 500 ships, and the United States barely held onto an eleventh place world ranking. The fiscal year 1984 federal deficit is projected to exceed $150 billion, and all government programs, including government support of the merchant marine, are receiving their closest scrutiny in over half a century. Perhaps most important, in the 1980s America is no longer the world's only superpower. It has been challenged on every front by the Soviet Union, particularly at sea, where the United States once dominated.

In such an environment, a book on merchant shipping must devote a large share of its pages to government policy, industry problems, and national security. This book does so and gives less attention to history and shipping operations. On the other hand, to emphasize that the merchant marine is a part of the total national logistic system—an emphasis that is long overdue—it includes chapters on ports and the intermodal transportation system.

One of the book's strengths is that outside authorities have contributed chapters in their fields of expertise. Key topics are treated more than once, and this overlap gives the reader different views of the knotty issues facing the industry in the 1980s. All the writers agree on this, however—the national security of the United States requires a significant American-flag presence at sea.

Many people made the book possible. A special thanks goes to Al May, Executive Vice President, Council of American-Flag Ship Operators; Emanuel Rouvelas of the law firm of Preston, Thorgrimson, Ellis and Holman, one of Washington's most knowledgeable maritime attorneys; Burt Kyle, former Director of Ship Operations at the Maritime Administration; Bob Bryan, Chief, Reserve Fleet, at the Maritime Administration; Esther Love, Deputy Director of Maritime Labor and Training at the Maritime Administration; Isaac C. Kidd, Jr., Admiral, U.S. Navy (Ret.); David Bess, Dean of the College of Business Administration and Professor of Transportation at the University of Hawaii; and Joe Walsh of the U.S. General Accounting Office.

Closer to home, I thank my wife Marion for her encouragement and never failing optimism, Betty Woodall, who deserves a large share of credit for everything I have written over the past ten years, and Mike Hickey, my graduate research assistant, for his untiring efforts in the Clemson University libraries. To those many others too numerous to mention, I can only say that their assistance is appreciated and not forgotten.

The opinions, conclusions, and recommendations made in the book are solely those of the authors and not those of the Naval Institute Press. By the same token, a contributor's inclusion in the book does not imply that the contributor agrees generally or specifically with the opinions, conclusions, and recommendations made in the book by the other contributors.

About the Contributors

Herbert Brand is Chairman of the Transportation Institute in Washington, D.C. Earlier, he worked for twenty years with the Seafarers International Union of North America, AFL-CIO, where he was Director of the Research, Education, and Publication Departments. He is a member of the Propeller Club of the United States and served for seven years on the Advisory Board of the U.S. Merchant Marine Academy.

Henry R. Del Mar (Major General, U.S. Army, retired) is Vice-President of Southern Pacific Transportation Company and President of the National Maritime Council. His last assignment in thirty-five years of army service was Commander of the Military Traffic Management Command. In this position he instituted origin-to-destination transportation management and began the Highways, Railroads, and Ports for National Defense Program. He has an undergraduate degree from New York University and a master's degree from Long Island University.

Andrew E. Gibson is President of Delta Steamship Lines. He was a Deck Officer and Master of U.S. Lines' ships and a U.S. Navy Lieutenant in the Korean War. He has worked in the Department of Commerce as Assistant Secretary for Domestic and International Business and Assistant Secretary for Maritime Affairs. He holds a master's degree in business administration from New York University and is a graduate of Brown University and of the advanced management program of Harvard University.

Ralph J. Nahra is Scientific Advisor and Assistant Chief of Staff for Analysis at Headquarters, Commander in Chief Atlantic (CINCLANT) and Headquarters, Supreme Allied Commander Atlantic (SACLANT) and has managed studies of defense issues and programs for over fifteen years. He received his bachelor's and master's degrees in electrical engineering from Case Western Reserve University.

Lawrence J. O'Brien has a private law practice and was Chief Counsel of the House Merchant Marine and Fisheries Committee from 1978 to

1981. After graduating from Georgetown University in 1968, he served four years as a Second Lieutenant in army infantry units in the United States, Korea, and Vietnam. He later earned law and master of law degrees from Georgetown University.

Paul R. Tregurtha is President and Chief Operating Officer of Moore-McCormack Resources, Inc. He is a member of the Cornell University Council Administrative Board and Council for the Graduate School of Business and Public Administration and has been a guest lecturer at Cornell and Harvard University. He holds a degree in mechanical engineering from Cornell and a master's degree in business administration from Harvard.

Abbreviations Used in the Text

CAR	Construction, alteration, and repair
CCF	Capital construction fund
CDS	Construction differential subsidy
DOD	Department of Defense
DWT	Deadweight tons
EUSC	Effective U.S. control (shipping)
FMC	Federal Maritime Commission
GAO	General Accounting Office
GT	Gross tons
JMC	Joint Maritime Congress
LASH	Lighter aboard ship
LDC	Lesser developed countries
LNG	Liquid natural gas carrier
LOOP	Louisiana Offshore Oil Port
LORAN	Long range navigation
LOTS	Logistics over the shore
MarAd	Maritime Administration, Department of Transportation
MOT	Military Ocean Terminal
MSC	Military Sealift Command
MTMC	Military Traffic Management Command
NADOT	North Atlantic deep-water oil terminal
NDF	National defense feature
NDRF	National Defense Reserve Fleet
OBO	Ore-bulk-oil carrier
ODS	Operating differential subsidy
OECD	Organization for Economic Cooperation and Development
OMB	Office of Management and Budget
RDF	Rapid Deployment Force
RDJTF	Rapid Deployment Joint Task Force

RO/RO	Roll-on/roll-off
RRF	Ready Reserve Force
SRP	Sealift Readiness Program
TEU	Twenty-foot container equivalent unit
ULCC	Ultra Large Crude Carrier
UNCTAD	United Nations Conference on Trade and Development
UNREP	Underway replenishment
VLBC	Very Large Bulk Carrier
VLCC	Very Large Crude Carrier

The U.S. Merchant Marine

1 The U.S. Merchant Marine Past and Present

Merchant shipping is one of North America's oldest enterprises. Its beginnings parallel the first English settlements. As the colonists were struggling to survive at Jamestown in 1607, the bark *Virginia* was being built on the banks of the Kennebec River in Maine. In 1631 the first seagoing vessel, *Blessing of the Bay*, was launched in Massachusetts.[1] The merchant-shipowners of the New England and the Middle Atlantic colonies became men of influence and wealth. In Maryland, Virginia, and the Carolinas the hallmark of a successful planter was that he owned his ships and was not dependent upon others to carry his tobacco, sugar, rice, and indigo to European markets.

A century and a half later, when war with England finally came, it was the colonies' merchant ships and merchant mariners that gave birth to the American navy. Merchant vessels operating as privateers or under letters of marque also contributed to the ultimate American victory. Over four hundred were at sea in 1781 and, while they could in no way directly challenge the English fleet, they ranged the Atlantic, showed the flag, and in so doing foretold the maritime greatness to come.

In the colonial period and first half of the nineteenth century, American ships and shipbuilders were more than equal to world competition. Between 1800 and 1840, U.S.-flag ships carried over 80 percent of the country's foreign commerce, while American shipyards could build their best ships for £ 3–4 a ton compared to £ 5–7 a ton in England.[2] Shipbuilding was a major industry. Order books were almost always full. An abundance of cheap and close-by timber, combined with good workmanship and innovative designs, gave American builders a significant competitive advantage.

Interestingly enough, it was in this early period of our maritime history that the federal government embarked upon a policy of protectionism for domestic shipping and shipbuilding interests. Acts passed in 1789 and 1790 levied heavy duties on foreign-flag, foreign-built vessels engaged in trade between American ports, the so-called coastal trades.[3] In 1817 this commerce was reserved exclusively for U.S.-flag, U.S.-built ships.[4] The legislation was later extended to include the intercoastal trade and trade between the United States and its offshore possessions and territories. With respect to foreign commerce, U.S. registry was denied to all but American-built vessels.[5]

The main purpose of these early protectionist laws was to pressure Great Britain and other European maritime powers into rescinding or modifying laws that excluded American ships from their trades. With the repeal of the last of the British Navigation Acts in 1849, America had to all intent and purpose accomplished its goal. U.S. exclusionary laws, however, were neither repealed nor modified.

The practical effect of our protectionist policy was to insure the existence of a domestic trade fleet in some form or other. Investment in this shipping would vary over time depending upon the extent to which it could compete with land transportation, i.e., the railroads and later long-haul highway trucking.

The foreign trade merchant marine was another matter. The requirement that U.S.-flag ships engaged in foreign trade be American built effectively tied the success of that part of the industry to how well U.S. shipyards could compete in price with their foreign counterparts.

If the 250 years since the launching of the *Virginia* in 1607 had been kind to American maritime fortunes, the latter half of the nineteenth century saw the beginning of a long-term decline. By and large, content with the good profits earned by wooden sailing vessels in an era that reached its zenith with the clipper ships, American owners and builders were late in accepting and developing iron (and later steel) hulls, compound engines, and the screw propeller. Rudyard Kipling was an accurate chronicler of this era of rapidly changing marine technology and its effect when he wrote in 1894:

> I knew—*I* knew what was coming, when we bid on the *Byfleet*'s keel—
> They piddled and piffled with iron. I'd given my orders for steel!
> Steel and the first expansions. It paid, I tell you, it paid,
> When we came with our nine-knot freighters and collared the long-run trade!
> And they asked me how I did it, and I gave 'em the Scripture text,
> "You keep your light so shining a little in front o' the next!"
> Rudyard Kipling, "The Mary Gloster"

In any case, the United States became a relatively high cost nation with respect to both building and operating a merchant marine. No longer was timber plentiful, close by, and cheap, and statutes protecting our infant iron and steel industry put the better quality and cheaper British product out of reach of our shipbuilders. Moreover, better pay and profit opportunities had beckoned men and capital into new manufacturing enterprises and western land development. The country's best young men no longer went to sea, nor did its best entrepreneurial talent invest in marine enterprises. Although America's merchant marine would later reach peaks of greatness in two world wars, it would also decline again when hostilities ended.

Whaling

No introduction to U.S. maritime history would be complete without noting the important part the whale fisheries played in developing and sustaining the American merchant marine during the eighteenth and nineteenth centuries.

In the seventeenth century, whales were found in abundance off the New England coasts; the first whaling vessels were relatively small, and cruises were generally no longer than six weeks. The industry was concentrated in New England, in particular the port of Nantucket.

Whaling activity in both the Revolution and War of 1812 declined to virtually nothing, but after both wars it recovered quickly. By 1821, American vessels were seen at all of the world's major whaling grounds. In this period the price of sperm oil rose from less than $1 a gallon to over $1.75. Voyage profits were high. One ship, the *Lagoda*, netted an average of 98 percent profit on six voyages between 1841 and 1860.[6] In the period of 1835–60 an average of 600 whaling vessels flew the American flag. A high point was reached in 1846, when 736 whaling vessels were registered at thirty-four U.S. ports.[7]

Year	No. of Vessels	Tonnage
1846	736	233,262
1856	635	199,141
1866	263	68,535
1876	169	38,883
1886	124	29,118
1896	77	16,358
1906	42	9,878

During the Civil War the whaling fleet declined from 514 to 263 ships. It would never again attain its prewar importance. While ship losses from Confederate raiders, especially in the Pacific, were costly, of greater importance in the demise of the fleet was that the opportunity for making large profits had passed. Whales were now much farther away, and voyages were of the order of two to four years. One authority concluded, "More than anything else, the increasing scarcity of whales in the established whaling grounds placed American whaling beyond the pale of profitable enterprise."[8]

Other factors also contributed to the decline of the industry. The value of whalebone was decreased by the invention of the steel spring, and in 1871 the entire New England arctic fleet of thirty-four vessels was crushed in the ice. But perhaps most important was the competition from another type of oil. In 1859 the first oil gusher in the United States (Pennsylvania) was brought in.

> The struggle between the two oils was short and sharp. Kerosene came rapidly in general use, lubricating oils were manufactured from the residuum, and the introduction of the wax or paraffin for making candles finally sealed the battle.[9]

While whaling continued into the twentieth century, it was on a much reduced scale. By 1906 the fleet was reduced to forty-two vessels registered in three ports. The earlier invention of the harpoon gun and the coming of steel and steamships all made a contribution to extending the life of the industry, but it was not enough. An era was coming to a close. The last U.S.-flag whaler, the *John R. Manta*, sailed from New Bedford, Massachusetts, in 1925.[10]

Merchant Ships and National Needs

Any student who has completed a first course in economic principles knows that a necessary condition for trade between individuals, regions, or countries is that both parties must benefit, i.e., gain from the exchange. In individual or local transactions, the exchange is made with little or no transportation charge being levied. Buying or selling a house or car, and purchasing legal or medical services, are common examples. However, when a significant distance separates the transacting parties, transportation is crucial. No matter that the colonial planter and English manufacturer would mutually benefit from an exchange of tobacco and ironware, the gain could not be realized unless there was a way—transportation—to bring the tobacco to England and the ironware to Virginia. In the colonial period the way was by ship. Three hundred years later the same is still true. In 1982, over 99 percent of U.S. imports and exports in terms of shipping weight moved in vessels.

Table 1.1 shows these aspects of U.S. oceanborne foreign trade in 1980: the number of tons carried, value, industry segment (i.e., liner, nonliner, and tanker), and percent moved in U.S. ships.

Although the needs of commerce have been the driving force behind investment in a merchant marine, other reasons exist for encouraging national-flag shipping. In addition to supporting commerce, Title I of the Merchant Marine Act of 1936, as amended, cites the national defense as a compelling reason for having a merchant fleet.

One way to gauge the need for a merchant marine is to consider those circumstances under which a nation might reasonably choose *not* to

Table 1.1. U.S. Oceanborne Foreign Trade, 1980

	Tonnage Carried	*Value of Cargo Carried*
Total		
All flags	777.2 million	$294.3 billion
U.S. flag	28.2 million	42.3 billion
U.S. percent	3.7%	14.4%
Liners		
All flags	59.3 million	136.9 billion
U.S. flag	16.2 million	39.2 billion
U.S. percent	27.3%	28.7%
Nonliners		
All flags	356.7 million	74.1 billion
U.S. flag	4.1 million	1.3 billion
U.S. percent	1.2%	1.8%
Tankers		
All flags	356.3 million	83.3 billion
U.S. flag	7.9 million	1.8 billion
U.S. percent	2.2%	2.1%

SOURCE: U.S., Maritime Administration, *Annual Report*, FY 1981, table 12.
NOTE: Figures exclude defense and U.S./Canada translake cargoes.

support national-flag shipping. While this approach is somewhat unusual, the exercise is useful and will serve as a frame of reference for arguments and analyses developed later on.

Those circumstances occur—

1. where a merchant marine does not serve as a naval auxiliary in time of war or emergency and the armed forces do not depend upon it for logistical support (the extreme case would be one in which all perceived merchant shipping needs in a contingency or war are supplied by government-owned and -operated vessels);

2. where shipping needs are supplied to the nonshipping nation by numerous countries, and these countries have such a diversity of national interests that they are highly unlikely to withdraw large blocks of shipping for any reason at any time;

3. where foreign-flag ships offer service sufficient in quantity and quality on all trade routes deemed essential to the nonshipping nation's commerce;

4. where enough competition exists among suppliers of shipping services that monopoly pricing and practices are unlikely;

5. where receipts from shipping services are not essential to a nation's balance of international payments and a merchant marine is not necessary to earn specific kinds of foreign currencies;

SS *Santa Clara* of Delta Steamship Lines is a break-bulk-type cargo vessel engaged in the U.S.–South American trade. Having an ability to load and unload cargo with its own cargo-handling gear makes the break-bulk ship especially valuable in support of military operations in areas where no port facilities exist. Delta Steamship Lines photograph

6. where a nation's resources can be fully employed without investment in shipping;

7. where, even if a nation had a merchant marine that carried a substantial part of its commerce, the merchant marine's contribution to the gross national product would be relatively insignificant;

8. where a merchant marine is not extensively used to further political goals and a nation's standing among nations is not determined by a continuous show of its flag in world ports.

In the case of the United States, our privately owned merchant fleet historically has been relied upon to serve as a naval and military auxiliary in time of war and, in the twentieth century, is the major sealift contributor to logistical support for the U.S. forces overseas, in particular, general cargo vessels. In a NATO war these American-flag ships would be the first to be loaded and sent across the Atlantic. On the other hand, government-owned ships, while quite numerous at various times in our history, have always been marginal contributors to military sealift support. Table 1.2 breaks down current U.S.-flag merchant-type tonnage into government owned and privately owned.

With respect to relying upon foreign-flag ships to serve U.S. bulk trade needs, it is unfortunate but true that the United States is not such an admired and followed world leader that it can risk depending, as it does today, on foreign nations to supply its nonliner tonnage requirements. American proposals and positions are routinely voted down in the United

Table 1.2. U.S. Private and Government-Owned Shipping, 1982

	No. of Ships	Deadweight Tons (millions)
Active fleet		
Privately owned	500	18.4
Government owned	16	0.1
Inactive fleet		
Privately owned	69	3.0
Government owned	250	2.7

SOURCE: U.S., Maritime Administration, *U.S. Merchant Marine Data Sheet*, as of 1 September 1982.

Nations, its views on what constitutes a stable world order are increasingly questioned by ally and adversary alike, and at the same time, what the United States sees as its exercise of options to increase its own security is condemned, in the developing world especially, as warmongering and a threat to world peace.

The case for a significant U.S.-flag presence in carrying strategic imports is obvious if it is granted that certainty with respect to an uninterrupted and secure movement of these commodities is a vital national interest. Although the odds favor some combination of foreign-flag carriers continuing to provide bulk shipping services should the United States find itself engaged in a major conflict, are favorable odds enough? Is a three-to-one bet that foreign shipping will stay in place an acceptable risk? Is a four-to-one bet, or a five-to-one bet? (Arguments for and against an extensive reliance on foreign-flag shipping are discussed in Chapter 18.) Table 1.1 shows how dependent the United States is on foreign-flag shipping at present.

On the other hand, it cannot be forcefully argued that the merchant marine contributes significantly to the U.S. gross national product or that the merchant marine's earnings markedly improve our balance of payments.[11] Nor can it be urged that in peacetime, competition would be lacking on major U.S. trade routes. Or that an American merchant marine is an instrument of national policy in the way practiced by the Soviet Union.

This is not to say that a merchant marine does not positively influence employment, GNP, or the balance of payments. Numerous studies have demonstrated such an impact. Or, for that matter, that Americans were not proud when the SS *United States* captured the Blue Riband, the award for the fastest Atlantic crossing, for the first time in a century or equally proud when the NS *Savannah*, the world's first nuclear merchant ship, was launched. In the final analysis, these considerations are not crucial to the nation's well-being and safety. Only the national security rationale for a merchant marine meets this test.

The U.S. and World Merchant Marines

In 1981 there were 24,867 oceangoing vessels in the world flying the flags of some seventy-five nations. Table 1.3 lists the number of ships and tonnage of the major maritime powers.

Table 1.4 breaks down the active American merchant marine by sector, e.g., foreign trade, foreign to foreign, domestic. Table 1.5 contrasts the growth of U.S. oceanborne foreign trade and the United States' share of this commerce between 1961 and 1980.

Conclusion

1. In the latter half of the nineteenth century, the United States gradually evolved into a high-cost producer of shipping services. In 1983 it simply cannot compete for world cargoes without government assistance.

2. Domestic trade shipping has been protected from foreign competition since the founding of the Republic. Like its foreign trade counterpart, however, it is a high-cost producer of transportation service. A main

Table 1.3. World Merchant Fleets, 1 January 1981

Country	No. of Ships	Deadweight Tons (millions)
Greece	2,928	69.6
USSR	2,530	21.8
Panama	2,437	38.0
Liberia	2,271	153.3
Japan	1,762	62.0
United Kingdom	1,056	42.3
People's Republic of China	695	10.1
Italy	622	17.2
Singapore	622	11.8
Norway	616	38.6
United States[a]	578	21.1
Spain	509	12.2

SOURCE: U.S., Maritime Administration, *Annual Report*, FY 1981, table 11.
[a]Privately owned.

reason is the requirement that protected trade vessels be built in high-priced U.S. shipyards.

3. Fashioning a maritime policy that will lead to a merchant marine capable of meeting our national security needs will require not only new ideas and concepts but a knowledge of what we have tried and where we

Table 1.4. Active U.S.-Flag Merchant Marine by Sector, 1982

Sector	No. of Ships	Deadweight Tons (millions)
U.S. foreign trade	195	4.5
Foreign to foreign	14	0.8
Domestic coastwise and intercoastal	172	7.6
Domestic noncontiguous	66	4.0
U.S. agency operations	53	1.5
Total	500	18.4

SOURCE: U.S., Maritime Administration, *U.S. Merchant Marine Data Sheet*, as of 1 September 1982.

Table 1.5. U.S. Foreign Trade for Selected Years, 1961–80

Calendar Year	Total Cargo Lifted (millions of long tons)	U.S. Percent
1961	272.4	9.7
1963	311.6	9.2
1965	371.3	7.5
1967	387.6	5.3
1969	427.5	4.6
1971	457.4	5.3
1972	513.6	4.6
1973	631.6	6.3
1974	628.9	6.5
1975	615.6	5.1
1976	698.8	4.8
1977	775.3	4.5
1978	775.6	4.1
1979	823.1	4.2
1980	777.2	3.7

SOURCE: U.S., Maritime Administration, *United States Oceanborne Foreign Trade Routes*, table 1; U.S., Maritime Administration, *Annual Report*, FY 1981, table 12.

have failed. Shipping is a complex business made up of many interest groups. A prerequisite to understanding the industry is knowing each of these groups and how they fit together to form the whole.

4. In an economy where every tax dollar has a thousand uses and in the tight budget environment of the 1980s, every effort must be made to insure that a dollar spent in support of a merchant marine is a dollar well spent.

5. The bedrock justification for significant government spending on national-flag shipping is national security. In the high-risk international environment of the 1980s, the United States must have a merchant marine large enough to logistically support American forces overseas, in both peace and war, and have a bulk/tanker carrying capacity large enough to insulate the U.S. economy from any foreign-flag boycott of its strategically important raw material and fuel trades.

2 The U.S. Shipping Industry

A great deal has changed in the business of shipping from the time when New England merchant-shipowners ranked among the colonies' wealthiest entrepreneurs and when, in the early nineteenth century, shipping along with shipbuilding was a dominant U.S. industry.

A century and a half later, in 1981, the five largest American firms in terms of assets included a utility, three banks, and an oil company. The largest, American Telephone and Telegraph, had assets of $137.7 billion.[1]

The largest transportation firm was a railroad, the CSX Corporation, with assets of $8.1 billion. In a ranking of the first 50 transportation companies (headed by CSX) the only shipping firm on the list was the Overseas Shipholding Group, with $1.2 billion in assets. It would not be ranked in a list of the 500 largest American firms and would rank only about 225th if it was fitted into the 500 largest industrial firms.[2] A final irony is that this shipping enterprise operates three times as many foreign-flag as American-flag vessels.

The other major changes in shipping since the nineteenth century have been in vessel technology—in particular, in propulsion, size, and design. Propulsion and size will be examined in Chapter 13. Here, interest will focus on design, since above all else it is the best indicator of how the shipping industry is organized.

From the colonial period well into the nineteenth century, ships were designed as general purpose carriers, "general purpose" including the carriage of passengers. The first major specialization could be said to have taken place when vessels were designed to primarily carry either freight or passengers, although each type did earn marginal revenues from carrying its nonspecialty—cargo or passengers, as the case might be.[3]

The latter part of the nineteenth century saw the move to more specialized cargo ships: sailing vessels built to carry grain and coal to the

West Coast and lumber schooners to bring the timber of the Pacific Northwest to growing California cities. The former were the forerunners of the steam-powered coal colliers seen in large numbers on the East Coast in the early twentieth century.

After the opening of the Panama Canal, in 1914, some general cargo ships were especially constructed with wide hatches to move steel from the East to the West Coast (Bethlehem Steel's Calmar Line), and vessels were built whose primary revenues came from moving lumber not only along the Pacific coast but through the Panama Canal to East Coast ports.

The tank vessel designed to carry liquid cargo, primarily oil, also appeared during this period, as did the ore carriers (Bethlehem Steel's Ore Navigation Company). Concurrently, vessels especially built to carry sugar, molasses, and fresh fruit (United Fruit Company's White Fleet) appeared in the American trades.

Design specialization slowed somewhat in the interwar period (1919–39), a time that saw a large part of the world's bulk cargoes carried in the lower holds of general cargo liner vessels or in tramps.[4] After World War II, however, specialized designs returned, particularly after the late 1950s. Combination bulk carriers (ore-bulk-oil carriers), which could efficiently transport a variety of bulk commodities—grain, oil, and ore, for example—made their appearance. Within the general cargo class, specialization was even more pronounced, beginning with Sea-Land's delivery of fifty-eight containers to Puerto Rico on a converted T-2 tanker in 1956.[5] This vessel, the SS *Ideal-X*, was the forerunner of today's modern container ships. The lighter aboard ship (LASH) and roll-on/roll-off (RO/RO) designs followed in order.[6]

In 1983, ocean transportation services can be categorized as follows:

Service	*Commodity Transported*
General cargo	All types of general, nonbulk freight, including autos, canned foods, paper products, TVs, textiles, and refrigerated cargo
Bulk cargo (liquid)	Crude oil, refined oil products, liquid natural gas, chemicals, and distilled products
Bulk cargo (dry)	Various ores, grains, coal, bauxite/alumina, and phosphate rock
Passenger	Passengers desiring transportation between specific points; cruise passengers

Suppliers of the above ocean transport services are of two types: those who solicit from the general public, whether large or small shippers, and those who meet their ocean shipping requirements by supplying their own in-house services. The former are classified as common carriers, the latter as private carriers. Firms in either category may own or charter the required tonnage or use some combination of both.

The oceangoing freighter is still the most versatile of all transport carriers. In addition to carrying hundreds of different commodities, it has a virtually unlimited ability to handle outsize deck cargo. Delta Steamship Lines photograph

In general, companies offering service to the public operate their vessels on fixed schedules and are known as liner operators. Those firms that solicit freight from the public but have no fixed schedules, i.e., will let the vessel's itinerary be entirely determined by the cargo offered, are termed tramp operators. Liner services derive their principal revenues from general cargo, although, as was noted above, bulk cargo such as ore may be carried in the lower holds. These firms typically operate container ships, LASH vessels, RO/ROs, and break-bulk ships. Tramp vessels carry either bulk or general cargo, depending on what is offered. There are no tramp lines under the U.S. flag.

Private carriers respond to the needs of the parent company. The size of the fleet and its use depend on parent company needs. The ships used are generally bulk carriers or tankers.

Passenger services under the U.S. flag are limited. At present, point-to-point passenger service is offered by the Delta Steamship Company on their *Santa Magdalena*–class combination cargo-passenger ships. One cruise firm, American-Hawaii Cruises, operates two ships between the

U.S. West Coast and Hawaii. A number of liner companies carry up to twelve passengers on their general cargo vessels.[7]

As was noted above, both common and private carriers may charter ships from third parties to supplement their tonnage requirements. In fact, some parent companies meet most of their shipping needs by chartering.

A final dichotomy in the American shipping industry divides firms into those that operate in the so-called protected trades (trade between U.S. continental and noncontiguous ports) and those operating in the foreign trade of the United States. Both private and common carriers sail these routes. The common carriers, by and large, offer general cargo service such as the Matson Navigation Company's service between the United States and Hawaii and Puerto Rico Marine's service to Puerto Rico. Private carriers primarily operate tankers between Gulf and Atlantic ports or move crude oil to the continental United States from Alaska. Examples would be the fleets of Exxon and Gulf Oil.

Firm Organization

Ocean shipping by its nature is a geographically dispersed operation. This "dispersion" is different for private carrier shipping and liner shipping. The former moves cargo primarily one way; for example, a Texaco tanker may transport crude oil from the Persian Gulf to the United States.[8] The important consideration in this type of operation is that cargo for the ship is assured. Company representatives at Persian Gulf ports, while handling a myriad of housekeeping details, are not responsible for obtaining cargo bookings.

On the other hand, booking foreign cargo for liner companies is all important. While outbound bookings from the United States can be reasonably monitored by the home office, and a non-cargo-producing agent at a particular port replaced, the problem is more difficult when the representative soliciting freight on the company's behalf is 5,000 miles away and operating in a foreign environment. How well he or she performs may well determine whether or not a voyage is profitable. United States Lines, for example, offers service between the United States and twenty-nine European and fifteen Pacific/Far East ports.

Given the far-flung nature of shipping operations, the fact that there are large and small companies, and that some liner companies are divisions of large conglomerates, it is reasonable to expect a variety of management organizations. For example, United States Lines, with four operating divisions—Eastern United States, Western United States, Europe, and Far East—is directed from its headquarters in New Jersey, where all worldwide activities are coordinated. In contrast, Delta Steamship Lines follows a decentralized management policy. Its three operating divisions are managed as separate profit centers, each with its own management organization (see Figure 2.1).[9]

Besides the centralized management practiced in tanker operations and the relatively decentralized management of the liner companies, two other examples of management organization are of interest.

One is the shipping operations of the Bethlehem Steel Corporation, the nation's second largest steel producer. Its Interocean Shipping Company owns two foreign-flag, dry-bulk carriers. The balance of company shipping requirements are met through a combination of bareboat and time-charter arrangements. Interocean's policy is to meet the parent company's ore requirements at the lowest net cost.[10]

In a company as large as Bethlehem, marine operations are only one of several activities that report to the vice-president of the Transportation Department. Figure 2.2 indicates the relations between the Interocean Shipping Company, Ocean Operations, and the corporate Transportation Department. Since Interocean's president is also the vice-president of ocean operations, the two groups coordinate their activities closely.

The other interesting management organization is that of Moore-McCormack Resources. Moore-McCormack is a conglomerate corporation with large shipping interests. Besides operating a thirteen-ship fleet of cargo liners, three oil carriers, two (planned) liquid natural gas carriers, and a Great Lakes fleet of several ore ships, the company has interests in oil and gas exploration, coal and iron ore mines, and concrete and cement product manufacture. Presidents with wide operating and marketing authority head the Bulk Transport, Great Lakes Shipping, and Cargo Liners divisions. They discuss corporate goals and policies at quarterly meetings of the full Board of Managers, a group that includes the subsidiary presidents and the key corporate officers. Through this type of management organization the company intends to generate the entrepreneurial aggressiveness of a decentralized structure while it insures that all managers understand and pursue corporate goals. Financial controls and reports are similar to those of more centralized companies.

Marine Operations[11]

In large shipping firms, operations or marine operations is headed by a vice-president. He is responsible for vessel operations, including vessel personnel activities, stevedoring, repairs, and dry-docking, and often has chief oversight responsibility for new construction. Reporting to him is a marine superintendent, who hires deck officers, except the ship's master (although his recommendation carries great weight), approves deck and hull repairs, and schedules the inspections required by government agencies. In larger companies he may be assisted by a port captain.

Also reporting to the operations vice-president is an engineering

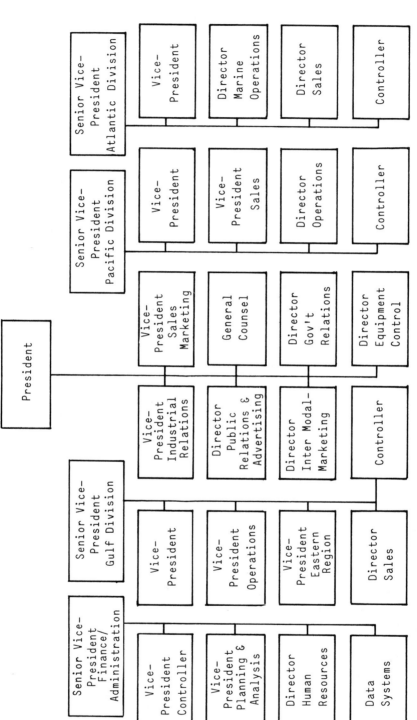

Figure 2.1. Organizational structure of Delta Steamship Lines. Courtesy of Delta Steamship Lines

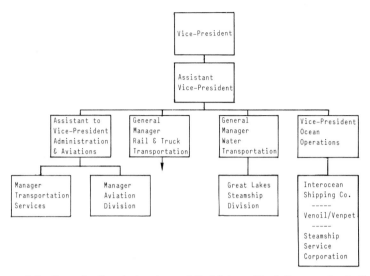

Figure 2.2. Organizational structure of Bethlehem Steel Corporation's Transportation Department. Courtesy of Bethlehem Steel Corporation

superintendent with almost the same responsibilities as the marine superintendent's except that his domain is the vessel's engine room. His authority extends to the hiring of engineering officers, and while his recommendation for a vessel's chief engineer must be approved, approval is generally only a formality. In larger companies, he may have a port engineer as an assistant.

Other key managers reporting to the operations vice-president are the steward superintendent, who sees to the housekeeping, including provisioning, aboard ship, and the terminal manager, whose chief job is to hire longshore labor and operate the company's pier(s) or terminal. More than any of his colleagues in the liner company, the terminal manager was affected by the container revolution.

In the 1950s and 1960s the terminal manager's territory was the company's covered, finger-type pier, reaching far out from the shore and capable of working two to six vessels simultaneously. His greatest problems were using a limited amount of storage space efficiently and preventing pilferage. In the 1970s the advent of the large container ports, such as Sea-Land's Elizabeth, New Jersey, operation, changed forever the way general cargo was loaded, handled, and stored shoreside. Mammoth container cranes, operated by one man and doing the work of a gang of stevedores, the acres of space needed for storing containers, and the huge company investment in cargo support equipment and facilities changed as well as added to the terminal manager's job.

In an industry long known for militant unionism, a major task of the operations vice-president and all those reporting directly to him is maintaining harmonious labor relations. In the 1980s, thus far, management and unions on the seagoing side have cooperated with each other more than they have confronted each other. However, with respect to insuring peace and productivity on the waterfront (a part of the terminal manager's job), the record has been uneven. A central problem has been container work rules and their enforcement, an issue considered in Chapter 16.

The Operating Environment

Like all other industries in an enterprise society, the shipping industry comes into contact with many entities—competitors, both foreign and domestic, harbor tugs and pilots, port authorities, independent agents representing the company's interest in many ports, inland transportation, labor, seagoing and shoreside, shippers, shipyards, and government. With so many "linkages," its operations can be brought to a halt (ships idled) more easily than those of most other industries.

Port congestion, shipyard delays, cargo not ready on time, a wildcat strike by stevedores, work stoppages by rail, truck, or harbor workers, not to mention a strike by only one seagoing union out of the four or five typically representing a ship's crew—all these can idle the vessel.

Another part of shipping's operating environment is determined by government. The Federal Maritime Commission, the Maritime Administration, and the Coast Guard loom large in the day-to-day operations of a company's ships. In particular circumstances, the quasi-official American Bureau of Shipping, the National Labor Relations Board, and the Federal Mediation Conciliation Service become extremely important. Their functions are briefly noted in other parts of the book.

The economic environment in which a shipping firm operates depends on the type of service offered. In the liner trades, competition is disciplined by some 350 shipping conferences worldwide. These cartels set rates and the amount of service to be offered on a particular route (see Chapter 4).

On the other hand, nonaffiliated bulk and tanker firms in foreign trade operate in the classic laissez-faire world of free and open competition. Nor can the subsidiary shipping operations of the large oil companies and steel and metal producers escape the all-pervasive effects of this competitive environment. For if an independent tanker operator can move crude from the Persian Gulf to the Louisiana Offshore Oil Terminal for $2 a ton less than a Texaco-owned vessel can, in the long run Texaco will move toward contracting out its shipping needs instead of supplying them in-house.

If it can be fairly said that the American-flag shipping firm operates in a complex environment, the U.S. company operating both American- and foreign-flag vessels faces even more problems, principally those involving government. Among them are the tax laws, which determine under what conditions and how much of the firm's foreign-flag earnings can be returned to the United States and the extent to which the firm will impose the stricter U.S. operating and construction standards on its own vessels. It is sometimes hard for a company to decide whether to trim operating costs in the short run and accept the increased chance of a large future liability (for example, a major oil spill) or to spend the money to maintain stricter operating standards. Table 2.1 lists those companies that operate both U.S.- and foreign-flag vessels.

Management Associations

As might be expected, shipping management shifts many day-to-day dealings with entities in its operating environment to management associations. These associations of steamship companies perform a variety of services. The most important are expressing their members' views on current issues before Congress, the executive branch, and the regulatory agencies and negotiating agreements with maritime labor, both seagoing and shoreside, on behalf of their members. A last important function is promotional, the primary reason most associations have headquarters in Washington, D.C.

Table 2.2 lists the major shipping management associations, their membership, and their responsibilities.

Table 2.1. U.S. Shipping Companies having U.S.- and Foreign-Flag Fleets

Company	No. of U.S.-Flag Vessels	No. of Foreign-Flag Vessels
Amerada Hess	1	4
Atlantic Richfield	12	3
Exxon	19	135
Gulf Oil	12	28
Mobil Oil	9	47
Ogden Marine	13	17
Phillips Petroleum	1	10
Reynolds Metals Co.	2	4
Texaco	14	59
Union Oil of California	8	2

Sources: "U.S. and World Shipping," p. 85; and U.S., Maritime Administration, *Foreign Flag Merchant Ships Owned by U.S. Parent Companies as of January 1, 1981.*

Table 2.2. U.S. Shipping Management Associations

Association	Membership and Functions
American Institute of Merchant Shipping	Membership is open to all owners/operators of U.S.-flag vessels. Represents members before Congress and government agencies. Provides technical/practical expertise to U.S. government representatives to the International Maritime Organization.
American Maritime Association	Represents unsubsidized shipping firms. Negotiates agreements with maritime unions on behalf of its members.
Council of American-Flag Ship Operators	Most members are subsidized U.S.-flag shipping firms. Represents members before Congress and government agencies. Promotes the merchant marine in general.
Maritime Service Committee	Represents owners/operators of dry cargo vessels on Atlantic and Gulf coasts in negotiations with maritime labor unions.
Pacific Maritime Association	Represents steamship, terminal, and stevedoring companies on the West Coast in negotiations with maritime labor.
Tanker Service Committee	Negotiates labor agreements for members who own/operate tankers.

SOURCES: U.S., Maritime Administration, *Seafaring Guide and Directory of Labor Management Affiliations*; and materials supplied by the associations.

Three other associations represent the maritime industry in general. The most important of these is the National Maritime Council, whose members include shipping management, maritime labor, and shipper representatives. The council was conceived by the Office of Market Development of the Maritime Administration. The original idea was that private funds would support the organization financially while the Maritime Administration would support it administratively, as needed.[12] Other organizations that represent both management and labor are the Transportation Institute and the Joint Maritime Congress. Both receive substantial financial support from seagoing unions.

Conclusion

The best reason for government support of a merchant marine, whether through subsidies, cargo preference, cabotage laws, or bilateral cargo-sharing agreements, is to preserve the national security. American shipping firms have more than fulfilled their obligation in this respect. In two world wars they saw their fleets decimated by enemy action yet went on to reinvest and rebuild when hostilities ended. In World War II, American firms managed some five thousand ships under the direction of the War Shipping Administration. They have acted as general agents for hundreds of government-owned ships that were taken out of the National Defense Reserve Fleet (NDRF) for service in the Korean and Vietnam Wars, and have willingly pledged their vessels for government use in less than mobilization situations under the Sealift Readiness Program (see Chapter 8). More recently, shipping companies have accepted the responsibility for overseeing the reactivation of vessels in the Ready Reserve Force of the NDRF. As more ships are upgraded to greater readiness levels, and dispersed to various ports in the country, the efficient performance of this function will be crucial in a quick-response emergency.

On the non–national security side, management of U.S. shipping has been made easier by Reagan administration moves to deregulate ocean transportation. Most notably the administration has allowed subsidized operators to buy their vessels in foreign yards and proposed relieving ship operators of the 50 percent ad valorem duty levied on repairs performed abroad.

A proposal that has received less attention but will affect the industry is to allow foreign ownership of U.S.-flag vessels to increase from the current 49 percent to 75 percent. Whether this increase would attract capital to the industry is problematical but it would open opportunities for financing new construction not heretofore available.

A deregulated environment opens other possibilities: a shipping firm could expand its reach by investing in other transportation modes (a concept discussed in Chapter 17) and a major ship repair facility and a liner company could be managed under a single corporate roof. The arrangement is not unique: oil and steel interests have combined such activities in the past. In 1983, for example, Bethlehem Steel operates both ships and shipyards.

3

Government Support of Merchant Shipping: 1845–1983

Direct government support for a nation's national-flag shipping can take several forms. This chapter considers only promotional support, support that directly and positively affects a ship operator's ability to compete in the movement of goods by sea. Promotional support includes vessel-operating subsidies, low-interest vessel construction loans, cabotage restrictions, and cargo preference enactments, including bilateral agreements. It does not include legislation such as the Trade Act of 1974, which allows the president to retaliate against nations that discriminate against American shipping; or the Ocean Shipping Act of 1978, the so-called Controlled Carrier Bill, which gives the Federal Maritime Commission (FMC) authority to suspend rates of state-owned carriers, such as those of the Soviet Union, when it finds them to be "unjust and unreasonable," that is, so low as to be deemed predatory; or the 1979 amendments to the 1916 Shipping Act, which strengthen the power of the FMC to prevent the practice of rebating in U.S. foreign trade ocean commerce.

This is not to say that legislation such as the 1974 Trade Act would not benefit American shipping. Obviously it does. The difference between a law such as the Controlled Carrier Bill and an operating subsidy is that the former acts as a response, which may or may not be activated, while the latter is an ongoing commitment to a national-flag merchant marine.

Mail Subsidies, Cargo Preference, and Bilateral Agreements

As was noted in Chapter 1, America's earliest laws to promote its merchant marine (and shipbuilders) imposed, in 1789 and 1790, heavy tonnage duties on foreign ships engaged in the coastal trades. In 1817 the law actually prohibited foreign tonnage in the U.S. domestic trades.

Also noted was the tardiness of American owners to adopt the newer marine technology (iron hulls, steam propulsion, the screw propeller) that was in use after 1830.

Mail Subsidies

A first measurable result of this failure was the almost complete British dominance of the North Atlantic packet ship services after 1840. Congress responded to America's almost nonparticipation in this service by passing a mail subsidy bill in 1845. More comprehensive mail subsidy enactments were later passed in 1864 and 1891.[1]

The theory was that guaranteed mail payments, in almost every case higher than the actual cost of providing the service, would induce American operators to establish steamship service on certain designated routes. These early subsidy laws were, in part, justified by national defense considerations. The 1845 act, for example, stated that preference would be given bidders for mail contracts who promised to deliver their vessels to the U.S. government in time of emergency. And the 1891 act stated that a mail-subsidized ship had to be convertible to a naval auxiliary and specified the type and speed of the ship.

As an instrument of government policy to arrest the decline of the merchant marine, the mail contract was a failure. In 1910, American-flag ships were carrying but 9 percent of the nation's foreign trade.[2]

Cargo Preference

In 1904 the first cargo preference legislation was enacted. Specifically, "transportation of coal, provisions, fodder, or supplies of any description . . . for use of the Army and Navy" was reserved to American-flag vessels unless the president found the rates excessive.[3]

In 1934 a resolution of Congress urged that freight procured with loans made by the U.S. government be carried in American ships.

Following World War II, a number of preference laws were enacted that culminated in the Cargo Preference Act of 1954. The 1954 law amended the Merchant Marine Act of 1936 and was intended "to provide permanent legislation for the transportation of a substantial portion of waterborne cargoes in United States flag vessels."[4]

Cargo preference laws, as a means of insuring an American presence on foreign trade routes in the highly competitive postwar period, could be considered moderately successful. Certainly, many U.S.-flag ships were at sea only because of them. However, as a means of insuring that the American merchant marine consistently carry a substantial part of America's foreign commerce, cargo preference laws were a failure. Moreover, the indirect costs were very high.

Aside from a 1961 amendment to the 1954 act to encourage construction in American shipyards, new cargo preference legislation was not seriously considered again until 1974. In that year President Gerald Ford pocket-vetoed a bill that required 30 percent of U.S. oil imports to be carried on American-flag vessels. At the time, less than 5 percent of this movement was in U.S. bottoms. Maritime unions strongly supported the measure. In 1977 a more humble proposal was made that would have guaranteed U.S. tankers 4½ percent of foreign oil import carriage the first year after enactment, to increase to 9½ percent five years later. The bill was defeated in the House of Representatives.

In 1978, Congress ruled that 50 percent of all foreign oil purchased for the Strategic Petroleum Reserve program had to be carried in U.S.-flag vessels. The impact on American shipping will depend upon whether and how fast the program is implemented. If petroleum reserves are built up slowly, as they have been in the past, the ruling is unlikely to lead to any new construction or the return of any foreign-flag tankers to U.S. registry.

In the post–World War II period, preference cargo accounted for 5 to 10 percent of all goods moved in U.S. foreign commerce. And as might be expected, the distribution of preference cargo was uneven. Outbound cargo made up the largest portion. Tramp shipping and tankers were very dependent on preference shipments; the liner companies were less so. For many U.S. firms, preference cargo accounted for 50 percent and more of their bookings. However, large disparities existed between trade routes and between companies. For example, during the Vietnam War, preference cargo (mainly military) handled by Pacific coast firms on Pacific routes was heavy. On the other hand, Farrell Lines, at the time primarily serving Africa, carried little preference freight, generally less than 10 percent.

In 1980, preference cargo accounted for approximately 3.32 million of the 28.2 million tons of cargo carried by U.S. ships in foreign trade.[5]

Bilateral Agreements

One form of cargo preference legislation is the bilateral shipping agreement between trading partners. Here, two countries formally agree to reserve a certain portion of the ocean cargoes moving between them to their national-flag carriers. The agreement will specify the types of cargo involved, the percentage reserved for each partner's national shipping lines, and the share allotted to third-country ships. Also spelled out will be the rights and enforcement responsibilities of each country and probably an arbitration procedure.

The United States has signed four major bilateral shipping agreements—with Brazil, Argentina, the Soviet Union, and the People's Republic of China. In 1970 the United States and Brazil agreed to share the northbound movement of coffee and cocoa on a 50 : 50 basis. The same shares were allocated on southbound cargo. The agreement has since been modified to allow third countries to share in 20 percent of the trade. The Argentine agreement, actually a memorandum of understanding, was signed in 1978. Under this agreement, each government recognized the other's right to carry a substantial share of the trade between them. Implementation was to be on a shipping firm–to–shipping firm basis.

The agreement with the Soviet Union (1971) is more comprehensive. It not only spells out the cargo-sharing arrangements between the two countries, but also for the first time specifically opens up a number of U.S. ports to Russian merchant ships. Two major motives induced the agreement. On the Soviet side was the desire to import American grain. On the American side was the desire not only to sell the grain but to give employment to U.S.-flag vessels. The agreement calls for each country to carry a "substantial share" of the bilateral trade between them. "Substantial" is defined as at least one third.

The latest bilateral agreement was signed with the People's Republic of China in 1980. It reserved to each country a one-third share of the bilateral trade between them, the remainder being available to third-country shipping. Ports of each country were to be opened to the other's shipping when due notice was received and specified conditions fulfilled.

In 1974, seventy-seven lesser developed countries (LDCs) presented to the United Nations for ratification the final draft of a Code of Conduct for Liner Conferences. The purpose of the UNCTAD (UN Conference on Trade and Development) code was to help developing nations to secure a share of international ocean commerce, in particular, trade between them and economically more developed trading partners.

The code says that ocean cargo between nations will be carried on a 40 : 40 : 20 basis; 40 percent will be carried by each trading partner and 20 percent will be left for third-flag carriers. The code deals only with liner shipping and, in fact, depends upon viable shipping conferences being in place to implement it.

Before President Reagan took office, American policy was hostile to the code, although the United States hardly spoke with a single voice. President Carter was unequivocally opposed to it and vowed that "we will continue to resist the imposition of cargo-sharing regimes whether bilaterally or multilaterally."[6] By and large, relevant congressional committees took a more flexible stance. American operators, although they opposed the code in its general form, believed that with some modifications it could prove beneficial.

Major U.S. objections to the code (from all parties) are as follows:

1. Transportation costs in international trade would increase because inefficient carriers would be protected from competition.

2. With the exception of military cargo, cargo preference laws presently in place would be invalid.

3. U.S. trades would become dumping grounds for shipping forced out of bilateral trades.

4. American companies would find entering and competing in cross trades difficult.

5. Settling disputes arising under the code would be expensive and time consuming.

Although technically the code has not obtained the number of ratifications necessary for it to come into effect (it must be ratified by countries having 25 percent of the world's merchant tonnage), Japan and the European Economic Community nations have said they intend to ratify; if they do, the tonnage requirement provision will be more than satisfied.

President Reagan is taking a more pragmatic view of bilateral agreements than did the former president. In announcing his maritime policy goals during the 1980 presidential campaign, then-candidate Reagan said:

> The United States has traditionally espoused free trade. However, the international shipping trade is laced with a network of foreign governmental preferences and priorities designed to strengthen foreign fleets, often at the expense of U.S. maritime interests. We must be prepared to respond constructively for our own interests to the restrictive shipping policies of other nations. A major goal of the United States must be to insure that American flag ships carry an equitable portion of our trade consistent with the legitimate aspirations and policies of our trading partners.[7]

Merchant Marine Acts of 1920, 1928, 1936, and 1970

The Merchant Marine Act of 1920 formally recognized the auxiliary role of merchant ships in wartime and emergencies. Section 1 of the act stated that the United States "shall" have a merchant marine capable of "serving as a naval and military auxiliary in time of war," a statement of policy that was to be repeated in succeeding major maritime enactments. The 1920 legislation also provided for the sale of government-owned ships and routes on which government-sponsored service had been established. A construction loan fund was provided to make available low-interest capital, in the hope it would stimulate shipbuilding. It did not.

The Merchant Marine Act of 1928 was more comprehensive. A larger construction loan fund was authorized; the Ocean Mail Act of 1891 was repealed; mail contracts were made, conditional on replacement of old tonnage; and all officers serving on mail contract ships as well as two thirds of the crew were required to be American citizens.

In his oft-quoted message to Congress in 1935, President Franklin Roosevelt opted to call a "subsidy by its right name" and proposed that the difference between American and foreign costs in a number of categories—construction, repairs, wages, insurance, and subsistence—

be paid by the federal government. Eligibility for subsidy payments was limited to liner (scheduled) shipping engaged in foreign trade. In return, ship operators were tightly bound by an agreement that, among other things, specified that their vessels must be built and repaired in the United States, that operators offer a specific number of sailings on assigned "essential" trade routes; that they adhere to minimum manning and wage scales and working conditions specified for subsidized ships; and that they submit plans for subsidized construction to the Department of the Navy for review. National defense features could be added at government cost if approved. President Roosevelt's proposals were incorporated into the most comprehensive piece of promotional maritime legislation ever enacted by Congress, the Merchant Marine Act of 1936.

The 1936 act also brought together and codified support of the merchant marine through the nation's tax laws.[8] Section 606(b) of the original act required a subsidized operator to maintain a capital reserve fund into which he was to deposit a sum equal to the annual depreciation charge on his vessels plus any insurance indemnities received. A special reserve fund was also set up into which a subsidized operator was to deposit earnings in excess of 10 percent a year and earnings in excess of the percentage allocated to the capital reserve fund. The first fund was to insure that monies were available for vessel replacement, i.e., insure the long-term viability of the subsidized merchant fleet. The second was to insure that the government was at least partially repaid for subsidy monies expended in those periods when the ship operator was making a better-than-average return on his investment. Section 605(f) exempted funds in both accounts from federal taxes.

The Merchant Marine Act of 1970, and later amendments, consolidated reserve funds and special reserve funds into a single capital construction fund, which served the same purpose as the earlier accounts. The 1970 act also made most segments of the merchant marine eligible for the tax treatment heretofore only accorded subsidized operators. Additionally, bulk carriers were eligible for construction and operating differential subsidies as were reconstructed vessels. Tankers and liquid natural gas carriers were eligible for construction subsidies.

The 1970 act attempted to control the increasingly high cost of supporting a merchant marine. Wages were indexed, and an upper limit set for subsidy payments: crew size was determined in the design/construction stage rather than negotiated after the vessel was in operation; and negotiated construction contracts were allowed in addition to competitive procedures. To increase efficiency, incentives were given to both the shipowner and the shipbuilder. The act envisioned a 300-ship building program over a ten-year period. However, considerably fewer than 200 ships had been built or were under construction in 1982. The high hopes of 1970, in fact, did not materialize.

U.S. Government Policy and Aid to Foreign Trade Ocean Shipping in 1982

U.S. Government support for U.S. foreign trade ocean shipping in 1982 included operating differential subsidies (ODS), construction differential subsidies (CDS),[9] tax benefits, loan and mortgage guarantees, trade-in provisions for older vessels, cargo preference enactments, and bilateral cargo-sharing agreements with several trading partners.

Table 3.1 shows the types of aid given by their governments to principal foreign-flag carriers engaged in U.S. foreign trade.

The Reagan administration announced its initial maritime policy in May 1982. It included the following items:

1. Operationally subsidized firms would have the continued option to buy vessels abroad.

2. Vessels returning to U.S.-flag registry would be immediately eligible to carry government-sponsored cargoes.

3. Foreign investment in U.S.-flag shipping would be encouraged.

Table 3.1. Aids Provided by Foreign Governments to Their Shipping Which is Significantly Engaged in U.S. Foreign Trade

Country	No. of Ships	Construc- tion Aid	Operating Subsidies or Significant Government Ownership	Tax Benefits	Cargo Preference
Greece	2,690	X		X	X
Japan	1,778	X		X	X
United Kingdom	1,210	X		X	
Norway	876	X		X	
Italy	607	X	X	X	X
West Germany	590	X		X	X
Spain	495	X	X	X	X
Netherlands	441	X		X	
France	382	X	X	X	X
India	363	X	X	X	X
Denmark	338	X			
Korea	301	X	X	X	X
Brazil	284	X		X	X
Argentina	187	X	X	X	X
Philippines	172	X	X	X	X

SOURCE: U.S., Maritime Administration, *Maritime Subsidies.*

NOTE: Flag-of-convenience countries are not included. For details on this shipping, see Chapter 18. The symbol X means yes; blank means no.

4. U.S.-flag ships would not be penalized for making repairs abroad.

5. The operating differential subsidy program would be more flexible.

6. There would be less federal regulation of foreign liner and noncontiguous domestic shipping (by the Federal Maritime Commission).

7. U.S. cabotage laws would have continued support.

8. Existing cargo preference laws would have continued support.

Ship operators' reaction to the initial proposals has been cautious, a wait-and-see-what-comes-next attitude with respect to bilateral trading agreements, cargo preference, and reducing the government's role in liner shipping regulation by curtailing the authority of the Federal Maritime Commission and the Anti-Trust Division of the Department of Justice.

On the other hand, the shipyard industry and organized labor have been bitterly critical of the initial proposals and have specifically cited the lack of administration concern or support for shipbuilding.

The Price of Government Aid: Intervention in Management Decision Making

It is axiomatic that governments seldom give anything away without getting something in return. As economists would put it—There is no such thing as a free lunch.

For example, while the federal government "gave" western railroads millions of acres in the form of land grants to encourage railroad building in the nineteenth century, the government also paid reduced rates for the rail services it received until 1946.[10] More recently, before deregulation legislation passed in 1978 and 1980, airlines and motor carriers were granted monopoly rights over many of the routes they served. A part of the price exacted for this benefit was that the amount and kind of service offered, and the fare or rate charged, were subject to government approval. And a route could not be abandoned without a government O.K.

The government has used the same carrot-and-stick method with American shipping. Our cabotage laws required U.S. operators to use American-built ships, and bidders on mail contracts had to follow naval auxiliary vessel design requirements. By and large, however, these limits on management actions were simple and straightforward, and their goals were easily understood.

When the Merchant Marine Act passed in 1936, the amount and kind of government aid increased significantly. But perhaps more importantly, the recipient shipping firm had to pay a high price—it had less freedom to make its own decisions.

While the following list does not definitively catalog and analyze all restrictions placed on subsidized shipping management by the Merchant Marine Act of 1936 and later legislation, it does show that these restrictions were numerous. Besides Buy American provisions and naval auxiliary suitability requirements, there were these constraints:

1. Compensation to shipping firm executives could not exceed $25,000 per year. This provision was later repealed.

2. The useful life of a subsidized vessel was set at twenty years. Vessel life was later extended to twenty-five years.

3. Subsidized operators were prohibited from having any beneficial interest in foreign shipping operations.

4. Subsidized operators were not allowed to operate their vessels in the protected domestic trade.

5. Minimum sailings were specified on a particular route for subsidized operators.

6. Subsidized operators needed government approval to move vessels from one trade route to another.[11]

7. The federal government controlled the entry of competing subsidized operators on already subsidized routes.

8. In approving subsidized services, the government had to try to meet equitably the foreign trade needs of all U.S. coasts—the Atlantic, Gulf, Great Lakes, and Pacific. This ruling indirectly limited the ports a subsidized carrier could serve.

9. Government approval was required for mergers, acquisition, or other forms of corporate control involving subsidized vessels.

10. Government approval was required to transfer vessels built under CDS (construction differential subsidy) to foreign ownership. Insofar as operationally subsidized firms were required to build in American yards and therefore to build under the CDS, options to dispose of vessels were limited.

11. A part of a subsidized operator's profit had to be deposited into a capital construction fund. While the present favorable tax treatment accorded these funds is hardly a constraint, the tax treatment could easily become less favorable at some future time if the fund requirement remains.

12. Minimum manning, wages, and working conditions were specified for subsidized ships.

After the 1936 act, as might be expected, shipping firms weighed the choice presented. By the time America entered World War II, twelve liner companies operating 176 ships had elected the subsidy option. Their fleets comprised about 50 percent of the dry-cargo, passenger, foreign trade merchant marine.

Both before and after the war, many firms believed the price asked was too high, and they operated without a subsidy and its attendant restrictions. However, by 1959 all eligible U.S. companies had applied for a subsidy.[12]

Conclusion

Most Western economists would agree that minimum interference by government in management decision making in an enterprise economy will produce the best results in the long run. And when constraints are imposed upon firms receiving government aid, the constraints should have a direct and easily perceived relation to the (government) goal being sought.

Only two goals compel government support of U.S.-flag shipping: (1) the logistical support a merchant marine provides to American forces overseas, whether in peace or war, and (2) the need to insure that our strategic import requirements never become hostage to a foreign-flag shipping boycott. With these goals in mind, what are justifiable constraints on a shipping company receiving direct government aid? In other words, what price should government exact when it helps build and maintain a privately owned merchant fleet?

First, government may reasonably require companies to make their ships available to the United States in a national emergency or war. At the same time, the government must agree to fairly compensate the vessel owner.

Second, the government may specify that national-flag vessels be constructed (or modified) so as to be as useful as possible in meeting military needs. However, its specifications should not significantly degrade the ship's commercial viability.

Third, vessels' officers and crews should be U.S. citizens, and, if necessary, key officers should be required to have a security clearance. If other restrictions—such as limiting the geographic areas a vessel may serve, specifying some minimum number of sailings, or mandating firm funds to specific accounts—are to be placed on management, the burden of proof must fall squarely upon those advocating the restrictions.

If it is true that the U.S. government should support the merchant marine, and if few government constraints on managerial decision making are better than many, a fair question is, How should the government implement its aid? In its economic survey of the merchant marine following passage of the 1936 act, a blue ribbon panel went to considerable lengths in detailing the difficulties of accurately determining the amount of operating and construction subsidy to be paid a shipping firm. It concluded that the criteria were so complex that amounts could only be aproximated with much room for disagreements.[13] If their conclusion is accepted, one option with much to commend it is a variable vessel bounty payment. The single requirement imposed on the operator would be to keep his ship on active status and in good repair *and nothing more.*[14] The notion of accommodating complexity within a framework of simplicity is not new. Occam's razor (rule) has been with us a long time.[15]

4

Rules
of the Game

The rules that govern the "game" of ocean shipping are, perhaps, the most pervasive and complex ever devised. They originate in the maritime tradition; national laws and regulations; international treaties, conventions, and understandings; and national and international legal decisions; which in turn give rise to precedents and private contractual arrangements, not to mention domestic laws and regulations that govern land transportation where it touches the ocean system. Add to this the growing number of bilateral trade agreements among nations, and the magnitude and scope of the rules of ocean commerce are staggering indeed.

Rules governing ocean shipping fall into three categories—those that are promotional, those that are economic, and those that affect vessel safety, in particular operating and construction standards. A particular rule, however, does not work in a vacuum; rather it affects many other rules, in the way a handful of pebbles thrown into a pond creates a meeting of ripples. Rules are made by people, not by God. They are made individually, through private agreements, or collectively, through government action.

Chapter 3 reviewed legislation whose purpose was to promote a U.S.-flag merchant marine. This chapter considers the other two categories of rules: the economic rules, which define the environment and specify the limits in which shipping management must operate, and the rules that accompany national laws on safety and standards and international treaties with regard to vessel construction and safety of life at sea.[1]

Private contractual arrangements, i.e., shipping conference agreements and labor contracts, and how they affect shipping operations, are also noted. Emphasis, however, is not on the reasons for a particular rule—whether it was instigated to promote a national-flag merchant marine, protect shippers, insure safety of life at sea, or provide seagoing employment—but rather on its effect on the business of shipping.

Economic Regulation: The Shipping Act of 1916

In 1914, after a two-year investigation, the House Committee on Merchant Marine and Fisheries under the chairmanship of Congressman Joshua W. Alexander issued a comprehensive and detailed report on alleged abuses by international shipping conferences.[2] Recommendations made in the Alexander Report led to the passage of the Shipping Act of 1916, the cornerstone of the economic regulations governing American foreign trade ocean shipping. The act stated its intent as follows:

> To establish a United States Shipping Board for the purpose of encouraging, developing, and creating a naval auxiliary and naval reserve and a merchant marine to meet the requirements of the commerce of the United States with its Territories and possessions and with foreign countries; *to regulate carriers by water engaged in the foreign and interstate commerce of the United States* [italics added]; and for other purposes.[3]

While the act exempted shipping conferences from American antitrust laws, it also imposed specific severe constraints on their American trade operations:

Section 14 of the act prohibited deferred rebates, i.e., the return by a carrier of any portion of the freight money to a shipper in consideration for future business beyond the completion of the original service. The section also prohibited the use of "fighting ships," i.e., ships used for the purpose of driving another carrier out of a particular trade by cutting rates. Prohibited was any type of discriminatory practice by a carrier against a shipper, such as refusing space when space was available and making contracts based on the volume of shipment.

Section 15 required all conference agreements to be filed with the Shipping Board and gave the board authority to modify or cancel any agreement it found to be discriminatory.

Section 16 detailed other discriminatory acts prohibited by the statute.

Section 17 prohibited discrimination between shippers or ports.

Section 18 required that rates be "reasonable" and that they be published.

Section 19 prohibited rate reductions whose effect would be to eliminate competition.

And while the 1916 act does not specifically require them, the Shipping Board and regulatory agencies that succeeded it have encouraged "open conferences," conferences that must admit any carrier wishing to join. In 1961, Congress made open conferences mandatory.

When deferred rebates were prohibited, conferences in the American trades turned to dual-rate contracts, contracts that gave an immediate reduction to shippers who agreed to use conference vessels exclusively.

However, in 1958 the U.S. Supreme Court held dual rates to be illegal. In turn, Congress temporarily validated the dual-rate practice. After two extensions, in 1961 dual rates were finally legalized but with stringent restrictions. Attempts to amend the Shipping Act of 1916, that is, loosen the restrictions on conference activities, are discussed in Chapters 5 and 9.

Safety of Life at Sea

International Law

The first international conference dealing with maritime safety was held in Washington, D.C., in 1889. It was not, however, until the sinking of the *Titanic* in 1912, with a loss of 1,493 passengers and crew members, that world attention seriously focused on the issue of safety at sea. International Conventions for Safety of Life at Sea (SOLAS) were held in 1914, 1928, 1948, 1960, and 1974. The 1974 convention came into effect on 1 May 1981, after it was ratified by countries controlling over 50 percent of the world's shipping tonnage.[4]

Safety of life at sea conventions set international minimum requirements for vessel construction and manning. Over the years, these have been periodically upgraded, and the United States has typically taken the lead in urging stricter standards. A 1978 protocol, for example, strengthened the 1974 SOLAS convention in a number of ways. In addition to periodic surveys called for by the convention, vessels were made subject to unscheduled inspections unless they were already subject to mandatory annual inspections. Stricter procedures were required to insure that corrective actions were taken when defects were found and that vessels were maintained in satisfactory condition between inspections. In general, over the past twenty years, most of the maritime world's attention has focused on tanker construction and operating standards.

Signatory nations to SOLAS conventions designate the government agency (or agencies) responsible for enforcing international requirements within their jurisdictions. In the United States the designated agency is the Coast Guard.

United States Law

Although the outbreak of World War I prevented the 1914 SOLAS convention from coming into force, many of its provisions respecting vessel safety were incorporated into American law with the passage of the La Follette Seaman's Act in 1915.[5]

The loss of the cruise liner *Morro Castle* in 1934, followed by the collision between the steamers *Mohawk* and *Tallisman* in 1935, triggered a detailed and thorough congressional investigation into American vessel operating and construction standards. The result was that the U.S. regulations were tightened, particularly with respect to vessel construction. Among other stipulations, the amount of wood used in construction was limited, sprinklers and fire doors were required, and crews had to be trained in fire fighting and abandon-ship procedures.

As a general rule, American construction standards are more stringent than international standards. In this respect, it is interesting to note the findings of the congressional committee that investigated the collision between the *Stockholm* and the *Andrea Doria* in 1956. The committee found in part—

> . . . that while facts at hand are not sufficient to state categorically that the *Andrea Doria* would not have sunk had she had the stability at the time of the collision required by the 1948 Convention, it seems quite certain . . . had she been in compliance with United States standards, she would have survived.[6]

As is the case for international law, the enforcing agency for U.S. regulations is the Coast Guard.

Private Arrangements

Not only do governments set the rules of the game in shipping, but numerous private contracts do too—shipping conference agreements, seagoing maritime union agreements, and longshoremen contracts also affect shipping firms' profit and loss statements.

The conference system began in 1879 with the emergence of the Far East Freight Conference, which regulated liner trade between India and Great Britain.[7] In 1983 there are approximately 350 different conferences worldwide. Fourteen serve points in North America and Europe.[8]

Equally important to a shipping firm's operations are seafaring labor contracts. These agreements specify crew size, wages, and working conditions. Twelve AFL-CIO chartered unions represent licensed and unlicensed personnel:

Union	Abbreviation
American Radio Association	ARA
Associated Marine Officers	AMO
Marine Engineers Beneficial Association	MEBA
Marine Firemen's Union	MFU
Marine Staff Officers	MSO
Masters, Mates, and Pilots	MMP
National Maritime Union	NMU
Radio Officers Union	ROU
Sailors' Union of the Pacific	SUP
Seafarers International Union	SIU
Staff Officers Association	SOA

Two unions represent stevedores. The International Longshoremen's Association negotiates for longshoremen on the Atlantic and Gulf coasts; the International Longshoremen's and Warehousemen's Union represents stevedores on the Pacific Coast.

On the other side of the bargaining table, four associations—American Maritime Association, Maritime Service Committee, Pacific Maritime Association (PMA), and Tanker Service Committee—negotiate with the unions on management's behalf.

The complexity of this aspect of the rules of the game—labor negotiations—can be seen from the following example. Lykes Lines, primarily a Gulf and East Coast operator, is represented by the Maritime Service Committee and negotiates with three licensed officer unions (MMP, MEBA, and ARA) and the NMU, representing unlicensed seamen. On the other hand, Sea-Land Services, a round-the-world-service liner company, and a competitor on some routes with Lykes, is represented by the American Maritime Association, which negotiates on its behalf with three officer unions (MMP, MEBA, and ROU) and one unlicensed union, the SIU.

Pacific Coast steamship operators, which include Sea-Land, are bound to the agreement reached by their management association, the PMA. Atlantic and Gulf operators (Sea-Land and Lykes), on the other hand, must individually ratify any agreement reached by their bargaining representative.

On the Atlantic and Gulf coasts, separate management groups negotiate with the longshoremen; on the Pacific Coast, the same association, the PMA, handles both seagoing and longshore labor negotiations.

In summary, these two shipping companies, represented by two management associations, negotiate with *four* officer unions, *two* unlicensed seamen unions, and *two* longshoremen associations.

A Simple Laissez-Faire Model

While there is no way to identify and measure the impact on management decision making of the myriad of rules under which ocean shipping operates, it is helpful to understand why some rules (laws) came into being, what the available options were at the time, and what the results were.

Consider a simple three-country model in which all things that affect the economics of ocean shipping are initially equal (so that changes can be introduced and their effects traced through to a new equilibrium).

Assume countries A, B, and C have cost-competitive merchant marines and compete in international trade. There is no requirement that their shipping investment be equal.[9] They trade among themselves and cross-trade. Foreign-flag shipping may engage in the coastal trade of each country without penalty. Safety requirements, construction standards, and crew size are set by international treaty and are the same in each country. No promotional legislation exists in any country such as cargo preference or preferential tax treatment for merchant shipping investment. The only departure from a laissez-faire environment is that each country's ships are crewed by its own citizens.

If the cost of ship construction in country A significantly increases, what are the options of A's shipowners when it comes time to replace their vessels? The answer is that they must build in either country B or C or eventually go out of business. In time, resources that went into shipbuilding in country A will seek other economic employments. Assuming country A adopts a hands-off policy, A's ships will be built at competitive prices and the size of A's merchant marine will not be affected.

What if vessel operating costs also significantly increase in A; for example, seagoing wages? With government again neutral, what options are open to the shipowner? Assuming the same level of service is to be maintained, the logical management strategy is to substitute relatively less expensive capital for relatively more expensive labor to the maximum extent possible under existing (crew size requirements) law.

Labor, however, can be expected to resist such a move; in particular, unionized labor will resist it. However, as is the case for any collective bargaining negotiations, bedrock positions will eventually be put on the table. What will be labor's position, assuming a hands-off government policy? Experience suggests that seagoing labor will ultimately agree to crew reductions on new tonnage. On the other hand, this same experience suggests that labor will be reluctant to accept much in the way of reduced crews on existing vessels. To the extent that A's shipowners can replace tonnage in a reasonably short time, A's shipping will remain competitive, although A will have somewhat fewer ships at sea. If operating costs other than labor costs increase in country A, ship operators will have the same option they had when vessel construction costs went up—to buy in the cheapest international market.

But what if country A continues to suffer an operating-cost disadvantage vis-à-vis B and C, that is, all the substitution possible between capital and labor has been made or, more likely, B and C shipowners have also substituted capital for labor, i.e., invested in automated vessels, to maintain their competitive advantage?

The last option open to A's shipowners is to work out a private agreement with those of B and C to collectively set rates high enough to allow A's owners to make a reasonable return on their investments. Or to guarantee a share of cargo to A's ships. At first it might seem that B and C ship operators would not benefit from such an agreement. But, first, a stand-pat position runs the always present risk that A's government will intervene, in which case it will not be a question of which nation is the most efficient producer of shipping services, but which is economically, or perhaps militarily, the strongest. Second, while the merchant fleets of B and C might become somewhat smaller if they allow a place for A, the return on their investment will probably be greater.[10] Third, if all suppliers are members of the cartel, the cartel's ability to set rates is considerably more secure.

While it can be correctly argued that such an arrangement would give the shipowners monopoly power over rates, this power would still be limited. In the long run, excessively high rates would decrease overall demand for shipping services, which in turn would make it attractive for some shipowners to withdraw from the agreement. Moreover, new operators not party to the agreement would see a profit opportunity and enter the market. Finally, in a laissez-faire world, shippers would also have the opportunity to organize and bargain with the ship operators over rates and services.

However, advantages in collective shipowner agreements, i.e., cartel arrangements, do not accrue entirely to the ship operator. A number of well-recognized and accepted advantages accrue to the shipper. Among them are certainty of service and long-run rate stability, the latter being of particular importance in international trade.

Several principles can be deduced from the laissez-faire model.

1. A country's national-flag shipping may still be competitive even if its shipbuilding costs are higher than in competitor nations. The same is true for repairs, insurance, and supplies. The prerequisite is that the shipowner be allowed to buy his vessel, supplies, and repairs in the cheapest international market.

2. A prerequisite to the unrestricted construction/repair option is that vessel seaworthiness requirements be uniform for all countries. It is no excuse that achieving such an agreement might be a long and tedious process; it must be pursued to a successful conclusion by the disadvantaged nation, whether it be by raising international standards or bringing national standards into line with world standards.

3. While government must be evenhanded in disputes between shipping management and maritime labor, it must unequivocally support technological innovations that will make its national-flag shipping more productive. In no case should government action discourage investment in new technology.

4. If ship operators faced with higher operating costs than their competitors can make a reasonable return on their investments through collective agreements, i.e., by participating in a shipping conference,

their national government must be supportive. An optimum policy, fair to shipowners and shippers, would support the integrity of shipping conferences, that is, endorse limited conference membership, mandate the option of individual-firm action within a conference, and encourage competition between conferences serving the same geographic area, e.g., North America–Europe.

A Not-So-Simple Promotional Legislation Model

This time, consider a not-so-simple model. Again assume nations A, B, and C are providing shipping services. None of them is burdened by excessively high construction or operating costs. Equilibrium conditions are the same as they were in the earlier example. Now let shipbuilding costs increase in A, but assume it is now A's policy to maintain a certain level of investment in its shipbuilding/repair industry.

Country A has several options. The one that apparently costs least is to exercise A's sovereign power and restrict domestic shipping to domestically built vessels. A could maintain some shipbuilding in this way, depending on how well domestic shipping was able to compete with existing land alternatives. A's foreign trade ship operators, as might be expected, would purchase their vessels in competitively priced foreign yards.

If the domestically built rule was extended to trade between A and its noncontiguous territories, some shipbuilding investment in country A is insured.[11] This scenario creates the interesting possibility that foreign-owned, domestically built vessels would be crewed by country A citizens, would fly A's flag, and would engage in A's protected trade. After all, if a profit opportunity exists, foreign investment in shipping is as likely as any other foreign investment in country A—that in automobile assembly plants, for example. In any case, if A is satisfied with a limited shipbuilding capability and a probably somewhat smaller domestic trade merchant marine, an equilibrium will have been reached.

Should A's vessel operating costs increase along with construction costs, domestic tonnage might find it more difficult to compete with its land competition. Any competitive edge would be determined by differences in mode operating costs.[12]

At this point A's government must make a decision. It can accept a shipbuilding industry/merchant marine whose size matches the size of its domestic ocean commerce, or it can actively support its foreign trade shipping. If A chooses the latter course, it has several options. (Assume the build-foreign alternative still exists for foreign trade shipping.)

1. A can reserve a share of cargo originating in A for A's shipping. A may do this in a number of ways. It could reserve all military cargo for A's

ships. It could set aside a part or all of government-sponsored cargo for A-flag vessels. It could enter into bilateral cargo-sharing agreements with A's trading partners.

2. A can provide direct subsidies to ship operators to compensate for higher operating costs.

3. A can indirectly reduce capital and/or operating costs for A's shipping. For example, accelerated depreciation for capital (vessels) and tax advantages for earnings are options.

A may employ these options singly or in combination.

Finally, if A decides that its shipbuilding base must be increased, its remaining alternative is to require that its foreign trade merchant fleet be domestically built. In this case, A must be prepared to subsidize shipowners for the difference between the domestic price and the world price.

However, unlike A's action restricting foreign participation in its domestic trade, A's direct support of its foreign trade merchant marine can be expected to invoke a response from B and C, particularly if they have increased their investment in international shipping to meet a growing demand or to compensate for a declining amount of A tonnage or both. They will hardly be willing to disinvest in shipping, particularly if A has been indifferent to its own shipping interests for any period of time. They are much more likely to support their own merchant marines through government actions similar to A's.

Country A, however, can no longer focus entirely on its shipping industry. Once the public purse is opened in support of a merchant marine, related maritime interest groups will demand a share of government attention. To the extent of their political influence, they will also shape maritime policy. Such interest groups would include maritime labor, suppliers, shipyards, the defense establishment, and port interests, both longshore labor and shippers.

In time a new equilibrium will be reached in which A, B, and C subsidize their merchant marines directly or indirectly and probably support maritime industries as well. As happens in any subsidy program, however, the subsidized item tends to become oversupplied. In the case of shipping, an oversupply of tonnage will exert a downward pressure on shipping rates. To deal with falling shipping revenues and to maintain their relative tonnage positions, A, B, and C will be forced to provide even larger subsidies. Resources devoted to international shipping are now inefficiently allocated; consequently, a higher cost is imposed on society.

This analysis has assumed a three-maritime-nation world. If that world included fifty or more countries that have their own aspirations for national-flag merchant fleets, that have a sovereign's power to promote their foreign trade (using all the options discussed above), and that have, as members of a collection of nations (the United Nations), power to impose standards on international shipping, the game of ocean shipping becomes not only complex in the extreme but also, perhaps more important, a high-risk capital venture.

The Cost of Rules: A Case Study

Under U.S. and international law a cargo vessel may carry no more than twelve passengers. If the thirteenth passenger is carried, the ship must be reclassified as a passenger vessel.

If reclassification added less to costs than the revenue generated by carrying additional passengers, there would be no problem. But this is far from the reality.

A study based on 1978 union wage and manning scales contrasted crew size and wages for a vessel operated as a cargo ship carrying no passengers and that same ship certificated as a passenger vessel carrying thirty passengers.[13]

When the vessel was classified as a cargo ship and carried no passengers, it required a crew of forty-four. As a cargo vessel carrying twelve passengers, it needed a crew of forty-seven, at an additional cost of $4,800/month. The potential passenger-carrying profit was $7,200/ month. When the vessel was classified as a passenger ship but carried no passengers, the crew increased to fifty-five, at an additional cost of $24,000. If thirty passengers were carried, the crew size was seventy-five and the total addition to wages was $63,000/month.

The thirty-one additional crew members (the difference between a cargo vessel and a passenger ship carrying thirty passengers) can be classified as follows.

Four crew members held positions required by U.S. statutes or treaties ($13,000). Eight held positions added because of certification as a passenger vessel ($19,900). Passenger vessels must meet more rigid construction and safety requirements than cargo ships. For example, they must have sprinkler systems, fire doors, extra pumps, lifeboats and rafts, and redundant electrical generation equipment. Eight more crew members operated and maintained this equipment. (Specific numbers are not, however, required by law.) The remaining nineteen crew members were added to serve passengers' and the larger crew's housekeeping needs ($30,100).

The study estimated the revenue from carrying thirty passengers at $60,000/month. Thus, wage costs alone exceeded potential revenues by $3,000. When subsistence and capital costs were added in, the cost of carrying thirty passengers was calculated at $77,000/month opposed to a revenue of $60,000/month.

What rules made the cost of carrying passengers so high that it became economically impracticable? First, U.S. statutes require a continuous radiotelegraph watch. This in turn requires employing two additional radio officers at a monthly cost of $9,800. Carrying a doctor on passenger ships is not required by international agreements. However, on U.S.-flag ships carrying over forty-nine passengers, a doctor is necessary. Traditionally, when a U.S. ship is certificated as a passenger ship and carries over twelve passengers, a doctor is also carried. The additional monthly cost is $1,600.

The number of crew members "required" to operate and maintain a vessel built and operated according to passenger ship safety standards is left to the discretion of the U.S. Coast Guard, which sets the minimum. Union agreements specify any additional crew. The nineteen members added for passenger and additional crew needs were entirely determined by bargaining.

With respect to construction and operating standards, the study concluded that standards already imposed on U.S.-flag cargo vessels (the world's highest) with few exceptions were sufficient for a ship carrying less than 100 passengers. An exception would be additional lifeboats and rafts. The study also concluded that safety requirements and crew/passenger needs for a vessel carrying 30 passengers could be efficiently and safely handled by an additional fifteen crew members at monthly wages of $25,000.

When estimates of subsistence and capital costs of $14,000/month are added to the $25,000 wage bill, it is seen that a potential profit of $24,000/month exists when thirty passengers are carried.

The study concluded that the regulations and union agreements that determine the cost of carrying passengers are archaic in view of advances in technology. Ships are faster and safer; navigation and communication systems are vastly more efficient, while remote computer-assisted medical advice and diagnosis has become a science. Neither law nor private contractual arrangements have recognized these advances. Al May, executive vice-president of the Council of American-Flag Ship Operators, summarized the operators' position:

> I can state positively that if obsolete rules with regard to the necessity for a doctor, three radio operators, large crews, etc., were eliminated, then many companies would give serious consideration to the economics of including increased passenger accommodations in the deck housing on new freighters.[14]

The study concludes, "It is ironic indeed that the crew and equipment on the flight deck of a 747 carrying upwards of 350 passengers is essentially identical to that on a 747 configured to carry cargo."[15]

Conclusion

The rules governing the game of ocean shipping are complex in the extreme. Rules designed to promote a merchant marine have been in many instances so restrictive as to be counterproductive. For this reason, many U.S. firms chose to operate without direct government subsidies between 1937 and 1940 and between 1945 and 1959 (see the discussion of the 1936 Merchant Marine Act in Chapter 3). When a nation, with the best of intentions, seeks to insure its place in the maritime world, the number of rules multiplies.

The question is how to relax the regulations, how to "deregulate" ocean shipping, so that the cost to the American taxpayer of maintaining a merchant marine is minimized.

5 The Making of Maritime Policy

To the observer far removed from the capital it may seem that nothing of consequence has happened to U.S. maritime policy since the Nixon administration's Merchant Marine Act of 1970, and—judging by "results only"—he or she could well be right. But appearances from afar can be, and often are, deceptive.

Despite the absence of stark change, the 1970s and early 1980s have been a time of creative tension within the national maritime policy system, and trial and error have led to refined assumptions and more focused conclusions. This chapter will consider those assumptions and conclusions, giving special attention to the historical context in which current policy choices arose; and it will state present and proposed policies and assess the political forces and coalitions that have influenced events in recent years, so that the reader will be left with a sense of where we have come from, where we are now, and where we are going.

The Postwar Context

The forty-six years since enactment of the landmark Merchant Marine Act of 1936 have been tumultuous ones. For example, the crash maritime shipbuilding program of 1941–45 contributed to total, unconditional victories over Germany and Japan in World War II. American shipping was the life support system for the Soviet Union's lend-lease resupply, and then it carried the postwar cargoes with which Marshall and MacArthur resurrected the vanquished nations.

Riding the economic high tide of the 1950s and 1960s, American ship operators—like the rest of American society—predicated their assumptions and expectations on an economy and a foreign policy that hardly knew a sense of limits. It was not until the Vietnam War in the late 1960s and the later inflationary downturn in the U.S. economy that such limits were even perceived.

During the Vietnam War, for the third time since Pearl Harbor, the American merchant fleet again bridged the Pacific Ocean. But during Vietnam, the Johnson administration tried to enjoy "guns and butter" simultaneously without mobilizing. There were no new shipbuilding programs: it was business as usual.

There had been no need for major capital investment in either our naval or merchant fleets between 1945 and 1965, since plenty of ships were leftover from V-E and V-J (victory in Europe and victory in Japan) days. Moreover, reinvestment capital for shipping assets was plentiful during the Cold War. But Vietnam changed that. For eight years (1965–73) the operating costs of the war preempted significant reinvestment in naval and commercial tonnage, and the timing could not have been worse.

The overheating of the American economy prompted by the Vietnam commitment coincided with the revitalization of the Japanese, German, and Korean economies, and each nation aggressively pursued maritime market shares. At the same time the Soviets, ably led by Admiral Sergei Gorschkov, took to the trade lanes with unexpected numbers of vessels. At home, "containerization" had arrived, creating competing demands for modernization capital.

Exacerbating matters were the 1973 oil embargo, the 1974–75 recession, and the inflationary spiral that compelled labor union leaders to seek higher survival wages for a seafaring work force whose real income was being eroded. Unable to find liquidity anywhere else, corporations sought relief in mergers and consolidations, and shipping was no exception. "I am often asked," one shipping executive would tell industry audiences, to gales of laughter, "if it is still possible to make a small fortune in U.S. shipping—and I always tell them 'yes—if you start with a large one.' "[1] Such gallows humor was to prove prophetic.

In short order, America's maritime leaders found themselves beset by obsolescence and the need to build new container fleets; higher fuel costs; wages inflating with the economy; and diminishing liquidity. They turned to Washington for assistance.

An appeal to the federal government was neither unexpected nor inappropriate, given that new foreign fleets were benefiting from foreign government subsidy and preference policies that favored home-grown shipping, to the detriment of American carriers. Moreover, federal policy had allowed tax advantages to those who reinvested in foreign shipping, had tied U.S.-subsidized operators to mandatory U.S. construction requirements, and—in the name of "flag" and in the interests of a reliable all-U.S. fleet—had denied U.S. companies the chance to go multinational to attract capital.

Maritime leaders sought federal aid for a simple, but precise, reason: If Uncle Sam is part of the problem, he can become part of the solution.

Standing Policy

The federal policy confronting the American maritime industry in the 1970s can only be described as antiquated. The elements mandated by the Merchant Marine Act of 1936 were straightforward: The government gave construction and operating differential subsidies (CDS and ODS) to liner shipping and (after 1970) to bulk operations as well, in order to offset the disparity between U.S. and foreign shipbuilding and ship-operating costs. In return, the government demanded that subsidy recipients abide by certain conditions, chief among them being that ODS recipients must build and replace their vessels through American shipyards.

The commercial behavior of liner operators was regulated by the Shipping Act of 1916, which, in effect, permitted agreements by members of shipping cartels (or "conferences") to be filed and policed by a Federal Maritime Commission. But under the late Chief Justice Earl Warren, the U.S. Supreme Court rode roughshod over the 1916 act's regulatory scheme and substantially limited operators' capacity for concerted action in conferences by allowing the Department of Justice to interpose between the Federal Maritime Commission (FMC) and conference members in litigation related to agreements. The ensuing court-created confusion led to a massive, and successful, antitrust attack on American liner companies operating in the North Atlantic in 1977 and demoralized ship operators, making liner shipping a perilous undertaking for those not advised by battalions of legal counsel.

At the same time, U.S. tax policy sent mixed signals to potential shipping investors. The federal government assisted ship construction financing by letting vessel operators defer taxes on ship operating profits by placing such profits in a capital construction fund (CCF). If CCF accounts were invested in U.S.-built vessels, operators could ultimately avoid all taxes. (Under Title XI of the 1936 act, the government acted even more directly by underwriting ship financing loans, another incentive to investors to build in the United States.) In spite of these inducements to Build American, the Internal Revenue Code set unfavorable ship depreciation rates (fourteen and a half years compared with one year in Great Britain) and permitted tax avoidance in situations where foreign income of American corporations was invested in foreign shipping.

Finally, American maritime policy itself was articulated in the 1970s from the Department of Commerce and not from the Office of the Special Trade Representative or the U.S. Department of Transportation (DOT). This was not inconsistent, since it was the maritime lobby of the late 1960s that had loudly resisted President Johnson's effort to incorporate the Maritime Administration into DOT.

At the heart of American maritime policy were two contradictory propositions. The first, found in Section 101 of the 1936 act, held that it was in the national interest for the United States to possess a merchant fleet capable of carrying a substantial portion of American commerce in peacetime and acting as a naval auxiliary in wartime; the second, having its origin in the pre–World War II Neutrality Act, permitted American corporations to own and operate vessels under foreign flags (usually Panamanian or Liberian). Moreover, underlying the first proposition was the presumption that American shipbuilders and ship operators should be mutually—and inextricably—intertwined by law.

The argument supporting this policy was rooted in what might be described as the "defense imperative": merchant ships and U.S. shipyards were needed in war, therefore the successful operation of the "shipping base" (vessels and shipyards) was in the national interest and should be encouraged. But at the same time the U.S. government did not block the paths of the corporations that sought low-cost foreign operating alternatives. In effect, and indirectly, the United States opted for two distinct fleets, each competing for capital.

In short, American maritime policy was internally contradictory.

Where Historical Trends and U.S. Policy Intersect

In a world of higher costs, larger containerized operations, labor unions fighting to keep pace with inflation, and work force expectations founded upon the attitudes of the 1960s, the size of the American-flag fleet declined in the 1970s. Military planners, who had been spoiled since 1945 by ready access to sufficient tonnage, discovered again how dependent any American force projection effort would be upon easily requisitioned U.S. ships.

Regardless of the reasons, the decline in numbers of ships was ominous. Doenitz and Hitler had nearly strangled England by targeting a relative handful of U-boats against the world's largest merchant fleet. With the Soviet Union capable of targeting a submarine force nearly five times the size of Nazi Germany's against a smaller number of larger ships (and better targets) carrying even more cargo, immediate action was necessary. A consensus, however, proved elusive.

Proposed Changes

If a consensus was difficult, the objective was clear—a larger, more competitive fleet. Unfortunately, the means to that end were less clear.

Distilled to their essence, the alternatives were, and historically had been, three:

1. a continuation of direct aid in the form of federal subsidies, perhaps at increased levels or on different terms;

2. indirect aid (with or without subsidy), for example, creating a climate conducive to investing in shipping or shipbuilding (e.g., tax relief or tax credits, rapid depreciation for shipping, and increased investment tax credits); reorganizing or consolidating government agencies concerned with shipping; granting relief from onerous bureaucratic regulation; or reforming the Shipping Act of 1916;

3. expanded flag preferences, a variant of alternatives 1 and 2, whereby the United States expands upon the Cargo Preference Act of 1954, reserving or allocating certain cargo for carriage by vessels of the United States.

Several combinations of these alternatives were tried in the 1970s during three successive administrations, but without success. Cargo preference bills twice failed to achieve passage. Finally, and in exasperation, a bipartisan Omnibus Maritime Bill was attempted in 1979 and 1980, but by the conclusion of the Ninety-sixth Congress, it also had been scuttled. What had happened? How could the combined efforts of so many bring forth so little success? What lessons can be applied to future reform efforts? Is consensus on maritime policy achievable at all, and if so, at what price? In delving for answers to such questions it may be possible to suggest what the current Republican administration can do.

Cargo Preference Legislation

Two attempts were made in the 1970s to expand standing cargo preference laws in order to encourage growth of the American bulk fleet. Each failed. With the benefit of hindsight, several reasons for the failures can be identified. A major one was opposing lobbies.

Opposition to cargo preference legislation came from a loosely defined group of consumers; American-owned carriers operating under foreign flags (deprecatingly denominated "flags of convenience" by their detractors); the major oil companies, whose product would be mandatorily carried on what they felt were more expensive U.S.-flag vessels; and last—but decidedly not least—Japanese and European carriers and their governments, who forcefully enunciated their views to the State Department.

Opponents of cargo preference legislation asserted that the legislation was needlessly protectionist. Specifically, they said that once U.S. operators monopolized a guaranteed market share, rates would inevitably skyrocket, at the expense of American consumers (most of the oil cargo would be imported), and that the American-flag fleet already received too much government largesse. Further, they argued, an outright preference would not affect such causes of American fleet decline as excessive crew levels, unaffordable worker benefits, and the unwillingness of subsidy-dependent managers to innovate or take risks. In sum, they said, to pass new cargo preference laws would be to protect an industry unable to compete for cargo in the marketplace.

Proponents of cargo preference called their proposal "cargo equity," claiming that cargo preference merely sought to put American shipping on an equal footing with fleets that already benefited from both statutory and "hidden" government preferences, and that it was naive to suggest that "free trade" was "free" at all. According to this view, opponents of U.S. cargo reservation (preference) (including many foreign operators) wanted a double benefit: the right to their own government's preference (or to some variation of the cargo-dividing UNCTAD Liner Code) and the enjoyment of unfettered access to open American trades.

Notwithstanding the strength of the U.S.-flag industry's case, opponents of preference succeeded twice in stopping the expansion of the preference act. First, in 1974, when at the behest of cross-trading foreign carriers and their embassies, President Ford vetoed a bill to reserve 30 percent of U.S. oil imports to U.S. vessels. And then, in 1977, when a 9.5 percent oil-carriage mandate failed in the House of Representatives.

The 1977 cargo preference fight became highly politicized and resulted in intensely negative national publicity for the shipping industry. The problem started when the Republican National Committee released an internal Carter White House memorandum in which the President's staff advised support for the measure as a means to repay maritime labor groups for backing Mr. Carter in the 1976 election. A partisan tone having been set, major oil companies and the flag-of-convenience lobby joined the fray, opposing cargo preference with their formidable war chests and publicity-generating capacity.

The debate became acrimonious, drawing editorial comment from coast to coast. Opponents persuaded many members of Congress that the consumer would be skewered by higher prices. Moreover, and perhaps more important, the opposition depicted the maritime industry as a monied "special interest" elite intent upon ruthlessly using its powerful political clout to exploit the man in the street. The maritime industry responded with its own media campaign, which unintentionally reinforced its image as a powerhouse lobby and further polarized the issue.

The policy goal of fleet development was lost in the fire of debate about the means of achieving it (i.e., cargo preference), and the House defeated the bill. This setback was to have enormous consequences.

First, and foremost, the Carter administration had been embarrassed in its first attempt at maritime legislation and retreated from maritime policy making. Second, the maritime industry, "big oil," cross-trading foreign carriers, and the flag-of-convenience group had checked the U.S.-flag sector's attack and stalemated policy formulation. Moreover, labor and management faced the worst of both worlds. In one world they were viewed as a powerful special interest group; in a second world they were viewed as little more than inept ward politicians.

Decisive legislative action traditionally requires two parts strong executive branch leadership, one part enthusiastic lobbying, and one part congressional cooperation. If the 1977 cargo preference fight accomplished anything, it was to diminish the Carter administration's appetite for further maritime combat. Thus, a crucial ingredient was lost.

Sensing the vacuum left after the 1977 debate, gradually concluding that the Carter presidency would provide no further maritime policy initiatives,[2] and convinced that the fleet would continue to decline, congressional Democrats and Republicans decided in 1979 to shift the locus of maritime policy initiation to the legislative branch and to write their own maritime policy.

The Omnibus Bill

In early 1979, a bipartisan coalition of House Democrats and Republicans introduced the Omnibus Maritime Regulatory Reform, Revitalization, and Reorganization Act of 1979 (H.R. 4769), a massive bill later reported out as H.R. 6899 by the Committee on Merchant Marine and Fisheries. While a narrower, more modest companion measure would be skillfully moved through the U.S. Senate by Senator Daniel K. Inouye, the Omnibus Bill would never reach the House floor. Paradoxically, critics outside the maritime sector would call it a giveaway to the special interests, while internal industry authorities would find it threatening or niggardly. Even today the question remains: How could such a bold conception have failed so thoroughly in the execution? Since the answer could well predict the success or failure of future initiatives, the question is worth investigating.

In broad terms the Omnibus Bill addressed those problems that oversight hearings had found to be central to maritime reform: (1) regulatory reform under the Shipping Act (later pursued as the Biaggi-Gorton Bill in the Ninety-seventh Congress); (2) reform of the 1936 Merchant Marine Act's promotional programs; (3) government reorganization in order to designate a chief maritime spokesman; and (4) substantial maritime tax reform. The intent of the drafters was to eliminate red tape, attract investment capital to shipping, restore competitiveness, and give political muscle to maritime policy makers within the government. Ironically, although there would ultimately be agreement on 90 percent of the bill, the discord associated with the remaining 10 percent would kill the bill.

From the point of view of the drafters and their staffs, the Omnibus Bill failed for eight reasons.

1. Coalition and compromise. To avoid a repetition of the 1977 cargo preference fight, a bipartisan coalition was essential. (This chiefly was composed of Democratic Chairman John M. Murphy, ranking Republican Gene Snyder of Kentucky, and Congressman Pete McCloskey of California.) Given the vast difference of opinions among the original sponsors, the language of H.R. 4769 was an exercise in compromise from the outset. Since neither side could have amassed enough evidence to support any single approach, consensus was needed. Each facet of the proposed program had to be acceptable to both Democratic and Republican views. While the legislative process is inherently one of compromise, this least-common-denominator approach to the Omnibus Bill resulted in provisions displeasing to some.

2. Yards versus operators. Ship construction in the United States had become progressively more expensive through the 1970s—prohibitively so, in the opinions of ship operators who availed themselves of government promotional programs and found themselves tied to Build American mandates. For shipyards, on the other hand, contraction and government regulations were also problems.

The construction differential subsidy (CDS) program was intended to offset the cost differential between U.S. and foreign construction costs by subsidizing up to 50 percent of the vessel cost. This ceiling and the underfunding of the CDS program acted as a deterrent to ship construction, according to the shipyard lobby. The problem was exacerbated by slack demand due to overtonnaging in certain trades and to the availability of foreign government–supported financing overseas.

Congress faced the competing objectives of maintaining a shipyard mobilization base, on the one hand, and increasing fleet size on the other. It identified two solutions. First, the House committee bill would lift the 50 percent limit, letting the CDS rate "float" from year to year, at the discretion of the government. This would give Washington the flexibility it desired. Second, the committee bill would permit subsidized operators to acquire a foreign vessel, on condition that operators would later buy a "matching" vessel in an American shipyard.

The drafters thought they had made every effort to accommodate the shipyard community by boosting CDS and by creating a matching-vessel requirement. In effect, they thought the prospect of "building foreign" would induce more U.S. building. Paradoxically, the Shipbuilders' Council of America adopted a benign neglect attitude, telling its lobbyists to neither advocate nor oppose the bill.

Shipyard apathy toward the bill angered operators, who privately claimed that U.S. yards were low in productivity, late in delivery, already en route to an expanded naval shipbuilding program, and merely shrinking from a postwar all-time high in numbers of shipyard workers. In short, operators believed that the shipyards were crying wolf. This split within the maritime sector dealt a fatal blow to the Omnibus Bill. Doubly vexing was the realization that while the bill did not tilt in either direction, both sides were disappointed.

3. *Labor union disapproval.* Citing crew costs and manning levels well above those of foreign competitors, Congressman McCloskey sought legislative limits on the crew levels of subsidized operators. The McCloskey proposal would have withheld all subsidies to operators' vessels exceeding the manning levels set by the government. The theory was that government had to back managers whose marginal cash flow positions had reduced their collective bargaining latitude.

Maritime labor viewed McCloskey's language as an intrusion into collective bargaining and felt that he blamed unions unfairly for fleet decline and overlooked recent union efforts to reduce crews. The opposition of maritime labor further subdivided the maritime community and added an "antilabor" aspect to what had been a strictly promotional effort.

4. *Essential trade routes.* Basing his approach on the testimony of liner shipping company managers, Congressman Snyder sought to eliminate "essential" trade routes (those routes allocated to subsidized operators under the law) in order to reduce government-imposed operational strictures. He assumed that his proposal was responsive to the industry's desire for greater freedom, an assumption later disproved when the liner operators opposed his amendment.

Trade routes had become alienable assets with market value (not unlike New York City taxi medallions, to paraphrase Congressman McCloskey), and cash-strapped liner managers wanted to convey them for profit. In short, "keep the trade routes" became a battle cry of liner operators, and another segment of the maritime industry turned against the bill.

5. *Shippers versus liner conferences.* Title II of the bill restated the antitrust exemption for liner conferences under the 1916 Shipping Act, reversing the erosion of the act's original intent. The shipper community felt that Title II would concentrate undue market power in the hands of liner conferences, so the committee authorized the establishment of counterbalancing shippers' councils.

Notwithstanding the conference/shipper council compromise, the Justice Department's Antitrust Division staff and their allies on the House Judiciary Committee persisted in opposing any restatement of the 1916 Shipping Act's qualified exemption, making no secret of their antipathy for even the original provision. In their view, a conference was a cartel and any continuation of Shipping Act freedoms flew in the face of both antitrust law and recent airline and truck deregulation trends whereby antitrust exemptions had been either abridged or abolished.

The opposition of the antitrust theorists—likened by some to "medieval theologians" for their emphasis on doctrinal orthodoxy and cant—led to the bill's referral to the Judiciary Committee. This procedural move derailed the proposal, and assured a similar debate on the bill's mirror-image successor, the Biaggi-Gorton Bill, in the Ninety-seventh Congress.

6. *Tax policy.* Title IV dealt chiefly with the broadening of access to the capital construction fund (CCF) and with accelerated depreciation for shipping and was eviscerated by the tax-writing House Committee on Ways and Means, where members were reluctant to distinguish shipping from other distressed industries, such as housing, timber, steel, and automobiles. Moreover, several members alleged that the shipping industry already benefited from tax-oriented stimulus programs (e.g., the CCF) and needed internal management reforms more than additional government assistance.

The reactions of the Ways and Means Committee members were not dissimilar to those of others inside and outside of the Congress and pinpoint two key antimaritime arguments that recur in each debate: (1) Why haven't previous programs worked? and (2) Why should shipping be distinguished from other industrial sectors? The answer, of course, lies in the defense aspect of shipping, a reality that must be repeatedly underscored.

7. *Lack of presidential pressure.* In response to the Omnibus Bill, the Carter administration formed a multiagency task force from the Departments of Commerce, State, and Treasury, but *not* the Department of Defense. A White House staff coordinator was designated, and he and the maritime administrator diligently pursued administration consensus on the bill: they wrote two presidential position papers and the maritime administrator appeared twice before the committee.

In general, the views of the agencies on the task force were not overruled by a majority, but were melded to form a consensus. Many industry and congressional observers considered that this approach was safe and overly cautious, but that the lack of boldness was not unjustified in an election year and in the wake of the earlier cargo preference debacle.

But maritime history teaches that it was only strong executive branch leadership in 1936 and in 1970 that produced meaningful legislation, and the absence of bold, enthusiastic presidential advocacy in 1979 and 1980 could hardly be compensated for by a bipartisan coalition of former opponents (Congressmen Murphy and McCloskey). Quite understandably, a "committee" was a pale substitute for an aggressive leader. The president's defenders, on the other hand, ascribed his tentativeness to a sense that having been once burned on cargo preference, his enthusiasm had been necessarily diminished.

8. *Congressional dynamics and legislative management.* The Omnibus Bill was vast in scope and steeped in detail. It appeared to many to be too much in one package. Moreover, since the original version (H.R. 4769) had prompted so much controversy, a passable rewrite (H.R. 6899) was needed. This change in the bill's content confused all but the most sophisticated observers. Finally, the committee's chairman and the bill's prime mover, Congressman Murphy, became embroiled in the so-called Abscam episode in February 1980 and had to surrender his chairmanship. Only a few months later, his successor, Lud Ashley of Ohio, pronounced the bill dead.

Conclusion

In military history many bold plans have failed in the execution. One recalls, for example, Field Marshal Montgomery's airborne thrust across the Rhine in 1944, which extended "a bridge too far" and failed to establish a northern passage into Nazi Germany. When asked about the flaws in his grand design, Montgomery distinguished the plan from the execution: the plan was fine, but the execution was lacking. The same can be said of the Omnibus Bill.

Lost in the smoke of its demise was the recognition that the Omnibus Maritime Bill debate had laid out an ambitious agenda, 80 to 90 percent of which was generally supported. Moreover, soon after the bill's burial the Reagan administration moved decisively to designate the secretary of transportation as the key government spokesman and he, in turn, proved to be a most forceful advocate of regulatory reform (Title II of the Omnibus Bill), in the Ninety-seventh Congress. Having pursued reform and reorganization (Title V of the Omnibus Bill) and having reduced the depreciable life of vessels from fourteen and a half years to five in 1981 tax legislation (a key part of Title IV of the bill), the Reagan team expansively construed congressionally initiated provisions of the 1982 Maritime Authorization that permitted ship operators to build overseas and still retain operating subsidy, thereby implementing a major plank of the Omnibus Bill. Finally, President Reagan has proposed a 600-ship navy in his Five-Year Defense Plan, offering an average navy shipbuilding budget of $21 billion in the bargain.

Despite the progress of 1981 and 1982, however, problems remain, and President Reagan has promised to proffer a promotional package to the Congress. Once again, the Omnibus Bill experience suggests what the content of such a package should be and how to proceed. (Title III of the Omnibus Bill was a fleet promotional proposal.)

With or without subsidies, any promotional package will have to contain a mix of direct and indirect aids to the fleet, justified by the unique defense role played by the merchant marine. Administration and congressional figures have discussed proposals to expand cargo preference; extend the 200-mile exclusive economic zone of the 1976 Fisheries Conservation and Management Act to include all maritime activity; offer tax credits; and authorize permanently foreign building or a build and charter program whereby militarily useful vessels could be acquired.

But if the experience of the Ninety-sixth Congress teaches anything, it is that form and procedure may be as important as substance. Thus it would appear advisable for future administrations to formulate plans in the comparative quiet of internal deliberations and permit "previews" for the maritime industry. Such an approach would anticipate and resolve intraindustry disagreements that would otherwise polarize matters were they to arise in public settings, where parties have less flexibility. Regardless of the scope or depth of deliberations, some debate is inevitable, but such a debate in Congress on American maritime policy may be long overdue.

With American defense policy focusing anew on the strategic mobility required to deploy and sustain a rapid deployment joint task force of multidivision strength, the sealift or defense imperative must provide the backdrop for maritime promotional legislation. But for its defense utility (vividly demonstrated by the Falkland Islands campaign's adept use of British merchant shipping), the American merchant fleet would remain just another means of commercial transport, not unlike the bus, truck, or train. Thus any future fleet development initiative must be preceded by an articulate explanation of the sealift needs of the United States; such a case could best be made by the Defense Department, an absentee from the Omnibus Bill debate in the Carter years.

While a precise definition of what the Reagan administration will offer by way of fleet promotion was not known as the Ninety-eighth Congress met in January 1983, one can discern what will probably not prevail, on the basis of the Omnibus Bill and cargo preference episodes.

No measure will succeed without strong, aggressive executive branch support that clearly and forcefully sets out the unique role of the merchant fleet in the execution of American strategy. At the same time, the interests of shipyards and ship operators must be balanced, even if policy persists in its formal disconnection of the two. If American operators are to have access to foreign shipbuilding, builders must have some counterbalancing benefit. The matching vessel compromise of the Omnibus Maritime Bill may still be the answer.

Finally, the self-destructive impulse to find fault or cast blame for the contraction of the U.S.-flag fleet must be repressed. Neither labor nor management nor government nor builders nor operators are solely responsible. Conversely, no one segment can chart a new course alone.

Having failed in their bold attempt to leap the Rhine by air in Operation Market-Garden, the Allied armies reorganized in late 1944 and forged ahead in a steady, driving coalition campaign. So, too, must maritime reform advocates now come together and press on with what promises to be as tough a legislative campaign as those of 1977–78 and 1979–80.

6   Domestic Ocean Shipping

Almost from the founding of the Republic the coastal trades of the United States have been reserved to American-flag vessels. Initially, this shipping was protected by the levying of heavy tonnage duties on foreign vessels. Later, foreign tonnage was explicitly excluded by statutes that limited U.S. coastal trade to ships not only registered in America but also built in America and crewed by U.S. citizens.

As the United States expanded its boundaries from the Atlantic to the Pacific Coast, built the Panama Canal, and later acquired noncontiguous territories and possessions, U.S. coastal trades expanded. Statutes excluding foreign shipping from these new trades followed. Two major exceptions were made for foreign vessels operating between the continental United States and the Philippines and Virgin Islands.[1]

A temporary exception was made by Congress in 1914 owing to shipping shortages on a number of American trade routes. The Allies had recalled their ships from these routes for service in the North Atlantic on their strategically more important trades. However, the prohibition against foreign-flag ships was reinstated by the Merchant Marine Act of 1920 and has never been seriously challenged since that time. (The Merchant Marine Act of 1920 (Section 27) is more commonly referred to as the Jones Act.) There is no doubt that cabotage legislation was chiefly responsible for the large percentage of the total number of American-flag vessels historically found in the protected (domestic) trades. Before World War II, over 800 vessels engaged in domestic ocean trade, twice the number of vessels engaged in foreign trade.

The author gratefully acknowledges comments and suggestions by David Bess, Professor of Transportation and Dean, College of Business Administration, University of Hawaii. Errors of fact or logic, however, remain the responsibility of the author, as do all conclusions and recommendations.

Profile of the Protected Trades

Table 6.1 breaks down U.S.-flag tonnage into domestic and foreign trades and contrasts the pre–World War II fleet with that of 1982.

In 1982 the major domestic ocean trade routes reserved to U.S.-flag ships were as follows (see Figure 6.1):

Route	Primary Commodity
Alaska–Pacific Coast	Crude oil, petroleum products, general cargo
Alaska–Gulf and Atlantic coasts	Crude oil, seafood
Pacific Coast–Hawaii	Petroleum products, general cargo, sugar, passengers
Pacific Coast–Gulf and Atlantic coasts	Lumber, petroleum products, chemicals, general cargo
Pacific Coast	Petroleum products, general cargo
Gulf–Atlantic Coast	Petroleum products, phosphates, bulk chemicals
Atlantic Coast	General cargo, bulk commodities
Atlantic Coast–Puerto Rico	General cargo, petroleum products, sugar, bulk commodities

Table 6.1. Domestic and Foreign Trade: U.S.-Flag Shipping, 1937–82

	1937		1982	
	No. of Ships	Gross Tonnage (millions of tons)	No. of Ships	Gross Tonnage (millions of tons)
Domestic trade				
Dry cargo (freighters)	506	2.3	44	0.6
Tanker	343	2.4	210	5.7
Total	849	4.7	254	6.3
Foreign trade				
Dry cargo (freighters)	374	2.3	164	2.8
Tanker	52	0.4	24	0.5
Total	426	2.7	188	3.3

SOURCES: 1937 statistics: U.S., Maritime Commission, *Economic Survey of the American Merchant Marine.* 1982 statistics: U.S., Maritime Administration, *U.S. Merchant Fleet Data Sheet,* as of 1 March 1982.

NOTE: Foreign trade includes foreign to foreign. It does not include eighty vessels on charter to government agencies.

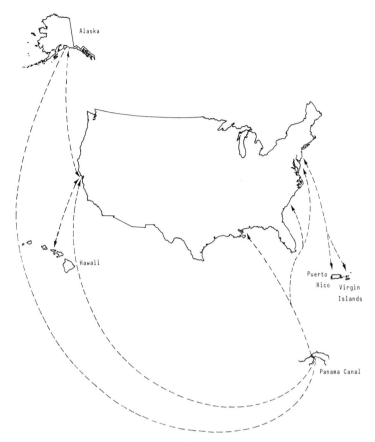

Figure 6.1. Major domestic ocean trade routes.

| Gulf–Puerto Rico | General cargo, bulk commodities, petroleum products |
| Virgin Islands–Gulf and Atlantic coasts | Petroleum products, general cargo |

Other domestic trade routes reserved to U.S.-flag ships are Hawaii–Atlantic and Gulf coasts, Pacific Coast–Puerto Rico, Alaska–Hawaii, and Pacific Coast–Guam.

Table 6.2 lists the larger companies (in terms of fleet size) serving these trade routes. Note, however, that the list is not exhaustive. At any one time, a number of companies with smaller fleets will be found on these routes.

Tonnage in the protected ocean trades increased between 1975 and

Table 6.2. Major Steamship Lines Serving Protected Trade Routes

Company	Type of Service
American-Hawaii Cruises	Passenger
American President Lines	General cargo
Apex Marine	Bulk liquid
Atlantic Richfield	Bulk liquid
Chevron Shipping Company	Bulk liquid
Cove Shipping	Bulk liquid
Exxon	Bulk liquid
Gulf Oil	Bulk liquid
Keystone Shipping Company	Bulk liquid
Marine Transport	Bulk liquid
Matson Navigation Company	General cargo
Mobil Oil	Bulk liquid
Maritime Overseas Corporation	Bulk liquid
Ogden Marine	Bulk liquid/dry
Puerto Rico Marine	General cargo
Sabine Towing & Transportation	Bulk liquid
Sea-Land Services, Inc.	General cargo
Sun Transport	Bulk liquid
Texaco	Bulk liquid
Trinidad Corporation	Bulk liquid
United States Lines	General cargo
Union Oil (California)	Bulk liquid

SOURCE: "U.S. Flag Ocean Going Fleet as of April 1, 1982," *Marine Engineering/Log* 87 (15 June 1982).

1979 from 234 to 314 million short tons. Table 6.3 shows how tonnage was distributed in coastwise, intercoastal, and noncontiguous trades. While this growth was a respectable 80 million short tons, it was almost entirely attributable to the increase in crude oil shipments from Alaska through the Panama Canal.

With respect to type of vessel, the share of cargo between non-self-propelled dry cargo and tank barges remained essentially the same in the coastwise and intercoastal trades. In the noncontiguous trades, although barge tonnage absolutely increased, its percentage share decreased.[2]

Land Competition

With the exception of the noncontiguous trades, primarily with Alaska, Hawaii, and Puerto Rico (where U.S.-flag carriers are virtually freight monopolists), domestic ocean shipping faces competition from land transportation systems. Historically, its major competitors have been the railroads. But while the nineteenth and first part of the twentieth century

Table 6.3. Domestic Ocean Commerce, 1975–79

Sector	Tonnage (millions of short tons)	
	1975	*1979*
Coastwise	170.5	163.1
Intercoastal	3.8	3.9
Noncontiguous	60.1	146.9
Total	234.4	313.9

SOURCE: U.S., Maritime Administration, *Domestic Waterborne Trade of the United States, 1975–1979*, p. 34.

has fairly been called the railroad era, domestic shipping was able to maintain a share of the market and was reasonably profitable.

On the Atlantic and Gulf coasts the cargoes were primarily bulk—oil, phosphates, and coal. On the Pacific Coast, lumber predominated. In the intercoastal trades, via the Panama Canal, primary cargoes westbound were steel, chemicals, paper products, and general merchandise. Cargoes eastbound were lumber and canned fruits and vegetables.[3]

One gauge of the importance of domestic shipping was that even in the depression years (1930–40), ships in the coastwise and intercoastal trades carried greater tonnages than their U.S.-flag, foreign trade counterparts.

The post–World War II period, however, was another story. Traffic that had been diverted to rail because coastwise and intercoastal ships had been taken from their trade routes to support the overseas war effort tended to say with rail. And although some shipping lines reestablished service, their return was relatively short lived. The traditional break-bulk ship was labor intensive, with respect to both shoreside cargo handling and shipboard manning. The ocean system as it was then constituted simply could not compete for general freight with the scheduling flexibility of the railroads in bulk movement or the long-haul trucks on the nation's newly built interstate highways. Furthermore, in the 1970s, tanker petroleum product shipments from the Gulf to the East Coast faced increased competition from pipelines.

Not even the advent of the container helped in the long run, for while containers had the potential to significantly reduce the cost of the ocean system, stevedore work rules limited any real savings. Moreover, the rail and truck modes quickly adapted to the innovation.

Even if the longshore unions had been more moderate in their wage demands and work rules and less inclined to work stoppages, the problem of vessel replacement was still there. In this regard, the first container ships, and the ones used in the domestic trades, were generally converted, war-built T-2 tankers and C-2 cargo ships. These vessels, mostly built in 1943–45, and acquired at bargain prices after the war, were approaching the end of their useful life by the mid-1970s. However, under the Jones Act, replacement tonnage had to be U.S. built, and by the late 1970s a U.S.-built ship cost twice as much as a foreign-built one. Since construction differential subsidies were not available for ships in the protected trades, the ship operator faced the formidable problem of earning a competitive rate of return on an exceedingly highly priced piece of capital equipment. In this environment, with rail and truck competition and prohibitive vessel replacement costs, Sea-Land Services, one of the larger and more profitable U.S.-flag shipping firms, in 1977 suspended its Atlantic and Gulf container ship service as well as its intercoastal operations. These ships were absorbed into the company's foreign and noncontiguous services.

Cost and Service Characteristics of Domestic Shipping and Its Competitors

Domestic ocean shipping offering service between continental U.S. ports faces three major surface competitors—rail, highway, and pipeline. A fourth competitor might be said to be non-self-propelled barges, although they are generally considered part of domestic ocean shipping. Recent innovations in barge movements are described in Appendix A.

Table 6.4 contrasts the advantages and disadvantages of the four modes making up the U.S. domestic freight system in terms of cost and service characteristics. Figure 6.2 relates the cost per ton mile and output over a range of outputs. Note, however, that the average cost per ton mile

Table 6.4. Advantages and Disadvantages of Domestic Ocean Shipping and Its Competitors

Cost and Service Characteristics	Modes in Descending Order of Relative Advantage
Ton-mile cost	[Pipeline, shipping], rail, highway
Capacity	Pipeline, shipping, rail, highway
Time	Highway, rail, shipping, pipeline
Flexibility	Highway, rail, shipping, pipeline
Dependability	Pipeline, rail, [highway, shipping]
Environmental impact	[Pipeline, shipping], rail, highway
Energy consumption per ton mile	[Pipeline, shipping], rail, highway

NOTE: Modes in brackets have approximately the same relative advantage.

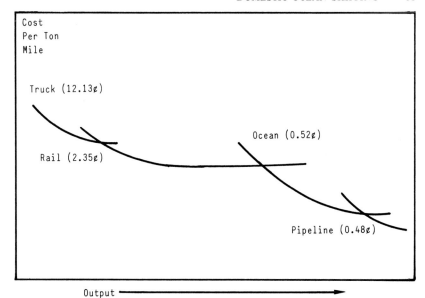

Figure 6.2. Cost-output relationships between transport modes. The average cost per ton mile is shown in parentheses. Sources: U.S., Maritime Administration, *Domestic Ocean Trade Area—Final Report*; U.S., Maritime Administration, *The Competitive Position of Domestic Shipping in the U.S. Transportation Market*.

shows that the ocean system is even more competitive than the curves suggest.

Table 6.4 and Figure 6.2 imply what the market is for ocean transportation in the present operating environment. It is in the volume movement of liquid and dry bulk commodities over relatively long distances. On the other hand, in 1983 the possibility of any significant increase in general cargo shipments must be considered remote for at least three reasons:

1. Deregulation of the railroads, together with the railroads' pricing flexibility, will make railroads much stronger competitors for long-haul movements. Equally important is the rapid development of large super railroads spanning greater distances. In 1983 the CSX Corporation and Norfolk and Southern straddle the East Coast from Canada to Florida; Conrail has been revitalized; and Burlington Northern's tracks run from the Pacific Coast to the Gulf of Mexico. Other large systems are certain to follow. As interchange delays between once competing and/or independent roads disappear, delivery times will become shorter.

2. The Jones Act requirement that domestic trade vessels be built in the United States places an almost prohibitive burden on an operator contemplating general cargo service. Railroads are under no such con-

straint, should the price difference between U.S.- and foreign-built rail equipment widen appreciably.

A related impediment to general freight movement in contiguous trade is lack of a suitably designed ship. Before World War II, general cargo vessels in the domestic fleet were much smaller than their foreign trade counterparts. This is generally the case today where large coastwise trades exist, e.g., the Baltic Sea, the Mediterranean Sea, the Japanese home islands, and the Southwest Pacific. A container ship of the handy size of the old Maritime Commission C-2 design has never been built in the United States, nor is such construction likely. The trend is to ever larger container ships such as Sea-Land's D-9 class. Moreover, the design speeds of ocean carriers have decreased. The trend now is the opposite of that of ten years ago. The slower but more fuel-efficient diesel engines are preferred. Unless prospective operators were given the option of buying their vessel in a foreign yard, a vessel sized to meet domestic general trade requirements would be hard to come by in the United States.

3. If there were to be a rebirth of general cargo shipments in the domestic trades, it would have to be in the container mode. However, present container work rules have driven up the cost of handling containers at U.S. ports to a point where the ship operator would find it difficult to compete with the increasingly efficient rail container system. (See Chapter 16 for a discussion of longshore labor in general and container work rules in particular.)

In 1979 the domestic ocean trade share of U.S. surface intercity freight traffic was approximately 314 million short tons or a little over 5 percent of the total movement.[4]

Mode	Short Tons (millions)	Percentage
Domestic Ocean	313.9	5
Great Lakes	151.2	2
Inland waterway	622.4	11
Railroad	1,560.0	27
Truck	2,240.0	38
Pipeline	978.0	17

Government Policy

While government policy toward protecting domestic ocean shipping has been as constant as the polar star, it has not been uncriticized.

When the Merchant Marine Act of 1936 was being debated, the question of improving the earning potential of coastwise and intercoastal operators was raised. The operators suggested they be allowed to build abroad and register their vessels under the American flag. They also proposed that construction subsidies be made available. Neither option, however, came to pass.[5]

Periodically, bills have been introduced in Congress to waive Jones Act requirements. In 1981, for example, H.R. 3577 proposed such a waiver. Under this bill, foreign-flag vessels would have been allowed to carry West Coast forest products to East and Gulf Coast ports and to Puerto Rico for a two-year period. American West Coast lumber interests claimed they were at a competitive disadvantage with Canadian producers using foreign-flag ships. The bill was strongly opposed by U.S. shipping interests and was never reported out of the House Merchant Marine Subcommittee. While there is little doubt efforts will be made to reintroduce this legislation, the outcome is likely to be the same. Jones Act waivers have been few and far between.[6]

Ronald Reagan, in his campaign and as president, has endorsed retention of the Jones Act. In 1982, the secretary of transportation, as the chief administration spokesman on maritime affairs, proposed (1) that the requirement that ships be U.S. built and registered be extended to offshore drilling rigs and their support vessels and (2) that cabotage protection be extended to include the U.S.–Virgin Islands petroleum trades.[7]

On the other hand, criticism of the Jones Act and the congressional ban against allowing the sale of Alaska crude oil to foreign nations has been increasingly vocal. One proposal that continually generates support in Congress is to allow Alaska crude oil to be shipped to Japan and have the United States make up the difference by importing more oil from other overseas sources. The argument was summarized in this extract from a 1981 *Wall Street Journal* editorial:

> Every day some 600,000 barrels of oil leave the port of Valdez, Alaska, on a silly and humongously expensive voyage. They start out in supertankers, are transhipped through the Panama Canal in smaller boats, then are transferred back into supertankers and end up on the U.S. Gulf Coast. The whole journey is in U.S. flag ships, and the transport costs amount to $5.50 to $5.60 a barrel.
>
> That same oil could be shipped to Japan in foreign tankers, at a cost of about 60 cents a barrel. Gulf Coast refiners could make up the difference by stepping up their imports, say from Mexico (cost in foreign tankers: 50 cents a barrel) or from the Middle East ($2 to $3 a barrel). . . .
>
> The biggest supporters of the ban have been U.S. shipowners and maritime unions, who well realize that U.S. shipping rates are roughly twice those of the international market. Since the Jones Act requires that all interstate shipping be done in American-made bottoms with U.S. crews, banning the export of Alaskan crude has essentially amounted to a costly subsidy of the shipping industry by U.S. oil producers, refiners, and consumers.[8]

What the editorial did not state was that a part of this additional cost was due to the need to tranship to smaller vessels because the Panama Canal cannot handle the large supertankers, whose crew size and costs are among the lowest in the U.S. fleet. Nor that Panama Canal tolls have been increased by 85 percent over the last decade. Nor, finally, that some part of the higher American cost can legitimately be charged to the national security.

With the opening of the deep-water Louisiana Offshore Oil Port in 1981, the Panama Canal bottleneck is the only remaining physical barrier to reducing the cost of Alaskan crude oil shipments to the Gulf Coast, although the lack of deep-water terminals on the East Coast is still a major problem.

In any case, the construction of a new sea-level canal at least has reached the planning stage. The concept is a joint venture between the United States, Japan, and Panama.[9]

Two other relatively recent government policy changes have had or will have an impact on domestic shipping. One is the reopening of the question of to what extent the ship operator must pay for harbor improvements and maintenance, e.g, dredging of channels. In the past, these costs have been borne entirely by the federal government. In 1981 and 1982, proposals were made to shift some of this cost to users. In 1983, several bills have been introduced, and it is reasonable to expect that some user cost-sharing scheme will eventually become law.[10] (See Chapter 16 for a discussion of the port charge–user issue.)

The second policy change occurred in 1977 when the Maritime Administration allowed Very Large Crude Carriers (VLCCs) that were built with construction differential subsidy (CDS) funds to participate in the Alaska crude oil trade. The initial ban was to insure that low-priced (to the firm) ships built with CDS did not unfairly compete with protected trade ships built without government assistance.

Faced with periodic shortages of "Jones Act tankers," that is, tankers built without construction subsidies, the decision was made to approve a VLCC's operation in the Alaska trade for up to six months in any twelve-month period. Operators are required to pay back a pro rata share of CDS monies for time spent in the Alaska trade. Some of the largest and newest U.S. tanker tonnage is employed under this arrangement.

National Defense Considerations

At the commencement of hostilities in both World War I and World War II, domestic shipping provided the largest portion of in-place tonnage. And as might be expected, with its ships instantly committed to wartime support roles, the destruction of this fleet was the most complete.

In 1982, as Table 6.1 shows, the domestic fleet was a tanker fleet with a

Table 6.5. Average Age and Tonnage of Contiguous
and Noncontiguous Domestic Shipping, 31 December 1979

Type	Contiguous			Noncontiguous		
	No. of Ships	Age (years)	Tonnage (dwt)	No. of Ships	Age (years)	Tonnage (dwt)
Dry cargo	10	31	17,000	35	23	15,000
Tanker	148	25	30,000	37	12	75,000

SOURCE: U.S., Maritime Administration, *The Competitive Position of Domestic Shipping in the U.S. Transportation Market.*
NOTE: Tonnage is in deadweight tons (dwt).

modest number of general cargo vessels, a considerably different composition from that of the fleet in 1937, when over 500 cargo vessels could be counted in the protected trades.

What does this changed fleet composition imply for national security? First, as has been said elsewhere, the types of vessels most suitable for military logistical support are RO/ROs, LASH, break-bulk ships, and container ships, in approximately that order. Less important would be tankers and bulk carriers, and least of all, the non-self-propelled barges.

A detailed 1980 Maritime Administration study of the competitive position of the domestic fleet in the U.S. transportation system examined the domestic fleet with respect to age, vessel type, and trade. Table 6.5 indicates the relevant relationships. Most important, from a national defense view, is that thirty-five of the forty-five dry cargo vessels, including the newer container ships and RO/ROs, are in the noncontiguous trades and that the same is true for most newer and larger tankers. Two and a half years later (1 March 1982) dry cargo numbers were down to twenty-seven. However, included in the later total were two cruise liners.[11] Tankers increased to forty-four.

The implication for national security seems clear. If a major justification for the Jones Act is, in fact, national security, then the justification rests on ships in the noncontiguous trades. For example, the privately owned U.S.-flag oceangoing fleet in 1982 had a total of sixteen RO/ROs, the military's most prized logistics support ship. Three companies operating in the noncontiguous trades accounted for nine of them.[12]

Conclusion

The single most important policy question with respect to domestic shipping is this: Should the Jones Act be kept? And if kept, should it be modified?

In arriving at an answer, the intercoastal/coastwise trades must be considered apart from the noncontiguous Alaska, Hawaii, Puerto Rico, Virgin Islands, and Guam trades. For, as was noted above, a large part of the national defense argument for keeping the Jones Act in place rests on the shipping the act supports in the latter group. Thus the question becomes how to maintain, and even increase, noncontiguous shipping at a minimum cost to the taxpayer.[13] The most efficient policy would be to maintain the U.S.-registry and U.S.-crew requirements for this shipping and gradually phase out the requirement that this tonnage be American built. The importance of the phase-out schedule cannot be overstated. It is the most important element in implementing such a policy. For example, it would be inequitable if the Matson Navigation Company suddenly had to compete in the Hawaii trade with foreign-built ships constructed for half the cost of Matson ships. Several solutions to the phase-out problem are possible. The problem is far from insurmountable. A beginning would be to implement a faster depreciation schedule for existing U.S.-built ships.

Assuming a case can be made for a government policy supporting noncontiguous trades on national defense grounds, an even better case can be made on political grounds. Namely, Hawaii and Alaska are sovereign states in the American federal system, while Puerto Rico's commonwealth status is as close to statehood as one can come. It is one thing to discount the domestic political ramifications should foreign-flag shipping be pulled off one or more U.S. foreign trade routes. It is quite another to have the ocean shipping links of two noncontiguous states severed.[14]

It is not valid to argue that any foreign-flag shipping on these routes might be U.S. owned. The same risks would exist in relying on this shipping in the noncontiguous trades as in foreign trade. (See Chapter 18 for a discussion of U.S.-owned foreign-flag shipping.)

The case for keeping Jones Act protection on the intercoastal and coastwise trades is considerably weaker. First, this shipping is primarily composed of relatively small, aging tankers. If, as will be urged in Chapter 7, a modest tanker and bulk fleet under the U.S. flag is justified on the grounds of national security, the present coastwise and intercoastal fleet is a poor foundation on which to build. A better option is to estimate our bulk and tanker national security needs and fill those needs by augmenting existing noncontiguous tonnage with a foreign trade fleet. Since our newest and best tanker tonnage is already in the noncontiguous and protected Alaska trade, it is the foundation on which to build. Moreover, with a policy allowing U.S.-flag tankers to be foreign built, as urged above, the cumbersome and inefficient policy of granting waivers to non–Jones Act tankers to operate in the Alaska trades for six out of twelve months would end.

On the other hand, several good reasons exist for allowing U.S.-owned, foreign-flag shipping into our coastal and intercoastal trades.[15]

First, the argument that this shipping was under effective U.S. control would have a certain validity, mainly because these vessels would be operating between ports and in waters under nominal U.S. control.

Second, this shipping would help maintain a degree of competition in our domestic bulk movements. With deregulation, railroads have made giant strides in reasserting their position as primary freight movers. As a nationwide system of six to eight large rail systems develops, domestic shipping is unlikely, under foreign flag or otherwise, to recapture any significant part of contiguous general cargo freight. The speed and flexibility of rail-truck systems will be too great to overcome. On the other hand, it is not in the national interest to allow the rail and pipeline modes to become bulk carrier monopolists between the Gulf and East coasts.[16]

The question is whether the present, aging, coastwise tanker fleet will be replaced under Jones Act restrictions. If not, how might a reasonably competitive environment in this trade be insured? The worst way would be to reregulate the railroads and pipelines. Far better would be to insure some amount of ocean competition with U.S.-owned tonnage, even under foreign flag.[17]

7 The Resource War: Bulk and Tanker Shipping

This chapter could be simply titled "Bulk and Tanker Operations." Such a title, however, would miss the main point of the chapter, which is, Why is it important to have a modest amount of U.S.-flag bulk and tanker tonnage engaged in the American foreign trades?

What has changed since 1936, when the framers of the most comprehensive piece of maritime legislation ever passed by Congress, the Merchant Marine Act of 1936, ignored bulk and tanker shipping by providing neither construction nor operating subsidies for it? Or put another way, what occurred in the next thirty-four years to make the Merchant Marine Act of 1970 remedy the deficiency?[1]

A good part of the answer to the second and third questions was the pre–World War II lack of demand for tanker services in U.S. foreign trade. Imports of foreign crude oil were minimal. On balance, the United States was an oil-exporting nation. If a national defense tanker tonnage requirement could be said to exist, it was met by a large domestic fleet composed of some 300 vessels—a fleet, moreover, protected from foreign competition by cabotage legislation.

The U.S. ocean bulk fleet was primarily composed of ore carriers serving parent company requirements, e.g., the large steel companies. Other bulk shipments were moved in the lower holds of liner vessels. No tramp fleet of any consequence existed, nor any government interest in promoting one. In fact, a blue ribbon panel charged with making specific recommendations to implement the Merchant Marine Act of 1936 concluded:

> It is clear that the trend in American overseas trade since the war [World War I] had been to an increasing degree to ship cheap and bulky cargoes by regular liner services.
>
> It is argued by some that the United States should have a good supply of bulk-cargo carriers to transport foodstuffs and supplies overseas in time of war. The speed of a convoy, however, is limited by the speed of the slowest ship and much difficulty was encountered in convoying slow-moving tramps to Europe during the World War. From the viewpoint of national defense it is far better to subsidize cargo liners.[2]

The Post–World War II Period

In the period since the end of World War II and particularly since 1960, the United States has become increasingly dependent not only on imported oil but also on nonfuel raw materials. The point was made in some detail by General Alexander M. Haig, Jr., then president of United Technologies, Inc., when he testified before Congress in 1980. He said in part:

> Personally, I have long been troubled by what is rapidly becoming a crisis in strategic and critical materials—a crisis rooted in our own and in our allies' dependence on imports for key materials.
>
> The United States is inordinately and increasingly dependent on foreign sources of supply for many of the raw materials critical to our defense and our economy. In 1950 only 4 of 13 basic industrial raw materials were imported in quantities of 50% or more. Today we have reached that level of import for 9 of the same 13 materials. But as serious as the problem is to us, it is far more so to our industrialized allies and friends around the world.[3]

Other authorities have voiced similar concerns.[4] In 1981, forty-one percent of U.S. petroleum needs were met by imported oil. Table 7.1 lists major oil suppliers and the amount of oil the United States depended on these suppliers for.

On the nonfuel side, General Alton D. Slay, Commander, Air Force Systems Command, testified before Congress in 1980 that the United States depends on foreign sources for twenty-three of the forty materials essential to the U.S. economy and national security.[5] Table 7.2 lists twenty of the most important minerals and metals, major sources of supply, and the percentage the United States depends on these sources for.

Overseas sources of fuel and minerals/metals critical to America's industrial base are summarized below. Each listed source is 1,000 or more statute miles from a continental U.S. port.

Algeria	Italy	South Africa
Australia	Jamaica	Southwest Africa
Bolivia	Japan	(Namibia)
Brazil	Korea	Spain
Dominican Republic	Kuwait	Sri Lanka
Europe (general)	Malagasy	Surinam
Gabon	Malaysia	Thailand
Guinea	New Caledonia	Turkey
Honduras	Nigeria	United Kingdom
Indonesia	Norway	Venezuela
Israel	Saudi Arabia	Zaire
		Zambia

Table 7.1. Petroleum Imports and U.S. Domestic Production
as of December 1981

Source	Average No. of Barrels (millions per day)	Percentage of Total Consumed
OPEC		
Saudi Arabia	1,128	8
Nigeria	622	4
Venezuela	404	3
Indonesia	364	2
Libya[a]	320	2
Algeria[b]	310	2
United Arab Emirates	83	0.6
Other	87	0.6
Total	3,318	23
Non-OPEC		
Mexico	523	3.5
Canada	445	3
Other	1,695	11
Total	2,663	18
U.S. Domestic Production	8,562	59

SOURCE: U.S., Department of Energy, Information Administration, *Monthly Energy Review* (Washington, D.C.: U.S. Government Printing Office, March 1982), pp. 34, 35, 50.
NOTE: OPEC is the Organization of Petroleum Exporting Countries. Other sources of U.S. petroleum imports include the Bahamas, Netherlands Antilles, Puerto Rico, Trinidad, Virgin Islands, Soviet Union, Rumania, and Angola.
[a]There were no Libyan imports in 1982.
[b]Natural gas imports in January 1982 were 95 billion cubic feet. The largest overseas source (of liquified natural gas) was Algeria, which supplied 3 billion cubic feet.

Figures 7.1 and 7.2 indicate the main shipping routes between the United States and these sources. Appendix B shows the distances between these sources and the United States as well as the estimated days the transporting vessel would be at sea (in wartime, this would be the time during which the ship is exposed to hostile naval or air attack).

While there is near-unanimous agreement that the United States must somehow make its foreign raw material sources as secure as possible, there is no consensus on how to do this.

Two schools of thought have suggested ways of maintaining a stable and continuous flow of raw materials and fuel imports. The first school might be called passive and diplomacy oriented, relying on the long-term

Table 7.2. Net U.S. Imports of Strategic Minerals
and Metals by Source in 1979

Mineral or Metal	Percentage Imported	Major Sources
Columbium	100	Brazil, Thailand, Canada
Mica (sheet)	100	India, Brazil, Malagasy Republic, Mexico, Spain
Strontium	100	Mexico, Spain
Titanium/rutile	100	Australia, Japan, India
Manganese	95	Brazil, Gabon, South Africa
Tantalum	95	Thailand, Canada, Malaysia, Brazil
Bauxite and alumina	95	Jamaica, Australia
Flourine	90	Mexico, Spain, Italy, South Africa
Cobalt	90	Zaire, Belgium-Luxembourg, Zambia, Finland
Chromium	90	South Africa, Soviet Union, Turkey, Zimbabwe
Platinum	90	South Africa, Soviet Union, United Kingdom
Asbestos	85	Canada, South Africa
Nickel	80	Canada, Norway, New Caledonia, Dominican Republic
Tin	80	Malaysia, Thailand, Bolivia, Indonesia
Cadmium	70	Canada, Australia, Belgium-Luxembourg
Potassium	70	Canada, Israel
Mercury	60	Algeria, Spain, Italy, Canada
Zinc	60	Canada, Mexico, Honduras
Tungsten	60	Canada, Bolivia, Korea
Antimony	50	South Africa, Bolivia

SOURCE: U.S., Congress, House, Committee on Armed Services, *Capability of U.S. Defense Industrial Base*, 96th Cong., 2d sess., 1980, pp. 456–58.

NOTE: Some examples of mineral or metal use in industry include the following: chromium, a basic input of ferrochromium, which in turn is employed in making stainless and alloy steel; nickel, used for electroplating and in stainless steel; asbestos, used in building materials; titanium, in aircraft; vanadium, in special steel products; manganese, in iron and steel; fluorspar, a flux in steel making; uranium, used in nuclear power generation; tungsten and mica, in electrical products.

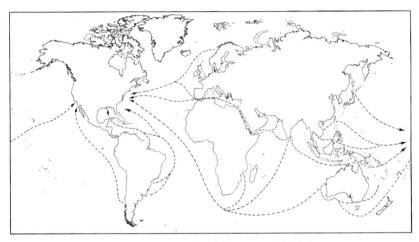

Figure 7.1. Principal ocean routes for U.S. strategic bulk imports.

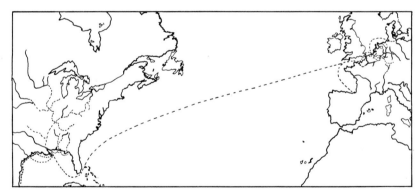

Figure 7.2. Principal ocean routes for U.S. crude oil imports.

good will of the suppliers. Here, American policy has been to provide financial and technical aid; encourage government-backed investment by U.S. business; identify with the political and economic aspirations of the developing nation suppliers, on the one hand; and promote free trade policies with the developed nation suppliers, on the other. Recent examples of this strategy include the reinstatement by the United States in 1977 of the Rhodesian chrome embargo and the 1977–80 U.S.-backed attempt

SS *Ultramar*, owned by Apex Marine Corporation, is a combination oil-bulk-ore (OBO) carrier of 82,000 deadweight tons. Maritime Administration photograph

to economically isolate South Africa. Our on again–off again policy of stockpiling strategic imports could also be fairly considered a passive strategy, as could major conservation programs, particularly energy programs.

The other approach is more pragmatic. Examples are President Reagan's position of "trade not aid," spelled out at the summit meeting between the so-called rich and poor nations at Cancun (Mexico) in October 1981; a more conciliatory policy toward South Africa, sometimes referred to as the "Persian Gulf of mineral wealth";[6] and a willingness to supply weapons and militarily support governments friendly to U.S. interests. Recent arms sales to Saudi Arabia and Egypt are other examples. Congressman James Santini fairly summed up the pragmatic approach:

> We must have an economic strategy relative to our relations with foreign nations that will give higher priority to mineral security aspects of those relations. We cannot wait until we are irrevocably trapped. Our foreign policy must work to re-establish traditional economic concepts under international law.
>
> The luxury of days past when we basked in the enlightened foreign policy of exporting human rights while we imported Russian chrome must come to an end.[7]

Insuring a continuous flow of strategic imports is a two-part problem. The first is to maintain in place governments friendly to the United States. The second is to secure the ocean transportation link between the raw material source and the United States. A threat to either, the source or the transportation system, is unacceptable. However, such a threat is real and likely. General Maxwell D. Taylor, former chairman of the Joint Chiefs of Staff, considers that the probability of the threat is "approaching certainty in some form, with a potential for serious damage to our trade and thereby to the national security."[8]

Transporting Strategic Materials and Fuels

Insuring an uninterrupted flow of essential raw materials and fuels from overseas sources is the main reason for supporting a U.S.-flag bulk and tanker fleet. It should be noted, however, that this sector of the merchant marine serves the national security interest somewhat differently than liner shipping does. Bulkers and tankers support our mobilization base day in and day out. The cargoes they carry originate at dozens of overseas supply sources, as noted above, and are discharged at continental U.S. ports. The trades, that is, the routes over which they sail, would be the same in peacetime, a contingency, or a national emergency. On the other hand, the defense mission of liner shipping, made up of container ships, LASH, RO/RO, and break-bulk vessels, is to provide direct logistical support for American forces overseas. In this role, military cargo would be loaded in U.S. ports and move to those places in the world where American forces are stationed or where U.S. interests are threatened. In a contingency or a national emergency, ships would be taken off scheduled services and concentrated to meet a particular shipping requirement. In a NATO war, for example, liner vessels in the South American and African trade would be used to supply U.S. and NATO forces in Europe. (See Chapter 8 for a discussion of liner shipping in its national security role.)

In conjunction with a policy of maintaining friendly governments in power at supply sources is the crucially important navy role of defending our strategic import routes. But our far-flung, long, and very well identified strategic routes will be hard to secure with even a 600-ship U.S. Navy and maximum cooperation by friendly power naval forces.

U.S.-Flag Tanker and Bulk Fleet

Table 7.3 shows current U.S.-flag and foreign-flag bulk and tanker tonnage. Table 7.4 shows the characteristics of this fleet.

While the data in Table 7.3 fairly reflect the almost complete U.S. dependence on foreign-flag bulk tonnage, the United States is even more dependent on foreign-flag tankers than the table shows. Most of the U.S. tanker tonnage shown is employed in the protected domestic trades. In 1982, only thirteen U.S.-flag tankers were engaged in foreign trade.[9]

On the other hand, the United States has been a leader in developing, and to some extent implementing, new technology. The 125,000–cubic meter LNG *Aquarius* was launched in General Dynamics' Quincy, Massachusetts, yard in 1977. In the same year the 265,000-dwt (deadweight tons) *American Spirit*, built by Bethlehem Steel's Sparrows Point yard for

Table 7.3. U.S./World Bulk and Tanker Tonnage

Type	No. of Ships	Tonnage (thousands of dwt)
Bulk		
U.S. flag	18	570
Foreign flag	4,778	184,604
Total	4,796	185,174
Tankers		
U.S. flag	291	15,483
Foreign flag	4,953	330,096
Total	5,244	345,579

SOURCE: U.S., Maritime Administration, Office of Trade Studies and Statistics. Foreign-flag bulk data are as of 1 January 1981, foreign-flag tanker data as of 1 January 1980, and U.S.-flag data as of 1 March 1982.

NOTE: U.S. tonnage (in deadweight tons) includes private and government owned. Bulk category includes oil/bulk/ore (OBOs) and colliers.

Gulf Oil, went into service on the Alaska trade route. In 1978 the *El Paso Southern*, a 126,000–cubic meter LNG, was launched by the Newport News, Virginia, shipyard.[10] And in 1979 this same yard delivered the largest U.S.-built tanker, the 390,770-dwt UST *Atlantic*.[11] The largest bulk carriers under the U.S. flag are the 82,000-dwt *Ultramar* and *Ultrasea*, built in 1973–74. In fact, the two ships are multipurpose bulk carriers (ships that can carry oil, bulk, and ore cargoes).

Port Requirements for Large Tankers and Bulk Vessels

One natural disadvantage the United States must cope with in regard to its strategic imports is the relatively shallow depths of American ports. An Ultra Large Crude Carrier (ULCC) can draw up to 100 feet, while U.S. port depths are generally in the 35- to 50-foot range. Such a deficiency is costly in economic terms and probably increases the risk to bulk and tanker shipping in a period of hostilities, since partially offloading the large ships into smaller vessels not only increases the number of ships needed and lengthens delivery time, but also increases the exposure of the entire system to hostile action.

A 1972 Maritime Administration–sponsored study on the feasibility of a North Atlantic deep-water oil terminal (NADOT) estimated that annual savings would be of the order of $500,000 per year if such a facility were constructed. Since then several regional studies have been done. All

Table 7.4. Characteristics of U.S. Bulk and Tanker Fleet
as of 1 January 1982

	No. of Vessels	Average Age	Average Tonnage (dwt)	Average Speed
Bulk				
Privately owned	18	25	47,300	14.8
General	15	27	24,600	14.8
Collier	1	37	24,300	13.0
Ore/bulk/oil	2	8	82,200	16.0
Tanker				
Privately owned	274	18	57,900	18
Major type	236	...	...	...
Minor type	6	...	...	...
Special products	32	...	...	...
Government owned	16	36	16,000	15

SOURCE: U.S., Department of the Navy, Military Sealift Command, *Ship Register*, January 1982.
NOTE: Both active and inactive vessels are included.

in all, twenty-four locations on the East, Gulf, and West coasts have been identified as potential deep-water ports.

In May 1981 the first U.S. deep-water port was opened to business. It is the Louisiana Offshore Oil Port (LOOP) which extends nineteen miles out into the Gulf of Mexico. A second deep-water port is planned on the Texas coast—the Seadock project. In 1982 its future is uncertain. (See Chapter 16 for a discussion of deep-water ports and the problems associated with them.)

Conclusion

The modern tanker and bulk carrier are not lovely ships to behold. They do not have the classical lines of ships. The best single world to describe them is "massive." By contrast, the Liberty ships of World War II, Franklin Roosevelt's so-called Ugly Ducklings, would inspire poetry.

Be that as it may, bulk and tanker shipping is vital to U.S. national security. It is also vulnerable. Rear Admiral Robert J. Hanks of the Institute for Foreign Policy Analysis recently observed:

> As a sailor, my concern is with the security of the sealanes across which these materials must flow, the threats to that movement, and the means required to protect the flow. Despite the remarkable advances which have been achieved in air transport across the years, it is a hard fact of life that the overwhelming bulk of all international trade must still travel by sea. And threats to such passage are myriad.[12]

He is right. It is also right to note again that even should the U.S. Navy reach 600 plus ships, it would still be spread extremely thin in trying to protect the sea lanes over which our bulk and oil imports move. This fairly raises the question of incorporating national defense features into any new bulk or tanker tonnage built for American registry, a question that heretofore has not received much attention, probably because we have come to accept the proposition that the best the United States could manage is the second best solution of relying on citizen-owned ships sailing under foreign flags.[13] Another reason for ignoring the question is the oft-stated navy position that bulk carriers and tankers have little, if any, defense value as logistical support ships. While this may well be true, it certainly does not imply that a modest amount spent for national defense features, such as navy compatible communications systems, helicopter pads, a minimum capability to replenish underway navy combatants, and submarine detection equipment, is a poor investment.[14]

U.S. coal exports may again loom large in the scheme of things, particularly if OPEC (Organization of Petroleum Exporting Countries) nations are able to agree on production limitations and are thereby able to maintain a relatively high price for world oil. And also, if the movement of Persian Gulf supplies is disrupted by conflict—a possibility that cannot be discounted. For whatever reason, a large coal export trade could be a new beginning for the bulk portion of the American merchant marine if—

automated vessels, requiring fewer crew members, could be obtained at the best world price;

maritime unions were willing to renegotiate downward wages and benefits for those remaining crew members; and

long-term bilateral agreements were in place to reduce the risk of private investment to a reasonable level.

If all this happened, American coal might not only lessen our dependence on foreign energy sources but also be the driving force to revitalize a crucial segment of the U.S. merchant fleet.[15]

8   Liner Shipping

> The Liner she's a lady, and 'er route is cut an' dried;
> The Man-o'-War's 'er 'usband, an' 'e always keeps beside;
> But, oh, the little cargo-boats that 'aven't any man,
> They've got to do their business first, and make the most they can!
>
>   Rudyard Kipling, "The Liner She's a Lady"

Liner shipping, sometimes referred to as scheduled or regular-service shipping, is the mainstay of the U.S.-flag, foreign trade merchant marine. It is also an important component in the U.S. domestic, noncontiguous trades. And while, in his 1894 poem, Kipling had the great passenger liners in mind, it is still true that the routes of present-day liners are, for the most part, "cut an' dried." In fact, the distinguishing characteristic of this fleet is schedule certainty. Sailing dates, ports of call, and services offered are as scrupulously maintained as the corresponding services of a well-run airline.

Schedule certainty is of particular importance, since a liner carries the freight of many shippers, with their own deadlines and timetables to meet. In fact, certainty of schedule is the hallmark of a well-managed liner company and a main consideration in determining a shipper's loyalty.

As common carriers, that is, carriers offering service to the public generally, liner companies are the most regulated segment of the shipping industry. The rationale for regulating them is no different from that for regulating common carriers in other modes. The necessary authority was upheld in the 1877 Supreme Court decision of *Munn* v. *Illinois*, where the court reaffirmed the long-held principle that it was a right of government to regulate those industries "affected with a public interest."

In 1983, liner shipping is entirely confined to those firms in the foreign and domestic noncontiguous U.S. trades. It was not always so, however. Before World War II, a number of liner companies offered regular service, including passenger service, on coastwise and intercoastal

The SS *United States* was the last holder of the Blue Riband for the shortest Atlantic crossing. Once the arrival of the great transatlantic liners in New York was a major news story and a much valued news assignment. No more. Passenger ships in 1983 are of the cruise ship variety, an as yet undecided possibility for the SS *United States*. Maritime Administration photograph

routes. Passenger vessels of the Savannah Line, the Eastern Steamship Company, and the Merchants and Miners Transportation Company called regularly at U.S. East Coast ports. (Technically, Eastern Steamship Company vessels were engaged in foreign trade. Their principal routes were New England ports to Nova Scotia.) Among these fleets were such passenger favorites as the *City of Chatanooga*, *Fairfax*, and *Evangeline*. Scheduled cargo services were provided by the A. H. Bull Steamship Company, the Newtex Line, the Calmar Line, the Luckenbach Steamship Company, the Isthmian Line, and other lines.

In 1937 there were 385 vessels engaged in the U.S. dry cargo/passenger foreign trade. Twenty-five principal liner companies operated 214 ships. Since there was no appreciable American tramp tonnage, the liner companies provided the general cargo service and showed the flag on the trade routes of U.S. foreign commerce.

The Merchant Marine Act of 1936

A main purpose of the 1936 act was to insure an American-flag presence on the liner trade routes of U.S. foreign commerce. Initially, in fact, operating and construction differential subsidies were limited to this shipping. Table 8.1 lists the major liner firms in 1937 and their status under the operating differential subsidy (ODS) provisions of the Merchant Marine Act of 1936.

As Table 8.1 shows, 155 liner vessels, owned by seventeen firms, were operationally subsidized. At the time, the United States' share of its dry cargo trade was 29.2 percent, of which subsidized vessels carried 16.6 percent.[1] By 1940 the number of subsidized firms had decreased to twelve, while the number of subsidized ships had increased to 176. However, the American share of its dry cargo foreign trade had fallen to 25.1 percent.

The Post–World War II Period

In the postwar period the United States stood almost alone as the world's predominant shipping nation. In 1946, American-flag vessels carried in excess of 65 percent of the country's foreign trade, dry cargo tonnage. Three years later, however, in 1949, subsidy payments to liner companies, which had been suspended during the war, were resumed. The active U.S. dry cargo/passenger fleet numbered 856 vessels, and the U.S.

Table 8.1. Subsidy Status of Dry Cargo, Passenger Firms in Foreign Trade, 1937

Line	No. of Vessels
Former mail contract lines subsidized	
under the 1936 Act	
American Diamond Lines	8
American Mail Line	4
American Scantic Line	7
American South African Line	4
Atlantic and Caribbean Steamship Company	5
Baltimore Mail Line	5
Columbian Steamship Company	3
Eastern Steamship Company	4
Export Steamship Company	18
Grace Lines	6
Lykes Lines	54
Mississippi Shipping Company	9
New York and Cuba Mail Line	3
Pacific-Argentine-Brazil Line	6
Oceanic Steamship Company	2
South Atlantic Steamship Company	6
United States Lines	11
Total	155

Table 8.1. (cont.)

Line	No. of Vessels
Former mail contract lines not subsidized under the 1936 Act	
American West African Line	8
American Line	3
Panama Mail Line	3
States Steamship Company	8
United Fruit Company	6
Waterman Steamship Company	13
Dollar Steamship Company	14
Munson Line	4
Total	59
Vessels not subsidized under mail contracts or the Merchant Marine Act of 1936	
Private carriers (subsidiaries)	134
Government owned and operated (nonmilitary)	37
Total	171
Grand total	385

SOURCES: U.S., Maritime Commission, *Economic Survey of the American Merchant Marine*; and U.S., Maritime Commission, *Report to Congress for Period Ending October 25, 1937.*

NOTE: Under the terms of the Merchant Marine Act of 1936, every line that applied for adjustment of its mail contract could seek to substitute an operating differential subsidy (ODS) agreement, which might cover all or part of its fleet.

share of its dry cargo trade had decreased to 38 percent. Thirteen liner firms, operating 256 cargo and passenger vessels, were under operating differential subsidy contracts, while twelve nonsubsidized companies operated about 200 vessels. The remaining dry cargo tonnage was tramp shipping.

1959–74

In 1959 the privately owned, dry cargo/passenger fleet numbered 489 vessels. Fifteen liner firms, operating 313 vessels, including 40 passenger and combination passenger/cargo ships, received operating subsidy payments, and all other liner firms eligible for operating subsidies had applications pending. The 109 nonsubsidized ships, when added to already subsidized tonnage, totalled 422 vessels. The remaining 67 ships were tramps or bulk carriers. All told, U.S. liner, tramp, and bulk shipping lifted about 15 percent of the nation's dry cargo foreign commerce.

Fifteen years later, in 1974, there were 258 active, privately owned, general cargo/passenger vessels engaged in U.S. foreign trade. Thirteen liner companies, of which eleven were subsidized, operated most of these ships. Of the total tons of dry cargo (general and bulk) moved, U.S.-flag ships lifted 6 percent.

1982

In 1982, the number of ships in the privately owned, foreign trade, general cargo fleet varied slightly according to source and the date a count was taken.[2]

The Maritime Administration estimated the total general cargo/passenger fleet to number 244 ships as of 1 September 1982, of which 201 were engaged in foreign trade, including 4 in foreign-to-foreign operations and 25 chartered to government agencies, primarily the Military Sealift Command.[3] Of these 201 ships, 139 were receiving operating differential subsidies.

In 1982 the U.S.-flag share of the dry cargo (general and bulk) that moved in foreign commerce reached a new low, less than 4 percent. The nation's share of its foreign liner commerce was approximately 27 percent.

Evaluation of Liner Operations, 1937–1982

In Chapter 15 the cost and benefit of operating differential subsidies are contrasted. Benefit is measured by the number of active liner vessels supported (kept at sea) by ODS payments.

Another measure would be the amount of foreign commerce liner tonnage moved in American ships. Table 8.2 shows the United States' share of its liner trade, 1962–82, as well as the size of the liner fleet. For purposes of comparison, it also shows the percentage of total tons of cargo moved in U.S. oceanborne foreign commerce.

Table 8.2. American-Flag Liner Participation in U.S. Foreign Commerce

Year	No. of Liner Vessels	Liner Tons (%)	Total Tons (%)
1962	497	26.2	10.0
1972	255	21.9	5.5
1980	205	27.3	3.7
1982	201	27.0[a]	3.5[a]

SOURCE: U.S., Maritime Administration, *Annual Reports*, FY 1962–81.
[a]Estimated.

In considering the data in Table 8.2 it cannot be overemphasized that U.S. support of its liner shipping is not restricted to providing operating differential subsidies. Indirect support programs, such as those discussed in Chapter 3 and elsewhere, are equally important. They include cargo preference for both military and nonmilitary government-impelled cargoes, the Title XI loan guarantee program, and favorable tax treatment for monies deposited in capital construction fund accounts. Noncontiguous, domestic liner shipping benefits, of course, from Jones Act restrictions, which reserve this trade to American-flag ships.

One conclusion to be drawn from Table 8.2 is that over the past twenty years the United States has secured a share of its foreign liner commerce much larger than that of its total foreign oceanborne commerce.

In 1982 the United States carried approximately the same share of foreign trade liner tonnage that it carried in 1937—in the range of 27–29 percent. Nevertheless, a question that must be asked is, Can a U.S. liner fleet of some size survive without ODS? Because, for better or worse, maritime policy in the 1980s seems to be heading toward eliminating ODS.

Before World War II, a number of firms moved in and out of the ODS program, a mobility that, in itself, showed that it was possible to survive without subsidies. Moreover, five years after the war in 1949, approximately 200 vessels operated in our liner trades without ODS. Many operated entirely without subsidy, for example, the Isthmian Steamship Line and Pacific Far East Lines, while some subsidized companies also operated nonsubsidized vessels, e.g., United States Lines, Grace Lines, Lykes Lines, and American Export Lines. As was noted earlier, however, by 1960 all eligible companies had either received or applied for a subsidy agreement, even such long time holdouts as the Isthmian Steamship Line, States Marine, Isbrandtsen, and the Waterman Steamship Company.

Today, one of the largest liner companies, Sea-Land Services, operates entirely without an ODS agreement. In 1982 its fleet numbered forty vessels of which thirty to thirty-five were engaged in foreign trade.

Whether a liner firm could survive in the long run without operating subsidies depends on several considerations.

First, is the shipping operation a part of a larger parent company? Sea-Land is a subsidiary of the R. J. Reynolds Company, Delta Lines is a part of Holiday Inns Inc., and Lykes Lines is a part of the LTV Corporation. This is not to suggest that shipping subsidiaries are not profitable or for that matter may not be the most profitable part of a conglomerate operation, only that having additional financial resources behind a shipping company is a plus.[4]

Second, to what extent can American liner companies in foreign trade reduce crew sizes and/or their wage bills? Chapter 15 argues that wage costs must be reduced; they cannot merely track wage settlements in other sectors of the economy. The more wage costs are reduced, the more liner firms are likely to survive without ODS.

Third, will the United States accede to the Code of Conduct for Liner Conferences, wherein each trading partner has the option of lifting 40 percent of the cargo shipped? Or alternately, will the United States actively pursue bilateral shipping agreements outside the code? Either way, should operating subsidies be terminated, some form of cargo preference must exist if the U.S. liner industry is to survive.

Fourth, will Congress put American companies on an equal footing with foreign carriers in liner conferences? Specifically, will U.S. firms be allowed to pool freight, remain members of conferences that restrict membership, and offer through-intermodal rates? Will the economic deregulation process, put into motion with passage of the Airline Deregulation Act of 1978, the Staggers Rail Act of 1980, and the Motor Carrier Reform Act of 1980, include ocean shipping? If it does, the odds will be better that U.S. liner companies can survive without operating differential subsidies.

Fifth, do significant economies of scale exist in shipping operations, i.e., do larger firms enjoy lower average operating costs than smaller ones? This issue was raised in 1937 when a blue ribbon panel, charged with making recommendations to implement the Merchant Marine Act of 1936, noted:

> The need for consolidation is suggested by a comparison with the large lines of other nations. Several of the foreign fleets are larger than our entire subsidized merchant marine. . . .
>
> The advantages these large lines obtain are, among others, flexibility of operation, assurance of more stable earnings by diversity of routes, and more economic utilization of overhead expense and capital facilities.[5]

Does the same hold true today? Unfortunately it is not a topic that has received much attention in the transportation literature. But, presumably, economies still exist for the same reasons described in 1937.

However, it is not enough for the Department of Justice to maintain a hands-off policy should U.S. liner fleets grow in size. It is equally important for the liner companies themselves to appreciate the opportunities in growth—as they evidently did not during industry testimony and positioning on the Omnibus Maritime Bill in 1980. (See the discussion in Chapter 5.)

While a positive response to each of these five considerations is not essential to the survival of a sufficient amount of American liner tonnage without an operating subsidy, American wage costs must be reduced and a comprehensive system of cargo-sharing agreements must be in place.

Being larger rather than smaller, having the backing of a strong financial parent company, and passing economic deregulation legislation, while important, are not crucial.

National Security Considerations

Do the liner ships that ODS and other programs support meet our national security needs? The answer depends on the types of vessels in the liner fleet and their military usefulness. Historically, the fleet was made up of break-bulk vessels, a type of ship that traditionally has proven its worth in logistical support roles. In 1983 the foreign trade liner fleet is composed of 21 LASH/Sea Barge vessels, 64 container ships, 8 roll-on/roll-off carriers, and 108 break-bulk vessels—a total of 201 ships.

For military logistic support, LASH, RO/RO, and break-bulk vessels are extremely valuable. Container ships are less valuable, because of their dependence on sophisticated port facilities, which may not be available in a contingency or war. Nonetheless, container ships are included in all sealift deployment plans, and efforts continue at the Department of Defense to increase their capabilities in a logistics-over-the-shore (LOTS) environment.[6] In view of the type of vessel used in the liner trades, the "military and naval auxiliary" requirement of the Merchant Marine Act of 1936 is reasonably met.[7]

If the ships supported by government programs are, in fact, militarily useful, another question that could be asked is, What was the opportunity cost of the annual millions paid for operating subsidies?[8] Table 8.3 contrasts the number of subsidized liner ships, the direct ODS cost of

Table 8.3. Economic Opportunity Cost of ODS Expenditures

Year	No. of ODS Liner Ships	ODS (millions)	Approximate Opportunity Cost
1972	200	$192	0.8 nuclear guided missile cruiser ($240 million)
1975	181	$265	39 F-16 fighter aircraft at $6.4 million each
1978	165	$293	2 fleet oilers and 2 ocean tugs ($300 million)
1981	139	$272	151 M-1 tanks at $1.8 million each

SOURCE: U.S., Maritime Administration, *Annual Report*, FY 1972, 1975, 1978, 1983; U.S., Department of Defense, *Annual Report*, FY 1972, 1975, 1978, 1983.

NOTE: ODS (operating differential subsidy) is overstated in that figures include payments to a relatively small number of bulk vessels.

supporting them, and alternate defense purchases that could have been made with the funds. While it is always a matter of opinion how best to spend monies for national security, the data show that it costs an average of $255 million annually to support an average of 171 vessels—perhaps not that poor a use of taxpayers' money.

Vessel Availability

To be useful in a contingency or national emergency, vessels must be available. In a national emergency, vessels will be available since the president has the authority under a number of statutes to requisition any American-flag or American-owned (foreign-flag) vessel.

In a less-than-mobilization contingency, a priori authority is contained in contracts between those steamship companies that carry Department of Defense cargoes (most liner companies) and the Military Sealift Command. Under the so-called Sealift Readiness Program (SRP) operators agree, as a precondition to bidding on defense shipments, to make a portion of their fleet available in a contingency. Historically, between 100 and 115 vessels have been pledged under the SRP.

However, a call-up of vessels under the Sealift Readiness Program has never been made, hence defense planning cannot rely on past experience. To implement the SRP in peacetime would mean that U.S. operators would risk losing cargoes on their regular trade routes.

A comprehensive study of the Sealift Readiness Program was completed by the National Academy of Sciences in 1975.[9] In the proposed Omnibus Maritime Bill of 1979–80, the SRP was noted as a viable defense arrangement and, in fact, its provisions were strengthened with respect to operator participation.

Although the Department of Defense has from time to time expressed reservations about the SRP program, there is no reason to doubt that those agreements would be honored. In fact, industry spokesmen have sometimes been quite critical of Department of Defense officials for seeming to imply otherwise.

Size versus Numbers

Liner vessels are getting larger. In 1962 there were 454 active, privately owned freighters in commercial operation with an aggregate gross tonnage of 3.7 million. In 1983 there are 247 such ships in the U.S. fleet with an aggregate gross tonnage of 3.9 million. In other words, the U.S. fleet has the same carrying capacity, but 207 fewer ships.

Whether this is good or bad depends upon the types of nonmobilization scenarios the Department of Defense envisions as being the most likely to occur over the next decade. In a general war, convoy doctrine, as yet undecided upon, would also be a crucial variable.

Meanwhile, two points are worth noting. First, larger ships yield operating economies, and so it is reasonable to expect that the move to larger general cargo vessels will continue. Second, at some point in the trade-off between numbers and size, numbers will be the more important consideration in defense planning. In other words, if the justification of a liner fleet is the national security, then in order for that fleet to serve the national security usefully, a minimum number of ships must be supported. (See Chapter 12 for a discussion of size and numbers.)

Conclusion

This chapter has urged that the liner segment of our merchant marine is essential to national defense and is probably a good buy for the taxpayer. However, because the maritime environment is changing, the next chapter asks (and answers) the question, What are the essential elements in putting together a viable U.S. liner shipping policy?

9 Essential Elements of a U.S. Liner Shipping Policy

Of the major trading nations, only in the United States does one encounter the endless challenge to justify the existence of a merchant marine on purely economic terms. Although assistance in various forms has been provided since the founding of the Republic, it has generally been begrudgingly given by those who view it either as infringing on the free enterprise system, as they perceive it, or as diverting limited resources from programs to which a bureaucracy has assigned higher priorities.

It has only been on rare occasions that our government has recognized that a merchant marine is important enough to merit the government's developing a coherent, high-level executive program and then implementing it fully. These occasions have been either in time of war or when we have had a president who could comprehend the relationship of sea power and America's interests. In this century, three presidents have demonstrated this understanding.

Theodore Roosevelt connected the two great oceans with the Panama Canal, a link that resulted in a major increase in American trade, and at the same time built a modern American navy—the "great white fleet." Then, in spite of substantial opposition (at that time from Congress), he sent the fleet around the world as a demonstration of America's political and economic interests as an emerging world power.

Franklin Roosevelt, who started his government career as assistant secretary of the navy, used the rebuilding of the navy in the 1930s as an economic tool, and then rebuilt the U.S. merchant marine. His efforts—naval and merchant—were key factors in our overwhelming victory in World War II.

Richard Nixon similarly supported sea power when he developed the 1970 maritime program. Given the opposition of most of the government agencies, the program would never have been developed if the president had been persuaded on the basis of narrow, doctrinaire arguments. President Nixon wasn't and, as a result, the Merchant Marine Act of 1970 was enacted to implement a far-reaching program. This was the president who also gave sea power its modern-day definition as "the ability of a nation to project into the oceans in time of peace its economic strength, in time of emergency its defense mobility. . . ."

President Reagan's commitment as he took office to renewing our merchant marine on the basis of sound national security and economic reasoning could not have been clearer. At the same time, traditional free trade and antisubsidy biases have strengthened the hand of the agencies in the executive branch whose long-standing opposition to any pro-U.S.-flag maritime policy is well known. As a result, for the past two years the president has repeatedly reaffirmed that we need a merchant marine, but few programs have been implemented to bring the president's commitment to fruition.

One might think that the 1982 Britain-Argentina Falklands conflict sharpened perceptions of the woeful inadequacies in our sealift capacity, but it did not. In an apparent attempt to discredit any administration effort to promote the American merchant marine, the Office of Management and Budget (OMB) in May 1982 circulated a staff memorandum questioning the need for a merchant marine, a subject on which Mr. Reagan had clearly already made up his mind. The OMB memorandum concluded, with a self-assurance that is frequently derived from profound ignorance, that there is little justification for a major power, such as the United States, to support a merchant fleet.

Fortunately, however, the conclusions reached in the OMB memorandum were put into focus by a detailed critique written by former Chief of Naval Operations Admiral James L. Holloway, III. Appendix F notes pertinent portions of the OMB paper and Admiral Holloway's critique.

From all this confusion have emerged isolated initiatives—the results of political compromise and not of a clear articulation of the principles of trade and defense on which our new maritime program would be based. Out of many deliberations, leaked memoranda, and public announcements, however, one thing has become clear and that is the administration's commitment to reducing and eventually ending all direct government subsidy to the maritime industry. To achieve this goal, the administration is prepared to abandon many of the premises of the 1936 Merchant Marine Act. It has already done so in the shipbuilding industry by eliminating all funding for ship construction differential subsidies.

However, Department of Transportation officials appear to recognize that if U.S.-flag operators are to survive, and even flourish, without direct government subsidy, they must become much more cost-competitive and that, to do so, they must be able to obtain the most efficient capital equipment available and be free to organize for its use just as foreign competition does. Indeed, in spite of years of substantial direct assistance, high fuel consumption due to inefficient steam plants, vessels too small to confer sufficient economies of scale, and high manning costs have combined to cripple the U.S.-flag fleet.

The maritime initiatives announced in 1982 by the administration, if translated into action, would begin to create an environment conducive to the rebuilding of the U.S. fleet. Under the administration's program, owners would be free to acquire and maintain ships in the world shipbuilding and repair market.

The Department of Transportation also announced support for regulations that would permit owners operating in the U.S. trades to organize the massive capital systems involved in ocean transportation to achieve efficient use and lowest cost, as foreign competition does. However, the legislation needed to implement most of the initiatives supported by the administration was never introduced, let alone debated, so that any action must come from a future Congress. Moreover, two of the knottiest issues—the cost of U.S. citizen crews and a coherent approach to cargo policy—have yet to be dealt with in any meaningful way.

At this point, it is appropriate to ask, What is the policy framework that underlies the initiatives announced thus far by the administration? What should it be? How does this framework take account of the competitive realities of liner shipping today? What is the relationship between maritime policy and U.S. trade policy as a whole? Will new directions in maritime policy give us a U.S.-flag fleet capable of supporting our national security interests? Who will invest in the renewal of our merchant marine and why? Do the actions of this administration taken together augur the beginning of a new and more successful era in maritime policy or the end of what remains of our fleet?

Major Areas of Maritime Policy

The remainder of this chapter will address the three major areas of maritime policy: the cost of U.S.-flag operation, access to cargo, and regulation of intercarrier agreements. These areas are examined in a broad defense and trade policy framework so as to highlight the relationships between them.

Cost of Operation

The Merchant Marine Act of 1936 and subsequent amendments (including the major revisions of the 1970 act) created a system of promotional programs designed to place the American-flag carrier at cost parity with foreign competition. Underlying the 1936 act was the assumption that the cleanest and least anticompetitive approach to merchant marine policy was to recognize that a cost differential existed in owning and operating

U.S.-flag ships, and to face that issue directly. Implicit in this approach is another assumption—that American operators, if their costs are comparable to those of their competitors and if they have fair access to cargo, can compete effectively in the international marketplace.

The promotional framework of the 1936 act was founded on the national security imperative of maintaining a trained cadre of U.S. citizen merchant seamen on U.S.-flag vessels and of maintaining an adequate shipyard mobilization base. In both building vessels in the United States and operating them with citizen crews, it was recognized that additional costs would be imposed on U.S.-flag operators, costs that they could not be expected to bear in meeting these national policy objectives and still remain competitive in the international marketplace. It was further recognized that a viable private fleet, primarily supported through commercial operation and available to meet national security requirements, was the most cost-effective way of insuring that our emergency sealift needs would be met. In comparison with maintaining a dedicated fleet for military logistic requirements, this dual-use, commercial merchant shipping was and is cheaper by an order of magnitude. One has only to look at the billions being spent by the navy on the relatively small T-ship logistic program to measure the cost of attempting to provide backup sealift in this way. Dual use of a merchant marine is the foundation of Soviet sealift strategy. Isolated from the broader issues of why the United States needs a fleet in the first place, the budgetary attack on the modest merchant marine programs is driving the policy process from the wrong end.

Similarly, in the context of trade policy, the cost parity concept has broader implications than whether and how to promote the U.S.-flag fleet. It is designed to improve rather than burden the position of U.S. exports in the international markets. The alternative is to leave U.S.-flag owners in the position of trying to recover their higher costs in the marketplace, thereby decreasing the competitiveness of U.S. exports and burdening domestic industry and consumers with more expensive imports. In the liner sector of the industry, the substantial presence of low-cost, American-flag tonnage on our trade routes tends to dampen increases in the rate-making process and in this way exercises leverage over foreign-flag rates as well, to the benefit of U.S. trade. This American presence also inhibits other nations with control over their merchant marines (either directly or indirectly) from skewing freight rates to the benefit of their own export marketing programs and to the disadvantage of American shippers. Properly administered, the cost parity program leaves American operators subject to the same competitive pressures as the foreign operators in any given trade and further contributes to cost efficiency.

Finally, the parity concept recognizes that if private capital is to be expected to provide the kinds of trade and national security advantages that a strong and efficient merchant marine confers, investment in U.S.-flag liner operations must yield a return comparable to the return other uses of capital yield.

The major cost categories in shipping are capital, financing, operations, and taxation. The maritime program implemented by the 1936 act addresses each of these areas. The revisions to the parity program contained in the Merchant Marine Act of 1970 corrected many of the deficiencies of the 1936 act that had become apparent at that time, and resulted in a brief period of growth and promise for the merchant marine. However, the program again ceased to function as intended during the international shipping collapse that followed the first Arab oil embargo. In the wake of that collapse, other governments moved aggressively to protect and promote their shipping and shipbuilding interests, while the United States failed to respond.

The most significant problem that had developed by the mid-1970s was the cost of capital equipment and the closely related issue of financing. The traditional linkage between U.S.-flag liner operation and U.S. shipbuilding is the requirement to build in the United States. This, coupled with arbitrary constraints on the amount of construction subsidy (CDS) that was provided for the U.S. shipyards, left American shipowners far short of capital equality with their foreign-flag competitors. That foreign shipbuilding benefits from extensive direct and indirect subsidy has been well documented. For reasons that make sense to them, many countries obviously regard support of a labor-intensive export industry such as shipbuilding, which drives many other basic industries, as a superior alternative to unemployment and welfare.

Moreover, the United States did not respond to the growing role of interest rate subsidies in international shipbuilding promotion. The Title XI guarantee program was, until the mid-1970s, one of the traditional strongpoints of the maritime policy framework. However, as capital costs escalated, and the inflationary spiral gripped the United States, Title XI offset less and less the subsidized financing provided by virtually every other shipbuilding nation in the world.

Table 9.1 summarizes the competitive position in which U.S. shipowners found themselves. Unless they built in the United States, they were foreclosed from most of the other U.S.-flag promotional programs—operating subsidy, capital construction funds, Title XI, and to some extent U.S.-flag preference in carriage of government cargoes. If they built in the United States with CDS, their net capital cost was more than 50 percent higher than that of foreign competitors. When the present value of subsidized foreign debt is considered, this competitive disadvantage reaches more than 75 percent. Table 9.1 uses the experience of

Table 9.1. Comparative Capital Cost of New 2500-TEU
Container Ship—United States and Foreign

	United States with CDS	Foreign
Shipyard price	120,000	42,000
Construction differential subsidy (CDS) (50%)	(60,000)	...
Construction interest (net)	6,000	1,000
Net capital investment	66,000	43,000
Financed investment	49,500	34,400
Equity investment	16,500	8,600
Interest rate	14%	8.75%
Financing term	25 years	8½ years
Annual depreciation	3,300	2,150
First-year interest	6,860	2,920
First-year capital cost—book basis	10,160	5,070
Present value of equity investment plus debt payments—cash basis (14% discount)	66,000	37,510

NOTE: Amounts are shown in thousands of dollars, unless otherwise indicated.

American President Lines in constructing three modern container ships
in the United States, and it contrasts prices during a comparable period in
Japan. Financing (in Table 9.1) is based on 14 percent Title XI as opposed
to standard OECD (Organization for Economic Cooperation and Development) shipyard financing, although many foreign yards routinely
offer even better terms.

Another capital cost disadvantage that U.S.-flag owners have traditionally been forced to bear is that associated with standards for U.S.-flag
vessels which are higher than international norms. Before a vessel can be
registered under the U.S. flag, U.S. Coast Guard specifications must be
met. Wiring, piping, and fireproofing standards for United States registry
are unique in the world, and there is no indication that these higher
standards make any significant contribution to safety or seaworthiness.
One U.S.-flag operator constructing new vessels in Japan estimated that
complying with U.S.-flag standards cost him about $2.5 million more per
vessel than complying with foreign-flag standards would have cost. To
upgrade an existing foreign-built vessel so that it may be brought under
the U.S. flag, the cost can be significantly higher even under recent
revisions to Coast Guard regulations.

With respect to operating costs, the ODS program has given, and continues to give, U.S. operators wage costs roughly equivalent to those of their foreign competitors. It may be argued that the operation of the ODS program has not resulted in the most efficient manning levels or competitive labor agreements that might have been negotiated. However, given the cost structure that has historically prevailed in the industry, in the absence of ODS much of the U.S.-flag liner fleet that exists today either would never have been built or would have been retired from service long ago.

A second major operating cost element in which most U.S. operators have become noncompetitive is fuel. Without belaboring the reasons for this, it is enough to say that the solution to this problem goes hand in hand with replacement of the capital base of the industry (in this case, more fuel-efficient ships), which is essential if the U.S. liner fleet is to survive. Another holdover from the traditional linkage between U.S. shipbuilding and U.S.-flag operation is the 50 percent ad valorem duty on repairs performed abroad. Like the limit on construction subsidy, this provision effectively shifts the cost of maintaining the shipyard mobilization base from the government to U.S.-flag operators, whose competitive position is further eroded.

The cornerstone of U.S. maritime tax policy, the capital construction fund, has never provided equivalency to the zero tax environment that much of the competition enjoys. However, it does, especially when combined with recent changes in depreciation schedules enacted for all U.S. industry, give U.S.-flag operators a reasonable and defensible tax environment compared with tax regimes abroad. Ironically, U.S. owners who build a vessel abroad for operation under a foreign flag at present enjoy more favorable tax treatment under Subpart F of the Internal Revenue Code than they would if they put the vessel under the U.S. flag.

A somewhat extended discussion of parity is necessary for three reasons. First, and most simply, an intelligent U.S. maritime program can emerge only from a thorough understanding of the costs of doing business. This is especially true in an administration where the philosophical bent is toward maximum reliance on free competition, since ocean liner shipping is a very competitive business. Second, the conventional wisdom in government these days appears to be that the 1936 act has failed. In the quest for simplicity (the most common alternative to serious thought), policy makers tend to reject all of our traditional maritime programs, especially those that might be labeled "subsidy," instead of examining where the programs have broken down and why. Finally, it is important to understand that the only substitute for a cost parity–based maritime policy is some form of cargo preference where the higher costs of U.S.-flag operation can be recovered through higher prices. This would be a maritime policy in direct conflict with the overall purposes of U.S. trade policy, namely to maximize the ability of U.S. exporters to compete in the international marketplace.

Table 9.1 demonstrates the magnitude of the related capital and financing cost problem that has faced the U.S. operator building in the United States. In view of the first-year capital cost disadvantage in excess of $5 million per vessel, it is no wonder that few vessels have been built in the United States for the international trade in recent years. If the government determines that additional work is needed in U.S. shipyards on top of a substantial naval program, it must completely revise the form of assistance to U.S. yards in competing for orders from shipping companies. The shipowner should be removed from the process altogether, a notion that was undertaken but not carried to fruition by the 1970 act. The delivered cost of the vessel and the financing available in the United States must be competitive with the owner's options abroad. If this is the case, without question U.S. owners will support domestic shipyards. However, they cannot be asked to subsidize these yards. If, on the other hand, the government is not willing to fund such a program, U.S. owners must be free to acquire their ships abroad.

Once the decision to sever the fate of the U.S.-flag operating industry from that of U.S. shipyards has been faced honestly, changes in other parts of the total parity equation follow naturally. The 50 percent ad valorem duty on foreign repairs should be repealed and if the U.S. ship repair industry is deemed essential for defense mobilization, the government should be prepared to give the necessary support to insure its survival. All tax benefits formulated over the years to promote the U.S.-flag fleet and U.S. industry in general should be extended to U.S.-flag ships wherever built. This would include the capital construction fund and certain conforming amendments in the Internal Revenue Code to allow U.S. owners to take full advantage of the leasing market for foreign-built U.S.-flag ships.

If these changes are made, the U.S. owner will be able to obtain parity in capital cost, financing cost (through access to subsidized foreign financing), and the tax environment. Investment in new tonnage would also solve the fuel consumption problem faced by U.S. owners at present operating steam-powered vessels.

The final parity issue is how, if at all, to deal with the higher cost of U.S. citizen crews. The Reagan administration's response thus far, encouraged by a few industry executives, has been that with large, modern ships, American operators can somehow deal with the crew cost problem themselves. The administration does not intend to continue the operating differential subsidy program beyond honoring contracts currently in existence. Admittedly, U.S. liner shipping has become significantly more capital intensive as the "containerization" of world trade has progressed. In the developed country trade where containerization is already fully implemented, crew cost, even of a U.S. crew under present labor agreements, has become a lower percentage of total cost than has historically been the case. This is true not only because of the extensive investment in containers, terminals, and marketing and control systems, in addition to vessels, but also because of the rapid growth in average carrying capacity of modern container ships.

Table 9.2 illustrates the economics involved. It compares an existing American-flag C-4-type break-bulk/container vessel with a fully containerized vessel of approximately the same size (800 twenty-foot container equivalent units (TEU)) and a new container vessel of twice that size. Comparison shows the total cost of operating two of the C-4 or 800-TEU vessels or one of the larger vessels, which would provide a rough equivalency of capacity.

The last line of Table 9.2 shows American wages as a percentage of total cost. It is assumed that the new vessels would be manned with an

Table 9.2. Comparative Costs of Three U.S.-Flag Vessels

	Existing C-4 Break-Bulk	New 800 TEU	New 1600 TEU
Number of ships	2	2	1
Revenue tons/voyage	18,000	18,000	36,000
Voyages/year	16	19	9
Revenue tons/year	288,000	342,000	324,000
Crew size	40	20	20
Vessel cost	$5,000,000[a]	$26,500,000	$35,000,000
Container cost	leased	$11,700,000	$23,400,000
Annual costs (thousands)[b]			
Wages	6,335	3,960	1,975
Fuel	4,370	3,745	2,155
Other vessel costs	4,110	4,010	2,385
Cargo handling and port costs	9,250	10,260	9,720
Container expenses	3,520	5,270	5,270
Terminal expenses	1,000	1,000	1,000
Vessel depreciation	1,000	2,385	1,575
Container depreciation	. . .	2,990	2,990
Total annual costs	$29,585	$33,620	$27,070
Average cost/revenue ton	$102.75	$ 98.30	$ 83.55
Wages as percentage of total cost	21.4%	11.8%	7.3%

[a]Net book value.

[b]Costs shown in columns 2, 3, and 4 are for two C-4 carriers, two 800-TEU ships, and one 1600-TEU ship, respectively.

economic-size crew (maritime unions are willing to negotiate in this respect). For the existing C-4 vessel, wages constitute 21.4 percent of total cost versus 11.8 percent for the 800-TEU container ship and 7.3 percent for the 1600-TEU vessel. For the still larger container ships (now in excess of 4000-TEU) being discussed for the East-West trades, the relative importance of crew cost is reduced even further. But even with a competitive-size American crew, a seaman's wage differential will remain. American operators will naturally seek to recover it to the extent that they can through freight rate adjustments. The trade policy implications of this in the liner rate-making process have already been noted.

Access to Cargo

In developing a successful cargo policy, it is first necessary to understand what cargo policy is not—it is not a substitute for cost parity. In the absence of a realistic approach to cost parity, the only real alternative to no action (and no merchant marine) is cargo preference, which may imply higher cost to the user of shipping services. Again, these relationships must be weighed in the broader foreign trade framework.

In formulating an effective U.S. cargo policy, it is necessary to appreciate the broad range of foreign cargo initiatives that have contributed to the decline of the U.S.-flag fleet. In the liner market, these range from unilateral cargo reservation or acceptance of the UNCTAD cargo-sharing formula to the more indirect, but no less effective, integration of cargo control within a total national trade program with the active support of the foreign government. Outright cargo reservation policies increasingly dominate trade with developing countries, although several industrialized nations—for example, France—engage in unilateral preference. The integration of Japanese government laws and promotional programs and close cooperation with the commercial practices of the major Japanese trading houses has long provided an exceptional example of the more subtle variety of national cargo policy. Additionally, the cross trade of other countries is being systematically closed to U.S.-flag operators, while our trade remains open to all.

The United States must adopt a U.S.-flag cargo policy that is both flexible and dynamic, capable of responding to the variety of cargo policies adopted by our trading partners. We must take an active stance instead of the reactive one that has characterized United States policy so far. Otherwise, we will continue to cede the policy initiative to other nations. And we must move quickly to establish some credibility in this area, because other governments are now adopting strategies to protect and further their own maritime interests in preparation for the coming into force of the UNCTAD Liner Code.

Above all, we must understand the relationship between parity and cargo policy. The goal of parity is to insure that U.S.-flag carriers can carry cargoes at competitive world market rates. The goal of a cargo policy is to insure that they have fair access to those cargoes.

Discussions of possible responses to the code and noncode cargo regimes in other nations have already consumed an enormous amount of time, both within the industry and within government policy circles. We really have only three options. We could do nothing, in which case the future of the U.S.-flag merchant marine is easy to predict. Or we could ratify the code or ratify it with reservations, as the European community is proposing to do. Or we could adopt a flexible policy that is presumptively in favor of cargo agreements benefiting the U.S. flag, commercial where possible, governmental where necessary, but not locked into any specific formula. There has also been some discussion recently of a fourth option, which is to treat U.S.-flag cargo policy in the context of a much broader multilateral conference to be convened to address the general area of trade in services. If history is any teacher, this last option is really no option at all as far as U.S. carriers are concerned. The United States representatives at such a conference would almost certainly place much higher importance on such areas as communications and data technology, in which the United States is still the acknowledged leader in the world. Most of their negotiating counterparts from other countries, on the other hand, are likely to have a much clearer perception of the importance of shipping to their respective political and economic strategies.

Of these alternatives, a flexible bilateral policy has a lot to recommend it. In the first place, the United States has substantial experience in this area. Moreover, bilateral strategy can be targeted to the specific conditions in our various trades, trades that differ dramatically. The zonal bilateralism that is the basis of South American shipping policy, for example, presents a rather more difficult cross-trading problem for the U.S. carrier than that faced by our East-West carriers.

Also, with little or no encouragement from the administration, a large number of beneficial agreements could be concluded by commercial means, thereby contributing to the goal of minimizing direct government involvement. Agreements taking the form of consortia, mutual space charters, and revenue pools in effect in many non-U.S. trades have the primary purpose of lowering costs through more efficient use of capital equipment, but they have the secondary purpose of providing a commercial framework within which to harmonize the maritime objectives of the participating flags. Ratification of the UNCTAD Code, on the other hand, with or without reservations, would foster the development of a new international bureaucracy and contribute to the conflict and confusion that are likely to arise from the complexity and legal imprecision of the code. The bilateral approach is also less in conflict philosophically with the traditional trading policies of the United States and could be effectively implemented by executive decision. Given the variety of conditions in our trades, legislation, in addition to producing inevitable and protracted delay, would have to be either so complex as to be unworkable or so general as to be meaningless. A coordinated strategy in the executive branch offers the only real hope for dealing with the less straightforward cargo policies of other nations such as the vertical integration of shipping with the other aspects of an export economy that exists, for example, in Japan. Finally, the bilateral approach would give the United States the ability to deal effectively with the variety of responses that the developed nations may make to the code and with the effect that these responses will have on U.S. trade and on U.S. carriers.

Wherever possible, official government involvement in negotiating cargo-related agreements should be minimized. In most cases, the role of the U.S. government should be limited to swift and decisive response to discrimination against U.S. carriers not resolved by commercial means. Ample authority and sanctions already exist under the Merchant Marine Act of 1920, the Trade Act of 1974, and customs statutes. A few instances of such a response would do more than anything else to convince our trading partners that the United States is indeed serious about its merchant marine, and this would, in turn, set the stage for resolution of most cargo access problems in the commercial realm. Without such a proactive stance by the administration, no other course of action will have any meaning.

This approach to cargo policy, while not in itself requiring new legislation, presumes a regulatory environment in which U.S.-flag carriers are free to negotiate agreements with their foreign-flag counterparts that deal effectively with conditions in their particular trades, both political and economic. If the U.S. government does not wish to take a leading role in fashioning a responsible cargo policy for our ocean trades, it must at least sanction and support the efforts of American carriers to maintain a fair share of U.S. ocean commerce through the use of cooperative agreements.

Regulatory Reform

The economic arguments for regulatory reform are equally strong. The pall that the Justice Department and the Federal Maritime Commission have cast over cooperative intercarrier agreements, easily implemented in all trades except those of the United States, has been the subject of intense debate since 1978. Three successive Congresses have attempted unsuccessfully to bring U.S. maritime regulation more into line with the realities of international liner shipping today. From the outset, a central purpose of the regulatory reform effort has been to increase the competitiveness of the transportation system serving U.S. exporters. This fact accounts for the overwhelming support for this legislation from the U.S. shipper community. Opposition to these reform efforts centers on a doctrinaire defense of unbridled competition between carriers at any cost, including the cost of U.S. exports of goods and services.

In this regard, it is important to remember that the national trade objectives being served by permitting effective rationalization of shipping services are those of U.S. commerce as a whole and not just those of the ocean carrier community. U.S. exporters compete for markets served by exporters of all other countries. The exporters of Europe, Japan, and the rest of the international trading community have long recognized the cost advantages to themselves deriving from the efficient use of the increasingly capital-intensive transportation system that serves them. Shipping services that have been rationalized between foreign countries and our export markets have resulted in transportation costs lower than costs in comparable nonrationalized services between the United States and those same export markets. An example is instructive. A healthy and increasingly containerized trade exists both between the United States and the west coast of South America and between Europe and the west coast of South America. As is usually the case, American exports compete with European exports in this market. These trades have traditionally been served by a large number of small multipurpose vessels such as the C-4 vessels cited in Table 9.2. Each trade is capable of supporting a small number of large, highly efficient, modern container ships. The shipper requirement for frequency of services, combined with the limited total volume of trade, makes it impossible for any single company to introduce such vessels. The European solution has been to form the Eurosal (Europe–South American Lines) consortium in which the principal carriers, both European and South American, will introduce approximately six 2,000-TEU container ships. This arrangement not only makes it possible to provide the most efficient and lowest cost transportation for the benefit of the trade, but also spreads the capital risk among several companies.

The analysis in Table 9.2 is, in fact, based on present conditions in this trade. The total volume of cargo carried between the United States and the east and west coasts of South America, combined with the requirement for frequency of service, would suggest that an individual company preparing to renew its fleet could replace its present break-bulk vessels with six self-sustaining container vessels of approximately 800 to 1,000 TEU. However, if it created a consortium with other carriers in the trade, it could introduce six vessels of 1,600 to 2,000 TEU. The inability to form such a consortium would logically result in carriers' introducing suboptimal vessels or, alternatively, continuing to operate older and even less efficient tonnage. As Table 9.2 shows, the consortium approach results in a substantial reduction in the cost of providing the service. Doubling the vessel's capacity adds only about 30 percent to the capital cost. Most vessel operating costs are modestly higher for the larger ship; crew cost per vessel is virtually the same. It is clear that European exporters will have the cost advantage of such a system through the Eurosal consortium. That the United States would deprive U.S. exporters of a comparable competitive advantage is difficult to comprehend.

However, in the name of competition, that is precisely what the House Judiciary Committee would have done to the regulatory legislation during the Ninety-seventh Congress. By severely restricting the ability to implement consortia, revenue pools, and space charters in the U.S. trades, amendments added to the reform bill by the judiciary branch reversed much of the good that the drafters set out to achieve. What remained would have done nothing more than to restate that Congress really meant what it said in the Shipping Act of 1916. But it would certainly not have led to the kinds of cooperative intercarrier agreements that would permit U.S. industry, both ocean carriers and the exporters they serve, to compete more effectively in the increasingly difficult realm of international trade.

These realities were recognized recently by the General Accounting Office in a report to Congress on liner regulation, which said in part:

> As advances in containership technology produce even larger, more costly vessels, the continued successful operation of the fleet may require that U.S.-flag companies form consortia similar to those formed by Japanese companies. These arrangements, in which capital resources are pooled, would enable U.S. operators to acquire the equipment needed to compete effectively against foreign-flag consortia while still retaining the possibility of interline competition.
>
> The Congress should also consider changing current maritime regulation to enable U.S.-flag liner operators to more easily form consortia to facilitate financing new vessels. By making this alternative form of vessel acquisition readily available, U.S.-flag carriers may be placed in a more favorable position compared with their foreign-flag competitors.[1]

Conclusion

Only by examining in detail a national security and trade policy framework for maritime programs can the close relationships between cost parity, cargo policy, and regulation of intercarrier agreements be clearly understood. No single one is a substitute for either of the other two. Unless our policy makers understand this integration, it is unlikely that anything of lasting value will be accomplished, and President Reagan's determination to renew American maritime strength will ultimately be frustrated.

10

Financing
U.S.-Flag Shipping

Until recently, the subject of financing U.S.-flag shipping was comparatively easy to comprehend, since only a limited number of well-known and extensively used U.S. government assistance programs were available to the industry. Chief among these was the Title XI program.

Pursuant to the terms of the Merchant Marine Act of 1936, Title XI provides a U.S. government guarantee on obligations issued by an American shipowner to finance up to 87.5 percent of the cost of building or reconstructing U.S.-flag vessels. The coupon rate paid by the issuer historically averaged about fifty basis points (0.5 percent) above the rate on a direct U.S. Treasury obligation of comparable maturity. In addition, the issuer paid the Maritime Administration an annual guarantee fee of between 0.5 and 1 percent. The total cost was 1–1.5 percent above the Treasury rate. In almost every instance, except perhaps for the major oil companies, this rate is substantially below the rate shipowners could obtain if issuing obligations supported solely by their own credit, if indeed they could market the obligation at all. A further major advantage of the Title XI program is that the guaranteed obligations can have a maturity equal to the statutory life of the vessel, in most cases twenty to twenty-five years. Long-term financing at such favorable rates is unobtainable anywhere else in the world, except in those rare cases where the general credit of the issuer is strong enough on its own to support long-term corporate debt. The Title XI program has given U.S.-flag shipowners an access to the long-term U.S. capital markets that they otherwise would not have enjoyed, and the program's success is demonstrated by the fact that over 3,000 vessels have been financed under Title XI guarantees; $7.9 billion of guarantees are currently outstanding against a statutory ceiling of $9.5 billion.

But times have changed. While the Title XI program is still in place, it is under attack, primarily from those who are philosophically dedicated to the curtailment, if not elimination, of all government guarantee programs. A good case can be made, however, that Title XI is unique among government guarantee programs: it is minuscule in comparison with the total government guarantees outstanding of some $362 billion; it costs the government nothing, since the issuer pays the full amount of the interest on the obligations. The government has, in fact, made money on the program by virtue of the initiation and annual guarantee fees it charges the users, which have far exceeded the insignificant defaults.[1]

These are all valid arguments, but somewhat beside the point. The fact is that the current (1981–85) administration, while publicly committed to making certain that the American merchant fleet and the U.S. shipbuilding industry survive and grow, is opposed to government credit support programs, particularly in light of the increasing concern of the financial and investment community over the huge projected budget deficits and their impact on the U.S. capital market. The continued availability of Title XI in this environment must, therefore, be viewed as uncertain, even though the former secretary of transportation, Drew Lewis, in his maritime policy recommendations formally advocated continuation of the Title XI program albeit with an annual ceiling of $900 million for 1983 in additional commitments.[2]

Current Status of the U.S.-Flag Fleet

A more fundamental question than that of the availability or nonavailability of Title XI funding is, Will there be any U.S.-flag ships to finance? The answer is that there will always be some, since under U.S. cabotage statutes, water transportation of cargo between points in the United States, including its noncontiguous states, territories, and possessions, is reserved exclusively for U.S.-built, -owned, and -operated vessels. This "Jones Act" fleet currently comprises about 300 vessels, of which about 240 are liquid bulk carriers.[3] Overall, however, the privately owned, U.S.-flag fleet has declined since World War II from 1,188 ships to 574, of which 300 are American-flag ships, because by law they must be, i.e., those ships operating in the protected trades.

In this same period, the U.S.-flag fleet's share of American oceanborne foreign trade has declined from 58 percent to roughly 4 percent. The reasons for this decline are not hard to find. The cost of building and operating American-flag vessels in international trade substantially exceeds the cost foreign competitors must pay. A standard container vessel of approximately 2,500 twenty-foot equivalent unit capacity would cost $118 million if built in the United States. The same vessel would cost $61.5 million if built in Japan.[4] The average daily crew cost of a U.S.-flag liner vessel is $8,200; the cost for a comparable OECD (Organization for Economic Cooperation and Development) flag vessel is $3,061, and that for a non-OECD (lesser developed country) flag vessel is $1,616.[5] No credit support program, no matter how favorable the terms, can possibly offset these huge differentials. The point is that Title XI, or for that matter any alternative financing scheme, cannot be examined in isolation. The total range of maritime support programs, and their consequent impact upon the return on invested capital, must be taken into account in order to come to an intelligent and informed conclusion over whether a particular ship investment should be made.

Before the relative merits of U.S.-flag financing alternatives, including Title XI, are analyzed, it is necessary to note the other segments of U.S. maritime policy that purport to place the U.S. owners/operators on an equal footing with their foreign competitors. In this respect, an assessment is made not only of what currently is in place, but also of what future changes will occur.

Government Support Programs for Merchant Shipping

Like any other investment decision, a decision to employ U.S.-flag vessels in foreign trade must confront uncertainty—uncertainty about market/economic factors and uncertainty about government policy.

Four major U.S. government support programs besides Title XI support American-flag shipping. These are operating differential subsidies (ODS); construction differential subsidies (CDS); the capital construction fund (CCF); and cargo preference legislation. Since these programs are discussed in greater detail in other chapters of the book (see Chapter 3), they are reviewed only briefly here, to show the background against which shipowners make their decision to invest in a U.S.-flag vessel.

The purpose of ODS is to equate the operating costs of U.S.-flag vessels with those of their foreign competition. Payments are made by the Maritime Administration pursuant to twenty-year contracts with various subsidized operators. Currently, about 150 U.S.-flag vessels receive on average $2.5 million per vessel per annum, aggregating about $400 million per annum. By far the largest component of these payments represents the crew wage cost differential. The existing contracts terminate between 1994 and 2001.

The present (1983) policy of the administration is to honor existing contracts but not to sign new contracts. By implication, existing contracts will not be renewed. Since few, if any, subsidized vessels report a book profit in excess of $2.5 million, it can be seen that these payments are crucial in maintaining even a minimum rate of return.

The purpose of CDS is to equate the construction cost of a U.S.-built vessel with the cost of a comparable vessel built in a foreign yard, subject to a statutory 50-percent ceiling. In the example of the standard container vessel referred to previously, this 50-percent limitation would not pose a problem, but for other types of vessels, for example, dry bulk carriers,

the U.S./foreign cost differential exceeds 50 percent. The present administration wants to eliminate CDS. No CDS appropriation was sought for
either 1982 or 1983, nor are any funds expected to be appropriated in the
foreseeable future. However, the administration has granted a temporary waiver, so that U.S. owners can build or reconstruct vessels abroad
and register them under the U.S. flag, and still be eligible to receive other
forms of government support. Thus, of these first two forms of government assistance, one has been drastically curtailed and the other virtually
eliminated. Regarding CDS, however, since the cost differential frequently exceeds 50 percent, U.S. shipowners may actually be better off to
build foreign. In this case, they are, in fact, paying only the current world
price. Further, neither ODS or CDS guarantees U.S. shipowners/oper-
ators a profit. At best, and then infrequently, it puts them on an equal
cost basis with their competitors, and only then can the relative merits of
financing alternatives be evaluated. For while an attractive financing
scheme may offset to some extent the failure of CDS or ODS to equate
vessel or operating costs to world rates, a good financial package will not
make a bad deal good. This is no less true in shipping than in any other
industry.

Capital construction funds are special funds into which earnings from
operations of U.S.-flag, U.S.-owned vessels may be deposited on a
tax-deferred basis. Taxes are also deferred on the income earned on these
deposits. Withdrawals may be made only to acquire, construct, or reconstruct U.S.-flag, U.S.-built vessels, including retirement of debt principal
incurred in connection therewith. Withdrawal reduces the tax basis of the
vessel by an equal amount and thereby triggers the recapture over time of
the original deferral via reduced depreciation for tax purposes. Withdrawals for any other purpose are immediately subject to tax recapture
plus interest, so that operators will not benefit by depositing more into a
CCF than they contemplate using for qualified purposes. Before the 1981
tax law changes, CCFs represented a significant tax, and thus cash flow,
advantage for U.S. shipowners in comparison with the advantage of
acquiring other domestic assets.[6] CCF brought U.S.-flag shipowners
closer to parity with foreign-flag shipowners, who deferred all taxes. The
1981 tax law changes did not reduce the benefits of maintaining a CCF,
but they did reduce the advantage U.S.-built vessels had in comparison
with other U.S.-built assets. While they are not relevant in comparing
U.S.-built and foreign-built vessels, any tax law changes encouraging
acquisition of U.S.-built capital assets, whether specifically geared to
vessels for foreign trade or capital assets in general, presumably give U.S.
shipowners a competitive advantage when pricing their services in the
world market, other things being equal.

Cargo preference cargoes are required by statute to be carried in

U.S.-flag vessels. In general, they include all military shipments, 50 percent of Export-Import Bank–financed shipments, and 50 percent of U.S. government aid shipments, as well as strategic petroleum reserve shipments. Preferred cargo can also include cargo covered under bilateral agreements such as those negotiated between the United States and Brazil and Argentina. The benefit of cargo preference laws is that they reserve some portion of the U.S. foreign trade for U.S.-flag vessels.

Other government programs to support and maintain a strong U.S.-flag merchant marine are comparatively insignificant. Many are being reviewed and revised, and all may be reviewed and modified in future.

In examining the financing of U.S.-flag shipping, however, the form of support programs is not the real issue. The real issue is that, absent government support, U.S.-built and -manned vessels are not, and cannot be, competitive in a world market—they cost too much to build and they cost too much to operate. Only when these differentials have been reduced to manageable proportions, through government aid or increased productivity or both, and when there is a reasonable assurance that the reduction is sustainable over time, can a prudent investor decide whether the net effect of the available financing and tax benefits can generate sufficient earnings and cash flow to justify an investment. It is assumed that a government program in support of a merchant marine, by whatever combination of options, will remain in place and succeed in reducing to manageable levels the cost disadvantage U.S.-flag shipping suffers in comparison with shipping in the rest of the world.

Title XI

Title XI continues to be the best vehicle available to the U.S.-flag shipowner to obtain long-term, low-cost, fixed-rate financing. Even the evolution of the conventional leveraged lease market in the early 1970s relied upon Title XI to provide the necessary borrowed funds. In the high interest rate environment of the 1980s the spread over comparable Treasury issues has widened considerably from the 50 basis points (0.5 percent) referred to earlier—in some cases to as much as 120 points. But so has the spread of general high-quality corporate debt yields over government obligations. Many Title XI issuers, like their corporate counterparts in other industries, have refrained from going to the market, instead waiting for long-term rates to recede. This, however, is a reflection of the market in general, not of any deterioration in the acceptability of Title XI debt. The simple truth is that the alternatives to Title XI are few.[7]

However, there is nothing in the U.S. market comparable to the standard financing package available in virtually all OECD countries for shipbuilding, where financing can be obtained for 80 percent of the cost of the vessel for eight years at approximately 11 percent. However, even though the OECD rate is lower than that currently obtainable in the United States, the eight-year maturity requires significantly greater cash outflows in the early years of the vessel's employment than does the U.S. twenty- to twenty-five-year amortization. It should also be noted that the OECD terms, like Title XI, are government sponsored and do not reflect free market conditions. The only real substitutes for Title XI are the financing options available to any U.S. corporation with a good credit rating, i.e., general purpose, long-term corporate debt, leasing, bank loans, etc. Unfortunately, the "good credit rating" standard is frequently lacking if the shipping company is viewed on a stand-alone basis, since shipping is generally a highly leveraged and cyclical business. Moreover, where the shipping company is owned by a credit worthy parent, the parent may be unwilling to use its borrowing capacity to finance a project that can just as easily, and probably more cheaply, be financed at the project level using Title XI. This is not to say that the credit standards to qualify for Title XI are deficient, but for reasons of public policy they are often more lenient than an arms-length lender would demand for such a highly leveraged venture. As was noted earlier, Title XI is available for financing up to 87.5 percent of the cost of a vessel, the average probably being around 70 percent. In return, the shipowners must not only demonstrate the economic feasibility of the proposed project and their ability to operate and manage the business, but must also submit to a number of restrictive covenants covering working capital, net worth, debt, equity ratios, and dividend restrictions. Further, they must grant the government a first preferred mortgage in the vessel financed.

As a rule, commercial banks are unwilling to lend for more than eight to ten years, and then only at floating rates. Thus, shipowners are subject not only to a much shorter repayment period, but also to the risk that their borrowing cost may rise to the point where the project becomes economically unsound. The main role that commercial banks have played and will continue to play in financing U.S.-flag shipping is in providing financing during the construction or reconstruction period. It is the policy of many shipping companies to borrow all the funds required during this period and then repay the bank at or near delivery by issuing Title XI debt plus contributing the equity, whether from unrestricted funds or from its capital construction fund. In this way the equity ultimately to be contributed to the project can be invested and earn current income until the asset has been completed and employed, while the interest expense during the period is capitalized.

Leasing

The only other long-term financing option available to U.S. shipowners is leasing. As in other capital-intensive industries, leasing provides an opportunity to finance 100 percent of the cost of the asset at a reasonably attractive rate when shipowners are not in a position to use the tax benefits of ownership, including investment tax credit and accelerated depreciation, as incurred. It is not strictly an alternative to Title XI, however, since the cost of borrowed funds in a standard leveraged lease, whether provided by Title XI or by the lessor, is passed directly through in the lease rate together with a return on the lessor's equity. Leasing has been extensively used in the shipping industry precisely because most shipping companies are not able to use the tax benefits of ownership as incurred.

It was initially thought that the 1981 tax law changes, particularly the safe harbor leasing provisions, would prove a boon to U.S. shipowners and that the 1981 law alone could stimulate and support new construction.[8] The new law certainly contained a number of changes that not only made it much easier to structure a lease transaction, but also made the transaction more attractive to both the lessor and the lessee. For example, the new law has lowered the minimum "at risk" investment that lessors must make from 20 percent to 10 percent. Thus, it is now possible for lessors to make an equity investment of only 10 percent of the purchase price of a vessel and still get 100 percent of the tax benefits. With the increases in deductions for accelerated cost recovery and use of the investment tax credit, lessors' 10 percent investment can be recovered almost immediately. The new tax law also allows lessees to purchase the asset at the end of the lease term at less than fair market value—a major change in the tax laws—and eliminates the requirement that the lessors must show that they entered into the transaction to make a profit. In addition, the so-called safe harbor provisions of the law resulted in an entirely new lease package as an alternative to the traditional leveraged lease. Briefly stated, the new law allows owners to "sell" their tax benefits to lessors. They can sell any or all such benefits, splitting out the investment tax credit from the accelerated depreciation, and can even sell the benefits for a portion of the ship. The value of these benefits to the lessors is a function of their ability to shelter their own tax at the earliest possible moment and is calculated by applying a discount factor to the cash saved through tax deferral in the years of saving. The discount factor selected is subject to market forces relating to the ultimate financial strength of the lessee selling the credits and the availability of purchasers of such credits. However, as is well known, this provision has come under severe and vocal attack for providing a windfall to a number of prominent lessors that went far beyond what was originally intended in the act. The recently enacted 1982 tax legislation drastically scaled back the benefits available to the safe harbor lessor, thus limiting its value as an alternative to conventional leasing.[9] Moreover, its provisions terminate at the end of 1983. The results of the other changes, included in the 1981 tax law upon lease charter rates, are not as dramatic as one might originally have supposed. To assess the impact of the 1981 tax law, as well as that of the interest rates on lease charter rates, a lease transaction entered into six years ago under the former tax laws (when interest rates were 9 percent) was recalculated. The results expressed as an annual factor, i.e., a percentage number that when multiplied by the capital cost of the asset produced the annual payment or lease cost, are as follows:

	Debt Rate	Annual Factor
Pre–1981 tax law	9.0%	8.5%
1981 tax law	9.0%	7.6%
1981 tax law	10.5%	8.5%
1981 tax law	16.0%	11.7%

The 1981 tax law at the same debt rate produced only a 10 percent reduction in the lease cost (from 8.5 to 7.6 percent), and at 10.5 percent debt cost, the entire benefit of the 1981 act is offset. One would have expected a greater reduction in lease expense given the much more rapid depreciation write-off period, but the capital markets are tight and a sufficient number of new purchasers of tax benefits have not yet been assembled.

The impact of interest rates is also readily apparent. At a 16 percent interest rate, the lease factor is 11.7 percent. Thus, over the period in our example, the lease cost rose 38 percent (from 8.5 to 11.7 percent) in spite of the granting of additional tax benefits under the 1981 tax law. Other tax law changes enacted in 1982 with respect to leasing, investment credit, and capital formation will further increase the costs of leasing.

In summary, it would seem that near-future leasing may not be as big an encouragement to shipbuilding in the United States as it was originally expected to be. There is some hope, however, if the current predictions of sustainable lower interest rates prove accurate. It can also be reasonably hoped that the laws of supply and demand will attract more investment capital to the leasing companies in the months to come and thereby ease the upward pressure on the rates they charge. Those developments depend, of course, on broad economic trends, many of which have proved difficult to influence in the past.

Conclusion

Title XI, whether alone or combined in a leveraged lease, remains the single best hope for U.S. shipowners to obtain financing upon competitive terms. As was pointed out, however, a government policy supporting an American-flag merchant marine must be in place before U.S. ship-owners can compete in the world marketplace. How a project is financed certainly plays a part in its economic viability; however, the fundamental cost/price relationships must be in balance before financing becomes an issue.

11 Government-Owned Shipping

While federal policy has long encouraged and promoted a U.S.-flag merchant marine, it was only after World War I that a large commercial fleet was owned and managed by the federal government. Earlier, the government met its needs for merchant shipping in national emergencies by requisitioning and chartering privately owned shipping and returned the vessels to their owners when the emergency ended.

Background

When war broke out in Europe in 1914, American shipping was at an all-time low. In 1910, U.S. vessels had carried less than 10 percent of the nation's oceanborne commerce. The war exacerbated the shipping shortage in American trades, for one of the first acts of the belligerent powers was to divert their national-flag merchant marines to wartime support roles. North Atlantic tonnage remained in place or even increased, but other ships were recalled from less crucial routes, with predictable results. In some cases, service was suspended outright. In others, freight rates increased significantly. For example, rates on cotton from a U.S. southern port to the United Kingdom rose from $2.50 to $60 a bale, and wheat from 5¢ to 60¢ a bushel.[1] There was no American tonnage to fill the void.

The response to this state of affairs was passage of the Shipping Act of 1916, cited in Chapter 4 as the basic law for the economic regulation of U.S. foreign trade shipping. A second purpose, of importance in this chapter, was to lay the basis for a government-owned merchant fleet. Section 11 of the act authorized the federal government to form one or more shipping corporations for the "purchase, construction, equipment, lease, charter, maintenance and operation of merchant vessels in the commerce of the United States."[2] The section also provided guidelines for the disposition of this fleet when the war was over.

Upon America's entry into World War I, an Emergency Fleet Corporation was chartered under provisions of Section 11. And although the war ended before the impact of new American construction could be felt, the building program nonetheless fathered a fleet of some 1,400 ocean vessels at a cost of over $3 billion. In 1921 the U.S. Shipping Board, the agency responsible for administering both the regulatory and management provisions of the 1916 act, controlled a fleet of 1,792 vessels aggregating 15 million deadweight tons.[3] The board's management of this large war-built fleet was not passive. Steamship lines were formed and service was established on trade routes the board felt were essential to U.S. foreign commerce.

The Merchant Marine Acts of 1920 and 1928 made it quite clear that the government was to get out of the business of shipping and gave specific guidance to the Shipping Board with respect to disposing of government-owned tonnage. It was not, however, until almost the beginning of World War II that federal merchant marine operations ended with the sale of the last of the government-owned shipping lines to private investors.[4]

World War II again found U.S.-flag shipping far short of wartime needs. And again a massive government building program was undertaken. At the end of hostilities in 1945, the government-owned merchant fleet totalled some 5,000 vessels.

The National Defense Reserve Fleet

The Merchant Ship Sales Act of 1946 authorized sale of government-owned ships to private investors, giving preference to American citizens. Authority to sell vessels ended on 15 January 1951. Ships not sold by that date were placed in a National Defense Reserve Fleet (NDRF) as outlined in Section 11(a) of the 1946 act. The fleet was to be maintained by the U.S. Maritime Commission and later by the Maritime Administration, now an agency in the Department of Transportation.

On 1 July 1946 there were 1,421 ships in the NDRF. Over the years the fleet fluctuated in size. Chartered ships were returned as the postwar demand slackened and other nations built new tonnage. Ships were broken out of the fleet during the Korean War and again with the closing of the Suez Canal in 1956. Many older, privately owned ships were turned in for credit toward new construction. In this period a review system was initiated to determine which ships should be preserved and which sold for scrap or nontransportation uses.

During the Vietnam War, 172 vessels, mostly Victory types, were reactivated and put into service. By November 1970 the last of these ships had been returned to the NDRF. At this time there were over 1,000 ships in the fleet. Four years later the number was less than 500, of which 320 were in the preservation program.

As the age of the NDRF increased, the rationale that it should be maintained as a source of emergency shipping became less convincing. The most often cited problem was the time required to break out a ship, i.e., have the ship reactivated, crewed, and ready to receive cargo. Conventional wisdom was that the minimum breakout time was forty-five days, far too long in an era where contingencies occurred overnight and additional shipping was needed in days, not weeks.

With this problem in mind, in 1974 the U.S. General Accounting Office (GAO) investigated the NDRF as a source of emergency shipping. A report issued in 1976 concluded that the types of ships found in the NDRF, mainly break-bulk cargo vessels, were particularly suited to Department of Defense emergency sealift requirements.[5] It also found that for ships that were better preserved breakout time could be shortened to a militarily acceptable five to ten days. The result of the GAO effort was a joint Department of Defense/Maritime Administration program to maintain thirty NDRF ships in a high state of readiness. This Ready Reserve Force (RRF) was initially funded in the FY 1977 navy budget and the Maritime Administration administered the program.

A number of trial breakouts have proved the value of the RRF. In fact, the fleet has been expanded and includes a variety of ships suitable to meet emergency sealift needs. In 1982 the NDRF consisted of 308 ships, 236 of which it retained for defense purposes, including ships in the RRF. Table 11.1 lists RRF ships by name, type, and location.

The concept of an RRF within the NDRF is no longer questioned. Present plans are to expand the fleet to as many as 77 ships. The very success of the program, however, has raised a number of issues. They will be addressed at the end of the chapter.

The Military Sealift Command

The Military Sealift Command (MSC), formerly the Military Sea Transport Service, was established in 1949. It is the successor agency to the World War II Navy Transport Service and Army Transport Service. The fleet commander is the executive agent of the secretary of the navy, who in turn is the single manager for the Department of Defense (DOD) sealift. The mission of MSC is to meet the sealift requirements of the armed forces in a national emergency and a nonmobilization contingency, as well as in peacetime. Its operations are industrially funded, i.e., the command bills the military customer for the shipping services rendered. In fulfilling its mission, MSC uses its own or chartered ships as well as contracting with commercial carriers. MSC-controlled ships are civil service crewed.

In time of war, the military has historically had an in-house sealift capability. At the end of hostilities, however, this shipping would be retired and the relevant command(s) disbanded. Not so since the end of

World War II. The MSC has remained in place, and at different times its controlled shipping has been expanded considerably, particularly during the Korean and Vietnam wars. However, the very existence of an active,

Table 11.1. Ships in Ready Reserve Force of NDRF as of 30 April 1982

Name	Type
Philadelphia, Pa.	
Lake	C-3
Pride	C-3
Scan	C-3
James River, Va.	
Adventurer	C-3
Agent	C-3
Aide	C-3
Ambassador	C-3
Cape Alava	C-4
Cape Ann	C-4
Cape Alexander	C-4
Cape Archway	C-4
Cape Avinof	C-4
Cracker State Mariner	C-4
Old Dominion Mariner	C-4
Lone Star Mariner	C-4
Great Republic	C-5
Young America	C-5
Ohio	Seatrain
Puerto Rico	Seatrain
Catawba Victory	Victory
Beaumont, Tex.	
Hoosier Mariner	C-4
Maine	Seatrain
Washington	Seatrain
Santa Ana	C-4
Pioneer Contractor	C-4
Pioneer Crusader	C-4
San Francisco, Calif.	
President	C-4
Lincoln	C-4
California	C-4

SOURCE: U.S, Maritime Administration, *Ships in the National Defense Reserve Fleet by Design*, 30 April 1982.

NOTE: C-3, C-4, C-5, and Victory are break-bulk ships.

government-owned merchant marine raises some questions. Should government-owned ships compete with private industry? What are the reasons for maintaining a government-owned merchant marine in peacetime in the first place? Are the reasons valid?

By and large, maritime industry spokesmen argue that commercial carriers can meet all DOD sealift requirements in wartime as well as in peacetime. Testifying before Congress in 1971, then–Maritime Administrator Andrew Gibson said:

> I have consistently advocated and continue to believe that the Government owned nucleus fleet should be composed only of special purpose vessels which are required to perform functions which the commercial fleet cannot perform. I further believe that military cargoes should be employed to support and strengthen berth line, common carriage shipping so that the commercial portion of this capacity can be diverted to military use in time of emergency.[6]

No maritime administrator since Gibson has been as candid. On the other hand, representatives of shipping firms and particularly maritime union leaders have had few qualms about stating the case for privately owned, contract-manned shipping.

The navy view is contrary. It has consistently maintained that a certain amount of DOD-controlled merchant shipping is necessary. It holds the same position in 1983 as it did thirty years ago, when Admiral William Callaghan, the first commander of the Military Sea Transport Service, testified before Congress.

> *Senator Magnuson.* You feel that the Navy must continue to operate a certain portion of military merchant marine.
> *Admiral Callaghan.* I do, definitely.
> *Senator Magnuson.* How long would you say that should continue?
> *Admiral Callaghan.* I should say that would continue until the world situation approximated that perhaps in the early twenties or early thirties before the threat of a second world war faced us.[7]

The MSC position is that it must have a surge shipping capability instantly available in a quick and dirty situation. However, in meeting its surge capability requirements in the past, MSC routinely chartered more ships than it needed. The result was that many chartered MSC ships were underutilized, and when no need existed at all, they were placed in a reduced operating status. The rationalization for this overtonnaging of the chartered fleet was the navy stipulation that MSC keep ten of its ships in a quick breakout status to meet contingency requirements. The time allowed for these ten ships to be on berth was the same as that mandated for Ready Reserve Force ships in the NDRF.[8]

Table 11.2 shows that part of the MSC fleet that provides merchant marine–type commercial services.

Table 11.2. Commercial-Type Merchant Vessels Operated
by the Military Sealift Command

Ship Type	MSC Vessel Classification	No. of Active and Inactive Ships
Department of Defense Owned		
Tanker	AO	31
Tanker, gasoline	AOG	5
Dry cargo	AK	5
Vehicle cargo (roll-on/roll-off)	AKR	4
Fleet ocean tug	ATF	6
Refrigerated cargo	AF	1
Stores ship	AFS	2
Total		54
Chartered		
Dry cargo	. . .	32
Harbor tug	. . .	2
Tanker	. . .	16
Total		50
Grand total		104

SOURCES: U.S., Military Sealift Command, *Ship Register*, January 1982: "Military Sealift Command," *Defense Transportation Journal* 38 (February 1982): 21–25.

Naval Fleet Auxiliaries

An historic role of the merchant marine is that of a naval auxiliary. In fact, successive merchant marine enactments have cited that mission specifically. The preamble to the Merchant Marine Act of 1920 is typical when it states "the United States shall have a merchant marine (capable of serving) as a naval or military auxiliary in time of war or national emergency . . . ."[9]

In the nineteenth and early twentieth centuries the requirement was that the ship be capable of serving as a naval auxiliary. In time of war it would be turned over to the navy, navy manned, and used to its best advantage, which included use as a combatant. In the Civil War many merchant ships were armed and became combatant vessels; others served in fleet support roles.

Thus, the navy has traditionally viewed the fleet auxiliary role as a navy role, although requisitioned or chartered merchant ships sometimes perform this role. In the pre–World War II world, before the United

States became a superpower with global commitments and the need for a large navy, the question of whether privately owned vessels, crewed by union seamen, could or should perform naval auxiliary missions was a moot point. The number of ships (and jobs) involved was not large.

The mission of naval auxiliary vessels is combat fleet support, i.e., to underway replenish (UNREP) an on-station fleet with stores, fuel, and ammunition as well as to provide repair, towing, and salvage capability.

The question of whether union-crewed merchant ships can provide some or all of these fleet support services has been a bone of contention between the industry, principally the maritime unions, and the navy since the late 1960s.

In 1972 a joint U.S. Navy–Maritime Administration test using a union-manned, handy-size tanker, the SS *Erna Elizabeth*, demonstrated that it was feasible to use civilian tankers in some UNREP roles. The *Erna Elizabeth* steamed some 13,000 miles and underway refueled forty ships, including the carrier *John F. Kennedy*. The mission received a congratulatory "well done" from the then chief of naval operations, Admiral E. R. Zumwalt, Jr. In discussing the test, he said:

> It proved the feasibility of using commercial tankers to consolidate Navy replenishment ships and to provide limited replenishment of combatant ships. The knowledge that this surge capability is available can expand the employment options of our Fleet.[10]

A later test demonstrated that it was also feasible to underway replenish an on-station fleet with dry stores. The test vessel was Prudential Lines' SS *Lash Italia*, which delivered a token load to the Sixth Fleet in the Mediterranean in 1972.

The result of these tests was that some navy-manned UNREP ships were turned over to the Military Sealift Command, principally the replenishment oilers (AO), stores ships (AFS), and towing and salvage vessels (ATF). These vessels were crewed with civil service personnel. In testifying before Congress, DOD officials said that the arrangement was extremely cost effective.[11] This, however, did little to still the controversy as far as the maritime unions were concerned.

In 1978 the navy issued a report, *Investigation of the Potential for Increased Use of Civilian Manning on Fleet Support Ships* (short title CIVMAN). The study did not make definitive recommendations but reached several conclusions that were central to the navy case for continued MSC or navy manning.

> In order to minimize risks which would immobilize a ship as a result of battle damage, weather damage, grounding, collision or machinery casualties, personnel are allocated to watch stations to exercise immediate casu-

alty control. Additional personnel are assigned to watch stations for training and to provide further redundancy.

This manning philosophy, essential to a combat ship, has been carried into the naval fleet support ships. Support ships perform operations (such as refueling, rearming, reprovisioning, and repairs) which sustain warships' fighting capabilities . . . .

Thus, the manpower requirements of support ships are commensurate with those found on warships.[12]

The report went on to contrast the differences between fleet support ships and privately operated merchant ships with respect to construction, manning, and operations.

In 1980 a draft report, *Civilianization of Navy Fleet Support Ships*, commissioned by the Joint Maritime Congress (JMC), an industry group with heavy maritime union representation, evaluated the 1978 CIVMAN study. The JMC draft report concluded:

Manpower cost savings for the entire fleet support fleet of 95 ships are estimated to be $209 million a year when compared to the Navy military manning option and $82 million a year when compared to the civil service manning option. This substantial savings is due to the fact that both the Navy and the Military Sealift Command (using civil service personnel) man their fleet support ships with an excessive number of personnel.[13]

In February 1981 a report prepared for the Office of the Chief of Naval Operations, *Analysis of a Study Entitled Civilianization of Navy Fleet Support Ships Prepared for the Joint Maritime Congress*, was released and took issue with the JMC findings. As did the earlier CIVMAN report, this report principally attributed the difference in crew sizes between navy-manned ships and service/union–manned ships to the mission of underway replenishment vessels. The report stated:

The differences in the number of personnel result from different manning philosophies between Navy Military and the two civilian options. The Navy provides a considerable number of personnel for range and depth in watch standers at ship operating and control stations, for maintenance, and for damage control. However, the Navy Civil Service and the commercial contract managers place reliance upon unattended equipment and the employment of off-watch personnel during underway replenishment (UN-REP) operations. The two civilianized options have limited capability to repair combat damage, fight fires, or sustain casualties.[14]

In 1981, Congress asked the General Accounting Office to evaluate the JMC report and the navy's 1981 rebuttal to it. GAO findings were inconclusive, mainly because the draft JMC report was undergoing revision. GAO auditors did, however, ascertain some navy priorities with respect to the manning of its auxiliary fleet. All ships that directly serve underway combatant vessels should be military manned. When this is not possible, the navy prefers that these ships be civil service manned under MSC control. Union-manned ships would be acceptable for point-to-point logistic roles, e.g., a tanker carrying aviation fuel from a refinery at Long Beach, California, to the naval base in Honolulu.

Historically, the Maritime Administration has supported the concept that privately owned and operated merchant vessels, union or nonunion manned, may perform routine MSC tasks and, to some extent, underway replenishment tasks, as the *Erna Elizabeth* did in 1972. Arguments have primarily rested on economic efficiency. On the other hand, as was noted before, the navy has resisted turning over any significant part of its fleet auxiliary requirements to the private sector. In fact, the 1981 report prepared for the Chief of Naval Operations concluded that in terms of total operating costs, the MSC civil service option was less costly than the contract manning option would have been for the three types of auxiliaries studied, an AF-58, AO-155, and ATF-158. [15]

The Rapid Deployment Force (RDF)

The Soviet invasion of Afghanistan in 1978 and the seizure of the American embassy in Iran in 1979 clearly demonstrated the need for a capability to rapidly deploy American forces to areas of the world where U.S. interests were threatened and a concurrent capability to sustain such a force. The military assessment was that the United States was short of both the necessary sealift and airlift.

In his FY 1981 annual report to Congress, Secretary of Defense Harold Brown requested $220 million to fund the first two of fourteen maritime prepositioned ships, the so-called T-AKX program.

> In peacetime, the ships would be stationed in remote areas where U.S. forces might be needed. Though not designed for amphibious assault, they will be able to debark their equipment over the beach, if necessary.[16]

Another option to improve U.S. rapid deployment capability was for DOD to purchase eight large, fast Sea-Land container ships (SL-7s) and to modify them as military logistic support ships, the so-called T-AKRX program.

These SL-7s were built in the early 1970s and had a maximum speed of 33 knots, a speed not economically efficient in an era of high fuel costs but highly valued from a defense viewpoint.

In 1980 it was felt that time was of the essence, and an off-the-shelf, seven-ship prepositioned force was sent to Diego Garcia, a British-owned island in the Indian Ocean. The force was composed of merchant-type ships—RO/ROs, break-bulkers, and tankers.

In 1981, approval was given for DOD to purchase the SL-7s and to go ahead with the T-AKX program. However, there was little unanimity on how best to put an RDF capability in place, i.e., how to fine-tune the two proposals. Areas of disagreement included whether to convert existing ships for the prepositioned force or to build new ones, the extent of modifications to make on the SL-7s, and to a lesser extent, how the ships would be crewed.[17]

By 1982 the two programs had advanced to a point where the design modifications of the SL-7s were complete. They would have a roll-on/roll-off configuration. With respect to the T-AKX program, the roll-on/roll-off design was again preferred. Shipowners were invited to offer existing ships in their fleets. Conversion work on accepted proposals was scheduled to begin in the fall of 1982. Present plans call for the ships to be operated by the Military Sealift Command.

Rationale for Government-Owned Shipping

The chief rationale for maintaining a government-owned fleet is the quick response capability it presumably would have in today's world of instant crises.

In 1982 the general cargo portion of the active U.S.-flag merchant marine numbered 244 vessels.[18] These are the ships that would be called upon primarily to logistically support a major American military overseas commitment.[19] The problem with counting entirely on this shipping in an emergency is twofold. First, the very nature of the shipping business dictates that at any particular time, company fleets will be scattered worldwide. Second, the total number of suitable U.S.-flag ships is relatively small. Figure 11.1 illustrates the problem. It shows the location on a particular day in 1975 of those privately owned general cargo ships that belonged to companies that had pledged a portion of their fleet to DOD in a less than general mobilization contingency. Of 228 ships, 56 were in or near U.S. Atlantic/Gulf Coast ports.[20] In a Mediterranean or Persian Gulf contingency, for example, DOD could reasonably only count on these ships as being available in the prescribed five to ten days.

If the United States is to rely entirely on its privately owned shipping, then the active general cargo fleet would have to be considerably larger than it was in 1982. How much larger is a fair question.

As was noted earlier, on 1 January 1982 there were 244 general cargo ships in the privately owned fleet. Assume that 25 percent, approximately 60 ships, are at or near continental U.S. Atlantic and Gulf ports on any given day and that half of this number are pledged to DOD. Are 30 ships enough?

Two options are open with respect to increasing numbers. One is to increase the number of ships a company pledges to the government in the event of a contingency. The other is to increase the size of the general

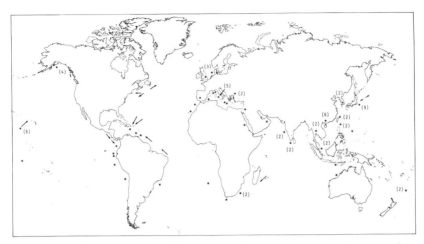

Figure 11.1. Location of privately owned U.S. general cargo vessels on a particular day in 1975.

cargo U.S.-flag merchant marine. While it is beyond the scope of this work to analyze in detail the costs and benefits of encouraging a larger U.S.-flag general cargo fleet versus the costs and benefits of maintaining an MSC civil service–manned fleet and a ready reserve component of the NDRF, there is no doubt that such an exercise must be performed in formulating an enduring U.S. maritime policy.

Issues

In 1982 there were twenty-nine ships in the Ready Reserve Force of the NDRF. How many more should be added and where should they come from? Which government agency should control the RRF?

The original concept for an RRF was to upgrade thirty World War II Victory-type vessels. In fact, the first ship to enter the RRF was the *Catawba Victory*, which was brought to quick breakout status for about $800,000. Before a second Victory could be upgraded, however, other types of ships were being turned into the NDRF that, from a military planner's point of view, had a greater defense utility than the Victories. These were Seatrains, C-3s, and C-4s. Ship operators turning in these older ships were given a dollar credit toward new construction under Section 510(i) of the Merchant Marine Act of 1936. As long as construction funds were appropriated by Congress, the system worked well. But in 1981, when construction subsidies were cut, the problem became how to compensate the owner of a desirable candidate ship for the RRF. The fall-back position was to give him the equivalent trade-in value in scrap tonnage. For example, an operator could trade in a C-3 for the scrap

SS *Meredith Victory*. This World War II, Korea, and Vietnam War veteran is now part of the National Defense Reserve Fleet anchored at Suisun Bay, California. To make her and her other 129 sister ships ready for sea would require thirty to forty-five days and cost about $1.5 million per ship. Maritime Administration photograph

value of five or six scrap candidate ships. As long as there was a sufficient amount of scrap tonnage in the NDRF there was no problem.

In 1982, serious consideration was given to increasing the RRF to 77 ships. However, present scrap tonnage is insufficient to compensate for approximately 50 more ships. One source of scrap tonnage would be the 130 Victories now being retained for national defense purposes. In 1977, the *Catawba Victory* was upgraded for less than $1 million; to upgrade a Victory in 1982 would cost about $2½ million. In the increasingly tight budget era of the 1980s, pressure on the Maritime Administration to scrap 130 Victories for 20 C-3s or C-4s is all but certain. But is such a course of action a bargain in the long run? In 1980 the Maritime Administration estimated the replacement cost of a Victory at $28 million. On the other hand, scrapping 6 Victories would net the owner of a traded-in C-3 approximately $1 million. The question is, Should the government buy the C-3 for $1 million and keep the Victory as a potential candidate for the RRF? The answer depends on several considerations—likely contingencies in the future, the likely number of non-Victory candidate ships for the RRF, the length of time during which the Victories can be minimally maintained and still be upgraded if need be, and, most of all, whether a maritime policy can be put in place that will increase the size of the active merchant fleet and conversely lessen the need for government-owned shipping.

The union-manned SS *Erna Elizabeth* refueling the aircraft carrier *John F. Kennedy* in 1972. Ten years later the question of whether, and to what extent, privately owned, union-manned merchant ships can replenish on-station U.S. naval combatants is still unresolved. Maritime Administration photograph

Another issue is whether an MSC-controlled fleet is justified. Or whether, as former Maritime Administrator Andrew Gibson maintains, the active merchant marine can, if necessary, be expanded to perform all MSC commercial functions. In considering the question, it must be remembered that on any given day, MSC ships, like the privately owned fleet, are scattered worldwide and only a part of this shipping would be in continental U.S. ports and available in a contingency.

The bottom line is whether the Military Sealift Command can serve any useful purpose in the 1980s.[21]

The last issue with respect to government-owned shipping is whether privately owned, union-manned merchant ships can perform some navy underway replenishment missions and be more cost effective than the present MSC/navy–manned ships. President Ronald Reagan believes it is a fair question to ask. As a presidential candidate in 1980, he proposed that the United States do the following:

> Improve utilization of (its) military resources by increasing commercial participation in support functions. The Navy today is facing a critical shortage of trained personnel. With the commercial industry assuming increased responsibility for many auxiliary functions, substantial cost saving can be achieved and a large reserve of manpower can be released to provide crews for a growing naval fleet. This is an example of the means by which we can increase defense mobility without adding burden to the taxpayer.[22]

Long-time maritime observers concede that not all of the ninety or so ships performing UNREP missions should be contract operated. Destroyer and submarine tenders are in this category. The question is whether some missions now handled by MSC and the navy can be more efficiently undertaken by the private sector. The results of the *Erna Elizabeth* tests simply will not go away, and at some time the navy must squarely face up to the issue.

Conclusion

In 1983 the United States is inextricably moving toward a large DOD-controlled merchant marine. The navy now funds the RRF and would like to see the program expanded and ultimately brought under MSC jurisdiction. At the same time, the MSC-controlled fleet is expanding. Plans are well advanced for MSC acquisition of an additional five point-to-point tankers as well as five new fleet oilers. Eleven ships, mostly tankers, have been added to the fleet since 1975.[23] Moreover, plans call for MSC to operate ships in the Rapid Deployment Force as they come on line.

With construction differential subsidies all but a thing of the past and with the remainder of the NDRF, one way or another, coming under

A portion of the James River, Virginia, National Defense Reserve Fleet. In 1982, there were 144 ships at this fleet site, including 6 transports, 52 military auxiliaries, 6 tankers, and 80 dry cargo vessels. Maritime Administration photograph

navy/MSC control, the time is not far off when some will raise the question of why an active, privately owned merchant fleet should be supported in the interest of national security when the government, in fact, already owns and operates a rather large merchant marine in addition to maintaining a reserve merchant fleet having a quick breakout time capability. The next logical step would be to abolish the Maritime Administration.

If in the best of all possible worlds the United States would have a relatively large merchant marine and would maintain it at a minimum cost to the taxpayer, in the worst of all possible worlds the United States would be supporting *two* government-owned merchant marines, one active and one inactive, under Department of Defense auspices, i.e., as part of the defense budget.

In 1983, government-owned shipping can be justified because of the relatively small size of our active merchant fleet. The name of the game is, or should be, to maximize the numbers in the privately owned merchant marine and, as circumstances permit, phase out all government-owned shipping operations.

12 Sizing a U.S. Merchant Marine for National Defense

For more than thirty-five years, Western Europe has formed the front line for the defense of American security. This imperative stems from the twin assessments by U.S. policy makers in the aftermath of World War II that the major threat to U.S. security interests was posed by the Soviet Union and that the best place to defend these interests was as far forward as possible, i.e., in the heartland of Europe.

On the basis of these assessments, new foreign and defense policy initiatives were taken, the results of which, like the threat, have endured. The North Atlantic Treaty Organization (NATO) was conceived, created, and steadily expanded; large numbers of U.S. armed forces were stationed permanently on European soil; and a commitment was given for these forces to join with those of its allies in defending against Soviet aggression. In this way, the Kremlin was confronted with a cohesive alliance armed with highly credible on-scene forces-in-being and located on the Warsaw Pact countries' very doorstep. The combination of these measures has played a major role in deterring hostile Soviet action in the NATO area and will continue to do so into the foreseeable future.

Clearly, much of the credibility of this conventional deterrent rests on Soviet perceptions of the will of the NATO allies to use the forces in actual battle. Equally important, however, credibility depends on allied capability to support such a battle. This means not only delivering military supplies to NATO forces in Europe, but also sustaining the civilian economies of alliance nations. This capability, in turn, rests almost completely on the combined merchant marines of the allied nations and the military forces that are available to protect them. In short, without adequate pools of merchant ships and protective maritime forces, the sea lines of communication cannot be relied upon, our ability to wage a war against the Soviets in Europe disappears, deterrence fails, and U.S. security is in peril.

In a similar vein, although to a lesser degree, American security may also be threatened in other parts of the globe. Indeed, a key U.S. planning principle is that "any conflict between NATO and the Warsaw Pact will be worldwide in scope."[1] The areas in which the United States may become involved and where U.S. forces and equipment may have to be reinforced, or to which they may have to be deployed, include Northeast Asia (e.g., South Korea), Central America, the Eastern Mediterranean, and the Persian Gulf. As was stated in the secretary of defense's annual report to the Congress for fiscal year 1983, the long-term goal for the United States is "to be able to meet the demands of a worldwide war, including concurrent reinforcement of Europe, deployments to Southwest Asia (SWA) and support in other areas of conflict."[2] Thus, the simultaneous consideration of other scenarios with that of NATO is prerequisite to an understanding of the total reinforcement and resupply task.

This chapter first formulates and discusses the requirements for the reinforcement of NATO Europe and the resupply of Europe and North America, extrapolates these to the wider global scenario, and translates them into merchant shipping requirements. Next, it assesses the factors that bear on these requirements, either to increase or decrease them, and extrapolates the requirements to a global context. Then, it compares the capabilities we require with those we actually possess. Finally, it draws some broad conclusions. Note that force planning and sizing is still very much an art and not a science.

Merchant Marine Tasks in Support of NATO

In general terms, the role of the merchant marine in defense is to augment the overseas lifting capabilities of the air force, navy, and marine corps for personnel, equipment, and stores, and at the same time to continue its normal rule of transporting the material needed to support the national economies of the United States and its allies. In the former role, the merchant marine can be said to form a tactical element of sea power; in the latter, its function is essentially strategic. So important are these roles to the preservation of U.S. security that the American merchant marine has often been called "the fourth arm of national defense."

More specifically, for a NATO crisis or war scenario, the merchant marine's role falls into four separate tasks.

1. U.S. military reinforcement and resupply. This comprises the transport of equipment, such as tanks, guns, and non-self-deploying aircraft, for the armed forces personnel who will be flying to Europe to bolster forces permanently located there, together with consumable stores, such as ammunition and petroleum, oil, and other lubricants (POL), needed both by the reinforcement forces and by those previously deployed.

2. Military resupply of non-U.S. NATO forces. This includes consumable stores and new or replacement equipment required from abroad.

3. Economic shipping for North America. This is the material, including raw materials and manufactured items, essential to sustain the wartime economies of Canada and the United States.

4. Economic shipping for NATO Europe. This is the nonmilitary material required by our overseas allies.

The extent or size of each of these tasks varies with the type of cargo, the quantity needed at the destination, and the amount of it that can be delivered by airlift. Airlift, because it provides the speed and flexibility needed to deploy and support the critical initial combat forces, is absolutely necessary in any contingency. There are practical limits to airlift, however, that severely inhibit its applicability to the four reinforcement and resupply tasks. For example, because of high fuel costs and consumption rates, airlift per ton mile is many times more expensive than sealift. If assembly, handling, and queuing times are taken into account, less time is saved by airlift than is normally imagined. Secure forward aircraft landing sites are often not available where and when needed. In sum, while airlift is crucial in the early stages of force projection, it is likely that in the future, as in the past, more than 90 percent of total reinforcement and resupply tonnages will be delivered by sealift.

The Cargoes

With respect to the maritime tasks and cargoes themselves, it is estimated that the NATO transatlantic reinforcement and resupply requirement will total more than 80 percent of the U.S. strategic reserve (twelve and a third armored or mechanized active and reserve divisions) plus a Canadian combat group of 6,000 troops and their equipment. This effort is expected to be completed within 180 days. Together these forces will comprise 30 percent of NATO's ultimate ground strength.[3] All but 2 percent of the nearly 1.5 million reinforcement personnel will be transported by air, but the vast bulk of their equipment and stores, except for prepositioned items, will go by sea. The equipment and stores, including ammunition, total over 8.5 million tons, and POL totals over 100 million barrels or 15 million tons.[4]

As a basis for estimating the military resupply requirements of the nearly fifty non-U.S. NATO divisions, and of allied naval and air force elements in Europe, it has been assumed that European nations will provide for one half of their needs and the rest will come from North America. A second assumption is that the non-U.S. units will require the same loads proportionately as those of the U.S. forces. Calculations then indicate that for the first 180 days of fighting the requirements are 7.2 million tons for dry cargo and 9.6 million tons for petroleum products, a total of 16.8 million tons.

Cargoes for the third of the four basic merchant marine tasks, that of providing economic shipping for North America, consist largely of oil and minerals. Using peacetime levels of the principal economic imports into North America, and assuming that the wartime requirements would be at least equivalent, a conservative estimate of the annual cargo tonnages would be as follows:[5]

Type of Cargo	Yearly Imports (millions of metric tons)
Crude oil	290
Bauxite	25
Iron ore	20
Phosphate	5
Other bulk cargoes	25
Total	365

(The category "other bulk cargoes" includes cement, sugar, salt, fertilizer, gypsum, nonferrous ores, wood products, etc., mostly shipped in bulk vessels of less than 40,000 deadweight tons.)

The following final groups of cargoes, those to meet the needs of the civilian economies of NATO Europe, have been calculated in the same way as those for North America.

Type of Cargo	Yearly Imports (millions of metric tons)
Crude oil	570
Iron ore	120
Coal	75
Grain	45
Phosphate	22
Bauxite	6
Other bulk cargoes	110
Total	948

The total cargo tonnage requirements for the four merchant marine tasks are as indicated.

Task/Cargo	Tonnage
1. Military reinforcement/resupply of U.S. forces	23.5 million tons in first 180 days
2. Military resupply of non-U.S. NATO forces	16.8 million tons in first 180 days
3. Economic shipping—North America	365 million metric tons per year
4. Economic shipping—NATO Europe	948 million metric tons per year

The routes on which the above cargoes will be shipped depend primarily on whether the cargo is military reinforcement and resupply or whether it is economic shipping. For the former, the routes follow those used in World War I and II, that is, from the United States or Canada to Europe and from the United Kingdom to the mainland. For the latter economic cargoes, however, the routes will no longer follow the North America to Europe pattern of previous wars but will originate mostly in other parts of the world. Thus, although items such as grain, coal, iron ore, and general cargo will continue to be transported from North America in quantity, by far the largest part of the economic shipping will travel to Europe from the Arabian Gulf, the Near East, and West and North Africa (oil) and from South Africa, South America, and Australia (minerals).

Shipping Requirement for NATO Tasks

The types of wartime shipping needed, the expected total cargo tonnages, and the routes involved having been outlined, the next step is to convert this information into a statement of the shipping capacity that is required. This capacity can be measured either by the total amount of deadweight tonnage of shipping needed to support the flow of cargoes over the given routes or by an approximation of the number of actual ships that will be necessary.

In reinforcing and resupplying U.S. forces, the military cargo to be carried from North America to Europe in the first 180 days is about 23.5 million tons (see the tabulation). To achieve this flow rate in the types of vessels available, i.e., tankers, break-bulk, container ships, roll-on/roll-off (RO/RO), and barge carriers, will require, according to the former NATO deputy supreme commander Atlantic, nearly 1,000 merchant ships.[6] For the resupply of the NATO European allies, it is estimated that another 700 vessels will be needed.

As has been indicated, the annual total of the principal economic cargoes for North America is about 365 million metric tons. To transport this cargo over the routes involved will require the following shipping capacities and numbers of ships:[7]

Cargo	Deadweight Ton Capacity (millions)	No. of Ships
Crude oil	37.4	299
Bauxite	2.3	95
Iron ore	0.7	6
Phosphate	0.3	15
Other bulk	3.0	100
Total	43.7	515

In a similar manner, the following are the shipping capacities and numbers of ships for the 948 million metric tons per year of economic shipping for NATO Europe:

Cargo	Deadweight Ton Capacity (millions)	No. of Ships
Crude oil	63.1	69
Iron ore	12.2	107
Coal	7.8	112
Grain	3.7	131
Phosphate	1.5	85
Bauxite	0.7	25
Other bulk	10.9	363
Total	99.9	892

The results of the above calculations of the shipping required for the four NATO merchant marine tasks are summarized as follows:

Task	Cargo Tonnage (millions of tons)	Ships Required
1. Military reinforcement/resupply of U.S. forces	23.5 short	1,000
2. Military resupply of non-U.S. NATO forces	16.8 short	700
3. Economic shipping— North America	365 metric	515
4. Economic shipping— NATO Europe	948 metric	892
Total		3,107

Note that the relationships between the second and third columns vary sharply. One reason is that the special nature of the military cargoes, e.g., tanks, guns, and ammunition, makes it impossible to load ships close to their deadweight tonnage carrying capacities. The economic cargoes, on the other hand, can be so loaded, and fewer ships are therefore required for a given tonnage. Similarly, the routes for the economic shipping for NATO Europe are shorter than those for North America and, again, relatively fewer ships are required.

Shipping Requirement for Global Tasks

The wartime tasks for the merchant marine outside the NATO area are essentially the same as those within it. In short, forces and their equipment will have to be moved overseas, over greater distances than those in the NATO scenario; these forces will have to be resupplied over similarly long distances; and the economies of the United States and possible allies will have to be sustained. What changes is the scale of the tasks, both the amount of the cargoes and the distances over which they have to be transported.

It is possible, because of multiassignments of U.S.military units to more than one contingency operation, that the need for sealift to NATO Europe might decrease to the extent American involvement increases elsewhere. For example, a sealift of the Rapid Deployment Joint Task Force (RDJTF) to Southwest Asia could draw off forces earmarked for NATO and thus reduce the number of ships required for European destinations. This possibility is offset, however, by the likelihood that global, non-NATO scenarios will occur in which the assistance of several, or all, of the allied merchant fleets will not be available. Within NATO, the United States is assured of the merchant ships of the world's largest ship-owning nations; in conflicts outside of NATO, this will probably not be the case. On balance, therefore, wartime commitments by the United States in global scenarios are expected to increase greatly the need for American sealift.

In theory, the number of additional merchant ships required for shipping outside NATO can be calculated step by step, as was done for shipping inside NATO. The difficulty is that the variables and data are so changeable in terms of the areas of possible conflict, the participants, and the forces involved that a reasonably accurate estimate is impossible. An alternative and simpler method of calculation is to use the NATO figures already developed for the North Atlantic and Mediterranean and to project these to cover the South Atlantic, Pacific, and Indian oceans on the basis of proportionality.

In peacetime, about 60 percent of NATO shipping is normally distributed in the North Atlantic and Mediterranean and about 40 percent in the South Atlantic, Pacific, and Indian oceans.[8] Assuming that roughly the same proportions will apply in wartime, and applying the same ratio to the number of ships calculated for the NATO area, i.e., 3,107, gives an overall requirement for a global war including NATO of 5,200 ships. Provided that this number is available, it should be possible in a global situation to sustain the military and economic life lines of both the United States and its likely allies and partners.

Factors Bearing on Achievement of Tasks

The factors bearing on the achievement of these shipping tasks range from the nature of the conflict itself to the availability of the required cargoes and transhipping facilities and the availability of adequate numbers of merchant ships and the attrition rates to which they will be subjected.

The first group of controlling factors includes the location of the crisis or conflict, the manner in which it arises, the speed of the events comprising it, the threat involved, and whether the war is conventional or nuclear. These factors will determine what the nature of the conflict is and thus whether the merchant marine tasks can be achieved. The following illustrations may serve to identify some of the questions and considerations that have to be faced.

Should the war be confined geographically to the NATO area, chances for success will increase. Merchant marine needs in this area are more predictable, risks relatively well known, and planning and procedures in place and well known and rehearsed. Should horizontal escalation occur or the war become global, on the other hand, the number of contingencies will be vastly higher, the uncertainties larger, and the outcome in greater doubt.

How the crisis or conflict arises is equally important. If the enemy has the initiative for controlling the escalation of the dispute, our courses of action will be very limited. If the initiative is ours, or we regain it, the range of options widens. Acting as an alliance, we could, for example, go most of the way toward guaranteeing a safe reinforcement operation by ordering the operation to start well before hostilities begin, so that the operation is largely completed before we suffer the first losses. Much depends on political will: without it, the tasks are extremely difficult; with it, they may become manageable.

Closely related to the question of who controls the events is the speed at which they occur. If lead times are inadequate on some of the tasks, it will be difficult, or even impossible, for us to fulfill them. Again, forceful and timely political decisions will be required from our leaders as the crisis mounts.

Another important element in the nature of the crisis is the type and size of the threat being faced. This applies both to merchant ships themselves and to the forces that protect them. Today's greatest and most probable threat is that posed by the Warsaw Pact countries, in particular, the Soviet Union. This threat is increasing alarmingly in both relative numbers and quality. In numbers of major combatants, including submarines and reserves, the Soviet navy has more than doubled from less than 400 in 1949 to over 800 in 1981. Meanwhile, the U.S. Navy has decreased from over 1,100 in 1949 to about 360 in 1981, so that from a numerical superiority of three to one the U.S. Navy has shrunk to less than half the size of that of the USSR.[9] At the same time, the Soviet maritime air force has also grown rapidly and with its large numbers of Backfire attack aircraft, equipped with up-to-date long-range air-to-surface missiles, threatens U.S. and allied surface ships over most of the North Atlantic.

In quality, the Soviet buildup has been equally menacing. Their diesel submarine fleet has been replaced by one that is now mostly nuclear propelled. Their newest classes of submarines are equal or superior to any others in existence. The Alfa, for example, dives deeper than any other, while the Oscar has a 250-mile-range missile that can be launched against surface ships from deep in the ocean. Moreover, the threat is being further strengthened by the introduction into service of larger and more formidable destroyers and cruisers and by a seaborne air fleet embarked in increasing numbers and types of aircraft carriers.

Once the shooting war commences, the success or failure of the merchant marine tasks may depend to a very critical degree on whether nuclear weapons are used and whether or not there is any advance warning. Provided that formations are alerted in time, they can be dispersed so as to reduce casualties. Otherwise, losses could be prohibitive. The use of enemy nuclear weapons against assembly and disembarkation areas could be an even more serious setback.

Short War/Long War

One of the more common predictions concerning a NATO war is that it will be a short one, i.e., less than thirty days. The war will be fought with the forces and resources already in place, and neither military nor economic shipping will have a bearing on the war's outcome.

Short war predictions are, of course, not new. History has recorded many similar ones in the past. Some examples from the current century include the following.

At the outbreak of war in 1914, "[t]here was a general opinion that the war would be short. After fighting a month or two, the belligerents would be exhausted, financially and otherwise."[10]

Also in World War I, "[t]he Russians, like all the other powers, had gone to war believing that they would have victory within a few months, and they were even less able than the others to adjust themselves to a long struggle."[11]

In World War II, German strategy and effort, both military and economic, rested on Hitler's conviction that the campaigns and each phase of the war itself would be short.

After the success of the Inchon landings in Korea, MacArthur and others believed the Yalu could be reached, the war ended, and Korea reunified within a few weeks.

In the fall of 1963, during a conference with the president on the Vietnam War, "Secretary McNamara and General Taylor reported their judgment that the major part of the U.S. military task can be completed by the end of 1965, although there may be a continuing requirement for a limited number of training personnel."[12]

In view of such past lessons, it would appear imprudent to base NATO strategy on the premise that the current prophets of a short war will be proven correct. Neither would it be wise to assume that shipping will not play as decisive a role in the future as it has in past conflicts.

A more compelling reason to prepare for a long war, however, is that by doing so we insure that short- and long-war possibilities are both covered. The converse is, of course, not true. Thus, if we prepare only for a short war while the enemy prepares for a long one, we will be unable to reinforce and resupply Europe to redress the imbalance of conventional forces there. In these circumstances, our only option would be to initiate the use of nuclear weapons and risk an even more costly defeat or outcome.

On the global front, the risks of the short war doctrine were pointed out recently by the undersecretary of defense for policy.

> Deterrence would be weakened if the enemy were misled into believing that he could outlast us in a conventional war. In particular, for a vulnerable and vital region like Southwest Asia, a U.S. strategy that promised our adversaries a 'short war' could be an invitation to aggression. If we were unprepared to sustain the conflict, the adversary might be encouraged in his expectation that we would seek a truce at the price of conceding vital territory to his control.[13]

Prepositioning

The next important factor affecting allied or American capability to reinforce and support overseas forces in battle is that of prepositioning. In an ideal world, it would be possible to preposition all the military equipment and stores that the forces would need in the areas where the battles would be fought. Troops would fly into the area from overseas, pick up their fighting apparatus, and start fighting almost immediately. In a parallel way, economic material would have been stockpiled where needed, and industry and food distribution, etc. would have been carried on virtually without interruption.

The world is not ideal, however, and there are practical limits to just how much prepositioning or stockpiling can do.

There are, for example, the high money costs and tactical risks of procuring large quantities of material in advance, choosing the optimum storage sites where the battles are expected to be joined, and then maintaining the material, including motorized equipment and ammunition, in serviceable condition.[14] Early enemy action may succeed in destroying or capturing the prepositioned items before the troops can reach them. There is also the risk that, owing to unpredictable contingencies, troops for whom the material is intended will be sent to another theater completely. Moreover, military equipment stored abroad would not be available to troops at home for training. Given these costs and uncertainties, prepositioning is not expected to cover more than a small percentage of the total military reinforcement and resupply requirement.

Availability of Cargoes and Transhipping Facilities

With respect to the shipping requirements estimated, it was assumed that cargoes would be available whenever needed by the ships and also that transhipping facilities would always be ready to load or unload the cargoes. Thus, no allowances were made for the delays that would undoubtedly occur and that would cause ships to be inefficiently employed. Either they would have to stand by idly awaiting cargoes to arrive in the departure port area or they would have to await dock space for loading or unloading equipment, some of which may have been damaged or destroyed by enemy offensive action.

To offset such situations requires a redundancy of ships that, although they will sometimes be used only as floating warehouses, are available when needed to use available port facilities at far higher rates than the normal shipping flow level would require. Thus, a substantial number of extra ships will be needed in the shipping pool. Without this reserve, interruptions and irregularities in the shipping flow will become critical.

Inventory of Available Merchant Ships

Without question, what finally determines whether the cargoes can be moved to their destinations is the availability of enough suitable merchant ships. Although wartime shipping calculations must be based on decidedly imprecise numbers, figures may be arrived at that will show the quantity of shipping that is likely to be available for the tasks at hand.

The types of merchant ships that may become involved in the wartime tasks are—

1. freighters, including general cargo carriers, container ships, roll-on/roll-off (RO/RO) vessels, and barge carriers;

2. tankers, including crude petroleum, petroleum products, chemical, liquid natural gas (LNG), wine, molasses, and whaling tankers;

3. bulk carriers, including combinations such as ore/bulk/oil;

4. combinations, ships with capacity for thirteen or more passengers.[15]

The trend over past years has been for the number of specialized ships (container ships, RO/ROs) to increase and for them to form an ever larger proportion of the total.

Based on the nation of registry, ships under flags of convenience being bypassed for the moment, the numbers and deadweight tonnages of suitably sized ships in the fleets of the maritime members of the alliance, including France and Spain, are as follows:[16]

Nation	No. of Ships	Deadweight Tons (thousands)
Belgium	63	2,607
Canada	62	852
Denmark	154	7,408
France	255	18,915
Germany	265	10,252
Greece	2,111	68,315
Iceland	2	3
Italy	435	16,418
Netherlands	192	7,245
Norway	476	37,413
Portugal	46	1,868
Spain	216	11,254
Turkey	69	1,732
United Kingdom	779	40,119
United States	759	23,569
Total	5,884	247,970

By themselves, these figures may appear impressive; however, they must be weighed in a larger, less favorable context. In relation to the world inventory of similar vessels, NATO's fleet has declined in deadweight tonnage from over 80 percent in 1950 to only 39 percent in mid-1981.[17] The NATO nation whose relative decline has been greatest is the United States. From a position as the world's leading nation, with 35 percent of the world's tonnage in 1950, the United States sank to seventh place in 1978.[18] Other measurements show that U.S. general cargo vessels decreased in number from 523 in 1970 to 256 in 1980, and from second place in deadweight tonnage to 1965 to eighth in 1979.[19] During the long period of the decline of NATO fleets, and U.S. fleets in particular, the share of world trade carried by these countries has also declined, along with concomitant reserves of trained and experienced national merchant ship manpower.

Another cause for concern is the aging of the NATO merchant fleet. Again, the case is particularly serious for the United States, where the average age of the 865 ships in the inventory at the end of 1979 was twenty-two years.[20] When this is coupled with the increased time required to build new ships, and the diminished output potential of the ailing U.S. shipbuilding industry, the situation becomes even more serious.[21]

Some reason for optimism can be found if the inventory is expanded to include vessels that are owned by companies and individuals in NATO nations but that are registered in other countries, i.e., the flag-of-convenience fleet. For the United States, for example, the fleet size almost doubles.[22] The problem with including these ships in the assets available to NATO, however, is twofold. In the first place, there is no certainty that the state of registry will accede to an ownership state that requisitions the vessels to meet a perceived security crisis. The second uncertainty is that of crew loyalty. Almost all flag-of-convenience ships are manned by citizens of states other than those of the owners, normally the registry state but sometimes third-party states as well. Experience with these crews is varied, especially in wars and confrontations that have occurred since World War II. Because of these two uncertainties, flag-of-convenience ships must be regarded only as a bonus and not relied upon as firm resources in security planning.

The final factor for discussion is that of attrition, both of ships and of cargoes. Faced with the combined air, surface, and subsurface threat that Warsaw Pact countries currently present to our shipping, we must be prepared for significantly high loss rates. These rates vary according to the study method used and depend on imputs such as the period examined, Soviet strategy and tactics, convoying policy, level of economic shipping, escort and support forces at hand, and mine warfare capabilities.

Analytical approaches are limited in forecasting events like attrition; however, based on a survey of studies that have been conducted on this subject, estimates of sea-lane attrition are 10–31 percent for the first thirty days, 5–10 percent for the second thirty days, and 3–5 percent thereafter.[23] Obviously, the number of merchant ships required to meet the reinforcement, resupply, and economic shipping tasks must allow for these losses.

Among the many facts and lessons arising from wars of the past four decades, the following are, perhaps, the most relevant to this discussion:

1. In World War I, 2 deadweight tons of shipping were needed to supply each U.S. soldier. In World War II, 7 deadweight tons were needed.

2. During World War II, 5,150 Allied merchant ships totalling 21,570,000 gross tons were sunk. Of these, 2,828 ships (14,687,000 gross tons), or 55 percent by number and 68 percent by tonnage, were sunk by submarines.

3. World War II U-boats averaged thirteen torpedoes per boat and patrolled about thirty-six days. Today Soviet submarines average close to thirty torpedoes and can patrol from sixty to ninety days.

4. At the start of World War II, there were fewer than ten enemy U-boats for every thousand Allied merchant ships. Now there are nearly fifty Warsaw Pact U-boats for every thousand NATO merchant ships.

5. During World War II, as many U.S. ships were sunk as there are in the entire U.S.-flag fleet today.

6. Although the Falkland Islands War of 1982 was relatively small, seventy British merchant ships were reportedly used to support the operations.

Adequacy of Present Resources

How does a smaller and aging NATO fleet, together with expected losses, affect the estimated numbers of ships required? Where the factors can be represented by actual numbers, i.e., merchant ship inventory and attrition, the answer is reasonably straightforward. Where the factors cannot be quantified, very subjective weighting multipliers would have to be used. Although venturing into such waters may tempt some, here it will merely be noted that their net effect is to increase the ships required by an indeterminate but significant amount. As a result, any judgments on the adequacy of present U.S. shipping resources must be based on a conservative estimate of requirements.

As was indicated previously, the worst attrition occurs in the first thirty days of hostilities, when we can expect casualties of between 10 and 30 percent. When an increment of 20 percent as an appropriate safety factor is added to the ship requirement already calculated, the increased or adjusted requirements for ships in a NATO war become the following:

Task	Ships Required	Attrition Increment	Adjusted Requirement
1. Military reinforcement resupply—U.S. forces	1,000	200	1,200
2. Military resupply— non-U.S. NATO forces	700	140	840
3. Economic shipping— North America	515	100	615
4. Economic shipping— NATO Europe	892	180	1,072
Total	3,107	620	3,727
Global war total (including NATO)	5,200	1,040	6,240

Comparing these adjusted ship requirements with the capabilities shown in an earlier tabulation gives the following results:

	NATO War	Global War
Adjusted requirement	3,727	6,240
U.S. inventory	759	759
Non-U.S. NATO	5,125	5,125
Total NATO	5,884	5,884
Inventory—others	not applicable	3,073

(The category "Inventory—others" includes all ships 1,000 gross tons and above for Japan (1,751), South Korea (361), Singapore (667), and Brazil (294) as of 31 December 1979.)

From the two preceding tabulations, several points emerge. First of all, in the NATO war scenario the total number of merchant ships in the allied inventory is adequate for the tasks envisaged. The United States, however, does not have the 1,800-odd ships needed to carry out by itself the two tasks that are essentially American, i.e., the military reinforcement and resupply of U.S. forces in Europe and the economic supply of North America. Furthermore, a more detailed examination of the U.S.-registered ships shows that of the 296 of these that were government owned on 31 December 1979, over 200 were World War II vessels. The great majority of these are ships of the National Defense Reserve Fleet, which reportedly require two to three months to be made seaworthy.[24] To make up the difference between U.S. capabilities and U.S. needs for military reinforcement and resupply, a pool of 600 ships of allied European registry has been earmarked by the respective national shipping authorities. To overcome the shortfall in ships for the economic resupply of North America, the United States will have to depend either on its allies or on flag-of-convenience shipping.

In the global scenario, the picture is not nearly so clear. If all the NATO allies cooperate with the United States and make their merchant ships available, there is no problem. On the other hand, should the United States be acting unilaterally, or with the support of only one or two nonallied partners, for example in South Korea or the Persian Gulf, the combined inventories would be much too small. If Japan's merchant fleet, or the fleets of the United Kingdom, Greece, or one or two other NATO allies are made available, the problem again disappears. Such uncertainties, however, are inconsistent with a sound national security posture.

United States action to reduce these uncertainties by strengthening its shipping capabilities for crises and war is finally under way. The Military Sealift Command is being built up by the acquisition over the next few years of a twenty-ship "fast sealift" fleet. This fleet will include ships purchased from industry, such as large SL-7-class container carriers, and chartered RO/RO-type vessels modified to meet military requirements. Some of the vessels would be used to carry military personnel and their weapons, while others would be stored with fighting equipment only and prepositioned near potential trouble spots where personnel of the Rapid Deployment Force could be deployed by air to link up with them when required. The vital question, as with all catch-up attempts, is whether such an effort will provide too little, too late.

Conclusion

Whether or not the size of the present U.S. merchant marine is large enough to meet the needs of national defense that will be placed upon it is a question that only history can answer. What can be derived from the foregoing, however, are certain conclusions about the size to which it should be increased in order to reduce the current dependence on the resources of possible allies. For, only if the fleet is substantially increased can the risks of overdependence be averted and the United States regain its ability to act independently in pursuit of its own overseas interests.

Given a reasonable set of assumptions, conservative assessments, and data obtained from standard sources, it has been shown that in a NATO war the amount of U.S.-flag shipping available would be less than half the amount required. Moreover, because of lay-ups and aging, much of this shipping must be regarded as slow to mobilize and undependable in performance.

If a war takes place beyond the NATO area, whether the alliance is involved or not, the gap between what America needs to move and what it can move widens. Only by using the ships of NATO allies, or of potential partners such as Japan, Brazil, and South Korea or of flag-of-convenience nations, can the gap be closed. Availability of flag-of-convenience ships is uncertain because of possible conflicts between the interests of the United States and those of the flag state or the ships' crews. In the case of assistance by allies and partners, the political and economic trade-offs and costs may be unacceptably high, and critical U.S. foreign policy goals may have to be sacrificed.

The consequence of this imbalance of needs and resources is that the United States has become weaker at sea than those nations that have read and heeded the lessons of sea power correctly and maintain merchant fleets commensurate with their overseas economic and security interests. It is not by chance that the USSR carries 50 percent of its trade in its own ships, the Japanese 39 percent, and the British 32 percent.[25] Nor is it by chance that these and other nations have so taken over American trade that the amount carried in U.S. ships has fallen from 20 percent twenty-five years ago to its present low of less than 5 percent.[26]

That the United States, with its historic awareness of the importance of the seas, demonstrated so regularly and vividly from its earliest days, has so neglected its merchant fleet is beyond comprehension. However, the numbers speak for themselves. They can no longer be ignored.

13 Marine Technology

The United States has a long history of marine technological innovation and invention, in both ship operations and vessel design.

The relatively small Baltimore clippers of the 1830s were followed by ever larger sailing ships of the same basic design, ships "of great length in proportion to breadth of beam, an enormous sail area, and long concave bows ending in a gracefully curved cutwater."[1] The high point in the clipper era was probably reached when Donald McKay launched his *Sovereign of the Seas* in 1853; at the time, it was the largest merchant ship ever built.[2]

And while the British must be fairly credited as leaders in developing and implementing the technologies of steam propulsion, iron hulls, and the screw propeller, it was still the American-built *Clermont* (1807) that first demonstrated the commercial viability of steam power and the American-flag *Savannah* (1819) that first used steam in an Atlantic crossing.

One hundred and forty-three years later (1962) with the launching of the namesake of the first *Savannah*, the United States demonstrated the feasibility of using nuclear power on merchant ships.[3] After a three-year demonstration phase of operation, the NS *Savannah* was bareboat chartered to First Atomic Ship Transport, a wholly owned subsidiary of American Export–Isbrandtsen Lines. The ship operated on an experimental commercial basis for the next four years. The average annual net operating cost (cost over revenues) was approximately $2.9 million per year. However, $1.9 million of this amount was a result of nuclear training, a nuclear shore staff, and a nuclear servicing facility, i.e., costs that had to be borne by the *Savannah* as a single-ship system.[4] Although the ship never came close to turning a profit, its primary mission of demonstrating a peaceful use of nuclear power was accomplished. The *Savannah* was taken out of service in July 1970. It is now on public display at the Patriot's Point Maritime Museum in Charleston, South Carolina.

The world's first nuclear-powered merchant ship was NS *Savannah*. Launched in 1962, the ship visited thirty-two U.S. and forty-five foreign ports in some twenty-five countries before being laid up in 1970. The *Savannah* is now on permanent display at the Patriot's Point Maritime Museum in Charleston, South Carolina. Maritime Administration photograph

In the area of ship design, it was American-flag companies that first introduced and operated container ships on the world's oceans.[5] And it was the U.S. Maritime Administration that developed the concept of the lighter aboard ship (LASH), which was later brought to its highest state of perfection with the introduction by Lykes Brothers Steamship Company of its "Seabee"-class vessel. The technologically complex liquid natural gas (LNG) carriers were also a product of American innovation and genius.

The United States has been, and undoubtedly will continue to be, a leader in maritime technology. Unfortunately it is not possible to patent the most successful ventures. Just as the British copied the American clipper ship, the *Cutty Sark* being perhaps the best known British clipper, so too did the traditional maritime nations copy the American container, LASH, and later, LNG vessels. It is hard to imagine the preeminent place U.S. liner shipping might have had today if the container ship concept could have been protected by a twenty-five-year patent.

The United States, however, does not stand alone in advancing maritime technology. In fact, it has sometimes been slow off the mark in adopting marine innovations, tending to be satisfied with the status quo and its predictable result. The historians Morison and Commager note American reluctance in the nineteenth century to move from sail to steam-powered and iron hull ships.

> By 1857 the British Empire had an ocean going steam tonnage of almost half a million tons, as compared with ninety thousand under the American flag. England had won back her maritime supremacy in fair competition, by the skill of her engineers and the sturdy courage of her shipbuilders.[6]

Since World War II, the United States has been slow to adopt diesel power and the automated (diesel) engine room, slow to develop a cost-effective shipbuilding technology to meet an increasing demand for the ever larger and more complex vessels being ordered by the world's shipowners,[7] and slow to apply automation to ship systems in general. The United States' situation with respect to shipboard automation has been fairly described as an "incongruous conundrum."

> Most certainly [the United States] has been in the forefront with regard to the development, manufacturing, and marketing of intelligent electronics, the common denominator and basic ingredient of nearly all modern auto-mated systems. There is little question that we are retaining a leadership role in this field by dint of continuing developments. Advanced micro-computers, microprocessors, microcontrollers, and complex sensors pro-vide examples of U.S. capabilities in this area. . . .
>
> In light of the demonstrated technological capabilities cited above, there can be no doubt that there exists within the United States all of the fundamental tools, hardware, facilities, and human talent necessary to produce, in rapid fashion, automated shipboard systems superior to those now available in the world marketplace. . . .
>
> Given this set of circumstances, which clearly identifies the relatively massive U.S. technological capability, it is difficult to rationalize the very limited progress that has been achieved by the United States in developing advanced automation systems for marine services and in applying these systems to American-flag ships.[8]

In general, Japan, Sweden, and Norway have been the leading innova-tors in shipboard automation.[9]

Industry Adoption of Marine Technological Improvements: Directions and Scope over the Next Fifteen Years

In forecasting the adoption of marine technology, or for that matter any new technology, attention must be paid to the environment in which the technology will operate. For example, a new method of cargo handling may be well within the state of the art or, in fact, already proven. If, however, a forecast of the operating environment shows that labor will be hostile, so that the new cargo-handling system will generate losses instead of profits, one cannot in good conscience forecast its adoption. Should adoption occur, the decision maker should be called a speculator rather than an investor. The operating environment of LASH ships is a case in point. LASH is a potentially profitable system. The ship and barges are well designed, and LASH has a definite advantage over containers in certain trades. The labor environment, however, is something else. While the system can operate with two men, the crane operator and a "talker," longshore contracts call for hiring two gangs (forty-two men) to work a LASH ship. On the other hand, for a container ship being worked with one crane, contracts calls for only one gang (twenty-one men). Given the benefit of hindsight, would Pacific Far East Lines have ordered LASH vessels instead of container ships? Pacific Far East Lines filed a bankruptcy petition in 1978.

Another major environment area that can affect the profitability of new technology is government regulation or government policy or both. An example here would be the legal prohibition against foreign-built ships operating in the U.S. protected trades. New, more efficient diesel-powered vessels could undoubtedly compete with land transportation for a variety of cargoes between a number of ports. The problem is that American shipyards are a high-cost option compared with their foreign counterparts; hence the capital investment would be exceedingly high in comparison with world prices. Railroads, for example, do not suffer from this disadvantage and may purchase their equipment at the best (world) price available. After putting the pieces together, a major resurrection of the coastal trades, at least with respect to general and many types of bulk cargo, simply cannot be forecast.

Other examples of regulatory and operating barriers to introducing potentially profitable, state-of-the-art technological improvements could be cited. The above two, however, make the intended point—not only must ship operators pay attention to the mechanics of a proposed innovation (Does it work? What does it cost? How soon can it be on line?), but also, equally important, they must forecast the environment in which the innovation will operate.

Which marine technological innovations might be adopted to a significant degree by the mid 1990s? Before these are considered, some that probably won't make it should be mentioned. Omission, however, does not imply that the innovation will never be adopted. It implies only that the political and/or economic operating conditions over the next fifteen to twenty years will not be favorable.

Nuclear Power
Despite a long Maritime Administration interest in nuclear research, the probability that even a demonstration nuclear ship, such as the NS

Savannah, will be built in the next two decades approaches zero. The economic/policy barriers are insurmountable. First, the international public is concerned about the safety of all things nuclear, including merchant ships. Second, research in nuclear propulsion systems, particularly commercial applications, has lost momentum. If it was going to be done, a second-generation *Savannah* should have been built ten years ago. Third, the capital cost of a nuclear merchant ship in, say, 1985 would be prohibitive without massive government subsidy, an unlikely event in an era of tight federal budgets. Fourth, to reduce operating costs to manageable levels, any new nuclear merchant ship would have to be highly automated. For the moment, American maritime unions are probably not prepared to accept the required drastic reductions in engine room personnel in particular and crew size in general.

Surface Effect Ships[10]

Like nuclear propulsion, and despite a continuing interest, surface effect ship (SES) technology is not competitive with respect to carrying capacity (gross tonnage) over even medium-distance trade routes. Again, like a nuclear merchant ship, a surface effect ship would require a significant government commitment, a commitment the government is unlikely to make when it doesn't know how to fund the social security system.

In the United States, investment in SES technology has come mainly from the Department of Defense and the Maritime Administration, which together have contributed over $500 million to SES research. Only one company, Boeing Aircraft, has shown any commercial interest. On the other hand, investment in the United Kingdom, a leader in exporting SES ships, has come mainly from the private sector and relatively little directly from government.[11]

A major problem in surface effect ship technology is designing commercially viable ships in the 1000- to 3000-displacement-ton range. While smaller vessels in the 100- to 300-ton range, with payloads of 60–90 passengers, give good economic performance, greater tonnages (with much larger investments) require operation at higher speeds to make the ship commercially profitable. But this in turn increases fuel consumption (operating costs) substantially.[12]

Prospects for ships in the 200- to 500-ton range (200–300 passenger or equivalent payload) are good. Applications would include passenger ferries, workboats for offshore drilling rigs, coastal patrol craft, fireboats, and various other types of harbor employments. The SES as an ocean cargo carrier, however, is still a considerable way down the road.

Sail

Who among us would not welcome a demonstration that sailing vessels might again be profitable? What shipping company executive office does not have at least one painting of a clipper ship? The sailing ship is a reminder of glories past and brings a warming glow to the cold realities of the 1980s.

The major problems that would be encountered with a sailing vessel are (1) building a vessel big enough to compete with fuel-powered ships and small enough to still be propelled by sail and (2) achieving schedule certainty. Of the two, schedule certainty is the more important.

Wind power advocates assume that in the movement of certain commodities, lower freight rates (brought about by lower operating costs) will compensate for slower transit times and less certain schedules. The question is, How much schedule uncertainty will a shipper tolerate? One week in either direction? Two weeks? A lesson can be learned from some northeast railroads. At one time they were virtual monopolists in carrying many of the commodities visualized for sailing vessels. But as their transit times increased and their delivery dates slipped two or three weeks almost routinely, they lost the traffic to other railroads and trucks and never fully recovered it.

Studies dealing with the question of transport scheduling invariably show that shippers want more certainty, not less, irrespective of the freight carried. And it must be remembered that the operator of fossil-fuel-powered vessels is not going to give up a profitable cargo without a fight, no matter how much nostalgia the competition evokes. If it comes to a showdown between a smaller sailing vessel and a large diesel-powered ship, the economist will have to go with the latter.

The extent to which sails might be profitably used as a source of auxiliary power to reduce fuel costs will depend entirely on vessel size. On small vessels that are employed in coastal trades and that have a completely automated sail system, i.e., the system does not require additional crew members, a profit potential probably exists.[13] On large ocean vessels, the initial cost and maintenance of a sail system are prohibitive.

Military-Commercial All-Purpose Ships

The last innovation that will probably not meet the economic profitability test over the next fifteen years is building and operating a "ship for all seasons" in the liner trades, i.e., one that meets both military and commercial requirements and, most important, is profitable.

In the period immediately after World War II, or for that matter in any period when demand for shipping space was high and supply relatively scarce, such a vessel could have succeeded. In fact, almost any type of vessel could have made money. It is a different matter now. Profit margins for general cargo vessels over the next fifteen years will be even thinner than they are today. Efficiency at the margin will determine which carriers survive. The hard fact is that in designing a military-commercial all-purpose ship, trade-offs must be made with respect to specific design features. A ship with a high utility for military logistic support would, by definition, have redundancy built into the design and incorporate features that have a limited commercial application (e.g., heavy lift gear, portable container cranes), that is, the features would add more to costs than to revenues. The only way out would be for the government to subsidize the ship with respect to both construction and operation. This is not the direction of the present Reagan administration.

Moreover, as bilateral agreements in the liner trades become the rule rather than the exception, low-cost vessels operating under the flags of developing nations will exert a continued pressure on established carriers to cut costs.

This does not mean that vessels designed to accommodate various types of cargoes in strictly commercial uses, such as a vessel having a break-bulk, RO/RO, and container capability, cannot be profitable. In fact, new construction includes such vessels.

If nuclear power, surface effect, sail, and military-commercial all-purpose ships do not meet the profitability test, at least for the foreseeable future, what technologies can be expected to be adopted over the next fifteen years?

There will be no technological leaps forward. Improvements will come at the margin of existing technology. Like aircraft technology, marine technology has reached a plateau. Like their airline counterparts, ship operators will adopt innovative ideas and technology only when such ideas and technology will reduce costs. And while ship operators won't be sanding paint off their ships to save fuel (as some airlines have done), the marginal approach will be the same. An improvement will be adopted only if it is demonstrated to be cost effective in its probable operating environment.

Diesel Power

Diesel power plants will be found in more and more new U.S. tonnage. In other words, the present trend toward diesel plants will continue and accelerate.[14] The primary diesel advantage is operating cost; the disadvantage, aside from somewhat slower speeds, is engine room crew size. At present, a steam turbine plant can be manned with two fewer crew members. However, this disadvantage can be overcome as new contracts are negotiated and automated engine rooms become standard on new construction.

In the past, a perceived drawback of any diesel plant was that it could not run efficiently on residual fuel (the heavy fuel that was left after the more refined products had been extracted from a barrel of crude). Since residual fuel was less than half the cost of a diesel distillate, the disadvantage of a diesel plant compared with a steam plant, which could burn residual fuel, was substantial. Moreover, as crude has increased in price, refineries have had to extract all of the higher valued product possible from a barrel of crude. And they have been succeeding. The result is that the residual contains even more contaminates.

While new diesel plants have shown that they can use residual fuels, the question is, Can they burn the heavy, relatively more contaminated fuels coming from the refineries today? The weight of opinion among marine engineers is that they can and any problems that exist can be solved.[15]

While the very real problem of higher residual fuel prices remains (because demand is constant and less residual fuel is left after refining), its effect on both plants will be the same—steam and diesel plants in the future will burn the same fuel.

Another change that will encourage a shift to diesel plants is the all but permanent lifting of restrictions prohibiting U.S. operators from building and repairing their vessels abroad. This policy change will expose the American shipowner to diesel technology more than before. In other words, as the U.S. firm evaluates foreign building options, it will be pressed by the foreign shipyard to consider the diesel option.

Whether U.S. manufacturers will make a greater commitment to diesels for oceangoing vessels is problematical, however. For without construction subsidies, they may not be able to sell their product.

Satellite Navigation

Most vessel operators are familiar with the LORAN A, and its successor LORAN C, navigation system. While LORAN C is highly accurate, it is a system with limited coverage.[16] This lack of worldwide coverage, coupled with the fact that it has long been known that satellite navigation was only a matter of time, probably best explains why LORAN C did not achieve universal adoption.

On the other hand, a conservative forecast is that by 1987 most U.S.-flag vessels will be using the now available, navy-sponsored, (worldwide coverage) Transit Navigation Satellite System. A number of manufacturers already market the relatively inexpensive equipment (receivers) needed to use it.

Equally important in hastening the adoption of satellite navigation is that the follow-on NAVSTAR Global Positioning System will be available for commercial use in the next decade. Today, present equipment can fix a ship's position within a tenth to a quarter of a mile; with NAVSTAR, accuracy will improve to within thirty feet. If accurate navigation can significantly reduce the number of nautical miles a ship must travel to reach point B from point A (and it can), and reduced miles mean more efficient vessel use, satellite navigation will more than repay its costs. In other words, it is a technological improvement that passes the economic cost-benefit test.

Satellite Communications

In 1981 a subcommittee of the International Maritime Satellite Organization voted to abolish the morse telegraphy requirement on ships in 1990. At this time an automated distress system is scheduled to replace it. The important point is that for almost seventy-five years radiotelegraphy (and the ship's radio officer) have been untouchable from a safety of life at sea point of view. The fact that this system is being replaced, albeit in the future, tells us something of the reliability of satellite communications.

In 1976 a Marine Satellite Communications System (MARSAT) became available to vessel operators. The system consisted of shore stations (on the U.S. East and West coasts), multifrequency orbiting satellites, and a shipboard terminal. In 1980 there were 500 terminals in use worldwide.

In 1982 INMARSAT (International Marine Satellite Communications) came on the market. This expanded system will serve the worldwide maritime community. Moreover, vessels with MARSAT equipment will be able to use their present terminals, since the two systems are compatible.

Like satellite navigation, satellite communications is an idea whose time has come, although adoption will be slower because (1) the present mandatory radiotelegraph system reduces the benefit of the system and (2) ship operators have yet to integrate the system into their shore operations. The ship operators in this case are like the early computer adopters. They were impressed by the computer's capability but were not sure what tasks it could perform or what tasks it should perform. It is also fair to point out that while shipping management is notoriously conservative and historically slow to accept innovations, it is certain that overall company efficiency can be markedly improved by having teleprinter/teletype/telephone capabilities aboard a company's vessels. The cost compared with the potential benefits is small. But shipping management must first identify the benefits.

Shipboard Automation

Shipboard automation and consequent crew reductions were explicitly recognized as a goal by the U.S. government when the Merchant Marine Act of 1970 ruled that excessive crews (as determined by the Maritime Administration) would not be subsidized under operating differential subsidy agreements. From that time, U.S.-flag manning scales have declined considerably. Nevertheless, they are still among the world's highest. On a LASH vessel, for example, the average U.S. crew numbers thirty-four, while for a similar type of ship under a foreign flag the average crew numbers twenty-eight. Similarly, U.S. wage costs are 42 percent higher than they would be under minimum Coast Guard manning requirements.[17]

Technological innovations, like automated engine room, bridge, and cargo-handling systems, have been able to reduce crew size for some time. The state of the art is such that a manning level of nine crew members has been proposed for a 200,000-dwt vessel.[18] Equally important, competent engineers and naval architects believe that such a ship would be safe. Today, a 4,500-dwt Norwegian bulk carrier with an automated engine room has a crew of thirteen. Normally, such a ship would carry a crew of seventeen.[19]

Given the tight federal budget and the likelihood of further decreases in merchant marine subsidy funds, it is reasonable to forecast that over the next fifteen years, crews will be reduced on American vessels. However, the smaller crews must be much more skilled than larger crews would have to be.[20]

Negotiating smaller crews for new construction will not be as much of a problem as reducing crew size on older vessels will be. If an older vessel, say one that is ten years old, was upgraded by automation but the crew was the same size, would the savings in increased productivity over the remaining life of the ship exceed the depreciated investment cost? Probably not.

Some authorities argue that the purpose of automation should be to improve operating efficiencies by reducing maintenance costs and unscheduled repairs and increasing crew job satisfaction; the purpose should not be to reduce crew sizes. Scandinavians invest in automated systems to improve operating efficiencies. On the other hand, the Japanese invest in automated systems to reduce shipboard manpower.[21]

Given the U.S. bias toward safety, not to mention union resistance, the purpose of increased automation on American ships will be the Scandinavian one; reduced crews will be a by-product. But crew reductions will take place. However, the movement will not come from any logical demonstration that certain crew billets are redundant, but rather from the fact that crew costs must be cut if American operators are to survive.

In the past, to the extent that American operators have adopted shipboard automation, it has been to increase operating efficiencies, not to reduce crew sizes. This is probably why the United States has lagged and why it will continue to lag in investing in automated shipboard systems. (The greater payoff for an American operator is a reduced crew size, not operating efficiencies.) However, while the United States will lag, it will not stop investing. In fact, a hard-nosed government policy with respect to limiting the amount of operating subsidies might bring about investment in automated systems much faster than is now forecast. In any case, automation on U.S.-flag ships will come about primarily by the new construction route. Little will occur on relatively older ships.

Very Large Bulk (Coal) Carriers

Commodity flows in world trade are the driving force behind ship design and overall tonnage on a particular route. For example, a present (and old) commodity flow will increase enough to encourage not only new tonnage, but also innovations in bulk carrier design. The commodity is coal. The flow is from the United States to Europe and the Far East, and to some extent from the United States to South America.

In 1981 a dramatically increased demand for coal and coal-port bottlenecks made headlines. Now demand has slackened, primarily owing to a worldwide recession and decreased oil prices, and port congestion is manageable; nonetheless, the long-run trend for coal exports is up. This is the key. When investing in new construction, particularly innovative construction for a particular commodity, investors must be able to reasonably forecast a demand for their ship. If they are convinced the long-run trend is stable, they are willing to ignore short-run fluctuations. This is true with respect to coal movements, and the industry is responding. New 100,000- to 150,000-dwt coal carriers are employed on the Japan-Australia run; British yards have evidenced interest in building new tonnage for U.S. coal exports; and Japan is building a 200,000-ton Very Large Bulk Carrier (VLBC) for its coal trade and has even larger ships in the planning stage.

Several notes of caution must be sounded, however. First, coal export facilities in the United States have marginal capability; they lack the deep draft ports needed to handle increased coal shipments. If the demand for coal had continued to increase at the 1980–81 rate, U.S. port facilities could not have handled the traffic. Second, on the assumption that East and Gulf Coast ports can compete in price with coal shipped from West Coast ports, the Panama Canal will be unable to handle new and larger coal ships. Third, American ship operators sharing in an increased coal export trade are absolutely dependent upon the U.S. government's (1) making bilateral agreements with the coal importing nations; (2) making a funded 100 percent CDS program available to the operator or allowing the U.S. operator a no-strings option to build abroad.

The forecast is that the long-term international movement of coal will be upward and that the VLBCs of the future will be of the order of 200,000 dwt, will be highly automated, and will be diesel powered or have coal-fired plants. Since no respected source in Washington is predicting a sea-level Panama Canal open to traffic before the year 2000, it is reasonable to expect that most U.S. coal exports to the Far East will originate at West Coast ports. A factor inhibiting this movement would be that larger and more efficient ships could be used to move the competitive Australian coal to Far Eastern markets.

While the form coal exports take—that is, whether the coal comes out of a slurry pipeline or off railroad hopper cars—may affect ship design, it will certainly affect the design of coal-loading facilities.

Coal-Fired Ships

As the price of crude oil continued to increase in the late 1970s and early 1980s, the use of coal, for example in coal-fired marine power plants, became more than an energy slogan. In 1980, two Australian firms placed orders in Japan and Italy for four 75,000-dwt coal-fired bulk carriers. With plentiful coal reserves in Australia to fuel the ships, it was a logical move. In the United States, one coal-fired vessel is under construction, a 36,000-dwt coal carrier being built for the New England Electric Company. The ship will carry coal from ports in Pennsylvania, New Jersey, and Virginia to the company's generating station in Massachusetts.[22]

As it did with diesel fuels, the Maritime Administration has taken a research interest in coal as a marine fuel. In 1981, it awarded $280,000 for research into the economic viability of coal-fired vessels. The ultimate success of coal-fired plants, however, will depend on the long-term price spread between Bunker-C, the residual now burned in fossil-fuel-fired steam plants, and coal, if the choice is for a steam turbine plant.

> Assuming Far East prices of $28 a ton for steam coal, about $44 worth of coal would be required to generate the same amount of heat as a ton of fuel oil. (If) fuel oil was assumed to cost $160 a ton . . . a coal-fired ship operating on a 30-day schedule between Australia and Japan for 11.5 months of the year would save $1.79 million a year using pulverized coal and $1.73 million using lump coal.[23]

However, if the spread narrows between coal and Bunker-C as it did in 1982, the shipowner will have second thoughts about building a ship that may cost as much as 20 percent more than an oil-fired vessel. Another constraint to the widespread adoption of coal is the lack of coaling stations. Many of the smaller bits and pieces of the British Empire came into being as coaling stations; but they are no longer there.

In the near term, coal-fired ships will more than likely be bulk carriers engaged in point-to-point operation between coal-exporting nations (the United States, Australia, and South Africa) and their customers. In the long run, those coal-fired ships that can convert from coal to oil or vice versa to take advantage of changes in relative prices will be the most profitable ones.

Conclusion

The environment in which a technological improvement must function is as important as the improvement itself. So that, to the extent that ship operators can favorably influence their operating environment, they must be prepared to do so. In the course of doing so, the shipping industry must come eyeball to eyeball with the longshoreman unions. The costs imposed on technology by the present work rules is staggering. And it is a great error for ship operators to assume that because their foreign-flag competitors bear the same port costs, everything equals out. It doesn't. The potential loss for the U.S. carrier is much greater. In the past, the operators (and government) blinked first. Now might be the time for operators to press the administration to take a long look at the entire port environment, and not just at who pays for what in port maintenance and improvements and how much.

14 The American Seaman

Since the days when primitive vessels first ventured beyond the sight of land, the seaman and his ship have been an inseparable combination. The seaman has depended on the seaworthy qualities of his vessel to bring him to safe haven. The ship has depended on the strength, the acumen, and the ability of the crew to safely transit the sea-lanes and deliver the passengers and cargo.

The courage and skill of the mariners, as much as or more than the seaworthiness of their seemingly fragile craft, took the seawise Polynesians over thousands of miles of the vast Pacific Ocean to explore new lands. The navigating ability and seamanship of the ancient Chinese enabled them to sail their lumbering, slat-sailed junks on year-long voyages to the Persian Gulf. And the Vikings must have been both physically tough and seawise to carry out their probing voyages across the North Atlantic and their daring forays into the Mediterranean. It is this human factor of the seafarers' courage and dedication that has given rise to the romance of the sea and inspired some of the most stirring sagas in human history.

More than in the days of Marco Polo is the seaman important to the ship and the ship's cargo. Brain is now more important than brawn and bravado. The accumulated nautical knowledge of the centuries has been printed, catalogued, and even computerized, so that the modern mariner has no excuse for not knowing the action of tides and currents, the location of shoals and reefs, and the exact position of his ship at any time anywhere in the world. Even for the deep-sea fisherman and the coast-wise navigator, who once were able to find their way through fog or mist by the color of the water and by the sound of fog horns, innate acumen has been largely superseded by electronics. However, even with all the scientific aids to navigation, the mariner must still know his ship. Many an officer who has neglected, or lost, the mariner's "feel" for the sea has paid a high price in strandings or collisions.

Nor is it just the officer who must have a rapport with the sea. When ships come to grief through storm or fire or another calamity, the lifeboat is still the crew's primary means of salvation, and handling a boat in any kind of weather requires skill. Electronics and automation are of little aid in such emergencies.

Machinery has been refined so that incapacitating breakdowns do not happen nearly as often as they once did—certainly not as often as in the days when ships were breaking down all over the oceans and all too many never made port because of a lost propeller, a broken shaft, or a burst steam line in stormy weather. No matter; despite technological advances, the seaman is still vitally important to the ship and the ship's safe transit; and knowledge of the sea and its vagaries remains his best ally in times of emergency.

The American Seaman

The American seafarer provides an essential service to the well-being of the nation. Our merchant marine and its crews are frequently referred to as the nation's "fourth arm" of defense, for during times of war or other national emergency, the merchant fleet is an irreplaceable component of our military capability. The navy is simply not able to transport all the troops and supplies necessary during war and relies heavily on the personnel, vessels, and shore facilities of U.S.-flag shipping companies for essential logistic and transport services. However, the vital services performed by American seafarers extend beyond times of emergency. During peacetime, the merchant marine facilitates reliable and safe ocean transport for our country's strategic imports, and provides the means to export our finished goods and agricultural products.

America currently requires almost 18,000 skilled seafarers to man its privately owned merchant fleet of 500 U.S.-flag, active oceangoing vessels.[1]

Vessel Type	No. of Ships
Combination passenger/cargo	6
Freighters	87
Bulk carriers	17
Tankers	240
Intermodal (container, LASH, RO/RO)	131
Tug/barge	11
Liquid natural gas carriers	8
Total	500

Note that 240 vessels, or almost 50 percent of the fleet, are tankers. Most are engaged in the domestic petroleum trade as opposed to our foreign trade.

As of 1 September 1982, this fleet of 500 vessels employed 17,347 American citizens, a figure that represents on-board employment exclusively.[2]

Vessel Type	Shipboard Personnel		
	Licensed	Unlicensed	Total
Cargo ships	2,821	6,140	8,961
Tankers	2,464	5,086	7,550
Combination passenger/cargo	122	714	836
Total	5,407	11,940	17,347

Examination of the above data reveals that some vessels require much larger crews than others. By simple division, it can be determined that the average crew size of the six passenger/cargo combination vessels is nearly 140. By comparison, the average tanker crew size is roughly 30. The obvious reason for this large difference is the fact that a passenger vessel requires waiters, chefs, housekeeping personnel, bartenders, etc., as well as the traditional licensed and unlicensed crew members. The point is that the modern-day seafarer is not necessarily a mate, engineer, or deckhand; he or she may be a maître d' or a laundryman. Nonetheless, all members of the crew must be trained and rated in various nautical skills, e.g., lifeboating.

The maritime labor force abroad American-flag ships is almost completely organized. There are twelve major AFL-CIO chartered unions that represent ocean shipping, seagoing labor in the American merchant marine.[3] Additionally, there are eighteen seagoing unions that represent only the licensed or unlicensed seamen of one particular company and that negotiate directly with their respective employers.[4] These unions are found aboard the domestic vessel fleets of the major U.S. oil companies. Finally, there are several unions that represent specialized skills used aboard passenger vessels such as nurses' and musicians' unions.

Employment in the merchant marine is volatile. Historically, it has been a feast or famine industry. During times of war or national emergency, the fleet and its accompanying crews grow rapidly. After the crisis, however, the demand for vessels falls significantly, and thousands of seafarers lose their jobs. During these ebb periods, many trained seamen seek employment in other fields and are permanently lost to the maritime industry. This phenomenon can be costly. It is important that seafarers remain in their profession in order to retain and upgrade their skills and certifications. During a national emergency, when there is a sudden need for additional sealift, recruiting able-bodied men and women to crew the ships is not enough—they must be trained at a time when there is no time.

In 1983, the U.S. merchant fleet is in an ebb phase, and seagoing employment opportunities are in a concurrent decline. If tomorrow, for whatever reason, the United States were to require significantly more merchant ships, it would be difficult to fill the new jobs with experienced personnel, because many one-time seafarers are gainfully employed in other occupations, and their licenses and ratings have expired and their nautical skills have faded.

The Education and Training of the American Seaman

Few occupations require the high standards U.S. seamen must meet and the demonstrated skills they must acquire in order to begin and maintain their career. In this regard, the U.S. Coast Guard specifies the training and experience standards for all levels of crewmen.[5] Comprehensive examinations must be passed by the applicant for most seafaring licenses and ratings. Moreover, with the increased technological advances taking place aboard ship, there is a genuine need for continuing, rigorous, and high-caliber nautical training. Fortunately, the seaman of today does not lack for facilities that offer training ranging from the fundamentals needed for ordinary seamen making their first trip to the technology needed for experienced technicians who must monitor the complicated instrumentation found in the control rooms of automated vessels.

State and Federal Training Schools

In the earlier years of the American merchant marine, men rose to officer status "through the hawse pipes," this being an old sailor's term for self-study and promotion through the ranks without benefit of academic training. When American clipper ships were the envy of the maritime world, the captain on the quarterdeck was a man who had started by heaving on the windlass, holystoning decks, and handling sails as a common sailor. There was no training school for shipmasters. Training was received entirely in the "hard school of the sea."

Times change, however. For more than a century, merchant marine officer training in the United States has been available at a number of state nautical schools. They have graduated thousands of merchant officers and company operating personnel. Today, all are branches of degree-granting state university systems. The Massachusetts Maritime Academy at Buzzards Bay, Massachusetts, and the State University of New York Maritime College at Fort Schuyler, New York, are about a century old. Some have closed. The Pennsylvania State Nautical School, which was one of the oldest U.S. training academies, was closed by the state after World War II. Other schools, namely, the California Maritime Academy at Vallejo, California, and the Maine Maritime Academy at Castine, Maine, have over a half century of service behind them. Maritime training schools, as part of state university systems, have also been started at the Texas A&M University (Texas Maritime College) at Galveston, Texas, and at Northwestern Michigan College (The Great Lakes Academy) at Traverse City, Michigan.

Shortly before World War II, the federal government became involved in merchant marine officer training with the founding of the National Merchant Marine Academy at Kings Point, Long Island, New York. More commonly known as Kings Point, this school is the "Annapolis of the merchant marine," where men and women train in a semi-military environment suggestive of those at the four military service academies.

While it is widely recognized that Kings Point provides as fine an engineering-scientific education for maritime careers as can be found anywhere in the world, the school is frequently criticized because many of its graduates who have received excellent educations at public expense do not pursue seagoing careers. The charge is correct. A number of Kings Point graduates have entered the shoreside sector of the maritime industry, joined the navy or the Coast Guard, or pursued business careers having little to do with the maritime world. However, many academy graduates accept shoreside employment because they cannot find jobs at sea.

The tremendous buildup in our merchant marine during World War II sparked a nationwide recruiting drive that brought back thousands of men from shoreside jobs and induced thousands of others to serve at sea. While many had prior sea experience, many more had never sailed on blue water. To meet this mammoth educational requirement, the government established emergency training schools on the Atlantic, Gulf, and West coasts for both unlicensed and licensed personnel. The unlicensed schools were mostly concerned with giving some seagoing fundamentals to young men who didn't know a tanker from a Missouri mule. The officer schools upgraded unlicensed personnel and helped provide the hundreds of officers, from third mates to masters, needed to keep the ships sailing. The last of these schools closed at the end of the Korean War.

Labor/Management Training Schools:
The Harry Lundeberg School of Seamanship

A fairly recent innovation in merchant marine training for both licensed and unlicensed personnel are schools operated jointly by the maritime unions and the companies with which they have contracts. The largest of these schools, as far as plant and facilities are concerned, is the Seafarers International Union's Harry Lundeberg School of Seamanship located at Piney Point, Maryland, near the mouth of the Potomac River on St.

Mary's Bay.[6] This impressive training center was recently expanded with the addition of a complex of classrooms and living quarters and a $3 million library. The school came into being as a result of the efforts of the late Paul Hall, one of the nation's most respected maritime labor spokesmen and a past president of the Seafarers International Union (SIU).

The purpose of the Lundeberg School is to provide trained seamen for SIU-contracted vessels and to enable union members to increase their earning power. Emphasis is on upgrading steward, deck, and engine room personnel. Entry rating personnel are trained on a continual basis with class sizes geared to current industry needs. With respect to entry ratings, a prime focus of the training at the Lundeberg school is to help the student adapt to the rigors and discipline of seagoing life. Students are prepared for life within confined quarters and the social, sanitary, and professional discipline that will be expected of them from their experienced shipmates. Lifeboat handling for all ship's personnel is an important subject. In fact the service crews of America's only deep-sea passenger ships, the SS *Constitution* and SS *Independence*, are trained at the Lundeberg school in lifeboat skills before being assigned to stewards department work on the passenger liners.

Other courses prepare men and women to handle the sophisticated engine rooms and equipment on everything from World War II vintage tankers to modern, highly specialized vessels, such as the liquid natural gas (LNG) carriers. There is also a training program to help provide engine room personnel in the American merchant marine's large-scale changeover from steam to diesel propulsion.[7]

An unusual feature of the school is a staff of qualified instructors that teach reading skills to young trainees in preparation for a high school equivalency program wherein students can obtain state-recognized high school diplomas. In addition to the opportunity for a trainee to obtain a General Educational Development certificate, the school offers accredited college courses in conjunction with the Charles County (Maryland) Community College.[8]

Other nautical schools that train seamen under joint labor/management auspices include facilities operated by the National Maritime Union; Districts 1 and 2 of the Marine Engineers Beneficial Association; the International Organization of Masters, Mates, and Pilots; the Radio Officers Union; and the American Radio Association.

Through these schools, American management and labor have demonstrated a commitment to effective, high-quality training programs that are responsive to the needs of the industry. Moreover, they have succeeded in recruiting minorities and women into seafaring trades. Indeed, it is no longer an uncommon sight to see women working aboard U.S.-flag vessels in all capacities and in all departments.[9]

The Changing Role of Seafaring Labor

Given the fact that the deep-sea American merchant marine is almost completely unionized, any discussion of industry problems and prospects must include consideration of the American seafaring unions and their role in U.S.-flag shipping.

The story of seagoing labor unions is perhaps the most colorful in all of American labor history. The earliest unions have a turbulent background born of the days in the mid and late nineteenth century when conditions for American seamen were far worse than the lot of the most ill-treated shoreside worker. Under the complete control of the ship's captain, seamen could be flogged, imprisoned, or starved for the smallest offenses, or no offense at all. For simply quitting his job, a seaman faced charges of desertion. Organizing with other seamen to better his condition could bring charges of mutiny. Also, the seaman was continually at the mercy of the "crimps"—brokers who virtually controlled the employment of seamen—and who took most of a seaman's meager pay in return for "placement services." The sailor was caught between bondage at sea and the vicious crimping system ashore.[10] And while reforms were instituted, seamen were still seen by the public not much differently from the way in which they were described by Chief Justice Story in 1836.

> They combine in a singular manner, the apparent anomalies of gallantry, extravagance, profusion in expenditure, indifference to the future, credulity which is easily won, and confidence which is readily surprised. Hence, it is that bargains between them and shipowners, the latter being persons of great intelligence and shrewdness in business, are deemed open to much observation and scrutiny; for they involve great inequality of knowledge, of forecast, of power, and of condition.[11]

In the twentieth century, spurred by Andrew Furuseth, leader of the International Seamen's Union and the Sailors' Union of the Pacific, Senator Robert M. La Follette introduced comprehensive reform legislation into Congress. His efforts were to become the Seaman's Act of 1915, more generally known as the La Follette's Seaman's Act.[12] It was not until this legislation that American sailors became "free" men in the same sense as shoreside workers, that is, in defining their rights with their employers and their general rights under the law.

The history of union organization among seamen was marked by an animosity and violence that bred a deep distrust and antagonism between the unions and the shipowners. This carried over into fairly recent years, resulting in an always fragile working relationship between labor and management.

The American maritime industry today, however, is characterized by a much better spirit of cooperation between unions and shipowners, and among the unions themselves. Too often in the past, maritime labor was more concerned with jurisdictional disputes than with the welfare of the industry upon which they were so dependent.

From their beginnings in the 1880s, American maritime labor unions were primarily concerned with obtaining better wages and working conditions and with seamen's rights under the law. They were less concerned with benefits such as vacations, pensions, and medical care. After World War II, however, these benefits became important union objectives. In recent years, having substantially achieved both wage/working condition and fringe benefit goals, unions are taking a much greater interest in the welfare of the industry upon which their existence depends. Preservation of existing jobs, and the creation of new jobs, rather than higher wages and more benefits, are the priorities of most union officials. Here, it would also be fair to point out that in addition to having made great strides in improving working conditions within the maritime industry, seafaring labor unions have also developed one of the most fair and democratic methods of awarding jobs to their members through the use of a rotary shipping policy, a policy that provides jobs on a first-come first-served basis to seamen on the beach.

Unions have taken the lead in introducing and influencing legislation in Congress for a stronger American merchant marine. A result of this concern about the economic well-being of shipping is that today's seamen are abreast of laws and regulations affecting their industry. More than in decades past, when seafarers had to fight just to be paid a living wage, career seamen are knowledgeable about and concerned with the political climate in Washington. A variety of union publications supply them with up-to-date information. Seamen are aware that the fleet's very survival may hinge on congressional actions; and in this regard, many seafarers have become effective voices in convincing legislators to support the merchant marine.[13]

To understand the subject of manpower aboard U.S.-flag ships, one must recognize that working at sea is different in many respects from working ashore. Seafarers who pursue a career on the high seas must adapt to a life-style that few people ashore understand. They must be prepared to commit themselves to their ship for at least the duration of the voyage. In the past, ships would remain in port for several days or even weeks while loading and unloading; during that time the crew could enjoy shore leave. Today, however, ships have a very quick turnaround in port, often only a matter of hours, which makes shore leave impossible.

Despite the strides made in working conditions aboard ships in recent years, it may be that life at sea is more difficult today than in the past. Before World War II, the professional seaman generally did not have strong family ties or deep roots within a shoreside community. The ship was his home; he was married to the sea. With the coming of social benefits such as welfare and pension plans, seamen today can support a family and can look forward to a decent retirement. One result has been a significant increase in the number of married men who have chosen the sea as their career. The positive result is a more stable and conscientious crew member; the negative side is that prolonged absences from home are more difficult and cause some of the industry's most capable employees to leave the profession.[14]

The Future of Maritime Manpower

The problems associated with automation and technological change confront the American maritime industry just as they do other industrial sectors in our economy. And these problems are creating dilemmas for both maritime labor and management. In general, fewer seamen are needed to transport a ton of cargo. Today, the industry is no longer labor intensive (as it was until recently) but is now capital intensive. Ever large investments are needed to build larger, more efficient, and more automated vessels. For example, the T-2 tanker, widely used during World War II and in the postwar period, was capable of carrying 17,000 tons of petroleum products. It required a crew of thirty-seven. By comparison, a modern 160,000-deadweight-ton tanker (which can carry 160,000 tons of cargo) requires a crew of only twenty-seven. In essence, it takes 90 percent less manpower to transport one ton of cargo on today's automated tankers than it took on tankers built only a few decades ago.

Another serious problem facing American seamen is the loss of jobs when American-owned vessels are registered under foreign flags. American seafarers were the first to suffer the effects of the "runaway shop." For years, they have witnessed a continual erosion of jobs aboard U.S.-flag vessels as American-owned companies registered their vessels under flags of convenience in nations such as Liberia, Panama, and Honduras to obtain the benefit of lower manning requirements, lower wages, and minimal taxes. This practice, considered by maritime labor to be an improper usurpation of American jobs, has created a keen awareness by both management and labor of the need to be as competitive as possible. One result of this awareness is that maritime labor is striving to improve the efficiency of its seagoing members through more training. In this respect, a not so well understood result of the shift toward more advanced technology on American ships is that new demands are being placed on individual men and women. While crews must be smaller in order to compete with foreign-flag vessels, they will also have to be better trained. The equipment they will use and maintain is simply too expensive and sophisticated to be trusted to unskilled hands.

Finally, in their struggle to keep American-flag ships at sea, some unions have been willing to negotiate reduced manning levels.[15] In the words of one union leader, it is a matter of "fewer jobs or no jobs at all."

National Defense Considerations

In 1983, and for that matter in most peacetime periods, an oversupply, not a shortage, of seamen is the problem. Not so in time of war. As history has shown, chronic shortages of seamen become the rule, not the exception. But this is an oversimplification and does not identify the most pressing problem relative to seagoing manpower in a war or major contingency in the 1980s and beyond.

In past wars, including Vietnam and Korea, there has been time to match additional manpower requirements with the additional ships needed. In World War II, the United States was able to train seamen at the same time that ships were being built. During the Korean and Vietnam conflicts, there was time to recruit former seamen from shoreside jobs as ships were taken from the National Defense Reserve Fleet and made ready for sea.[16] However, these types of scenarios, where American forces were built up over a period of weeks, months, and years, are far less likely to occur in the coming decades. The contingencies being planned for in 1983 are those demanding an instant response. Even in a NATO war, the effective warning time could be as little as forty-eight hours.

All this means is that we must go with what we have and with what can be quickly acquired—with respect to both ships and seamen. In a contingency where the United States acts alone, in terms of ships, it means we must rely on the active privately owned merchant ships, active ships of the Military Sealift Command (MSC), and the government-owned reserve fleets. In the case of the active merchant marine and MSC ships, existing levels of seagoing manpower could meet manning requirements, although a higher number of days worked per person would be expected.

Manning reserve ships in a nonmobilization situation, however, creates shortfalls. If a nonmobilization situation occurred in 1984 in which reserve ships were needed, the Maritime Administration calculates the following shortages would occur.[17]

If only ships in the Ready Reserve Force of the National Defense Reserve Fleet (25–35 ships) were broken out of lay-up, there would be a shortage of 168 officers but no shortage of unlicensed personnel. If all reserve ships, including navy reserve vessels, troopships among them, were broken out (estimated to number 209 in 1984), 11,631 billets would have to be crewed: specifically,

	No. Required
Deck officers	1,081
Engine officers	1,332
Radio officers	238
Staff officers	85
Unlicensed deck personnel	2,571
Unlicensed engine personnel	2,732
Stewards department personnel	3,592[18]

Assuming no increase in the supply of mariners, no recall of on-the-beach seamen, and no other special actions taken, crew shortages would be as shown in the following tabulation. These crew shortages are based on maintaining normal peacetime men-per-billet ratios for all ships.

	Shortage
Deck officers	1,681
Engine officers	1,831
Radio officers	327
Staff officers	50
Unlicensed deck personnel	1,177
Unlicensed engine personnel	1,048
Stewards department personnel	1,952[19]

In a mobilization situation, with national emergency powers in place, crew shortages are less severe but nonetheless substantial.[20]

In summing up the seagoing manpower problem in a mobilization, the Maritime Administration has noted:

> During a mobilization emergency, where shortages of seafarers could occur in the commercial, MSC and reserve fleets, two critical issues surface. The first issue pertains to federal manpower claimancy for seafaring personnel and the second to emergency federal training programs. Review of the Maritime Administration's claimancy authority reveals that this agency has claimancy authority for ships but not for seafarers. There is no effective emergency authority which can force seafarers to man priority ships.
>
> With regard to training programs, during a mobilization emergency, the Maritime Administration would rely primarily on existing industry and academy training instructions to generate needed additional seafaring personnel.[21]

Whether seamen would return to sea in the service of their country should have been answered for all time in World War II. With casualties on a per person basis second only to the Marine Corps, the ships continued to sail. Every major theater commander noted with commendation the devotion to duty of the merchant seamen. President Truman, and later President Eisenhower, were particularly strong in their praise.[22]

Conclusion

In its 1978 study on maritime manpower (based on 1976 data), the Maritime Administration estimated the median age of the overall seagoing workforce, including officers and unlicensed personnel, to be fifty years. And as might be expected, older seafarers have a much higher attrition rate than their younger colleagues. In this respect, the Maritime Administration determined that "of officers who actively sailed in 1976, approximately 45.3 percent of the deck officers, 45.4 percent of engine officers, 39.6 percent of radio officers, and 43 percent of the staff officers will be lost due to attrition between 1977 and 1985."[23]

Of the unlicensed seamen who were sailing in 1976, approximately "55 percent of the unlicensed deck, 63.3 percent of the unlicensed engine, and 57.4 percent of the stewards departments workforces will be lost due to attrition" during this same period.[24]

There is no shortage of seamen in 1983, and the likelihood of shortages' occurring in a strictly peacetime environment is remote. However, in a major contingency such as a deployment of a division-size American force to the Persian Gulf, seamen shortages would pose serious problems.[25] In other words, while the seagoing workforce is more than adequate in peacetime, it is barely adequate in a minor contingency, and absolutely deficient in a major U.S. overseas commitment. There is no easy answer to the problem. The most efficient way to insure that an adequate seafaring workforce will be available in an emergency is to have a strong and financially healthy U.S.-flag merchant fleet. The industry, both shipowners and seafarers, has done its part in attempting to keep an American merchant fleet at sea. It is now up to the federal government to enact laws that will not only halt the further decline of the fleet, but also, one hopes, add to its numbers. In any case, one thing is certain. As long as there is a national security requirement for an assured source of merchant shipping in both peace and war, there will be a need for the American seafarer.

15 Manning and Wage Scales on Subsidized U.S.-Flag Ships

The bedrock justification for public support of a merchant marine is its contribution to national security. This justification, however, like all expenditures for national security, has a dollar limit. In the long run, the public will subjectively equate benefits with costs, and should costs be perceived to exceed benefits, the expenditure will be denied or curtailed.

A long-standing criticism of public financial support for the merchant marine has been the dollar amount of direct and indirect subsidies necessary to maintain in place a reasonable-size U.S.-flag fleet. This chapter analyzes one part of this government expenditure, operating differential subsidies with respect to seagoing wages, as authorized in Title VI of the Merchant Marine Act of 1936, as amended. How the cost to government is determined is set forth in Section 603(b).

> [T]he amount of the operating differential subsidy . . . shall equal the excess of the subsidizable wage costs of the U.S. officers and crews . . . over the estimated fair and reasonable cost of the same item of expense . . . if such vessel or vessels were operated under the registry of a foreign country whose vessels are substantial competitors of the vessel or vessels covered by the contract.[1]

The initial flaw in the 1936 legislation was the lack of an explicit procedure for determining what was a "fair and reasonable" wage. In the ten years following World War II, what was accepted as fair and reasonable was, by and large, what the unions were able to negotiate with the shipping associations. Notwithstanding disclaimers to the contrary, the latter, with a large representation of operationally subsidized companies, lacked the necessary incentive to bargain hard with the unions, since the

The assistance, comments, and suggestions of Esther M. Love, Deputy Director, Office of Martime Training and Labor, Maritime Administration, are gratefully acknowledged. Errors of fact or logic, however, are solely the responsibility of the author, as are the conclusions reached.

difference between whatever wage scale was negotiated and the wages of foreign competitors was paid by the federal government. These wage agreements were, as a rule, endorsed by the Maritime Administration.

A 1956 congressional investigation into this state of affairs concluded:

> The Maritime Administration has failed to carry out its responsibility with respect to the determination that items for which subsidy is paid are "fair and reasonable." It is the duty of the Administration under section 603 (b) of the 1936 act to disallow for subsidy purposes any excessive amounts included in bills submitted by the lines in connection with payment of operating subsidy. This obligation extends to all items for which subsidy is paid, wages, subsistence, repairs, insurance, and maintenance. The mere fact that the item of expense is covered by a contract or collective bargaining agreement does not, ipso facto, make it fair and reasonable. The Maritime Administration conceded during the hearings that it has failed to carry out its responsibility in this regard.[2]

A major recommendation of the committee was as follows:

> In its consideration of amounts reimbursed under subsidy contracts for wages paid to officers and crews, the Maritime Board shall make a completely independent determination that the amounts paid are fair and reasonable under the statute, and the mere fact that payment was made pursuant to a provision in a collective bargaining agreement shall not be regarded as conclusive evidence of fairness and reasonableness, although weight should be given to such circumstances. *Particular attention should be directed to penalty or overtime payments.* [Italics supplied.][3]

The above recommendation, however, was difficult to put into practice. Federal courts consistently upheld (for subsidy purposes) wage agreements negotiated in the collective bargaining process. It was not until passage of the Merchant Marine Act of 1970 that a serious attempt was made to discipline the subsidized wage bill.

The 1970 act provided that subsidizable American wages be tied to an index computed on the basis of wage changes in shoreside transportation and nonagricultural industries and that crew sizes for vessels constructed or reconstructed under construction differential contracts be determined before the contract award.

With respect to wages, the General Accounting Office has concluded that Section 603(b) as amended, of the 1970 act, was, in fact, a restraining force. A 1981 GAO report stated:

> Our review of the relative increases in the subsidized seamen's wages before and after 1970 showed that the wage index system has been effective in keeping these wage increases in line with those of other U.S. workers. However, annual American seamen wage and fringe benefit increases in major union contracts, including cost of living increases, have still averaged 9.4 percent since the wage index system went into effect.[4]

With respect to crew size, the same report stated: "As of July 1980 . . . the average manning per vessel for the entire subsidized liner fleet was about 41 while the average manning per vessel as of December 1970 was about 56."[5]

However, in 1983 the subsidized seagoing wage bill is again under intense scrutiny and increasing criticism. A comparison of 1981 U.S. and foreign seagoing wages shows that American monthly crew costs exceed those of other nations with relatively high living standards by margins as high as 3 to 1.[6]

Country	Master	Second Engineer	Able Seaman
United States	$17,387	$8,212	$3,301
Japan	9,705	3,920	3,643
West Germany	7,401	4,174	2,200
Sweden	8,695	4,813	2,605
Denmark	5,945	2,899	2,428

Table 15.1 contrasts the cost of operating differential subsidies in the context of results achieved, i.e., the number of active U.S.-flag ships supported under the program. From Table 15.1, it is deduced that the average annual operating subsidy paid per ship, 1977–1981, was $1.65 million. Of this amount, $1.43 million, or 87 percent, was for wages. If the average crew size on U.S.-flag vessels is taken as forty-one, the cost to the government to support the average crew member is $35,000.

Analysis

There are two ways in which the subsidized wage bill can be lessened. First, crew sizes can be cut. Second, wage scales can be reduced.

Table 15.1. Cost and Benefits of Operating Differential Subsidies

	No. of Liner Ships	No. of Bulk Ships	Total	Regular ODS (millions)
1977	165	21	186	$300.3
1978	165	21	186	293.0
1979	156	21	177	276.2
1980	138	27	165	313.1
1981	139	26	165	272.5
Average	153	23	176	291.0

SOURCE: U.S., Maritime Administration, *Annual Reports*, FY 1977–81.

NOTE: Regular ODS does not include accruals for Soviet grain shipments. As of 30 September 1981, twenty-four U.S.-flag (thirty-one vessels) operators held short-term ODS agreements for grain shipments to the USSR.

Crew Size

As is noted above, crew sizes have been reduced on subsidized U.S.-flag ships over the last decade. However, they are still larger than those on comparable foreign vessels. Table 15.2 contrasts American and foreign crew sizes in general, i.e., it broadly classifies ships by type. Table 15.3 shows American crew sizes for a particular class of ship. Table 15.4 shows the actual crew numbers on vessels of an American-flag subsidized operator. In 1981, this firm accrued an operating differential subsidy in the amount of $33,046,000.[7] If $29 million (87%) of this amount is attributable to wages, the average annual subsidy per crew member works out to be $47,368 ($29 million/16 ships = $1.8 million per ship for wage subsidies and $1.8 million/38 crew members (average) = $47,368).[8]

Disciplining crew sizes on American ships is a two-dimensional problem. In the long run, there is strong evidence that seagoing labor unions will accept smaller crews on the newer, automated vessels. In this respect, agreement has been reached by U.S. Lines for a crew of twenty-one to twenty-two on fourteen planned large, diesel-powered container vessels. (The Maritime Administration has conditionally given approval for construction of these ships overseas.) This crew size compares favorably with crew sizes on the newer foreign ships, for example, the Japanese-built (1980) *Nichigoh Maru*, a fully automated container ship, which employs a crew of eighteen.[9]

Table 15.2. Comparative Crew Sizes

Ship Type	Country	Crew Size
Container ships	Japan	25
	Germany	34
	United Kingdom	34
	France	23
	United States	37–45
RO/RO	Norway	18
	United Kingdom	36
	United States	40
LASH	Germany	26
	Norway	30
	United States	32–38
Break-bulk	Japan	34
	Germany	22
	United States	34–36

SOURCE: U.S., Office of Management and Budget, *Staff Review of Maritime Programs and Policy*, 3 May 1982.

Table 15.3. Manning Scales and Daily Wages on Selected U.S.-Flag Vessels

Vessel Type	Crew Size	Daily Wages
C-3 break-bulk	48	$8,220
C-4 break-bulk	40	8,030
C-4-S-1a	57	9,730
C-4-S-58a	46	8,390
C-5 container ship	37	8,010
C-6 container ship	40	8,725
C-7 container ship	37	8,180
C-8 container ship	39	8,690
C-5 RO/RO	39	8,495
C-7 RO/RO	35	7,920
C-8 LASH	38	8,585
Tankers		
(20,000–250,000 dwt)	25–28	5,730–6,190
Bulk (29,500 dwt)	23	5,345

SOURCE: U.S., Maritime Administration, *Estimated Vessel Operating Expenses 1980*, September 1981.

Table 15.4. Actual Crew Sizes in an American-Flag Fleet, 1982

Type and Ship	Design	Crew Size
Cargo		
Mormacaltair	C-6	39
Mormacargo	C-4	39
Mormacdawn	C-4	39
Mormacdraco	C-6	39
Mormaclynx	C-4	39
Mormacmoon	C-4	39
Mormacrigel	C-4	39
Mormacvega	C-4	39
Mormacglen	C-3	44
Mormacsaga	C-4	45
Mormacsea	C-4	45
Mormactide	C-4	45
Mormacwave	C-4	45
Tanker		
Mormacstar	T-6	25
Mormacsun	T-6	25
Mormacsky	T-6	25
Average		38

SOURCES: U.S., Department of the Navy, Military Sealift Command, *Ship Register*, 1982; *Marine Engineering/Log*, 15 June 1982; and Council of American-Flag Ship Operators.

Sea-Land's new diesel container ships, the D-9 class, carry a crew of thirty-five, two to five fewer crew members than most U.S.-flag container ships carry.

The more difficult, short-term problem, is crew size on existing U.S.-flag ships, in particular the older, break-bulk vessels. Tables 15.3 and 15.4 show that, in general, the older break-bulk ships (C-3s and C-4s) have larger crews than the newer intermodal vessels (container ships, RO/ROs, LASH) do. However, even on the newer U.S. intermodal ships, crew sizes are considerably larger than on foreign-flag ships coming into service in the 1980s, e.g., the *Nichigoh Maru*.

Table 15.5 indicates the relative age of U.S.-flag ships. The preponderance of older vessels in the fleet highlights a major hurdle in trimming crew costs, since, as was previously noted, it is far easier to negotiate smaller crews on new construction than to reduce crews on existing (older) ships.

It cannot be stressed too strongly, however, that crew reduction is entirely a matter of contract negotiations between the operators and unions. Moreover, there is room to negotiate. A Maritime Administration–contracted study determined "that union agreements concerning crew size add an additional 42 percent in crew costs as compared to what would be incurred if U.S. Coast Guard requirements (alone) were followed."[10] On the other hand, the study found that "vessel operators would voluntarily choose a crew complement that cost more (approximately 10 percent) in crew wages than is required by the Coast Guard."[11] It is in this range of reduced costs, between 10 and 42 percent, that negotiations can and must take place to reduce manning scales on U.S.-flag ships.

Table 15.5. Age of U.S. Merchant Fleet

Type	Under Nine Years Old	Nine Years or Older
Break-bulk	2	101
LASH/Seabarge	13	8
Container	28	72
RO/RO	12	8
Bulk	6	12
Tanker	80	194
Total	141	395

SOURCE: U.S., Military Sealift Command, *Ship Register*. Excludes coastal types and passenger vessels.

Wages

As was shown earlier (in the tabulation based on GAO estimates), the monthly crew costs on a typical U.S.-flag ship are two to three times higher than on comparable foreign vessels for certain selected crew positions, i.e., the master, second engineer, and able seaman. Table 15.6 breaks down the cost of these particular billets on an actual ship for the years 1978 and 1982.

In Table 15.6, note that the outlays shown are contractually determined between the unions and shipping associations. They do not include employer contributions for social security or federal and state unemployment taxes.[12] Nor do they include the shipboard cost of room and meals.

Note also that GAO's estimate of monthly American crew costs in 1981 seem to be somewhat high with respect to an able seaman and low with respect to officers (master, second engineer). In any case, the GAO inference that the Merchant Marine Act of 1970 is, at present, disciplining ship officer costs to an average of 9.4 percent annually must be viewed with skepticism. In the case of the *Sealand Adventurer* second engineer, his wage cost rose from $6,729 in 1978 to $10,412 in 1982. If the cost of the position had increased by 9.4 percent it would have come to $9,635. In the case of the master, a 9.4 percent annual increase would have put that position at $16,378 in 1982, not the actual cost of $20,300. On the other hand, the GAO estimate is quite close with respect to an able seaman's wage cost. If the cost of this position was increased from the 1978 figure by 9.4 percent, it would equal $3,126 or be within $81 of the actual position cost.

Another statistic of importance shown in Table 15.6 is the high pension cost of the master and second engineer. These two positions, however, are not unique. Licensed officer monthly pension costs for the *Sealand Adventurer* in 1982 were as follows:

Position	Pension Cost, Including Feinberg Award
Master	$ 4,209.08
Chief mate	2,354.87
Second mate	2,164.61
Third mate (2)	3,948.56
Radio officer	2,463.00
Chief engineer	4,717.22
First assistant engineer	3,041.23
Second assistant engineer	2,791.01
Third assistant engineer	2,540.69
Third assistant engineer (2)	5,081.38
Total	$33,311.65

To assert that fringe benefits in general and pension costs in particular seem excessively high in the case of merchant marine officers would be an understatement. While there is no strictly comparable shoreside job for a

Table 15.6. Contract Costs of Selected Crew Positions, 1978 and 1982

Category	1978	1982
Master		
Base wage	$ 3,632.62	$ 5,436.85
Nonwatch	1,017.19	1,522.39
Vacation	3,523.58	7,943.75
Pension	2,369.66	4,209.08
Welfare/medical	232.20	374.70
Training	150.00	100.20
Automation	464.98	695.92
Hiring hall	16.50	16.50
Supplementary pension	30.00	. . .
Total	$11,436.73	$20,299.39
Second engineer		
Base wage	$ 1,738.90	$ 2,421.00
Overtime[a]	1,035.85	1,442.17
Vacation	1,829.22	2,925.45
Pension	1,593.98	2,791.01
Welfare/medical	187.50	420.00
Training	151.80	151.80
Automation	173.89	242.10
Hiring hall	18.78	18.78
Total	$ 6,729.92	$10,412.31
Able seaman		
Base wage	$ 866.34	$ 1,296.63
Overtime[a]	413.36	618.66
Pension	352.20	375.00
Training	108.60	231.60
Hiring hall	37.50	43.50
Transportation Institute	30.00	15.00
Vacation	376.50	466.50
Total	$ 2,184.50	$ 3,046.89

SOURCE: U.S., Maritime Administration, Office of Maritime Labor and Training, *Maritime Contract Impact System Personnel Cost Report for SS "Sealand Adventurer,"* 1978, 1982.

NOTE: In some instances, categories were combined and retitled for purposes of clarity. Added to pension cost is the so-called Feinberg Award, which mandates a fund for shipping company contributions for vacation days. Special account costs are incorporated into training costs.

[a]Overtime for an able seaman is average for unlicensed deck personnel. Overtime for a second engineer is average for engineering officers.

seagoing position, contrasting the wages and benefits as a percent of total cost for a heavy power equipment operator (a relatively high risk employment) in New York with those for a second engineer and able seaman is still a valuable exercise. In 1978, the hourly employer-contracted costs of a heavy power equipment operator were as follows:[13]

	Amount
Hourly wage	$12.64
Insurance	0.93
Pension	1.95
Vacation	0.70
All other nonlegally required contributions	0.20
Total	$16.42

Here, pension costs are seen to be 12 percent of the employer's total contractual responsibility. In 1978, a second engineer's pension costs were 23 percent of the employer's total contractual costs, while the able seaman's were 16 percent.

Refer again to the GAO comparisons between monthly crew costs of U.S. and foreign operators. Note that the U.S. able seaman cost is not too far out of line and is even less than the Japanese able seaman cost. In the case of the second engineer, it is another matter entirely. The base wage of the second engineer is approximately twice that of the able seaman, yet the employer's contribution to his pension is six times as great.

While there may be valid reasons for a company to contribute a greater percentage to an officer's pension, it is certainly fair to suggest that the burden of justifying such payments rests squarely on the officer unions and the ship operators with whom they negotiate.

Table 15.7 traces the growth of the seafaring fringe benefits over the period 1972–81. After becoming familiar with the trend shown in Table 15.7, consider that for American industry as a whole, it is estimated that fringe benefits in 1980 (again excluding any legally required payments) accounted for 22.9 percent of the total wage cost.[14] As is shown in Table 15.7, seafaring fringe benefits in 1980 exceed base pay in every category for which a calculation was made.

A final issue with respect to seagoing pension plans is the way in which present statutes have adversely affected the efficient operation of government-owned shipping in time of a major contingency such as the Korean War or Vietnam War. The impact of these statutes and the problem they pose are discussed in Appendix D.

Table 15.7. Seafaring Monthly Wages and Employer Contribution to Employee Fringe Plans for Selected Ratings, 1972–1981

	1972		1973		1974		1975		1976	
	Base Wage	Fringe	Base Wage	Fringe	Base Wage	Fringe	Base Wage	Fringe	Base Wage	Fringe
Master	2,749.12	2,766.49	2,914.31	2,944.48	3,147.29	3,086.96	3,304.68	4,007.13	3,539.22	4,883.98
Chief mate	1,492.36	1,644.21	1,581.96	1,772.28	1,708.44	1,828.40	1,793.86	2,369.93	1,921.26	2,966.08
Chief engineer	2,449.66	1,904.44	2,965.62	2,502.93	2,804.35	2,837.85	3,084.80	3,791.11	3,303.81	4,280.03
First assistant	1,492.36	1,489.65	1,581.89	1,604.71	1,708.51	1,819.69	1,879.28	2,407.03	2,012.72	2,717.36
Radio	1,184.88	1,565.92	1,255.41	1,693.81	1,343.78	1,856.06	1,478.16	2,429.64	1,588.11	2,967.75
Able seaman	554.88	737.19	582.62	725.47	611.75	753.32	688.22	996.73	737.08	1,064.92

	1977		1978		1979		1980		1981	
	Base Wage	Fringe	Base Wage	Fringe	Base Wage	Fringe	Base Wage	Fringe	Base Wage	Fringe
Master	4,046.71	5,221.72	4,350.25	5,464.15	4,863.58	6,550.47	5,634.08	7,600.85	5,634.08	9,795.39
Chief mate	2,196.71	2,661.76	2,361.46	5,594.33	2,640.06	3,837.42	3,058.37	4,422.99	3,058.37	5,292.30
Chief engineer	3,605.83	4,848.44	3,876.27	5,641.09	4,333.65	6,514.18	5,023.24	9,017.05	5,396.76	10,292.35
First assistant	2,196.71	3,096.25	2,361.46	3,600.52	2,640.06	4,157.57	3,058.37	4,951.76	3,287.74	5,732.71
Radio	1,727.81	3,466.85	1,857.39	3,888.88	2,076.57	4,446.31	2,405.54	5,364.23	2,726.92	6,972.71
Able seaman	804.45	1,109.01	864.78	1,205.81	966.83	1,321.90	1,120.00	1,392.90	1,204.00	1,598.78

SOURCE: U.S., Maritime Administration, Office of Maritime Labor and Training. Prepared 17 June 1982.

NOTE: Wages and fringes, in dollars, are as of 1 January for each year. Base wage includes nonwatch allowance for master, chief mate, chief engineer, and first assistant engineer. It does not include overtime for radio officer or able seaman.

16   Ports

While few would have trouble with the idea that shipping companies are competitors, many would have trouble with the idea that ports are competitors. Their disbelief would be both right and wrong. In a laissez-faire environment, ports would, in fact, be fierce competitors. The economic payoff is there—jobs, industrial development, and general economic growth for the port and the region it serves.[1] In fact, in the early days of the Republic, competition between port cities and between the states they served was heated.

The state of New York completed the $7 million Erie Canal in 1825. The canal linked the port of New York to the rapidly developing areas of the old Northwest. Pennsylvania's response was a massive canal-rail project connecting its port of Philadelphia with Pittsburgh on the Ohio River. This so-called Pennsylvania Public Works Project was completed in 1834 at a cost of $10 million. Virginia spent $10 million to link the James and Ohio rivers. Ultimate beneficiaries were to be its port cities at the mouth of the Chesapeake Bay.[2] At various times before the Civil War, public and private interests sought to connect Charleston, South Carolina, to Cincinnati by rail via a series of tunnels through the Appalachian Mountains. The project was never completed.

This early competition between the states and their ports was not no-holds-barred competition, however. Federal favoritism and unbridled state competition are restrained by the Constitution, various acts of Congress, and private and voluntary arrangements. For example, the U.S. Constitution, Article 1, Section 9, says:

> No preference shall be given by any Regulation of commerce on Revenue to the ports of one State over those of another; nor shall vessels bound to, or from, one State, be obliged to enter, clear, or pay duties in another.

Table 16.1 lists those federal enactments and court decisions on port development in the United States that mitigate port competitiveness.

Table 16.1. Statutes/Court Decisions that Mitigate Port Competition
in the United States

Statute/Decision	Purpose/Effect
Constitution, Article 1, Section 9	Mandated equal federal treatment of ports of the several states. Constrained port competition by the states.
General Survey Act of 1824 (4 Statute 32)	Appropriated funds for river and harbor improvements, and gave U.S. Army Corps of Engineers responsibility for these. Since these expenditures were authorized by a Congress made up of representatives of the several states, equity with respect to such expenditures was further insured.
Gibbons v.*Ogden*, 1824	Limited state authority to interfere with commerce on navigable rivers of the United States, i.e., forbade New York State to grant a water transportation monopoly to a domestic corporation serving its ports.
Rivers and Harbors Act of 1882	Affirmed the policy that no tolls or operating charges were to be levied on vessels using "improvements of navigation" (locks, lighthouses, etc.) belonging to the United States.
Act to Regulate Commerce of 1887	Prohibited (railroad) discrimination between persons, places, and traffic. Became basis for Interstate Commerce Commission jurisdiction in cases where discrimination between ports is alleged, e.g., a railroad charging less for shipments to a port a greater distance from the origin than for those to a closer port with comparable services.
Merchant Marine Act of 1920, Section 8	Asserted a positive federal role in developing and promoting "ports and transportation facilities in connection with water commerce." Be-

Table 16.1. (cont.)

Statute/Decision	Purpose/Effect
	came the authority under which the Maritime Administration has promoted U.S. ports.
Merchant Marine Act of 1936, Section 211	Directed the Maritime Commission to determine essential trade routes in the movement of U.S. foreign trade. Implicit in this charge was that ports on all coasts would be served by essential routes. In 1937, 23 routes from the Atlantic, Pacific, and Gulf coasts were determined essential. In 1981, 33 routes served U.S. ports, including those on the Great Lakes.

Because the Constitution limited port competition at the state government level; because legislation made harbor improvements an early federal responsibility and restrained land carriers from discriminating between ports; because labor costs, by and large, were standardized through union agreements, and the rougher attributes of competition disciplined by mutual agreement within port authority associations; it might seem that the potential for port competition would be quite limited.[3] Although this is true, it is not the whole story. Figure 16.1 illustrates why a natural competitiveness among U.S. ports exists. Note that a St. Louis exporter, for example, could reasonably ship to Europe or South America via New York, Baltimore, Norfolk, Charleston, Savannah, Jacksonville, Mobile, New Orleans, or Galveston, and the list is not exhaustive. A Denver exporter shipping to a destination in the Pacific basin could reasonably use the ports of San Diego, Los Angeles, San Francisco/Oakland, Portland, or Seattle.[4]

Over the years, while the federal government has not always shown an interest in port development and has even questioned whether port improvement was a local or federal responsibility, federal policy has been evenhanded.[5]

Profile of U.S. Ports

The Maritime Administration has identified 189 major ports in the continental United States, Hawaii, Alaska, Puerto Rico, and the Virgin

Figure 16.1. Some port alternatives for cargo originating at inland U.S. points.

Islands. These ports have 1,456 terminals with 2,939 deep-water berths of 20 or more feet on the Atlantic, Gulf, and Pacific coasts and 18 or more feet on the Great Lakes.[6] These ports are listed in Appendix G. If, however, berths in poor condition and those with a depth of less than 26 feet, the working depth for the average vessel engaged in ocean commerce, are excluded, the number of berths is reduced to 2,311. Table 16.2 summarizes ports and terminal facilities by region.

The Atlantic and Gulf coasts, and to some extent the Pacific Coast, of the United States are blessed with probably the largest number of deep-water ports per coastline mile in the world. In many regions, however, this is not the case. A few deep-water ports must serve large geographical areas. For example, the west coast of Africa (Tangier to Cape Town) is three times the length of the U.S. coastline from Portland, Maine, to Brownsville, Texas, yet it has only a third the number of ports.[7]

Although the continental United States is well served in numbers of ports, it suffers from a lack of deep draft ports, i.e., ports capable of handling supertankers and the ever larger bulk carriers coming on line in increasing numbers. Of the 2,939 berths at U.S. ports, only 11 have berthing depths of 55 or more feet. All are on the Pacific Coast.[8] If those with depths of 46 or more feet are added, the total would increase by only 45. In summary, the total number of berths at all U.S. ports with depths of 46 or more feet is 56 out of almost 3,000.[9]

Table 16.2. Berthing Facilities in U.S. Ports by Region

| Region[a] | No. of Ports | Berths | | | | | | |
		Break-Bulk	Con-tainer	RO/RO	Barge	Dry Bulk	Liquid Bulk	Total
North Atlantic	27	325	45	14	5	87	175	651
South Atlantic	24	113	11	26	2	29	75	256
Gulf	30	258	13	3	10	94	180	558
South Pacific	37	190	48	12	7	42	134	433
North Pacific	43	200	19	7	1	87	84	398
Great Lakes	28	138	1	0	0	439	65	643
Total	189	1,224	137	62	25	778	713	2,939

SOURCE: U.S., Maritime Administration, *National Port Assessment 1980/1990*, table 1.

[a]South Atlantic includes ports in Puerto Rico and the Virgin Islands; South Pacific includes ports in Hawaii; North Pacific includes ports in Alaska.

SS *Massachusetts*. This 265,000-deadweight-ton American-flag supertanker was built in 1975. While medium size as supertankers go, fully loaded she still cannot enter many American ports. Maritime Administration photograph

The economic costs the United States has to pay for its lack of deep draft berths can be seen in Figures 16.2 and 16.3. Note that the relationship shown in Figure 16.3 holds true for shipments of dry bulk cargo as well.

The most efficient way to handle deep draft tankers is the single-point mooring (SPM) system. In this system, one or more buoys are securely anchored to the ocean floor in a depth of 100 or more feet, a depth that can accommodate vessels in the 500,000-deadweight-ton class. A rigid submarine pipeline runs to the buoy's anchor point from onshore storage facilities. A flexible pipeline runs from the rigid pipeline at the buoy's base to the buoy on the surface and connects to the ship. The ship, moored to the buoy, can swing in a 360-degree circle as required. It discharges its cargo through the flexible pipeline into the rigid pipeline connected to shore. A two-buoy SPM system can handle a 600,000-barrel-per-day throughput.

Superports

The problem of providing deep draft berthing facilities for supertankers was addressed by Congress in the Deep Water Port Act of 1974.[10] This act designated the Department of Transportation as the lead agency in licensing offshore, deep-water terminals. The first so-called superport was the Louisiana Offshore Oil Port (LOOP), which began operation in 1981. This $640 million project, located 19 miles off the Louisiana coast in the Gulf of Mexico, can handle 1.4 million barrels of crude per day and accept tankers up to 700,000 deadweight tons.

The Louisiana superport is the only deep-water terminal operating in 1983, although two other projects have received initial approval and are well advanced in planning—the Texas Oil Port (TOP), to be located 12 miles off Freeport, Texas, and the Pelican Terminal Corporation

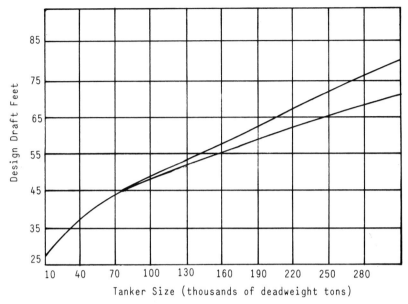

Figure 16.2. Relationship between deadweight size and vessel draft. Source: U.S., General Accounting Office, *American Seaports—Changes Affecting Operations and Development*, p. 10. Note: (1) For safety purposes, required channel depths must generally be 5–10 feet greater than the maximum draft of vessels using the channel. (2) Beyond 100,000 dwt, available data indicate a range of possible drafts depending upon the design characteristics of the vessels involved.

(PELCO) project, which is envisioned as an onshore facility. The plan is to dredge a 55-foot-deep channel 32 miles into the Gulf of Mexico. The concept includes shore facilities not only for oil imports but also for other bulk commodities.

Although the licensing procedure for deep-water ports is in place, another more subtle problem must be dealt with, namely, the reluctance and sometimes outright hostility of coastal communities to host deep-water terminals (Figure 16.4). A part of the problem is apprehension of oil spills and the resultant damage to nearby coastlines. Of equal concern is the fact that oil refineries will be built near the deep-water port. The more throughput a terminal has, the larger the refinery. And it is sad but true that while most citizens appreciate the need for refineries, they do not want them in their own backyards. The most pressing need for a superport is not in the Gulf of Mexico but on the North Atlantic Coast. The concept of a North Atlantic deep-water oil terminal has been around for a long time. In 1972 the Maritime Administration investigated the feasibility of such a terminal and concluded that the savings in oil transport costs would be substantial. The suggested location for the terminal

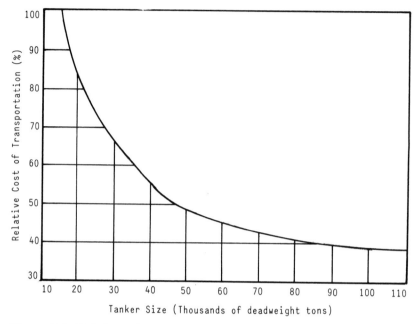

Figure 16.3. Relative unit cost of petroleum transportation by ocean tanker as vessel size increases. Source: U.S., General Accounting Office, *American Seaports*, p. 8.

was at Cape Henlopen outside of Delaware Bay. The project ran into severe criticism from environmentalists and in 1983, to all intent and purpose, is dead.

General Cargo Facilities

Table 16.2 shows that there are 1,448 general cargo (break-bulk, container, RO/RO, and barge) berths at U.S. ports. Facilities with berthing depths of 36 or more feet break down as follows:[11]

	Berthing Facilities
Break-bulk	160
Container	58
Roll-on/roll-off	21
Barge system (LASH)	6
Bulk (grain, coal, ore)	73
Other dry bulk	44

As of 1 July 1982, the largest number of vessels by type in the U.S. foreign trade fleet are container ships. There are ninety-eight container

Figure 16.4. *Washington Star-News*, 31 July 1974. By permission of the cartoonist, G. M. Crockett

ships in the fleet. Container ships are also the fastest growing component in our liner trades. Of importance to port authorities is the fact that these ships are getting significantly larger.[12] In a 1980 report, the U.S. General Accounting Office noted that "ports concentrating on general cargo (i.e., containerships) have requested the Corps of Engineers to dredge to a depth of 45 feet while ports concentrating on bulk cargo have requested depths of 50 or more feet."[13] Dredging, however, is not a free service. For example, to dredge the inner port of Baltimore and the approach channel to a depth of 50 feet from its present 42 feet will cost an estimated $230 million. And to increase the depth of the New York/New Jersey Port Newark Elizabeth Channel from 35 to 45 feet will cost $160 million.[14] The GAO report concluded:

> If the Nation is to realize the reduction in transportation costs that is possible through using larger vessels, harbors and channels will have to be deepened or new deep water ports will have to be developed. Many problems are associated with the deepening of harbors and channels, including going through rock in a growing number of east coast ports, disposal of the material excavated in an acceptable environmental/ecological manner, and constraints imposed by the Corps of Engineers budget.[15]

Port Investment[16]

In 1980 it was estimated that U.S. ports handled approximately 1.6 billion long tons of foreign and domestic waterborne cargo. This amount is expected to increase 32 percent by 1990. Since the end of World War II, over $3 billion has been invested in modernizing American port facilities. It is estimated that the replacement cost of all types of marine terminal facilities in the 189 U.S. ports is $54 billion.

About 49 percent of the berthing facilities in the United States are publicly owned (state government 25 percent, local government 75 percent). Privately owned berths handle primarily single bulk commodities, e.g., ore and grain. Of the estimated $396 million spent to improve terminal facilities in the United States between 1973 and 1978, the largest share went to dry and liquid bulk facilities.

Facility	Percentage of Improvement Money
Bulk	57
General cargo	
Break-bulk	27
Container,	
RO/RO, barge	16
Total	100

Overall, 87 percent of U.S. port facilities are in good or fair condition. However, it is estimated that by 1990 we will need 247 new facilities, as follows.

	New Facilities Needed
Container berths	111
Break-bulk berths	27
Petroleum berths	22
Coal berths	15
Grain berths	10
Ore berths	12
Liquid natural gas (LNG) berths	6
Other	44
Total	247

The total capital required for these new facilities is over $5 billion.

Port Costs and Revenues

For a port to be viable from day to day, its revenues must exceed or at least equal its costs for a particular accounting period. A General Accounting Office survey taken in 1977 determined that by and large most public ports operate in the black. The survey noted, however, that servicing the debt on capital improvements will become an increasingly important problem as port authorities seek funds to expand facilities. Table 16.3 shows the financial condition of representative U.S. ports in 1977.

Statistics that will become more important over time are port costs mandated by federal legislation (environmental protection, employee health/safety, and cargo security). Between 1970 and 1976, local public ports spent $194 million to remain in compliance with federal standards. Future mandated costs are expected to increase by 53 percent. On average, these costs accounted for 6 percent of a port's operating budget.[17]

In 1975 the ocean transport cost of international world trade was about $50 billion.[18]

	Amount (billions)
Ship turnaround (port) costs	$20.0
Stevedoring	8.0
Other direct charges against ship (navigation fees, pilotage, etc.)	2.8
Ship transportation	19.2
Total	$50.0

Note that the two major "land" costs in ocean transportation are ship turnaround and stevedoring costs. Together they exceed the ship charge for moving the cargo over many thousands of miles.

Ship Turnaround (Port) Costs

The chief area in which ports compete is service.[19] This is because the port that will be most attractive to the shipper and the ocean carrier will be the port that can significantly reduce port turnaround time, reduced turnaround time being a substantial benefit to both shipper and carrier.[20] In this regard, it is estimated that if the world's ports were to match their ship, feeder, and cargo transfer capacity (technology) to that of the existing ship and feeder technology, approximately 60 percent of port time costs would be saved.[21]

Areas where ports compete, and where efficiency in operation translates into lower shipper and carrier costs, include the following:

Table 16.3. Sample of Port Financial Conditions, 1977

Port	Fiscal or Calendar Year	Amounts (millions of dollars)				
		Income	Expenses	Gross Profit[a]	Debt Servicing[b]	Long-Term Debt
Chicago	FY	$ 1.3	$ 0.4	$ 0.9	$1.2	$ 16.8
Cleveland	CY	0.7	1.2	(0.5)	0.1	0.8
Corpus Christi	CY	5.3	4.6	0.7	0.8	34.7
Hampton Roads	FY	3.8	2.8	1.0	2.6	44.9
Houston	CY	22.3	19.0	3.2	8.6	102.8
Long Beach	FY	22.8	9.0	13.8	3.5	26.8
Los Angeles	FY	32.5	16.5	16.0	4.1	35.3
New Orleans	FY	20.9	13.6	7.3	6.1	86.3
Sacramento	FY	6.0	5.1	0.9	1.7	16.6

SOURCE: U.S., General Accounting Office, *American Seaports—Changes Affecting Operations and Development*, p. 19.
[a]Before interest and depreciation expense.
[b]Includes principal and interest.

Shoreside equipment, from multimillion-dollar container cranes to the fork lift shown loading a Delta Lines freighter, is essential to efficient port operations. Delta Steamship Lines photograph

1. Availability of facilities. This means having enough berths to accommodate all types of cargo moving through the port and having the ability to cope with peak demands. It means having enough transit sheds, warehouses, and storage areas for containers and having adequate equipment, container cranes, and heavy lift gear.

2. Security for cargo. Historically, significant pilferage has been the rule rather than the exception at many American ports. Pilferage raises insurance costs, which in turn are paid by the shipper and ultimately the consumer. Security also includes adequate protection against fire and weather hazards.

3. Documentation and information control. Ideally, a documentation and information system would be one with real time control over all port operations, including cargo flows and inventory, storage location, and manpower and equipment assignments. The ability to quickly locate "lost" shipments in the port area would be a significant plus.[22] Capable

The U.S. Army was a pioneer in developing container shipping systems beginning with the introduction of the smaller container express (CONEX) containers used in the Korean War. At present, the Military Traffic Management Command has an inventory of about 5,500 twenty-foot military containers (MILVANS), which have the capability of safely transporting ammunition, a capability not found in the commercial dry van container. Courtesy of Military Traffic Management Command

and responsive port administration personnel would also be included in this category.

4. Port support. Good port support includes reliable tugs and pilotage, minor repair facilities, availability of shipment consolidation facilities, and efficient public or private transportation or both in the port area.

5. Port infrastructure. Good land access to the port would include uncongested highways leading into the dock areas as well as rail connections to most berth positions. The wider the selection of motor carriers and railroads serving the port, the better.

Stevedore (Port) Costs

The second largest item of port costs is longshore labor. The fact that stevedoring is a casual type of labor employment, i.e., depends on number and type of ships in port on any given day, makes it expensive on a per hour/daily basis. Moreover, this port function, which was once exceedingly labor intensive, has now become much more capital intensive.

The two major longshore unions are the International Longshoremen's Association (ILA), representing stevedores on the Atlantic and Gulf coasts (75,000 members), and the International Longshoremen's and Warehousemen's Union (ILWU), representing longshore and warehouse labor on the Pacific Coast (15,000 members).

To maintain specified levels of employment and share in the economic benefits of labor-saving technology, longshore unions have relied upon a number of tactics in dealing with ship operators. Over the years, strikes have shut down entire coasts, specific ports have been closed, work

In many trades, cargo is still loaded and unloaded on pallets as seen in this photograph of stevedores working the hold of a Delta Lines freighter. In a container operation, a crane operator and a spotter would provide all the labor necessary to work a single vessel hatch. Delta Steamship Lines photograph

slowdowns have taken place, certain cargoes have been boycotted, and individual ships have been picketed. Apparently, no task was too large. After the Russian invasion of Afghanistan, the ILA boycotted all U.S. cargoes going to or arriving from the Soviet Union.

In early disputes over containerization, particularly on the West Coast, longshore unions negotiated agreements whereby employers contributed fixed amounts to funds to provide compensation and retirement benefits to workers displaced by containerization.

Agreements on all coasts typically specified that wages be paid for work not performed, i.e., wages that would have been paid without the advent of container ship and LASH technology. These contract provisions came to be nothing more nor less than mechanisms by which employers purchased the right to use labor-saving equipment. A 1979 National Academy of Sciences report on innovation in the maritime industry concluded:

> Although the LASH ship is highly automated, the loading and offloading of a barge is performed by the giant crane, operated by one man with the guidance of a "talker." The longshoremen's contract requires that the ship hire two gangs, a total of 42 men, for this work. By comparison, a containership loading with one container crane can hire one gang of 21 men. It is ironical that a system feather-bedded to the extent of LASH must pay a royalty into a fund intended to compensate for unemployment of longshoremen.[23]

The most complex and vexing "make-work" rules deal with marine containers; who will load and unload (stuff and strip) them, and where and under what circumstances. The issue has been overriding in ship operator–ILA negotiations since 1957. Bitter and lengthy strikes have resulted when negotiations broke down and the issue wound up on the docks. (The Port of New York was struck for 57 days and Gulf Coast ports for 100 days in 1968. The strike was finally resolved by presidential mediation.)

Present-day container work rules were adopted in 1969 and stricter union interpretations were added in 1973 (the so-called Dublin Supplement) and 1975. These rules require that containers that are owned or leased by shipowners and that originate or are destined to a point within 50 miles of the center of an ILA port be stuffed/stripped by longshore labor. A $1,000 fine is levied on each container that is not stuffed or stripped on the dock. There are, however, three major exceptions: (1) containers whose contents are owned by one beneficial owner and that are loaded or unloaded at his facility by his employees; (2) import containers that are stored at a public warehouse for at least thirty days; (3) containers containing mail or household goods of military personnel changing residences.

Containers that must be stuffed/stripped at the pier include those going to or from non-vessel-operating common carriers (NVOs), consolidators, forwarders, and other shippers and consignees who do not use their own employees to load and unload their containers. Hardest hit are the NVOs with places of business within 50 miles of an ILA port whose principal business is to consolidate the freight of small shippers into full container loads. Such shipments move on a single bill of lading and are able to take advantage of significantly lower container rates.

When the latest agreement between shipowners and the ILA, an agreement incorporating all the provisions listed above, was put into effect in early 1981, warehousers and truckers challenged its legality in the federal courts. The issue was further complicated over the question of whether the National Labor Relations Board or the Federal Maritime Commission had primary jurisdiction. Were the work rules an unfair labor practice and in restraint of trade (NLRB), or were they discriminatory with respect to shippers, a violation of the Shipping Act of 1916 (FMC)?

As of 1 July 1982, a court injunction has prevented the rules from being enforced. However, an appellate court decision in May 1982 affirmed the jurisdiction of the FMC to rule upon the validity of the proposed agreement. Presumably, the issues surrounding this particular contract will be resolved in 1983, although the general issue of container work rules promises to be around for many years to come.

Another labor cost that has increased significantly is the cost of worker compensation insurance under the Longshoremen's and Harbor Workers' Compensation Act (LHWCA) of 1927. Under amendments enacted in 1972, LHWCA benefits have far outstripped those in other industries. Critics of the 1972 amendments argue that the purpose of the original act, which was to provide compensation for work-related injuries suffered by maritime employees who, under the Constitution, could not be covered by state programs, has been abused beyond all reason. For example, the cost of workers' compensation insurance for a New York stevedore is estimated to be over $20,000 per year. Since benefits under the act are financed by private insurance, the additional costs are reflected in higher labor port charges.

However, considerable pressure for legislative reform has been exerted by covered employers, including stevedore firms, shipbuilders, small boat builders, marina operators, and ship repair facility firms, as well as trucking companies and warehouse operators.

In April 1982 the General Accounting Office issued a report suggesting reforms of the 1972 amendments. GAO noted that benefits have increased over 600 percent since 1972.[24] On 27 July 1982 the Senate passed reform legislation (S. 1182) that puts a 5 percent cap on the annual escalation of benefits, eliminates benefits for non-work-related deaths, and exempts a number of smaller marine-related businesses (small boat builders, etc.) from the 1927 act's provisions. The House Committee on Education and Labor did not mark up S. 1182, and it died in committee on 1 December 1982. The bill was reintroduced in the Senate (S. 28) on 26 January 1983.

National Defense

The Department of Defense maintains a considerable in-house shipping capability (the Military Sealift Command fleet and the Ready Reserve Force of the National Defense Reserve Fleet). However, military planners must rely almost entirely on state/local and private port facilities. Only two military ocean terminals (MOTs) are in active use in 1983. One is located at Bayonne, New Jersey, and the other at Oakland, California.

With respect to the role ports play in national security, there is both good and bad news. The good news is that the number of ports (on all coasts) from which military supplies can move overseas makes the always present congestion problem manageable. Weighed against that, however, is the tendency to concentrate specialized general cargo facilities in a relatively few ports. The result is that ports from the Virginia capes to Maine account for one third of the total container berths in the United States, and the state of California accounts for another third (see Table 16.2). Bolstering this tendency are the economies of scale associated with volume operations such as those in the New York–New Jersey area.

Some more bad news is the lack of deep draft ports and facilities for supertankers and Very Large Bulk Carriers. As the United States comes to depend more and more on overseas raw materials to support its industrial base, transhipping this cargo becomes more of a problem. First, the cost is very high—witness the high cost of transhipping Alaska crude through the Panama Canal bottleneck. Second, in a national emergency, speed—quick port turnaround time—is crucial. Cut port turnaround time significantly, and the number of vessels needed on a particular route decreases.

Thus, the large number of ports and berthing facilities available to the United States in wartime can be misleading. Port congestion is an all too real possibility, as history shows. In the Spanish-American War, for example, Tampa was designated the chief port of embarkation. However, as army historian James Huston so aptly notes, it was "hurry up and wait." Port congestion reached a point where within a few weeks a thousand railroad cars with military supplies "were backed up on sidings as far away as Columbia, S.C."[25] In World War I, "two hundred ships lay in New York harbor awaiting cargoes and fuel while 44,320 carloads of freight (nearly two million tons) backed up on the Atlantic seaboard as far west as Buffalo and Pittsburgh."[26]

World War II, however, was a two-ocean war in which all of the nation's ports were used and congestion such as that experienced by New York in World War I did not materialize on a large scale. According to Huston, seldom were freight cars held up at a port for longer than ten days. It should be noted, however, that ten-day delays would be unacceptable in the rapid deployment scenarios envisioned for the 1980s.

In 1978 the Department of Defense studied a selected number of U.S. ports to determine their ability to support the deployment of major U.S. Army tactical units in an emergency. Study objectives were to (1) assess the adequacy of predesignated commercial facilities, (2) identify any needed additional facilities, (3) identify the best suited facilities in the same port area, and (4) identify suitable backup facilities.

Study assumptions were that (1) only one unit at a time will move through a port, (2) all suitable U.S.-flag ships will be available for use, (3) intermodal containers will not be used, (4) the arrival rate of unit equipment at the port is not a constraint, (5) the five-day port clearance clock starts on the day after the first unit increments arrive and ends when all ships are loaded, (6) sufficient stevedore gangs will be available, and (7) deploying unit personnel will be transported by air.

The report concluded that most of the ports studied had adequate facilities "to support the separate deployment of U.S. Army division size units within a 5-day port clearance constraint."[27]

While the results of the 1978 study were generally satisfactory from a military viewpoint, there has been increasing concern in Congress that the U.S. port infrastructure is not only deteriorating but overburdened with federal regulations. A number of bills whose purpose was port improvement have been introduced. Two of the most far-reaching being considered by the Ninety-seventh Congress (1981–83) are S. 1692, National Harbors Improvement and Maintenance Act of 1981, and H.R. 4267, Port Development Navigation Act of 1981.[28] Of the two, H.R. 4267 is the more comprehensive with respect to the national defense. In opening the hearings on H.R. 4267, Congressman Mario Biaggi, vice-chairman of the House Merchant Marine and Fisheries Committee, stated that a major purpose of the bill was to undertake "the first significant overhaul of federal port policy since the adoption of the U.S. Constitution nearly 200 years ago."

Who Shall Pay for What and How Much?

Historically, the cost of developing the nation's ports has been shared by the federal government and the port industry. As a rule, the federal government has paid for the construction and maintenance of major shipping channels (Corps of Engineers budget) and navigation aids in and at port approaches (U.S. Coast Guard budget). Local/state authorities, and in some instances private monies, have paid the cost of dredging from main channels to berths. Public or private funds have paid for the berths and land support facilities.

The federal government has spent over $4 billion in dredging since the beginning of the nineteenth century. In 1978, annual harbor maintenance costs, averaged over five years, ranged from $18.2 million for Baton Rouge, Louisiana, to zero for San Diego harbor. Intermediate figures were $10.4 million for Savannah harbor, $5.3 million for Mobile, Alabama, harbor, and $1.4 million for Anchorage, Alaska, harbor.[29]

In 1980, under provisions of Public Law 95–502, sometimes referred to as the Waterway User Tax Bill, users of the inland waterway system were required to pay a small fuel tax to help defray operation and maintenance costs. Passage of the legislation was the culmination of a movement President Franklin Roosevelt began to require users to pay a share of this heretofore all-federal expense.

One of the first acts of the Reagan administration when it took office in 1981 was to introduce legislation to increase user fees on inland waterways and to recover full dredging costs from the ports. The Reagan administration rationale is straightforward: reduce so-called government subsidies to private sector users and collaterally reduce federal deficits, i.e., balance the federal budget. Since the beginning of 1981, over twenty bills dealing with this issue have been introduced in Congress.

In responding to administration proposals to recover all or part of the costs now borne by the federal government in maintaining the nation's deep-water ports, the American Association of Port Authorities (which represents the interests of the country's ports in Washington) can hardly speak with a single voice.[30] The difficulty is that the association represents both large and small ports and many of the proposals to recover federal construction, operation, and maintenance costs would have a markedly different impact, depending on port size.[31]

To illustrate the dilemma facing both the administration and the ports, consider the case of two ports, A and B, that historically have required the same amount of federal dollars to keep them economically viable, e.g., by maintaining main channel depths. Now assume that one million tons of cargo pass through port A annually and 100,000 tons through port B. Recovering costs by imposing a user charge on cargo passing through a port would penalize the smaller port. Assuming no other source of revenue, the smaller port would theoretically have to impose a user fee ten times greater than that of its larger sister port to raise an equal amount of income. If channel maintenance costs are high, in the long run, cargo would be diverted to those ports handling larger tonnages. This was the approach of the administration-backed S. 809 and H.R. 2959, introduced in 1981. Needless to say, this approach was anathema to smaller and medium-sized ports.

An opposite approach would be to "tax" cargo an equal amount without regard to which port it passed through. Revenues collected would go into a common fund that would be used to defray federal port expenses at all ports. Ninety percent of new construction costs would be paid from these monies. By definition, large tonnage ports would "contribute" substantially more to the fund that smaller ports. This technique was a key provision in S. 1856 and H.R. 4691.

If the revenues so generated were used only to maintain the status quo, i.e., for maintenance, objections from larger ports would probably be considerably less. However, when common fund monies are also to be used for new construction, as S. 1856 proposed, a concern of larger ports is that the "political process" would have a great deal to do with which projects are funded (as is now the case), irrespective of any legislative safeguards that might be imposed. As the large ports see it, funds they themselves generate could quite easily be used to improve competing smaller ports, while their own improvement plans were put on hold.

Several variants of the above proposals have also been put forward. One would impose a user fee on traffic passing through a port to defray ongoing maintenance costs at that port but limit the port's share to a specific percentage and/or establish a maximum per ton user charge. With respect to new construction, costs would be from nonfederal interests. Presumably, a port authority would calculate the costs and benefit of any new project and act accordingly. This was the approach taken in S. 1692.

Another proposal would simply transfer money from one government account to another. In the case of ports, a part of the annual $6 billion received in custom receipts would be used to fund the annual $300 million dredging costs. This was a key position of S. 2857, introduced in August 1982. While the bill would continue the current federal responsibility for maintaining existing channels between 14 and 45 feet, the cost of deeper channels would be shared on a 50:50 basis with nonfederal interests as would the additional operation and maintenance cost. The custom receipt sharing provision is opposed by the administration because it does not shift port maintenance to primary beneficiaries and, equally important, will do nothing to decrease the present extremely high federal deficits.

An amendment to S. 1692 that was introduced in October 1982 seeks to avoid the operation and maintenance controversy by keeping in place federal responsibility for maintenance but shifting new construction responsibility to the ports. Ports would be allowed to recover new construction costs by imposing differential user fees to reflect the service (the new improvement) rendered.

In urging a significant federal participation in maintaining and improving the nation's ports, local port authorities unanimously stress the following:

1. The nonfederal investment in the nation's ports is very large. It is estimated at $41 billion. Between 1946 and 1978, local port interests invested over $5 billion and are expected to invest an additional $10 billion through the year 2000.

2. Ports serve not only local and particular state economic interests but also broad regional interests, e.g., the port of Savannah, Georgia, serves not only Georgia but also a dozen or more midwestern states. See Appendix H for a smaller port view on the funding controversy.

3. In an era in which the most likely military contingencies will require a rapid deployment of forces, a geographic dispersion of ports is essential. In a large-scale deployment, moving supplies through a limited number of ports could cause unacceptable, if not disastrous, delays.

The port user fee controversy was not settled in 1982 and may or may not be settled in 1983. When action is taken, the most likely outcome is a compromise that will include a greater contribution to port development and maintenance costs by nonfederal sources, although not the complete nonfederal responsibility first advocated by the Reagan administration, and a compromise between large and small port interests that will insure the continued economic viability of the latter.

Conclusion

The most forceful argument supporting small to medium-size port viability and growth is the national security rationale. The large tonnage ports on the Atlantic Ocean are concentrated in the northeastern United States; consider the consequences if a winter storm hit that area with snowfalls of 10–15 feet and, at the same time, word came down to begin a massive deployment of U.S. forces to Europe. In such a case, the option of moving greater than planned tonnages through the southeastern range of ports would be almost beyond price. Yet a few years ago, the option did not exist. Jacksonville, Savannah, and Charleston had no modern facilities. These ports were sleepy southern towns, and it would have been charitable to assume their port throughput capable of supporting a military assault on the Bahamas.[32]

17 Intermodal Transportation

Few, if any, products that move by ship are produced at dockside. Some other mode delivered them to the pier, in many cases from great distances. A recent Maritime Administration report accurately describes how land transportation, the nation's ports, and ocean shipping come together to form an intermodal transportation system.

> It must today be recognized that the function of a port is not to provide a separate and distinct service, but it is to serve as an integral part of a chain of transport links which form an integrated transport system designed to move cargoes from origins to destinations. Ideally, therefore, the port should provide a capability of continuous flow transfer between land (feeder) and ocean transport modes.[1]

The Nature of Intermodal Transportation

Intermodal freight transportation can be viewed in two ways. Both involve the use of two or more transport modes to move goods from A to B. In the traditional concept, the freight itself—crates, boxes, automobiles, bales of cotton—is handled at modal interchange points. For example, a truckload of canned Hawaiian pineapples is delivered to a transit shed at dockside. The cartons are stored until the ship arrives, at which time they are brought aboard on pallets and stowed in a hold. Three characteristics of this type of intermodal movement should be noted. First, and most important, the freight itself is being handled, i.e., the cartons of pineapples. Second, the freight must be protected from the weather and made secure, that is, it must be stored in a safe and dry place. Third, the unit of freight is typically small; cartons contain between twenty-four and forty-eight cans. In some cases, however, the unit being transported may be quite large, outsize, or heavy; may not require

In this chapter the sections National Defense Considerations: Strategic Mobility and Conclusion were written by Major General Henry R. Del Mar, U.S. Army (Ret.).

protection from the weather; or may not need so much security. An example might be a rail flatcar delivering a large piece of earth-moving equipment to the pier, where it will stay in an open storage area until it is loaded aboard ship. These examples describe what is commonly called break-bulk shipments.

The second, and more recent, intermodal concept, while still dependent on two or more transport modes to make the movement from A to B, differs from break-bulk handling in several important ways. First, freight is consolidated into relatively large lots and shipped in a sealed, weather-resistant, reusable "package." Here, it is the package that is handled in a transfer between modes, not the freight itself. For example, an 8 × 8 × 40 foot steel or aluminum box may be loaded with cartons of tinned pineapples at a packing house, sealed, and then picked up by truck or rail and transported to dockside. The box is weather resistant, so that it serves as its own warehouse until it is taken aboard the ship. Weighing perhaps ten tons, the cargo is relatively secure in an open storage area. The steel or aluminum box is called a "container," and the movement is called a "container shipment."

Other intermodal systems in which cargo is loaded into large, reusable packages and the package itself transferred from one mode to another are trailer on flatcar (TOFC), lighter aboard ship (LASH), and roll-on/ roll-off (RO/RO).

In a TOFC shipment the package is a highway trailer that is loaded at a truck shipping platform at point A, driven to point B, loaded onto a railroad flatcar, and moved by rail to point C. At C the shipment returns to the highway mode and is driven to its destination. In LASH move-

SS *Delta Sud* of Delta Steamship Lines can carry both LASH-type barges and containers. Delta Steamship Lines photograph

ment, a large barge, the package, might be loaded at St. Louis, Missouri, towed down the Mississippi to New Orleans, and then loaded aboard a LASH vessel and transported to Rotterdam, where it is unloaded and towed to an inland destination on the Rhine River. A LASH barge is 61 × 31 × 13 feet and can carry 375 tons. The RO/RO mode is nothing more than a seagoing ferry. The package is a truck or trailer that is driven on and off the vessel. As is the case for TOFC, the package is the highway trailer or truck. RO/ROs are extensively used in movements from the U.S. East Coast to Puerto Rico and from the West Coast to Hawaii.

Figure 17.1 illustrates the concept of intermodal transport.

Profile of Land Systems

Air and pipeline transportation do not play even a minor role in cargo movements involving ocean ships. Pipelines are one-way carriers and, as far as petroleum products and coal slurry movements are concerned, are competitors of ocean carriers and not complementary transport systems. The same applies to air-ocean movements, but a brief comment on the air mode is in order.

While one of the most efficient ways of shipping general freight by sea is in containers—in fact, ocean carriers were the "founding fathers" of containerized movement—container shipping by air is another matter. The weight of an empty marine container (its "tare") is critical in calculating what can profitably be shipped by air. On the other hand, container tare weight is relatively insignificant in ocean transportation.[2] A second reason why ocean-air through movements do not exist is that the type of cargo that can be profitably shipped is not the same for air and sea.[3] Air

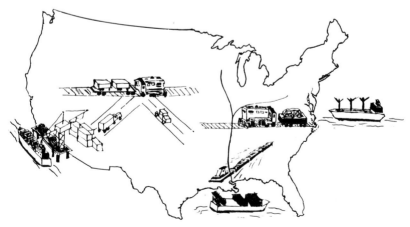

Figure 17.1. Intermodal transportation.

freight is typically high value in relation to its weight and bulk or is time sensitive or both. Ocean freight is typically less valuable in terms of weight and bulk, and transit times are figured in days and weeks. Indeed, ocean transit times are getting longer, because the newer, diesel-powered ships are somewhat slower than their steam turbine predecessors and because vessel operators are deliberately slowing vessel speeds in order to conserve fuel. In 1983, at least, it is difficult to conceive of any type of cargo that would make one part of a movement by fast, high-cost air transport and the other part by a relatively slow, low-cost ocean carrier.[4]

Railroads

In 1981, railroad investment in the United States totalled $34.9 billion. The rail system was made up of 179,000 miles of line haul track, 1.7 million freight cars, and 456,000 employees. The rate of return on investment for all railroads was 3.98 percent.[5]

In 1982, there were thirty-nine class-1 railroads. Assuming final court approval of the Union Pacific, Western Pacific, and Missouri Pacific merger, eight of these railroads will account for over 90 percent of all railroad revenue ton miles and 85 percent of the trackage. Companies with over 12,000 miles of main-line track are the following.

	Miles of Track
Burlington-Northern	28,000
CSX	26,000
Union Pacific/Western Pacific/Missouri Pacific	22,000
Norfolk-Southern	18,000
Conrail	15,000
Southern Pacific	13,000

Railroads connect with ocean shipping at all of the nation's larger ports. In the bulk cargo category, railroads deliver dockside the lion's share of agriculture exports, grain in particular. Other primarily rail bulk traffic, either to or from ports, includes ores and refined petroleum products. And as coal exports increase, it will be the railroad-owned coal terminals that will handle most of the traffic.

In terms of general cargo, railroads are moving an increasing number of containers (COFC, container on flatcar) and trailers (TOFC) to the ports. This increase in port traffic is a function of an increase in rail movement of trailer and trailer-size containers in general. As railroads increase their overall share of this freight, the amount delivered by rail for overseas shipments will increase proportionately. While there is no exact count of containers delivered dockside by rail, in 1981, overall trailer and trailer-size container loadings totalled 3.1 million, an increase

The SS *American Astronaut*, built in 1969, is a steam turbine, 20,000-deadweight-ton non-self-sustaining container ship. Not having the ability to unload its containers with its own cargo-handling gear, the non-self-sustaining container ship is absolutely dependent upon sophisticated shoreside container port facilities. Maritime Administration photograph

of almost 1 million over the 1971 figure.[6] Almost all outsize and very heavy types of cargo, e.g., diesel locomotives, are delivered to the pier by rail.

A relatively new form of ocean-rail movement is land bridge service, introduced by Seatrain Lines in 1972. In a land bridge movement, a container that is shipped from Japan to Europe, for example, moves by water from Japan to a U.S. West Coast port and crosses the United States on a rail flatcar to an East Coast port, where it is loaded onto a ship for the final water movement to Europe. In essence, the continental United States is used as a "bridge" between the Atlantic and Pacific oceans. Since 1972, land bridge traffic has increased by 350 percent.[7] The land bridge option is 3,000 miles shorter than the all-water Panama Canal route, and earns a commensurate savings in energy per ton of freight moved.

Two variations of land bridge are also used. A minibridge movement is one in which a container shipment from Japan destined for the U.S. East Coast would move from a West Coast port across the United States by rail to its destination instead of taking the traditional all-water Panama Canal route. A microbridge movement is one in which that same shipment is sent from a West Coast port to an interior destination, e.g., Kansas City.

Highways

The 3.9-million-mile U.S. highway system serves all 189 deep-water American ports, not just the larger ones. Using this highway system are approximately 35 million non-government-owned commercial vehicles, primarily trucks. Approximately 60,000 firms operate 10 or more vehicles; 17,000 of these are regulated by the Interstate Commerce Commission (ICC), and of these, about 1,000 are class-1 motor carriers. The three largest in terms of gross revenues, in order, are Consolidated Freightways, Roadway Express, and Yellow Freight.[8]

Freight moved by truck to the nation's seaports is in the general cargo category. Trucks deliver the largest number of containers to the ports and almost all the trailers that move on RO/RO vessels. Relatively little overseas bulk cargo moves to or from ports by truck.

Inland Waterways

The 25,000-mile inland waterway system connects with the ocean carrier through those ports located primarily at the mouths of navigable rivers and/or on the intercoastal waterway, a more or less continuous inland system running along the Atlantic and Gulf coasts. The most important part of this intercoastal system in terms of traffic is that portion on the Gulf of Mexico between Corpus Christi, Texas, and Mobile, Alabama.[9]

About 1,800 companies make up the barge and towing industry. The main transport vehicle in the system is the hopper barge, which has the cargo-carrying capacity equivalent of fifteen 100-ton-capacity rail cars or fifty-seven trucks with a capacity of 26 tons each. Bulk products predominate with respect to freight carried. As a percentage of total barge traffic, the largest commodity groups (in order) are petroleum and petroleum products, coal, building materials, and grain and grain products.

The modern intermodal movement that links the oceangoing vessel and the inland waterway network is the LASH system described earlier, a system entirely dedicated to general and neo-bulk cargo. Even in terms of general cargo, LASH is one of the intermodal systems with the smallest lift capability. In 1982 there were twenty-one LASH vessels in the U.S. oceangoing fleet. A large LASH ship carries 80–90 lighters. If all ships and all barges were actually being moved at a given time, the total lift capability would be about 2,000 lighters. In contrast, there are over 24,000 dry cargo barges in use on the nation's inland waterways. Figure 17.2 shows the routes of Lykes Lines Seabee (LASH type) ships and how they connect with the inland waterways of the United States and Europe.

Increasing System Efficiency: Multimodal Transportation Companies

Historically, the U.S. transportation system has evolved in a single-mode, single-ownership pattern. If there is a unifying thread to the myriad laws and regulations that have discouraged ownership of different transport modes under a single corporate roof, it is the always present congressional fear of railroad monopoly power, particularly in the first half of the twentieth century. With respect to railroads and water carriers—

> Congress sought to protect the conceived but unborn Panama Canal. The theory was that rich and powerful railroads would buy up shipping companies, divert their traffic to rail, and leave the Panama Canal bereft of tolls. The devised preventive was to preserve the independence of the

SS *Delta Mar* of Delta Steamship Lines, built in 1973, is a 41,000-deadweight-ton LASH-type vessel. In addition to carrying lighters, it can also carry containers. Delta Steamship Lines photograph

The SS *Doctor Lykes* is one of three Seabee-type vessels operated by Lykes Brothers Steamship Company. These vessels can carry up to thirty-eight Seabee barges. Each barge is 97 feet long and 35 feet wide with a cargo capacity of 835 long tons. In addition to its barges, the *Doctor Lykes* can carry 800 twenty-foot equivalent containers on its upper decks. Maritime Administration photograph

Panama Canal users and their coastal and inland connectors, thereby preserving intermodal competition.[10]

With respect to motor carriers and surface and air forwarders—

[s]eparately, in weak and chaotic condition, they sought protection against their own excessive in-fighting. The prescribed cure was rest—preservation of the status quo. To make sure the convalescents were not disturbed, the alleged big bullies (railroads) were fenced out or fenced in. The regulatory agencies watched over the recoveries, limiting movement until health was restored.[11]

In the recent past, succeeding secretaries of transportation have called for a critical examination of the prohibitions against forming multimodal transportation companies. In 1975, Secretary of Transportation William Coleman stated:

The exploitation of the inherent efficiencies of modes working in combination has been inhibited by an array of physical and institutional barriers, such as inadequate cross modal terminals and regulatory inhibitions against through ticketing or multimodal ownership.[12]

In 1978, Secretary of Transportation Brock Adams concluded, "We ought to see whether a truck line should be allowed to own a railroad as well as a railroad allowed to own a truck line and a barge line."[13]

In 1982, with deregulation of railroads, trucking, and airlines an accomplished fact, the question of multimodal transportation is again on the "front burner." Advantages of multimodal ownership include the following:

1. Shippers would have one-stop shopping—one bill of lading, one freight bill, etc. In general, rate structures would be simpler.

2. Multimodal transportation firm earnings would be less cyclical. For example, a prolonged coal strike would have less revenue impact on a coal-carrying railroad that is a part of a multimodal firm.

SS *Doctor Lykes*, shown under way during sea trials. This 38,000-deadweight-ton, steam turbine, Seabee-type vessel was built by General Dynamics at its Quincy, Massachusetts, yard in 1972. Maritime Administration photograph

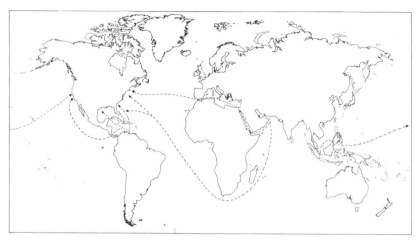

Figure 17.2. Lykes Steamship Company Seabee system. Courtesy Lykes Steamship Company

3. Larger and more diversified transportation firms would find it easier to attract investment capital.

4. Government-created inequities between modes would be fewer.

5. Multimodal firms would tend to be more energy efficient. Energy-conserving piggyback shipments could be expected to increase.

6. Multimodal firms would be better able to use the inherent advantages of containerization.

7. A truly national transportation policy would be easier to identify and implement.

8. A stronger transportation industry would be less dependent on government subsidies. When one mode is aided, the argument by others for "equal" treatment would be less persuasive.

9. Multimodal firms could be expected to identify and channel more R&D (research and development) funds into intermodal operational areas.

10. Multimodal firms would better serve defense requirements in a contingency or emergency, where time and reliability are imperative.

Railroads traditionally have favored loosening the barriers to multimodal ownership. The Association of American Railroads has consistently supported the idea. The president of the Norfolk-Southern Railroad, the nation's financially strongest and best managed road, is a long-time believer in multimodal ownership.[14]

While the regulatory climate for creating multimodal transportation firms is definitely improving, barriers still exist. In a survey published in

1982, railroad presidents perceived existing ICC regulations as being the most formidable bar to rail-based intermodal ownership. Limited railroad earnings, i.e., having the necessary capital to acquire other modes, was cited as being second most important.[15]

What about ocean-rail combinations? Little has been said and less written on the subject. At a 1978 conference on multimodal ownership two different views were expressed. Charles Hiltzheimer, president and chief executive officer of Sea-Land Services, stated,"I do not see any real advantage that would make us want to go out and buy a railroad or own a number of truck lines in the United States or overseas at this time."[16] On the other hand, W. James Amoss, president of Lykes Brothers Steamship Company, felt that some advantage might be gained from multimodal operations on an international scale and "would like to see the subject continue to be developed and discussed."[17]

While ocean-rail combinations have attracted relatively little attention in the deregulation discussions and debates of the last ten years, this lack of interest has not always existed. In a textbook published in 1909, written by one of the country's leading transportation economists at that time, existing ocean-rail combinations were noted and justified.

> The railroads leading to the North Atlantic seaports of the United States were constructed after the ocean transportation business was well developed; but the railroads to the Pacific ports were not thus served by ocean lines; consequently the leading steamship lines from the Pacific ports of the United States have been established and are now operated by the transcontinental railroad companies. By doing this, our railways to the Pacific have made it possible for the people in the Central West and eastern portions of the United States to exchange commodities directly with the people of the Orient, and facilities for through shipment without rebilling have been provided.[18]

There are good arguments for again considering ocean-rail combinations, especially with respect to land bridge traffic. One argument is that further economies in time and freight charges may be achieved. Under present arrangements, containerized shipments from Europe to the Far East, for example, are handled by a minimum of three different companies and, more likely, by four or five. Shipping firm X will carry the shipment from Europe to an American East Coast port. Railroad A will move it perhaps a third of the way across the continent, where railroad B, and maybe a third railroad C, will transport the shipment to a West Coast port. Here, it will be loaded onto a vessel of either the original shipping firm or, equally likely, the ship of another company to complete the final ocean leg of the journey. Interchanges such as these are time costly in that there is no pressing economic incentive for rail carrier A to precisely coordinate a freight interchange with shipping line X or railroads B and C. Time lost at interchange points can be, and often is, substantial. Common management of the ocean and rail carriers involved could be expected to considerably lessen this time lost.[19]

The rationale for ocean-rail combinations from a corporate-strategic point of view was well stated in a *New York Times* analysis of the Union Pacific, Western Pacific, and Missouri Pacific merger.

> With the deregulation of so-called piggyback traffic (TOFC) . . . the ability to control freight over long distances has become important and the larger railroads have been capturing a larger market share.
>
> Some analysts believe that the larger railroads have the potential to become companies that would acquire truck and barge capabilities and *possibly link up with steamship companies* [italics supplied], increasing their ability to control the movement of freight from customer to customer.[20]

Increasing American Exports

It has been urged in general and specifically in the case of land bridge traffic that intermodal transportation can be improved by the formation of multimodal transportation companies. By "improved," it is meant that transport costs can be lessened. If transport costs are less, the price of the delivered good is less. And—if a negatively sloping demand curve has any meaning—at a lower price, more of the good should be purchased. In essence, lower transport costs should increase American exports, and increased exports should benefit the U.S.-flag merchant marine.

Section 212(b) of the Merchant Marine Act of 1936 specifically mandates that the Maritime Commission, now the Maritime Administration, devise means by which "the importers and exporters of the U.S. can be induced to give preference to vessels under U.S. registry."[21] Investigating the possible benefits of U.S. rail-ocean combinations in this respect would seem to follow logically.

One reason that the government agencies responsible for promoting U.S. exports (Department of Commerce) and promoting the merchant marine (Department of Transportation) have not coordinated their efforts as well as they might have is the generally accepted belief that if the price of American exported goods is lowered, foreign-flag shipping will benefit equally with their U.S. competitors from heavier outbound bookings. In other words, while the pie may become larger, the relative share for U.S. operators will stay the same. In essence, it is reasoned that the U.S. exporters, all things being equal, are indifferent to which vessel carries their goods. This view, however, is not unanimously shared. At least one marketing authority believes that the U.S. shipping firm has a decided edge. If that is true, it is up to the ship operator (and the

Maritime Administration) to devote time and resources to exploiting the advantage.[22]

National Defense Considerations: Strategic Mobility

Strategic mobility has been the subject of countless forums, seminars, publications, studies, and formal military and think-tank courses. Invariably, the subject matter is treated in isolation, because military transportation thinking is rigidly disciplined by individual-mode responsibility. Only rarely is the military subject, "strategic mobility," addressed by a well-qualified overall distribution manager. More often, the subject is addressed by an individual or a panel of individuals eminently qualified as separate-mode operators. This single-mode emphasis is pervasive throughout the Department of Defense. On the other hand, one will rarely find a "Fortune 500" company whose separate land, ocean, and air transport managers maximize the efficiency of an individual mode to the detriment of total transportation system efficiency.

The Strategic Mobility Requirement

What is meant by the term "strategic mobility"? Simply put, strategic mobility is the capability to effectively deploy and sustain military forces worldwide in support of a national strategy. It is not the airplanes, ships, trains, trucks, ports, and infrastructure alone, but all of these elements, each well managed and molded into an integrated, smoothly functioning system. The job to be accomplished is the timely deployment of U.S. forces from a point of origin, in either the continental United States or an overseas area, to a final destination in a theater of operations. However, timely deployment is not the only essential consideration; sustaining these forces in combat is equally imperative. If strategic mobility is not viewed from this total perspective, there is a very real danger of systems failure when a crisis occurs.

The difficulty of insuring strategic mobility is compounded by the difficulty of building and maintaining a deployment capability in an austere funding environment. In this environment, those responsible for strategic mobility must make maximum use of existing resources and prudently use the funds available in accomplishing their task. They must aim at a maximum increase in total origin-to-destination transportation system capability for each dollar spent. Parochial concerns with one particular mode cannot play a part in the decision process. Rather, hard-nosed, objective trade-off analysis based on the total systems approach is required. No currently proposed mobility enhancement programs should be exempt from such a reevaluation. All should be tested against the question, Are we getting the maximum return in increased capability for each dollar spent?

The U.S. transportation network is analogous to the vascular system of the human body, in which arteries, veins, and capillaries each serve a specialized function but also cooperate in a total system. The vascular system is effective because of its total systems approach. In this context, any examination designed to reveal deficiencies in the strategic mobility system must first look at its component parts. How do they fit together? Do they fit together well enough to accomplish the task at hand?

Department of Defense Strategic Mobility Organization and Planning

If it is true that Department of Defense thinking focuses on single transport modes to the detriment of the total system, what are the deficiencies in our defense organization, strategic mobility operations, and planning that inhibit our ability to derive maximum benefit from existing assets and available dollars?

Mobility responsibilities are now fragmented and redundant within the Department of Defense. The services (army, navy, air force, and marines) and the transportation operators (Military Airlift Command, Military Sealift Command, and the Military Traffic Management Command), as well as other commands and agencies, now play an active role. All are involved in planning for the deployment of mobility resources and in analyzing capabilities. If the army wants to do a mobility analysis, they do it. If the navy wants to do one, they do it, and so on. Most of these unilateral analyses, of necessity, are based upon parochial assumptions and limited in scope. Usually the result is enhancement of one portion of the system to the detriment of the total system. At present, no one agency has the real time capability of compiling its men and materiel requirements and objectively analyzing what transportation resources are necessary and available to deliver them from origin to final destination. In fact, no federal agency is, or is capable of, pursuing the objective of computing total transportation requirements in time of war, i.e., military requirements, support of the national mobilization industrial base, and civilian requirements. While the procedural mechanism exists to apportion transportation network capacity in accordance with agreed-upon priorities, without the knowledge of total requirements, the outcome in time of emergency cannot be predicted. For example, during the Vietnam conflict, because of the North Vietnamese attacks, ammunition flow had to be increased by a factor of five within a three-week period. This additional demand occurred, however, during the harvest season, and the problem was whether rail gondolas would carry ammunition to the port or transport the harvest. During wartime when requirements exceed capacity, such paradoxes commonly occur.

No one agency at present has a total system capability. The Office of the Joint Chiefs of Staff concentrates on intertheatre lift; Military Airlift

Command looks at airlift; Military Traffic Management Commmand concentrates on continental U.S. land transportation and ocean terminals in the continental United States and overseas, and the theater commanders in chief look at the intratheater networks. To exacerbate the the difficulties posed by this fragmentation, movement requirement data lack accuracy and necessary detail. "Real" origin data are not made available. Tonnages are generally gross estimates. Combat unit deployments are generally reliable, but usable requirement data on mobilization of reserve units, resupply and ammunition tonnages, and specific origin points are nonexistent. That we cannot quantify civilian population requirements or what is needed to support an industrial base casts suspicion on the reliability of our mobility analysis.

Equally important, are we buying mobility enhancements on the basis of fragmented, unreliable knowledge? Can the justification for mobility enhancement programs stand up to critical audit? It is generally agreed that ocean vessels will carry over 90 percent of the wherewithal to deploy and sustain U.S. forces in theaters of operation. However, examination of the Department of Defense annual budget reveals that the airlift enhancement packages consume the vast majority of available funds and sealift enhancement is allocated an infinitesimal amount. Only recently has the Military Sealift Command been fortunate enough to obtain funds for specialized and highly productive vessels designed to support the Rapid Deployment Force (see Chapter 11). However, once the force is deployed, is the U.S. Merchant Marine capable of sustaining that force over time?

The Private Transportation Sector

National transportation policy dictates that the Department of Defense place primary reliance on the commercial transportation industry. This is as it should be, since the United States simply does not have a military transportation capability to meet all Department of Defense requirements in both peace and war. Any attempt to maintain a dual national transportation system—one for commercial and civilian requirements and one for fluctuating defense requirements—would be utter folly, as it would be economically wasteful in the extreme. The best solution for fulfilling DOD peacetime and wartime transportation requirements is an economically viable, privately owned and operated transportation network consisting of all modes. However, closer examination of the commercial transportation sector shows that U.S. capability to support deployed forces is questionable. While many railroad systems have merged for financial and efficiency reasons, and parallel lines and duplicative service have been eliminated in the hopes of creating an efficient and reasonable means of transporting people and materiel, many military bases and military industrial complexes have been left without rail service for raw materials, finished products, and wartime missions. The strength and redundancy of the U.S. rail system that served so well during World War II have diminished.[23]

In 1978 the airline industry was deregulated. This action was taken to stimulate competition, remove government regulatory limitations, and reduce air fares. And while government regulation regarding airline routes has been abolished, air fares and freight rates have skyrocketed due to inflation and fuel costs. Service overall has declined, and only small feeder airlines seem to be prospering. Several major carriers, both scheduled and nonscheduled, have declared bankruptcy, and a half dozen others are teetering toward that end. When major carriers operating wide-bodied aircraft disappear and their assets are sold, the harm to our strategic mobility is evident.

The American trucking industry has been seriously affected by inflationary fuel costs and must also deal with the progressive state of disrepair of our highways. Moreover, since the deregulation of common carrier trucking in 1980, ease of entry into the competitive freight market has played havoc with rates. These factors, together with the downturn in economic activity that began in 1981, have forced a number of old and established highway carriers into bankruptcy. In general, the American trucking industry's ability to fully support a major mobilization, as it has done in the past, is now questionable.

The hardest hit transportation mode, and possibly the most important for long-term support of deployed forces, is the maritime industry. Immediately after World War II this industry employed upward of 200,000 men in over 2,500 ships and many thousands of men and women ashore both in shipyards and terminal activities. The United States had the greatest merchant marine the world had ever seen. In 1983 that once great fleet has been reduced to 500 oceangoing ships employing about 18,000 seagoing personnel. Once deemed the fourth arm of defense, today the merchant marine would be hard pressed to sustain deployed forces for a long time in distant locations such as Southwest Asia.

Conclusion

There is little question that U.S. strategic mobility has deteriorated within the last decade. America's capability, whether with allies or unilaterally, to deploy and sustain forces over great distances anywhere in the world for prolonged periods is in jeopardy. Solutions, while simple to enumerate, are extremely difficult to implement. A beginning, however, would include the following:

1. A total national transportation policy embodying the total systems concept should be developed. Economic and efficient accomplishment of

origin-to-destination requirements would be the objective in lieu of promoting any one mode.

2. The Department of Defense should support the maxim "Total traffic management equals total systems approach from origin to destination, optimizing the advantages of each mode." Regardless of the location within the Department of Defense of the mode operators—land (Military Traffic Management Command); sea (Military Sealift Command); and air (Military Airlift Command)—a Department of Defense and/or Joint Chiefs of Staff traffic manager should direct DOD movements in both peace and war by selecting the most economic and efficient alternative from available services and cost options. Mode operators should not act as traffic managers, since they have no real alternative but to use the mode they manage.[24]

3. The Department of Defense should recognize that in supporting any sizable and prolonged exigency occurring in distant areas of the world, the vast material resources necessary to sustain these deployed forces would be transported by ocean carriers. This fact should be reflected in the actual funding amounts in the sealift and airlift enhancement budget line items.

As was noted earlier, our transportation capability has deteriorated and requires immediate remedial action. Such a restoration is essential not only from a military perspective but also from a total economy perspective. A nation that is blessed with ample raw materials and that is the major producer of manufactured goods but that cannot transport either to where they are needed can hardly expect to maintain its position as a world power. It has been said many times that "America is the democracy of opportunity and the aristocracy of achievement." In this context, the task of rebuilding America's transportation industries and supporting infrastructure that are so crucial to insuring strategic mobility is before us. Completing the task means nothing less than the nation's survival.[25]

18

U.S.-Owned, Foreign-Flag Shipping

Flag-of-convenience shipping—an arrangement in which a vessel owned by nationals of one country flies the flag of another—is not new. There are three motives for the arrangement. One is furtherance of a nation's foreign policy. A second is shielding a vessel from attack or seizure in time of hostilities. The last, and most important in peacetime, is realization of a higher return on capital investment.

In the colonial period and well into the nineteenth century, American owners engaged in U.S. foreign trade had no economic incentive to fly another flag. American operating and building costs were more than competitive.

The first mass transfer of registry from the U.S. flag occurred in the Civil War. The Confederacy, having no navy initially and being ever more tightly squeezed by the Union blockade of its ports, resorted to building naval vessels whose principal mission was to attack Northern merchant shipping. In this way it was hoped to pull Union warships from their blockade stations.[1]

The most famous of these Confederate raiders was the CSS *Alabama*, captained by Raphael Semmes. In the course of her three-year cruise, sixty-nine Union merchant vessels were sunk, burned, or ransomed.[2] Insurance rates of Northern shipping skyrocketed. And while the Confederate raiders did not perceptibly weaken the blockade, they did cause large numbers of Northern owners to transfer their vessels to foreign registries.

The next large move of U.S. vessels to foreign flags occurred just before World War II and came in a roundabout way.

Although the Roosevelt administration was openly sympathetic to the Allied cause when war broke out in 1939, actions in support of the Allies, and later Great Britain alone, were hampered by the Neutrality Acts of 1935 and 1937. And while a revised Neutrality Act passed by Congress in 1939 allowed sales of arms and supplies to belligerents, it prohibited

American ships from entering war zones. One way out of the dilemma was to transfer American-owned ships to Panamanian registry, Panama being at that time virtually a vassal state of the United States. Transfers, however, posed a problem, because maritime unions foresaw a loss of jobs and the more neutral segment of the American public thought the tactic an evasion of the Neutrality Act and likely to drag the United States into war. As a compromise to public opinion, transferred tonnage had to be "sold" to the neutral or Allied country purchaser. All told, 267 American-owned ships were transferred to foreign flags between September 1939 and 1 July 1941.[3]

In the pre–World War II and immediate postwar years, the preferred nonmaritime nations of registry for American-owned shipping were Panama and, to a lesser extent, Honduras. This changed, however, in 1949, when Liberia passed a well-planned, well-executed, and well-financed maritime code that offered considerably more stability than the oft changed and variously interpreted maritime laws of Panama. By 1956 Liberia had surpassed Panama in ship registries and tonnage, and a few years later Liberia became the world's leading "maritime power" in terms of registered tonnage.[4]

The Post–World War II Growth of U.S.-Owned, Foreign-Flag Shipping

The number of American-owned, Panamanian-flag vessels varied in the 1930s but was never large. In fact, the total number of ships under Panamanian registry in 1939, including the beneficially owned tonnage of all nations, was only 159.[5] Even at the end of World War II the total amount of tonnage registered in Panama and Honduras, then the main flag-of-convenience countries, was not large. In 1946 it was less than 2 percent of the world total. However, thirty-six years later (1982), flag-of-convenience tonnage, headed by Liberian tonnage, had increased to account for over 30 percent of the world's total. Of this, a significant part was American owned. Since there were no overriding foreign policy considerations or a threat to shipping, caused by hostilities, what economic motives caused such a massive flight from the American flag?

Two motives were important.

One was that other countries like Liberia placed fewer regulatory constraints on ship operations and fleet management. As was noted in Chapter 3, regulations impose heavy costs in areas such as vessel construction, repairs, manning, and scheduling; and they are expensive when owners cannot freely add to or lay up tonnage, depending upon market conditions. In addition, the United States has complex and pervasive regulations on incorporating a business, disclosing and reporting financial information, taxing profits, and registering vessels. The maritime code of

Liberia was drawn up specifically to give shipowners the maximum degree of freedom and incentive in these areas.

The second motive can be traced to the failure of the Merchant Marine Act of 1936 to provide construction or operating subsidies for tankers or bulk carriers. In the 1930s this was understandable, because most U.S.-flag tanker tonnage operated in the protected domestic trade. And while a number of U.S. international oil companies had tanker tonnage under various foreign flags, this was not considered important to American national security. Foreign-flag, U.S.-owned bulk carriers were almost nonexistent in this period.

In the latter part of the 1950s and the decade of the sixties, as the United States became increasingly dependent on foreign oil, notice was taken of the growing size of the American-owned, foreign-flag tanker fleet. By March 1970 this tonnage totalled 272 vessels of 14.3 million deadweight tons.[6] And just as the sixties heralded a growing U.S. dependence on foreign oil, the seventies brought home to the public our growing dependence on imported strategic minerals and a correspondingly increased demand for bulk tonnage. Like the oil companies before them, parent firms such as Bethlehem Steel, Alcoa, and U.S. Steel, as well as independent operators, registered their vessels in flag-of-convenience nations. By 1970, U.S.-owned, foreign-flag bulk carriers numbered 87 vessels of 3.8 million deadweight tons.[7]

During the fifteen-year period 1955–69, a rapidly widening differential between U.S. and foreign seagoing labor costs and between U.S. and foreign construction costs, coupled with a lack of compensating subsidies, insured a continued and large U.S. investment in foreign-flag tonnage.

The Merchant Marine Act of 1970 attempted to redress the earlier discrimination against tanker and bulk tonnage. Construction subsidies were authorized and operating subsidies were made available on the condition that U.S. operators divest themselves of their foreign-flag tonnage. While the 1970 legislation acted the role of a carrot to entice U.S.-owned, foreign-flag shipping home, the Tax Reduction Act of 1975 played the part of a stick. Before the act, taxes on profits of U.S.-owned, foreign-flag shipping subsidiaries were deferred until they were returned to the parent company as dividends. Since there was no time limit, to all intent and purpose these earnings were tax free. After 1975, however, the only way in which taxes on subsidiary shipping earnings could be deferred was for them to be reinvested in shipping assets even if they were not remitted as dividends to parent company stockholders.

All in all, the most that can be said of the Merchant Marine Act of 1970 as legislation designed to encourage U.S.-owned tanker and bulk tonnage to return to the flag was that it was well intentioned. But it did not work. When all benefits and costs were assessed, it was still much more profitable for shipowners to operate their vessels under the Liberian or Panamanian flag.

Table 18.1 lists the number, type, and tonnage of U.S.-owned, foreign-flag ships registered in Liberia, Honduras, and Panama in 1981.

Although Liberia and Panama account for most U.S.-owned tonnage registered under foreign flags, the flags of other nations also fly over American-owned ships. In 1981 this additional U.S.-owned shipping was estimated to be 277 ships of 2.1 million deadweight tons.[8] Countries of registry included the United Kingdom, France, the Netherlands, West Germany, Italy, Norway, Spain, Belgium, Australia, Canada, Greece, Venezuela, and Denmark.[9]

The distinction between ships registered in Panama, Liberia, and Honduras and those registered in other countries is that the former have agreed not to interfere should the United States requisition American-owned ships in an emergency. Actually, all U.S.-owned, foreign-flag ships can be requisitioned under Section 902 of the Merchant Marine Act of 1936. The problem is enforcement. Only Liberia, Panama, and Honduras have a priori agreed to such requisitioning. These agreements are basic to the concept of effective U.S. control of foreign-flag shipping owned by its nationals, a concept that will be discussed in detail later on.

Points of View

As might be expected, affected groups hold strong policy positions with respect to U.S.-owned, foreign-flag shipping. Their positions on key issues are summarized below.

U.S. Owners of Foreign-Flag Ships [10]

1. By and large American owners of foreign-flag ships consider their fleets a part of the U.S. merchant marine. In recent years a conscious effort has been made to encourage this identification in the mind of the public. Interestingly enough, the Soviet Union also holds the view that this tonnage is part of the U.S. merchant marine.

2. The vast majority—about 85 percent—of U.S.-owned, foreign-flag ships are tankers or bulk carriers. As would be expected, American owners of this shipping do not look with favor on any U.S. policy that would subsidize the construction and operation of a U.S.-flag tanker and bulk fleet. Rather, they urge that subsidy monies be invested in those ships that would be of most use in logistically supporting American forces overseas, e.g., RO/ROs, break-bulk carriers, LASH, and to some degree, container ships.

3. The strongest policy position taken by American owners of foreign-flag shipping is one against cargo preference laws, whether of U.S. or international sponsorship. Attempts in Congress in 1974 and 1977 to

Table 18.1. U.S.-Owned Shipping Registered in Liberia, Panama, and Honduras as of 30 June 1981

Registry	Freighters		Tankers		Bulkers		Passenger	
	Number	Tonnage	Number	Tonnage	Number	Tonnage	Number	Tonnage
Liberia	36	317	260	38,676	91	5,962	...	...
Panama	15	64	60	5,395	9	237	2	17
Honduras	7	41	...	...	...	...	1	9
Total	58	422	320	44,071	100	6,199	3	26

SOURCE: U.S., Maritime Administration, *Effective U.S. Control (EUSC) as of June 30, 1981.*

NOTE: Tonnage is shown in thousands of deadweight tons. The total number of vessels registered was 481; the total registered deadweight tonnage was 50,722,636.

mandate that a certain percentage of U.S. oil imports be carried in American bottoms were strongly and successfully opposed. In 1982 all stops were pulled out in opposing H.R. 4627, a bill that would require that 40 percent of U.S. bulk imports and exports be ultimately carried in American-flag ships.

Of even more concern is the attempt by a majority of the so-called Group of 77 developing countries to impose a cargo-sharing arrangement on the bulk and oil trades similar to the all-but-ratified UN-sponsored Code of Conduct for Liner Conferences, which mandates a 40 : 40 : 20 split of general cargo between the merchant fleets of trading partners—40 percent for each partner with 20 percent left for cross traders.[11] A very recent concern is that expanding U.S. coal exports is a tempting target for cargo-sharing advocates.

4. An important concern of American as well as other Western users of flags of convenience is the proposal by many lesser developed countries to phase out open registry shipping, i.e., foreclose the option of registering foreign vessels in flag-of-convenience countries. Their primary targets are Liberia and Panama, the two countries that register the great majority of this type of tonnage. The developing nations, however, are split on the proposal. Some, such as Sri Lanka, propose establishing their own open registry systems.

5. American owners of foreign-flag ships, particularly those registered in Liberia, are adamant in their contention that flag-of-convenience ships are safe with respect to both construction and operation. The contention is that ships (and firms) should be judged individually, not collectively. They argue that there is more variability between ships within a registry than there is between registries. In particular they note the stricter inspection standards imposed on Liberian vessels within the last five years.[12]

6. U.S. owners of vessels registered in Liberia, Panama, and Honduras have consistently argued that their ships are under effective U.S. (government) control and would be available in a national emergency. Their assertion that these ships are, in fact, a part of the U.S. merchant marine rests squarely on this premise.

U.S. Government: Executive Branch

Two policy positions tend to remain consistent irrespective of the administration in office. The first is an unwillingness to endorse cargo preference proposals as a means of building up the U.S.-flag merchant marine. The Carter administration was firm in this respect.[13] The first test for the Reagan administration came when it strongly opposed Title IV of H.R. 4627, the Maritime Dry Bulk Trade Act, which specified that a percentage of U.S. bulk imports and exports be carried in American vessels.

Over a ten-year period the U.S. share would gradually build to 40 percent. Agreements would be worked out bilaterally betweeen the United States and its trading partners. Administration opposition was unanimous. Letters to the chairman of the House Committee on Foreign Affairs from the Departments of Agriculture, State, Transportation, and Treasury condemned the bill.[14] Other cabinet-level departments, as well as the U.S. Trade Representative and the National Security Council opposed it as well.

The second policy position is a belief that this shipping is under effective U.S. control. The position dates from 1947 when the Joint Chiefs of Staff laid down criteria for determining "effective U.S. control." Although the criteria have been interpreted slightly differently at different times, U.S.-owned ships registered in Panama, Liberia, or Honduras have met the prescribed test over the years.[15] In 1981, Secretary of Defense Caspar Weinberger gave a lukewarm endorsement to the effective control concept.

U.S. Government: Congress

Historically, Congress has been far more receptive to supporting a merchant marine with public monies than have presidents. The only notable exception in modern times has been President Franklin D. Roosevelt.

In general, Congress has tended to favor cargo preference legislation as a means of increasing U.S.-flag participation in its own trade. In 1974 an oil cargo preference bill, the Energy Transportation Security Act of 1974, was passed by both the Senate and House only to suffer a pocket veto by President Gerald Ford. The most recent cargo preference proposal was embodied in Title IV of H.R. 4627.

With respect to effective control, Congress has been the branch of government to question the concept most closely and has generally found it wanting. For example, the Committee to the House of Representatives on the Energy Transportation Security Act of 1974 found that the present reliance of the United States on the effective U.S. control (EUSC) fleet was never intended and that overreliance (on it) was dangerous and contrary to the commercial and national security interest of the United States. In a later 1980 report, "The Strategic Implications of the Omnibus Maritime Bill: A White Paper," the House Committee on Merchant Marine and Fisheries concluded:

> Another serious question concerns the responsiveness of the EUSC fleet to national security requirements. Incidents associated with the sealift buildup of the Vietnam War and the 1973 Middle East War tend to support the contention that reliance on the EUSC fleet would be a mistake. These incidents, one a result of direct foreign government intervention, and

another stemming from the refusal of the crew to sail into the combat zone, provide an adequate basis for the position taken by a previous Assistant Secretary of Defense, who, before a Congressional Subcommittee, stated the view that the EUSC fleet should not be considered a substitute for U.S. flag shipping in meeting defense needs.[16]

Maritime Unions

Of all interest groups, the maritime unions most strenuously oppose the idea that U.S.-owned, foreign-flag shipping is a substitute for, or an adjunct of, the U.S.-flag merchant marine. Union actions opposing flag-of-convenience shipping have ranged from direct action boycotts to detailed analyses arguing against the EUSC concept. The most recent union efforts have focused on the effective control issue and the alleged substandard construction, operating, and inspection requirements of flag-of-convenience nations.

Shippers

Since the U.S.-owned, foreign-flag fleet is mainly made up of tankers and bulk carriers, shippers requiring this type of service are the ones that would be primarily affected should flag-of-convenience fleets be significantly altered in terms of tonnage or cost of operations.

Tankers, for the most part, are owned by shipping subsidiaries of the major oil companies. Here, increased shipping costs would be reflected in the price of the final product, a point continuously made by the oil companies in defending their flag-of-convenience fleets. The impact of increased shipping costs would be the same where parent corporations in industries such as steel and aluminum operate their own bulk carriers.

Two nonsubsidiary user groups also have a lot at stake if bulk shipping costs go up. One group is composed of independent commodity importers and exporters. They view any action that would increase ship operating costs as one that would also increase shipping rates, which in turn would negatively affect demand for the commodity in question. Coal exporters, for example, are extremely concerned that cargo preference legislation mandating the use of higher priced American ships would significantly decrease the overseas demand for U.S. coal.

The second group is made up of U.S. government agencies that are large buyers of bulk and tanker shipping services. The Department of Agriculture has long pointed out that higher shipping costs mean that less of a product, grain for example, can be shipped under such programs as Food for Peace. More recently, the Department of Energy has expressed concern about the shipping costs involved in stocking the national petroleum reserve.

Developing Nations, the Soviet Bloc, and the EEC

Developing countries for the most part favor bulk cargo–sharing arrangements similar to those agreed upon for the liner trades. Their proposals were presented to the Shipping Committee of the UN Conference on Trade and Development (UNCTAD V) in May 1979. With the exception of the Soviet bloc, the industrialized nations strenuously opposed these cargo-sharing proposals. At later meetings in 1980, the developing nations themselves could not reach a consensus on how to achieve their ends.

The developing nations, the so-called Group of 77, are even more divided on the issue of phasing out open registries. Most favor the proposal based on the notion that if Liberia and Panama somehow can be made less attractive as open registry nations, Western shipowners will consider other less developed nations as places of registry in their search for low-cost ship-operating environments.

The Soviet bloc favors, for no discernable economic reason, phasing out flags of convenience. Presumably, the Soviets' view is that their merchant marine will be able to compete with tonnage registered under Western flags better than they will with that registered in lower cost flag-of-convenience countries. On cargo preference, the Soviets' position is somewhat contradictory. They oppose cargo sharing in principle, but they have a long-standing grain cargo-sharing arrangement with United States–flag tonnage.

On the other hand, shipping communities in the European Common Market strongly oppose bulk cargo sharing and the phasing out of open registry. Their position, however, is being increasingly challenged by European Economic Community (EEC) maritime labor unions, particularly on the open registry issue. Labor sees the end of open registry as a step toward returning more shipboard jobs to national-flag shipping.

Effective Control?

Historically, most decision makers in the Departments of State and Defense have endorsed the concept that U.S.-owned ships registered in certain nations are under the effective control of the U.S. government and available in time of emergency. Their case rests on the following:

1. Section 902 of the Merchant Marine Act of 1936, which allows the United States to requisition American-owned shipping in time of war and national emergency;

2. agreements between the United States and individual flag-of-convenience nations stating that flag-of-registry governments will offer no objection to such requisitions;[17]

3. the (military) inability of Liberia and Panama to impose their sovereign will on EUSC shipping even if they chose;[18]

4. an interim war risk insurance program, under which the Maritime Administration has the option of issuing war risk insurance binders to flag-of-convenience vessels in exchange for the vessel owners' agreement to make the ship available in time of emergency and to periodically report the position of the ship to the relevant U.S. government agency.

Although there have always been a fair number of supporters in the executive branch of government for the effective control concept, there have also been some notable dissenters.

The well-known naval analyst Norman Polmar has contended that "their [EUSC ships] availability to support U.S. foreign policy goals in time of peace or carry combat loads in wartime is highly speculative."[19] In testifying before the House Merchant Marine and Fisheries Committee in 1975, Acting Assistant Secretary of Defense John J. Bennet stated that for a number of reasons "the effective U.S.-controlled fleet should not be considered a substitute for U.S.-flag shipping to accommodate defense needs." He further noted that "while these vessels *may* [italics supplied] prove valuable for transporting critical materials in time of crisis, their direct military utility is limited."[20] In testimony before this same committee in 1978, Admiral Isaac C. Kidd, Jr., supreme NATO commander Atlantic, said that he was left with something less than a completely comfortable feeling about flags of convenience. He said that the ship's company in flag-of-convenience ships is almost totally international, and that few are passport-carrying members of NATO countries. From this he concluded:

> One would have to ask oneself what would be the degree of enthusiasm which the nation owning those passports would have with their nationals involved in any conflict not necessarily of their choosing or making.[21]

Admiral Kidd precisely identified the most worrisome question about effective control—what would be the crew response if hostilities, either limited or general, broke out between the United States/NATO and the Soviet Union,[22] or if an unyielding Iran chose to make the Persian Gulf a combat area?

Granting that all the legal aspects of transfer to U.S. control will take place as envisioned, what still cannot be known is the crew response. In denying that a problem exists, EUSC partisans are on extremely shaky ground. It is misleading in the extreme to infer from the role of Panamanian-registered ships in supporting the Allied war effort in 1939–41 that foreign-registered ships would support the United States in 1983. Even worse is to offer Korea and Vietnam as examples of EUSC crews' willingness to support U.S. military and foreign policy objectives. These "wars" were not naval wars. There was little if any risk to a seaman in sailing ships to Korea or Vietnam. Moreover, U.S. world military supremacy was not in dispute. Statistically, seamen on these runs were safer than workers in a coal mine.[23]

If war should break out in the 1980s, U.S./NATO merchant shipping would face a formidable Soviet submarine threat. Imagine an Indonesian seaman on a flag-of-convenience tanker. Assume the ship is in the South Atlantic when hostilities break out, and according to present NATO plans, the ship enters a designated "safe" port, e.g., Cape Town. Will he and the rest of the crew complete the voyage to the United States or Europe? Or will crew, ship, and cargo remain in port? No one knows the answer since the situation has no precedent. One certainty is that in reaching a decision the crew will quite humanly give their own safety a high priority.[24] In assessing the situation, the analyst must recognize that the odds are at least even that the ship will not sail.[25] That is the nub of the flag-of-convenience issue—Can the United States accept the risk that the availability of its tanker and bulk shipping in time of emergency figuratively depends on the flip of a coin?

Conclusion

No one disputes that the primary reason for which American companies register their ships under foreign flags today is economic. And that the primary cost consideration is seagoing labor. On average, payroll costs on a U.S.-flag vessel are two or three times as high as those on a flag-of-convenience ship.

Nor does any one disagree that it costs less to manage a vessel under a convenience flag. Or that American law imposes higher construction and operating standards on vessels under its registry and that it costs more to meet these standards. In a laissez-faire marketplace, which fairly describes international bulk and tanker trades, American-flag firms simply cannot compete without operating subsidies.

In 1982 the maritime administrator reportedly asked representatives of U.S.-owned, foreign-flag bulk and tanker tonnage, "What would it take to return [some of] this tonnage to the American flag?"[26] The question is not new. In 1981 it was directly put to the executive secretary of the Federation of American Controlled Shipping, the Washington, D.C.–based lobby group that represents flag-of-convenience operators, by the chairman of the House Subcommittee on the Merchant Marine. In each case the controlling answer was that American costs were prohibitive in a competitive world environment. Be that as it may, it is urged here that the wrong question was asked in light of the fact that the cost to the U.S. government of putting any significant amount of returned flag-of-convenience tonnage on a par with its international competition would be in the tens of billions of dollars. What should have been asked is, What can the United States do to encourage the building of some modest amount of American-flag bulk and tanker tonnage for operations in its foreign trade, the amount of the tonnage to be sized entirely by national security considerations?

First and foremost, labor costs on American ships must be lowered. In the tight budget years ahead, government will not participate in building a bulk and tanker fleet unless the maritime unions agree to sizable manning and wage concessions. Before Congress will agree to subsidize a foreign trade bulk and tanker fleet of fifty to seventy-five vessels, seagoing labor costs will have to be reduced substantially.[27]

However, a program to insure some minimal amount of bulk and tanker tonnage under the U.S. flag must not be driven by bilateral trade-sharing arrangements per se. Bilaterals may be negotiated and in place, but government participation can be justified only on numbers of ships, not on a particular share of trade.

An equally important question about flag-of-convenience shipping is, What can be done now to improve the odds that these ships will, in fact, return to U.S. control in an emergency? Two suggestions are worth considering.

1. The Department of Defense could insist categorically that before any ship is deemed to be under effective U.S. control, its master, chief engineer, and chief officer be U.S. citizens with basic security clearances. This precondition would be initially nonnegotiable. It would be waived only when the shipowner could demonstrate that no American officers were available.

The problem of what these officers should be paid in a case where government sets standards is admittedly a thorny one. On the one hand, an owner could make an unreasonably low offer expecting it to be refused. On the other, he could legitimately balk at being blackmailed into offering the prevailing American wage, which for senior American merchant marine officers is over twice that of their European counterparts. However, reason suggests that American officers in their own self-interest will not make unreasonable demands, realizing that the Defense Department could waive the U.S. citizen requirement;[28] and that the owners would not be so insensitive to public opinion on a national security issue as to "force" on the officers a wage patently less than that paid for comparable shoreside skills. In other words, the government could let the marketplace decide what equitable wages for U.S. officers on EUSC ships are.

2. EUSC ships could be equipped with some minimum amount of national defense features (NDFs). It has been correctly pointed out many times that bulk and tanker ships would be of little use in a military logistic support role and that adding national defense features to remedy the deficiency would be quite costly. But some passive types of defense

features can still be justified, such as radio equipment for communicating with naval vessels, minimum-capability features to underway replenish naval combatants, submarine detection equipment, and redundant critical spare parts.

The cost of such NDFs could be offset by tax credits against the earnings of a flag-of-convenience vessel when such earnings are returned to the U.S. parent company.

However, these two suggestions—requiring some minimum number of U.S. citizen officers on EUSC vessels and adding national defense features to EUSC vessels—are not substitutes for a modest bulk and tanker fleet under the U.S. flag. At best, they only improve the odds that in time of emergency some flag-of-convenience ships will, in fact, return to U.S. control.

19 Merchant Marines of the Soviet Union and Developing Nations

At first glance, it might seem strange to dichotomize the shipping world into the Soviet Union and emerging nations on the one hand and the developed Western nations on the other. Actually, Soviet Union shipping and Third World shipping have more in common than not. Historically, neither was a supplier of ocean shipping service before World War II. And while the Soviet Union had a relatively large number of ships, they were mostly smaller vessels engaged in the coastal trades. Nations that are developing in 1983 were, for the most part, colonies and territories administered by the European powers in 1939. Their shipping requirements were met by the mother country. Table 19.1 shows the merchant fleets of the principal maritime nations as of 1 September 1939.

In 1939, forty-three countries had ships of 1,000 or more gross tons registered under their flags. However, the thirteen nations shown in Table 19.1, excluding the Soviet Union, accounted for 88 percent of the world's ships and 91 percent of its deadweight tonnage.

In 1951, fifty nations had one or more oceangoing vessels of 1,000 or more gross tons registered under their flags. The thirteen Western nations (including Japan) shown above accounted for 82 percent of the world's seagoing ships and 85 percent of its deadweight tons. The traditional maritime powers, by and large, still dominated the shipping scene.

In 1951 the Soviet merchant fleet stood at 554 vessels including those of Estonia, Latvia, and Lithuania, as well as 83 U.S. government–owned ships transferred to the USSR under lend-lease. However, in addition to the growth in Soviet tonnage and a continued dominance by the developed Western nations as suppliers of world shipping, a phenomenon not indicated above was becoming discernible. Vessels registered in Panama, Honduras, and Liberia in 1951 totalled 702 ships aggregating over 7.1 million deadweight tons.[1] The growth in tonnage of flag-of-convenience "maritime" nations had begun.[2]

Table 19.1. Principal Merchant Fleets of the World,
1 September 1939 (1,000 Gross Tons and Over)

Country	No. of Ships		Deadweight Tons (millions)	
British Empire	3,319		24,054	
United States	1,379		11,682	
Japan	1,180		7,145	
Norway	1,072		6,931	
Germany	854		5,177	
Italy	667		3,911	
France	555		2,999	
Netherlands	537		3,425	
Sweden	484		2,033	
Greece	436		2,791	
Denmark	379		1,576	
Finland	232		826	
Spain	217		1,052	
Total	11,311	(88%)	73,602	(91%)
USSR	354		1,597	
Rest of the world	1,133		5,402	
Total	12,798		80,601	

SOURCE: U.S., Maritime Administration, *Merchant Fleets of the World: September 1, 1939–December 31, 1951.*

Growth in Trade and Number of Nations, 1951–1982

Demand for ocean shipping service is a derived demand that depends upon world trade. As the world's population and what it produces increase, and as the economies of the world become more interdependent, trade between nations and regions increases, and with it the demand for shipping services.

Table 19.2 indicates the growth in world trade and population between 1938 and 1981.

An equally important growth taking place in the post–World War II period, which would have a significant impact on the suppliers of world shipping, was the growth in the number of nations. On 26 June 1946 the United Nations charter was signed by 50 nations. As of July 1981 this number had grown to 154. The increase was almost entirely accounted for by the emergence of the so-called Third World, or less developed, nations.

Table 19.2. Growth in World Trade and Population, 1938–1981

Year	World Population (billions)	World Trade (current dollars, billions)
1938	2.3	21.2
1951	2.5	76.7
1981	4.6	1,850.0

SOURCE: *Colliers Encyclopedia Yearbook 1953* (New York: P. F. Collier and Son), p. 376; *Colliers Yearbook 1982*, p. 293.

NOTE: In constant dollars, world trade was $73.3 billion in 1938 and $955.6 billion in 1981. This is a 6.1 percent compounded annual growth rate, i.e., thirteen times greater than in 1938.

The Soviet Union and Its Merchant Marine

Historically, the USSR was not a world supplier of shipping services. In 1939, with 354 ships, it accounted for less than 3 percent of the world merchant fleet in numbers and less than 2 percent in deadweight tons. In 1981, with 2,530 oceangoing vessels, it accounted for over 10 percent of the world's merchant ships and 3.3 percent of its deadweight tons.[3] While the data correctly suggest that the Soviet merchant marine is made up of smaller ships, the accomplishment is nonetheless impressive.[4] On the other hand, the Soviet merchant marine has not achieved the size forecast by some U.S. projections made in the early 1960s. For example, a congressional staff study in 1963 forecast that the USSR merchant fleet could be as large as 4,365 vessels of 27 million deadweight tons in 1980, while the U.S. fleet would shrink to 489 ships of 7.1 million deadweight tons.[5]

The Soviet Union supports its merchant marine for the following reasons:

1. Its merchant marine earns foreign currency and conversely minimizes the outflow of convertible currencies to pay for shipping services. In 1965, for example, foreign ships were carrying 50 percent of Soviet foreign trade. (This was due in part to the large amount of Soviet tonnage that was used to support the North Vietnamese during the Vietnam War.)

2. A traditional role of the Soviet merchant marine is to act as a naval auxiliary in time of both war and peace. As Norman Polmar has pointed out,

> A final factor in measuring seapower concerns centralized direction and coordination. This the Soviet Union has done to a high degree. . . . Naval

officers regularly serve with the non-naval fleets; merchant tankers are employed as a matter of course to refuel warships; the Ministry of Shipbuilding is responsible for building all ships; naval, merchant fishing, research, and inland transport. . . . [6]

Soviet fish factory ship *Baltisnaya Slava* at anchor off the coast of Virginia. These highly automated vessels represent some of the best in Soviet marine technology. While they have an electronic surveillance capability, their main mission is to prepare and preserve the catch of smaller fishing vessels. U.S. Naval Institute photograph

Soviet merchant trawler *Leniskiye Gory*. These relatively small 3,500-ton vessels comprise a large part of the Russian oceangoing merchant marine. Major areas of operations for these ships are the Baltic and North seas. U.S. Naval Institute photograph

3. A Soviet merchant marine establishes a presence in Third World countries, i.e., "shows the flag." The typically smaller Soviet ships can enter many developing country ports that larger Western ships cannot negotiate and, in many cases, avoid, because of the relatively small amounts of cargo offered.

A modern Soviet general cargo vessel under way in the Gulf of Mexico. The ship is comparable in size to an American C-2-class break-bulk vessel. Once a rarity, Soviet merchant vessels are routinely seen on most of the world's trade routes. U.S. Naval Institute photograph

A small Soviet general cargo vessel of the *Vitegrates* class. Note the helicopter landing pad on the stern, a feature not found even on the largest American freighter. U.S. Naval Institute photograph

Soviet general cargo vessel *Partizanskaya Iskra*. Although Soviet freighters are generally smaller than those of the Western maritime nations, their relatively shallow draft allows them to call at the smaller ports of many developing nations. U.S. Naval Institute photograph

General cargo vessel *Pridneprousk*. These smaller Soviet vessels are used extensively in the Baltic Sea and Far East coastal trades. U.S. Naval Institute photograph

4. As was noted in Chapter 7, "The Resource War: Bulk and Tanker Shipping," the United States has become increasingly dependent on overseas sources for its fuels and minerals and is almost entirely dependent on foreign-flag vessels to move these imports. To a lesser extent, the Soviet Union is also dependent on overseas sources for a number of its critical raw material imports. Five cited in recent congressional testimony are bauxite and alumina, flourine, tin, tungsten, and antimony.[7] In any case, the Soviets seem to have no intention of being dependent on foreign-flag shipping for their strategic imports, now or in the future. As of 31 December 1979, there were 156 bulk carriers and 470 tankers in the Russian merchant fleet.[8] During the following year, 5 freighters, 2 bulk carriers, and 1 tanker were delivered.[9]

However, while the buildup of the Soviet merchant marine has offered opportunities, it has presented at least one major problem—excess capacity and what to do with it. One estimate puts the Soviet fleet lift capacity available for cross trading, i.e., employed in trade between third countries, at 75 million tons annually. In 1975 the U.S. Maritime Administration estimated this excess fleet capacity to be between 5 and 6 million deadweight tons.[10]

It is sometimes pointed out that there is no bottom line in determining profit or loss for Soviet merchant ships, since all are government owned and instruments of government policy. One should not infer from this, however, that Soviet shipping will always be employed irrationally in an economic sense. Such an assumption would ill serve private U.S. shipping managers in their long-term fleet utilization planning and government officials responsible for developing a long-range American maritime policy.

V. G. Bakayev, minister of the Soviet merchant marine, said in 1966:

> Our shipping is planned to obtain maximum possible income. Our merchant marine has moved from inefficient planning of international services in tons and ton miles to net profit planning.[11]

Plainly stated, excess Soviet shipping will go where the cargo is. And a large part of the world's oceanborne commerce has the United States as an end point.

In the early 1970s Soviet ships began to appear in large numbers in the American trades. The 1972 U.S.-USSR Maritime Agreement opened forty U.S. ports to Russian ships. Between 1971 and 1976 Soviet parti-

Soviet freighter *Murgash* at anchor in Hampton Roads, Virginia. Note the modern cargo-handling gear. U.S. Naval Institute photograph

Soviet break-bulk freighter *Muehck* in the Tonkin Gulf en route to Haipong, North Vietnam. Soviet merchant vessels played a key role in support of the North Vietnam war effort. U.S. Naval Institute photograph

cipation in the U.S. trades had increased twenty-two times, from 261,000 to 5.7 million long tons.[12]

Not only did Soviet ships participate in the U.S. bulk trades, but also, to an increasing extent, penetrated the liner trades. Service was established on the four U.S. coasts. The Far Eastern Shipping Company operated from the Pacific Coast, the Baltic Shipping Company from the Atlantic and Gulf coasts to Northern Europe, and the Black Sea Shipping Company from the Atlantic/Gulf and Great Lakes to the Mediterranean and Black Sea. Other lines not in the U.S. trades included the Odessa Line, offering service between Europe and the Far East, and the Besta Line, serving East Africa.

The Shipping Act of 1916 requires that shipping conferences in the U.S. trades be open, i.e., any firm can join. Thus, the option of joining or not, depending upon expected benefits, was a discretionary decision for the Soviet marine minister. In some cases, the Soviets applied for conference membership; in others, they operated as independents outside the conferences. In any event, while Western nation shipping firms could accept the Soviet goal of maximizing their shipping income, how they went about it was another matter entirely and was not acceptable.

Almost from the beginning, American liner companies charged that Soviet rates in the U.S. trades were predatory, i.e., so low as not to even cover the admittedly lower cost of operating a Soviet ship. As a result, many Soviet rates were quoted at 10 to 15 percent below conference rates. Under American law, the recourse of U.S. operators was to complain to the Federal Maritime Commission (FMC), the agency charged with administering the economic regulatory parts of the Shipping Act of 1916. However, as complaints about Soviet rate cutting mounted, the USSR in turn accused conference members of "rebating," i.e., returning a part of the shipping charge to the shipper.

An understanding of sorts was reached in 1976 whereby the Soviets agreed to offer rates no less than those of the lowest non-Soviet independent company operating in the trade. However, from the FMC viewpoint, two main problems remained: first, obtaining from Soviet authorities the necessary information on which to base a decision respecting rate reasonableness; second, enforcing any judgment handed down with respect to rates. Continued agitation over alleged Soviet rate-cutting practices and the companion issue of rebating by conference members resulted in two pieces of U.S. legislation. The first, the Ocean Shipping Act of 1978, gave the FMC authority to suspend a rate it found to be unjust and unreasonable on the basis of the "constructive costs" of providing the service.[13] This provision, in effect, largely circumvented the need to obtain shipping information from reluctant foreign governments. Also, the burden of proof as to whether a rate was reasonable was placed on the carrier. The act also allowed the FMC to suspend a rate for a maximum of 180 days.

The second bill, an amendment to the Shipping Act of 1916, strengthened prohibitions against the practice of rebating in U.S. foreign ocean-borne commerce.[14]

United States foreign trade is not the only trade in which the Soviets compete nose to nose with Western shipping. Another is the Far East–Europe trade via the Mediterranean. Here, the competition is double edged. European shipping firms must compete with not only the Soviet Trans-Siberian Railroad (TSR) but also Soviet merchant ships that offer service over the all-water route. Allegations of Soviet predatory rate practices on both the land (TSR) and water routes have been voiced by European shipowners.[15] In their view the threat posed is serious and long term. Speaking at the general annual meeting of the European Common Market Shipowners Association in 1975, Karl-Heinz Sager, deputy chairman of Hapag-Lloyd A. G. stated:

> No one can deny the impact of various discriminating activities in many developing countries. More imminent, however, and possibly more detrimental in its effect on liner shipping of the Common Market and other OECD member countries, appears to be the tremendous expansion of the COMECON (Communist bloc) fleets, particularly the activities and the long term program of the Russian merchant navy.
>
> The dumping policies exercised by them in a number of trades are the most serious threat to the existence of liner shipping in its present form in the Western world.[16]

As was noted earlier, U.S. growth projections for the Soviet merchant fleet can be somewhat wide of the mark. Also, U.S. knowledge of what constitutes the Soviet merchant marine is not firm. In a 1977 analysis of the Soviet merchant fleet, the Maritime Administration, using a U.S. Navy –estimated base of 1,665 Soviet merchant ships in 1976, estimated the Soviet fleet would number 1,717 vessels of 18.4 million deadweight tons in 1981.[17] Later, however, in its 1977 annual report, the Maritime Administration cited the Soviet fleet at 2,420 vessels of 18.7 million deadweight tons.

A part of the discrepancy can be explained by the fact that the 1976 U.S. Navy estimate excluded Soviet vessels over 1,000 gross tons that were engaged in coastwise and fishing trades as not being relevant when analyzing deep-sea operations. On the other hand, Maritime Administration statistics invariably include these ships when estimating the rank, size, and tonnage of the world's merchant fleets.

Developing Nations and Their Merchant Marines

In 1939, shipping of the nonindustrialized countries totalled approximately 500 vessels of 2.1 million deadweight tons. Table 19.3 lists this tonnage by country of registry.

The nonindustrialized countries' merchant fleets constituted 4 percent of the world's total ships and 2.7 percent of its deadweight tonnage in 1939. By 1964, twelve additional developing nations had oceangoing vessels registered under their flags.[18] However, in terms of deadweight tonnage these fleets accounted for only 6.8 percent of the world total and, if the tonnage of Nationalist China and Israel are left out, only 5.7 percent.

Table 19.3. Nonindustrialized Country Shipping, 1939

Country of Register	No. of Ships	Deadweight Tonnage (millions)
Argentina	45	268
Brazil	122	542
China	100	276
Cuba	12	22
Dominican Republic	1	2
Egypt	23	128
Mexico	10	32
Nicaragua	2	4
Peru	7	31
Thailand	2	2
Uruguay	5	14
Venezuela	27	93
Yugoslavia	98	604
Total	504	2,199

SOURCE: U.S., Maritime Administration, *Merchant Fleets of the World*.

NOTE: Figures do not include 130 Panamanian or 27 Honduran ships that, in 1939, were almost entirely foreign owned.

While differences might exist as to what countries to include in a developing nation list, in general the relative position of Third World shipping has declined since 1965. One authority cites the decline as being from 7.3 percent of the world total in 1965, 6.9 percent in 1970, 6.1 percent in 1972, and 5.4 percent in 1974.[19] In 1980, developing nations' tonnage constituted less than 6 percent of the world total.

Partly in response to this state of affairs, the UN Conference on Trade and Development (UNCTAD) was established in December 1964. Its purpose was to hasten the economic development of less developed countries by revising international trade policies. In 1974, under UNCTAD auspices and at the behest of the less developed nations, a convention on a code of conduct for liner conferences was adopted by seventy-four votes to seven with five abstentions. From the viewpoint of the developing nations, it was hoped that a provision in the code dividing the movement of liner cargoes between the developed and less developed countries on an even basis (40 percent for each trading partner) would spur the growth of developing country merchant marines. In 1983 it is all but certain that the code will obtain the necessary number of maritime nation ratifications to come into force.[20]

Implications of Code Adoption for U.S.-Flag Shipping

U.S.-flag shipping and that of developing nations have one thing in common. In 1983 they carry relatively small amounts of their own foreign commerce. In the U.S. case, the principal reason is the high cost of providing shipping services. With the option in 1983 of purchasing their vessels in foreign yards, higher U.S. costs are mainly due to higher seagoing wages. Without government assistance, most U.S. firms are not competitive, particularly with flag-of-convenience, foreign-crewed ships.

For the less developed country, the problem is investment capital. Ships in 1983 are much larger and more expensive than they were in 1974, when the commitment was made to help developing nations through modification of existing trade policies. In the liner trades the support equipment, particularly for container ships, is a large investment. Perhaps of even greater consequence for the developing countries is that in developing a modern merchant marine, trading off relatively cheap labor for capital is not feasible. In other words, it is simply not possible to build a competitive, labor-intense vessel in 1983. On the other hand, the traditional maritime nations see automation, substituting capital for labor, as their best hope for remaining cost competitive. The result is that the developing countries must build or buy very expensive ships if they wish to stay in the game.

Two approaches to this knotty problem are feasible. First, a developing nation may opt to go the flag-of-convenience route, as Liberia, Honduras, Panama, and, to some extent, Sri Lanka and Singapore have done. In this scenario, they can expect some revenues from fees collected from the vessel owner, employment opportunities for their nationals, and whatever prestige goes with being a flag-of-convenience maritime power. In this option, vessel ownership and profits remain under foreign control.

Second, a developing nation may not only provide a place of registry for the vessel but also share in the ownership and profits. This approach means obtaining investment capital. In the decade of the 1980s this will not be easy. If there is to be any reasonable chance of success of obtaining foreign capital assistance, present flag-of-convenience registry must be discouraged, if not prohibited outright. Exxon, for example, will hardly opt for some type of partnership arrangement with a lesser developed and probably politically unstable country, when it can obtain greater benefits by registering its ships under the flags of the more amenable and historically stable flag-of-convenience nations.

In 1983, the lesser developed nations are split over the issue; the majority favor a UN convention to prohibit open (flag-of-convenience) registry. The U.S. position on cargo sharing is unclear. Some powerful interest groups, including some American liner operators and seagoing labor unions, favor cargo sharing. Others, including shippers and firms with large flag-of-convenience fleets, bitterly oppose it. The dilemma for the latter group is vexing: either return some ships to the U.S. flag and share in a particular trade from that vantage point or register ships among a dozen or more developing nations, probably sharing ownership and profits, under the best terms possible.

For the American-flag operator, the developing countries, and American companies with large investments in foreign-flag fleets, the stakes are enormous. U.S. oceanborne foreign trade in 1979 was estimated at 823 million long tons worth approximately $242 billion.[21] Table 19.4 lists the U.S. import and export tonnages with its top thirty trading partners.

People's Republic of China

In 1939, China's merchant fleet was reported as 100 vessels of 276,000 deadweight tons, composed of 16 combination freight/passenger vessels, 83 freighters, and 1 bulk carrier.[22] Admittedly, at that time China was fighting a full-scale albeit undeclared, war with Japan, and developing a merchant marine was undoubtedly far down on the priority list. Moreover, after World War II, preoccupation with a civil war precluded the Chinese from paying much attention to maritime affairs.

However, in 1961, more than a decade after securing the mainland, the merchant fleet of the People's Republic of China (PRC) still numbered only 146 vessels of 721,000 deadweight tons. In terms of tonnage it was in a class with Australia, Belgium, Turkey, Poland, Lebanon, and Portugal. Ten years later the PRC fleet had increased to 237 ships of 1.7 million deadweight tons but was still ranked with second-order maritime nations. Vessels were relatively small, on average about 7,000 deadweight tons, and engaged primarily in the coastal and nearby foreign trades.

In 1981, a decade later, the PRC merchant marine was one of the world's largest, with 695 ships of 10.1 million deadweight tons.[23] It ranked seventh in number of ships and fourteenth in deadweight tonnage. Moreover, the fleet was reasonably well balanced in terms of its commerce requirements.

	No. of Ships
Freighters	478
Bulk carriers	85
Tankers	87
Passenger/freighters	17
Other	28
Total	695

Of 695 ships, 184 were built in 1971 or later. Thus, on average, the PRC fleet is an aging one and for it to maintain its present world rank, the

country will have to support a sustained building program. The evidence
suggests this is happening. In 1980, 16 freighters and 6 tankers were
delivered.

The interesting thing about PRC maritime policy is its flexibility. In
1980, for example, 16 of the new ships added to the fleet were built in

Table 19.4. U.S. Waterborne Foreign Trade—
Top Thirty Trading Partners (Calendar Year 1979)

Rank	Country	Total Tons[a]	Import Tons	Export Tons
1	Japan	82,669	14,023	68,646
2	Canada[b]	73,166	41,330	31,836
3	Saudi Arabia	67,393	65,420	1,973
4	Nigeria	54,561	53,361	1,200
5	Venezuela	52,085	47,856	4,229
6	Algeria	37,461	36,724	737
7	Libya	33,536	33,408	128
8	Mexico	32,899	27,448	5,451
9	Indonesia	22,732	21,173	1,559
10	Netherlands	21,504	3,130	18,374
11	USSR	21,167	1,124	20,043
12	United Kingdom	19,317	11,939	7,378
13	Iran	17,988	16,180	1,808
14	Italy	17,078	3,757	13,321
15	Brazil	17,056	6,758	10,298
16	West Germany	16,757	5,621	11,136
17	Bahamas	14,781	14,332	449
18	Republic of Korea	14,588	2,131	12,457
19	United Arab Emirates	14,510	14,269	241
20	Netherlands Antilles	14,445	14,158	287
21	France	12,292	4,041	8,251
22	Belgium	12,045	1,430	10,615
23	Trinidad/Tobago	11,803	11,320	483
24	Spain	9,958	1,937	8,021
25	Jamaica	9,105	8,251	854
26	Republic of China (Taiwan)	8,970	2,238	6,732
27	Australia	7,747	5,119	2,628
28	Norway	6,662	5,439	1,223
29	People's Republic of China	6,469	1,083	5,386
30	Egypt	6,222	2,684	3,538

SOURCE: U.S., Maritime Administration, *United States Oceanborne Foreign Trade Routes.*
[a]Thousands of long tons.
[b]Includes translake (U.S. Great Lakes/Canadian Great Lakes) cargoes.

Japan and Yugoslavia. In the past, the PRC has not been hesitant to register its state-owned tonnage under other flags, in a sense using the flag-of-convenience concept, or to undertake joint ownership ventures.[24] It has also concluded a number of bilateral shipping agreements with its trading partners, including agreements with the United States.

How much the United States can gain from the PRC's maritime policy flexibility will depend upon nonmaritime high-level policy decisions, i.e., decisions on the extent to which the United States will formalize its de facto military alliance with the People's Republic of China. Assuming the present movement toward stronger ties between the two countries continues, the United States would seem to have opportunities for (1) further bilateral agreements, (2) joint ownership arrangements, and (3) agreements to build PRC naval vessels in American yards, which indirectly will lessen the political pressure to require a certain amount of merchant ship construction in the United States.[25]

Conclusion

The traditional maritime nations can no longer discount the impact of Soviet and developing nation shipping in world oceanborne trade, or for that matter, the fast growing PRC merchant marine.

The successful eight-year effort by the developing nations to force a sharing of the world's liner trades shows they are a political force to reckon with. Whether their attempt to mandate a share to themselves of the bulk trades and their move to do away with open registry will be successful are questions open to speculation. However, their efforts must be taken seriously.

For the moment, the developing nations have an ally in the Soviet Union, which supports their cargo-sharing goals and hostility to flag-of-convenience registry. The anomaly is that from the point of view of increasing the share of its own trade, U.S. policy should be roughly parallel to that of the developing countries and the Soviet Union. However, as was noted earlier, the fact is that while the shipping industry would generally support such a policy, other powerful interest groups are opposed—in particular, U.S. companies with large foreign-flag fleets and American exporters and importers, who argue that bilaterals will raise the ultimate price of the imported or exported good and thereby decrease demand. Historically, the latter view has prevailed.

With respect to what impact the Soviet merchant marine has had on the traditional suppliers of shipping services, events in the last few years seem to suggest that while the USSR merchant fleet is here to stay, it can be disciplined, at least in the American trades. Aside from the greater leverage the Ocean Shipping Act of 1978 gives the Federal Maritime Commission in determining what is an unreasonably low rate, the boycott of Soviet ships on the Atlantic and Gulf coasts by the International Longshoremen's Association following the invasion of Afghanistan, and the generally harder line followed by the Reagan administration, have obliged both the Soviet Ministry of Marine and those shippers using Soviet ships to reassess their policies. American ports opened to Soviet ships in 1973 could again be closed. Rationalizations would not be hard to find, e.g., the continued Soviet backing for the military government in Poland. Shippers, on the other hand, must consider what could happen to their cargoes if American-Soviet relations deteriorate. Possibilities include closing of ports to Soviet ships, stevedore boycotts, and finally, the removal of Soviet ships by the Soviet government. Because the Soviet merchant marine is centrally directed, Soviet ships can be pulled off a trade with little or no notice and employed in less hostile environments. In fact, Soviet participation in the American trades has declined markedly from its earlier 1977–78 volumes. This suggests that the much heralded Soviet maritime threat to U.S. shipping is less of a threat than was at first supposed.

Flag-of-convenience shipping, Third World shipping, and the Soviet merchant marine are here to stay, and effort spent to somehow limit their size is the least productive of policies. American ingenuity had far better concentrate on how to build up the U.S.-flag merchant fleet. World trade is growing and will continue to grow. This bigger pie should be considered as a challenge and an opportunity for U.S.-flag operators.

20   In Search of an Enduring Maritime Policy

As is noted throughout the book, the bedrock justification for a U.S.-flag, citizen-manned merchant marine is the role it has traditionally played, and the role it is expected to play in the future, in enhancing the nation's security. But unless the benefits of our maritime policy are perceived to outweigh the costs, that policy will be criticized and our merchant marine reduced and ultimately eliminated.

In this concluding chapter the main issues discussed in the book are summarized and a policy position stated. The sequence in which issues appear does not imply their rank. All are crucial to an enduring U.S. maritime policy.

The Merchant Marine Act of 1920 should be amended to allow American-owned, foreign-built, foreign-flag vessels to operate in the U.S. coastwise and intercoastal trade. At present, the great majority of vessels in this trade are aging tankers, vessels that can be expected to have increasing difficulty competing with pipelines, tug-barge systems, and the super rail systems now being formed. A policy that will encourage investment in ocean carriers to compete with land transport alternatives ultimately benefits the economy. It would almost certainly lower domestic prices for refined oil products, since this cargo is now moved in protected, higher cost, U.S.-flag vessels. And the amendment would benefit the national security, as U.S.-owned, foreign-flag ships trading in American waters would be truly subject to effective U.S. control in a national emergency.

On the other hand, the noncontiguous U.S. trades, those between the United States and its offshore states and territories, should continue to be reserved for U.S.-flag, though not necessarily U.S.-built, ships. Present ships on these trades include, and will continue to include, our most modern tankers and some of our most valuable military logistic support vessels. In this case, the added cost of operating these ships under the American flag is outweighed by their contribution to national security.

Bilateral trading agreements (or U.S. accession to the UNCTAD Code of Conduct for Liner Conferences) must be put into place to insure cargo support for a privately owned, foreign trade fleet composed of approximately 400 ships. The main difference between this fleet and the present one would be the inclusion of a modest tanker and dry bulk segment. Sized to meet minimum national security requirements, this fleet would include 250 general cargo vessels, 75 large tankers, and 75 large dry bulk carriers. This tonnage would be in addition to that in the noncontiguous trades and would comprise the U.S. "national security" merchant marine. While the fleet would decrease slightly in size from the present 500 oceangoing vessels, the benefit would be the establishment of a modest amount of foreign trade tanker and dry bulk shipping under the American flag. This tonnage would provide some minimum insurance that our required strategic imports would never become hostage to the policy of an unfriendly foreign power in a contingency or be cut completely in a general war. The cost of the option might be somewhat higher prices for U.S. imports and exports, although this is far from certain. For one thing, the smaller percentage of higher cost American ships would be averaged into final prices; for another thing, if the developing nations succeed in banning open registry, as they have vowed to do, automated American-flag vessels might well turn out to be the low-cost option on a number of trade routes.

American-owned, foreign-crewed ships in our foreign trades cannot be factored into our war or contingency plans with any degree of certainty. Past administrations have partly rationalized the decline of the merchant marine by citing the existence of flag-of-convenience shipping and attributing to it a national security role. They had far better simply acknowledge the fleet as an example of the right of investors in a free society to employ their resources where they will.

The wage cost of licensed officers on U.S.-flag vessels must be renegotiated downward over time to a point where they exceed comparable foreign wage costs by roughly the same percentage as American unlicensed seamen's wage costs exceed those of their foreign counterparts. This may be done for particular trade routes, as mandated by the Merchant Marine Act of 1936, or an across-the-board average may be taken.

Between 1978 and 1982 the position cost of the ship's master on an American-flag ship increased from $11,436 to $20,299; that of the second engineer went from $6,729 to $10,412; while that of the able seaman went from $2,184 to $3,046 (Table 15.6). No new responsibility and no greater skill required during those four years can justify this disparity.

If a second engineer's wage cost is renegotiated on the basis suggested, it would be $6,764 per month, not $8,212 as shown in the tabulation of U.S. and foreign seagoing wages in Chapter 15. This is roughly a 15 percent across-the-board cut.[1] While this approach avoids a value judgment of what is an acceptable wage differential between U.S. and foreign-flag officers, it strongly suggests that the licensed officer wage bill on U.S.-flag ships is excessive.[2]

The trend is toward larger and more automated vessels, and though it is true that labor as a percentage of operating costs will decline, it will not decline so much that the cost of officering an American ship becomes inconsequential.

In 1983 it seems all but certain that the operating differential subsidy as a means of supporting a merchant marine is over. While existing contracts will be honored or bought out, as the case may be, by the Maritime Administration, no one in the industry expects any new ones to be signed. Seagoing labor must recognize this fact above all else. Benefits to be derived from a more pragmatic treatment of American wages include a more cost-competitive merchant marine and, equally important, a perception by the public that the industry is truly striving to be competitive and deserves support.

Until the wage issue is resolved, future graduates of our national and state maritime academies might reasonably ask, Will we have jobs at sea at somewhat lower wages or no jobs at all?

The President must unequivocally specify the responsibilities of the Military Sealift Command in relation to the privately owned merchant fleet, and in particular, its long-term role in owning/operating sealift assets. At no time since the height of the Vietnam conflict has the Military Sealift Command (MSC) had such a high profile. New tanker construction has been funded; the MSC-controlled thirteen-ship maritime prepositioned ship program (T-AKX) has been approved (an increase of one ship over the twelve earlier authorized), as well as the conversion of eight SL-7 container ships to fast logistic support ships (T-AKRX program), which will be maintained and operated under MSC auspices; while the navy-funded Ready Reserve Force (RRF) within the National Defense Reserve Fleet (NDRF), now planned to include some seventy ships, is a prime candidate for an MSC takeover. The NDRF and its RRF component are now the responsibility of the Maritime Administration, but the logic of a transfer of the RRF is cold, hard, and irrefutable in the context of how government programs operate. Essentially, if they are navy funded, they are navy (MSC) controlled. Should such a transfer occur while MSC continues to increase its sealift assets, it is quite possible that the MSC–merchant marine roles will be reversed. In a contingency or national emergency the primary source of merchant ships would be from a government-owned fleet, and the privately owned merchant marine would be relegated to a supplemental role. Couple the above with a halfway convincing argument that U.S.-owned, flag-of-convenience shipping has a substantial national security value, and a case can be made for abandoning government support of a privately owned U.S. merchant marine entirely.[3]

Patently, this is not President Reagan's intention; nonetheless, there is a real possibility the United States could drift into such a state of affairs. In contemplating such an event, it is worth considering again the words of Alfred Thayer Mahan when he commented upon the efficacy of a navy without a merchant marine.

> Can this navy be had without restoring the merchant shipping? It is doubtful. History has proved that such a purely military seapower can be built up by a despot, as was done by Louis XIV; but though so fair seeming, experience showed that his navy was like a growth which having no root soon withers away.[4]

The President must decide whether, and to what extent, the merchant marine can be used in a U.S. Navy underway replenishment (UNREP) role. In his 1980 campaign, President Reagan called for increasing commercial participation in (navy) support functions. But the issue is so mired in charges and countercharges that even the venerable General Accounting Office opted out of becoming involved (see Chapter 11). A clear-cut policy statement is past due, particularly if an effort is going to be made to expand the foreign trade tanker sector of U.S.-flag shipping.

A deregulation act for ocean shipping must be passed. Efforts to do this were made with strong administration support in 1982. Such efforts must continue until a bill is achieved. A higher cost maritime nation can exist within a rational conference system (see Chapter 4). Those opposing deregulation of conference activities in the American trades urge that this would be granting shipowners unbridled power over rates and service. This argument, however, makes little sense at a time when the shipping world to all intent and purpose has embraced the UNCTAD Code of Conduct for Liner Conferences. Strong conferences, strongly supported by the traditional maritime powers, may be the most effective way of disciplining the shipping practices of over-eager and increasing numbers of Third World maritime nations. No one would assert that it was the strength of conferences in the U.S. trades that invited the dumping of Soviet tonnage onto these routes a few years ago.

The United States must take a leading role in establishing universal construction and manning requirements for all types of oceangoing vessels. Historically, the United States has had higher standards than the maritime world generally. This is not to suggest a lowering of standards but rather to move for international acceptance of standards that the United States can endorse. Such an American position would have a lot going for it. The United States is at one end of the world's largest set of trading routes. It has demonstrated by enforcing stricter tanker pollution controls that it has the will and capacity to act.[5]

Over the past ten years the Marine Safety Committee of the Inter-Governmental Maritime Consultative Committee (IMCO) has debated construction and manning requirements and has met with some success in raising international standards. The organization is now on dead center, which would seem to be an excellent time for the United States to exert forceful leadership to insure that the world's maritime nations start even with respect to construction and manning standards. As maritime technology moves toward larger ships and smaller crews, the importance of this issue will increase. There is not a better time than now to address it—when the United States is striving to frame a lasting maritime policy.

Shipyards

A United States maritime policy cannot endure without a defined role for the privately owned shipyards, both large and small.

In 1983 this role is one of building naval vessels, sharing with the naval shipyards in construction, alteration, and repair (CAR) work, building for the protected domestic trade, and repairing both U.S.-flag and foreign-flag ships engaged in foreign trade.

This book has endorsed the option of allowing U.S. carriers in all trades to build and repair their vessels at the best world price available. This does not imply, however, that the United States should allow its shipbuilding/repair base to deteriorate so much that it could not support allied shipping in a general war. What is accepted for the moment is that by rebuilding the U.S. Navy to 600 ships, building and overhauling for the MSC programs described above, having a fair share of naval CAR work, and making a concerted effort to be competitive in merchant ship repair, a shipbuilding/repair mobilization base can be sustained. Moreover, the option of building naval vessels for foreign account should be fully explored. The option was well stated in a 1981 *Marine Engineering/Log* editorial, which said in part:

> It is a market in which American yards can compete, on fairly even terms, with the world at large. Indications of this are existing orders for frigates for the Royal Australian Navy and for gunboats and patrol craft for Saudi Arabia.
>
> What is preventing American yards from simply going out and scooping up hatfuls of export contracts? For one thing, most administrations are a little fussy about where warships may be sold. For another, when the role of politically acceptable customers is called, there are few with mission requirements as demanding as the U.S. Navy's. Their needs are thus for somewhat less sophisticated ships.

These sorts of constraints on U.S. competitiveness could ease. . . .

Warship exports may never add up to a big bonanza. But from the shipbuilding viewpoint, the work would be well worth having.[6]

The naval authority Norman Polmar holds a similar view. While he notes the export potential of ship systems, he also says, "The widespread use of U.S. developed ship systems has overshadowed the fact that several nations have bought U.S. ships and ship designs over the past few years."[7]

If a case is made that a shipyard base cannot be maintained without some form of construction differential subsidies (CDS) for merchant ships, the administration and Congress will have to bite the bullet and appropriate the funds necessary.[8] That case, however, has not been made, and particularly not in the worldwide shipping and shipbuilding recession that began in 1981 and is causing as much grief to shipyards overseas as to shipyards in the United States.

Conclusion

The 1980s have already seen some major changes in maritime policy: the end of the CDS program and the phasing out of operating differential subsidies. More changes will surely come. Change, however, is not necessarily bad if managed correctly. That is the key consideration and one that the shipping community cannot lose sight of, even for a moment.

Larry O'Brien has noted that obtaining agreement within the maritime industry on major legislative initiatives is difficult (see Chapter 5). But "difficult" should not imply that it cannot be done and that an enduring maritime policy cannot be fashioned. The pieces are all there and need only to be fitted together.

Perhaps things today are not so very different from things in 1937, when a blue ribbon panel was struggling to implement the radically new maritime policy of the Merchant Marine Act of 1936. In its report the panel concluded:

> We are about to start again, not in a riot of enthusiasm, not with an expenditure of billions, but with a carefully planned program that gives due regard to the factors of need, method, and cost. Therein, we believe, lies our hope for the future of the American merchant marine.[9]

Appendices

A   Tug-Barge Operations in Domestic Ocean Shipping

Traditionally, barge traffic has accounted for a significant amount of coastwise tonnage movement. Non-self-propelled dry cargo and tank barges carried approximately 35 percent of this cargo in 1979. The flexibility of the system and relatively small crews have tended to insure its profitability. In the past decade, tank-barge tonnage has grown, while dry cargo barge tonnage has remained about constant. Intercoastal barge movement is relatively insignificant.

The newest technology in barge systems is the ever larger barge in which the tug is semirigidly attached to the barge. Over the past ten years these integrated tug-barge (ITB) systems have grown in size until in 1983 the cost of an equivalent capacity tug-barge combination approaches the cost of a self-propelled ship. However, crewing requirements remain small in comparison. Speeds for a large ITB combination can approach 15 knots.

Probably the largest single integrated tug-barge movement was that performed by the Crowley Marine Corporation's Northwest and Alaska Division. It was this ITB fleet that delivered approximately 800,000 tons of supplies between 1968 and 1978 in the building of the Alaska pipeline.

The largest petroleum ITB combination is operated by Belcher Oil Company. It is composed of a 510-foot barge and a 167-foot tug, which fits into the barge's notched stern. The barge is 54,000 deadweight tons with a 417,000-barrel multigrade capacity. The tug is equipped with a 15,200-horsepower turbo-charged engine.

As of 1 March 1982, Maritime Administration data show there are twelve tug-barges of 383,000 dwt in the U.S. oceangoing merchant marine.

B Distances/Days at Sea from Mineral/Fuel Sources to Selected U.S. Ports

Mineral/Fuel Source	Statute Miles	Days at Sea (at an Average Speed of 15 Knots)
To New York		
Lagos, Nigeria	5,615	13.5
Oslo, Norway	4,401	10.5
Dakar, Senegal	3,835	9.5
Singapore	11,693	28.0
Valparaiso, Chile (Bolivia)[a]	5,335	13.0
Rio de Janeiro, Brazil	5,965	14.5
Manila, Philippines	13,086	32.0
Panama Canal	2,323	5.5
Yokohama, Japan	11,169	27.0
Cape Town, South Africa	7,814	19.0
Buenos Aires, Argentina	6,761	16.5
Calcutta, India	11,290	27.5
Bombay, India	9,413	23.0
Hamburg, West Germany	4,166	10.0
Istanbul, Turkey	5,788	14.0
Algiers, Algeria	4,164	10.0
Liverpool, United Kingdom	3,539	8.5
Port Said, Egypt	5,895	14.0
Kuwait	9,759	23.5
Matadi, Zaire	6,215	15.0
Barcelona, Spain	4,271	10.5
Beira, Mozambique (Zambia)[a]	9,614	23.0
Colombo, Sri Lanka	9,941	24.0
Melbourne, Australia	11,452	28.0
Maracaibo, Venezuela	2,110	5.0
Bangkok, Thailand	11,420	27.5
Kingston, Jamaica	1,695	4.0

Mineral/Fuel Source	Statute Miles	Days at Sea (at an Average Speed of 15 Knots)
To San Francisco		
Panama Canal	3,735	9.0
Valparaiso, Chile (Bolivia)	5,919	14.5
Melbourne, Australia	8,011	19.5
Singapore	8,467	20.5
Manila, Philippines	7,164	17.5
Colombo, Sri Lanka	10,289	25.0
Bombay, India	11,247	27.0
Yokohama, Japan	5,223	12.5
Bangkok, Thailand	8,262	20.0
To New Orleans		
Panama Canal	1,650	4.0
Rio de Janeiro, Brazil	5,965	14.5
Valparaiso, Chile (Bolivia)	4,663	11.5
Kingston, Jamaica	1,310	3.0
Maracaibo, Venezuela	2,002	5.0
Buenos Aires, Argentina	7,233	17.5
Cape Town, South Africa	9,382	23.0
Beira, Mozambique (Zambia)	11,182	27.0
Lagos, Nigeria	5,783	14.0

NOTE: A statute mile is 5,280 feet; a nautical mile is 6,080 feet. At 15 knots, a ship averages 17.25 miles per hour times 24, or 414 statute miles a day.

[a]Landlocked Bolivia and Zambia use the ports of Valparaiso and Beira, respectively.

C Marine Technology Bibliography

Marine technology is not only a specialized area of research but one worldwide in scope and continually changing. The following selected reference sources should prove useful for the reader who wishes a more detailed discussion of the technologies discussed in Chapter 13 as well as a number of technologies that were omitted.

Bunker, John. "Coal Burning at Sea." *U.S. Naval Institute Proceedings* 107 (January 1981): 64.

Linder, Bruce R. "Pegasus: Winner or Also Ran." *U.S. Naval Institute Proceedings* 107 (September 1981): 39.

Maclean, W. M.; Hutchison, T. C.; and Carver, Leon. "Use of Simulators in Ship Design and Operation." *Naval Engineers Journal* 89 (April 1977): 85.

Marine Engineering/Log.

"Aids to Marine Navigation." 86 (October 1981): 65.

"Back to Coal for Power." 85 (July 1980): 32.

Blenkey, Nicholas. "Diesel Fuel Qualities." 86 (March 1981): 38.

"The Bright, Near Future." 86 (January 1981): 45.

Delaney, Rachelle. "Coal-Fired Ships." 86 (September 1981): 38.

———. "Future Bunker Fuel." 86 (November 1981): 58.

"Diesel Repair and Maintenance (R&M)." 87 (August 1982): 46.

"Enhancing Diesel Capabilities." 86 (January 1981): 40.

Heil, Gene, and Barrett, John. "Marine Navigation." 85 (February 1980): 57.

Luse, James D. "Marine Communications Satellites: A Look at the Next Generation." 83 (September 1978): 71.

Lynch, John G.; Jain, Maybank; and Varshney, Deepak. "Will Medium Speed Diesels Adapt to Heavy Fuels?" 86 (May 1981): 61.

Ovechka, Greg. "Sail Cargo Ships to Arrive in 1980s?" 85 (February 1980): 50.

———. "U.S., English Hydrofoil, ACV Roundup." 84 (May 1979): 53.

"Steam or Diesel? No Contest between Medium and Slow." 86 (February 1981): 52.

Sullivan, Fran. "Developments in Deck Machinery." 87 (August 1982): 40.

"Tomorrow's Bulk Carriers: World's Loneliest Ships?" 85 (November 1980): 67.

"U.S.-Built Low-Speed Diesels." 86 (April 1981): 50.

Maynard, Earle V. "The Case for Nuclear Powered Merchant Ships." *U.S. Naval Institute Proceedings* 107 (October 1981): 64.

National Academy of Sciences. *Innovations in the Maritime Industry*. Washington, D.C., 1979.

————. *Innovations in the Maritime Industry,* Washington, D.C., 1979, appendix.

Critelli, Francis X. "Contra-Rotating Propulsion Systems for U.S. Merchant Ships," p. 169.

Dashnaw, Frank. "Highly Skewed Propeller," p. 125.

Ebel, Francis G. "Evolution of the Concept and Adoption of Marine and Intermodal Containers," p. 1.

Ellsworth, William. "Air Cushion Vehicles," p. 183.

Fielding, Sterling A. "Development of Gas Turbine Propulsion: G.T.S. *John Sergeant*," p. 127.

Gorman, David L. "Innovation in the Maritime Industry: Landbridge Services," p. 109.

Jenstrom, Linda L. "The National Shipbuilding Research Program: A Case Study of Innovation in the Maritime Industry," p. 37.

Johnson, Robert J. "Hydrofoils in the U.S. Maritime Industry," p. 173.

Kern, Donald H. "History and Current State of Shipboard Automation," p. 133.

Penrose, William H. "Barriers and Incentives to the Adoption of an Innovation: Maritime Satellite Communications," p. 67.

Renehan, L. Arthur. "The Innovation and Implementation of LASH," p. 73.

Wirt, John G. "A Federal Demonstration Project: N.S. *Savannah*," p. 29.

Naval Engineers Journal 94 (April 1982).

Broome, Granville W.; Nelson, David W.; and Tootle, William D. "The Design of Variable Payload Ships," p. 147.

Plato, James G., and Rein, Robert J. "Is Automation The Magic Potion for Manning Problems?," p. 127.

Roche, John J.; Corkrey, Ronald; and Benen, Lawrence. "Sealift Capabilities and SEA SHED," p. 61.

Tattersall, E. G. "The History and Future of the SES in the United Kingdom," p. 267.

Thompson, Daniel H., Jr., and Thorell, Lennart M. "The Construction of Variable Payload Ships," p. 179.

Nuclear Utilities Services. *Utilization of Uranium Cost/Benefit Study for Nuclear Powered Merchant Ships*. Rockville, Md., 1977.

Seitz, Frank C., Jr. "Shipboard Manning Reduction—How Few Will Do?" *U.S. Naval Institute Proceedings* 107 (October 1981): 50.

Stanford Research Institute. *Transportation in America's Future: Potentials for the Next Half Century*. Stanford, Calif., 1977.

U.S., General Accounting Office. *Costs of Operating the Nuclear Merchant Ship Savannah*. 1970.

————. *Nuclear or Conventional Power for Surface Combatant Ships?* 1977.

Vego, Milan. "The Potential Influence of Third World Navies on Ocean Shipping." *U.S. Naval Institute Proceedings* 107 (May 1981): 95.

D Seagoing Pension Plans and Their Impact on NDRF Viability

In 1974, Congress passed the Employee Retirement Income Security Act (ERISA). The broad purpose of the legislation was to "protect" the pensions of retiring employees. A Pension Benefit Guaranty Corporation (PBGC) was set up to guarantee employee benefits. In furtherance of this goal, a funding liability for employers was established.

Under the 1974 law, employers could terminate their plans until 1978. If the termination option was exercised, their maximum funding liability was 30 percent of their net worth. However, a more than expected number of small single-employer plans were terminated; the result was that PBGC ran a deficit of approximately $15 million between 1974 and 1978.

To stop this drain and insure that large multiemployer pension plans remained in the system, in 1980 Congress passed the Multi-Employer Pension Plan Amendment Act. Under this legislation an employer faced a 100 percent net worth liability for both termination and withdrawal from a pension plan.

Shipping companies are part of multiemployer pension plans for their seagoing employees. Under present law, when a shipping firm enters into a general agency or reserve service agreement with the Maritime Administration to operate a vessel or vessels taken from the National Defense Reserve Fleet (NDRF) and hires a crew, the firm incurs a pension liability for the additional employees hired, even though the ship is government owned and returned to the NDRF after the emergency or contingency is over.

The economic impact of this arrangement would be so substantial that a prudent vessel operator would decline to operate NDRF vessels for government account in a contingency or national emergency. The national security economic loss is that having existing companies break out and operate these ships is by far and away the most cost-effective means of getting this additional tonnage to berth.

During the Vietnam conflict, 170 ships from the NDRF were operated for the government by private firms under general agency agreements. And even though the 1974 and 1980 legislation was not yet on the books, shipping companies still incurred large additional pension liabilities under existing union agreements. Many expressed a reluctance to participate in any future breakout of government-owned shipping. With the present 100 percent net worth liability, only a foolhardy operator would agree to operate more than a few ships, and these for a very limited time.

Criticism of the present statutes has been particularly harsh, not only from shipping firms, but from other transportation industries such as trucking, whose member companies also contribute to multiemployer pension funds. However, no industry has quite the same impact on national security as shipping does.

No law seems to bar the Maritime Administration from agreeing beforehand to be responsible for a fair share of any future pension liability occasioned by a breakout of NDRF vessels, although such cannot be stated as an absolute certainty. Assuming an a priori agreement to be valid, the problem is how to determine the government's share for pension liability and what safeguards need to be incorporated into these agreements so that the solvency of a participating shipping firm is not threatened at some time in the future.

One approach would be to amend the law. With this intention, hearings on "corrective" amendments to the 1980 act were scheduled in 1982. No bill, however, was reported out of committee. Lacking an amendment to the statute(s), the legal staff of the Maritime Administration should determine whether a binding agreement limiting pension liability for seamen employed on NDRF ships could be negotiated. If that is not an option, then the Maritime Administration should initiate, and write if necessary, legislation to correct this specific deficiency in our national defense.

E U.S. Companies and Their Foreign Affiliate—Owned Shipping, 1 January 1981

U.S. Parent Co. Foreign Affiliate	No. of Ships
Aluminum Co. of America	5
Amerada Hess	4
American Marine Industries	6
Ashland Oil	1
Atlantic Richfield	3
Bahamas Line	4
Bank of California National Association	5
Bethlehem Steel	2
Castle & Cooke	13
Charter Shipping	1
Citizens Trust Co.	2
Connecticut Bank & Trust	2
Conoco	5
Consolidated Aluminum and Revere Copper & Brass	3
Co-ordinated Caribbean Transport	1
Del Monte	12
Dolores Navigation	1
El Paso Natural Gas	3
Equitable Life	2
Euro Trading Co.	1
Exxon	135
Fairfield-Maxwell	6
First Trust Co. of St. Paul	1
GATX Corp.	20
Getty Oil	13
Grand Bassa Tankers	5
Greyhound Leasing	1
Greyship Corp.	1
Gulf Oil	28
Halliburton Co.	2
Hugo Neu	3

U.S. Parent Co. Foreign Affiliate	No. of Ships
ICC Industries	1
IU International	2
International Shipholding Corp.	5
Itel Navigations	7
Kaiser Cement	2
Koch Industries	2
Levin Metal Corp.	1
Ludwig D. K.	2
Manufacturers Hanover Trust	4
Marathon Oil	6
Marriott Corp.	2
Maru Shipping	2
Mobil Oil	47
Morton-Norwich Products	1
Northeast Petroleum	1
Ogden Marine	17
Overseas Shipholding	53
Phillips Petroleum	10
Republic Steel	2
Reynolds Metals	4
Sea Containers	23
Security Pacific National Bank	1
Standard Oil of California	23
Standard Oil of Indiana	14
Steuber Group	2
Sun Company	2
Texaco	59
Texas Commerce Bank National Association	1
Trans Union Ocean Shipping	9
Tropigas International	2
Union Bank	7
Union Oil of California	2
United Brands	19
U.S. Gypsum Co.	5
U.S. Steel	14
U.S. Trust Co. of New York	7
Utah International	12
Wilmington Trust Co.	2
Total	666

SOURCE: U.S., Maritime Administration, *Foreign Flag Merchant Ships Owned by U.S. Parent Companies as of January 1, 1981*, pp. 2–13.

F Critique of Office of Management and Budget (OMB) Memorandum on the National Security Justification for a United States–Flag Merchant Marine

OMB allegation: U.S. Merchant Marine would not be useful in a short war. In a short-term war (less than 30 days) the U.S.-flag merchant marine as currently configured is not likely to have an impact outcome because vessels do not have the speed nor are they the type of vessels likely to be required.

Response: Short war is no longer even considered relevant to sealift planning. A short-term war (less than 30 days) is no longer considered in the formulation of military requirements. Secretary of Defense Weinberger has said, "Another fallacy in defense policy regarding conventional warfare has been the short war assumption—the notion that in planning our strategy and designing our forces we could rely on the assumption that a conventional war would be of short duration. I have therefore instituted changes in our defense policy to correct this fallacy. It goes without saying that should our policy to deter aggression fail and a conventional conflict be forced upon us, the United States would bend every effort to win the war as quickly as possible. The essential purpose of our conventional warfare is to prevent war by deterring aggression. Deterrence would be weakened if the enemy were misled to believe that he could easily outlast us in a conventional war. If we were unprepared to

OMB allegations are followed by extracts from the OMB 3 May 1982 memorandum. Responses are followed by extracts from "Critique of OMB Staff Review of Maritime Programs and Policy" by Admiral James L. Holloway III, dated 30 June 1982.

sustain the conflict, the adversary might expect we would have to seek a truce by conceding vital territory to his control. The efforts that I have initiated to overcome the short war fallacy—improved sustained ability for U.S. forces, a strengthened capability to expand defense production, and appropriate changes in strategy and tactics—are essential to reduce the likelihood of war. They are essential in particular for vulnerable regions protected neither by the presence of U.S. forces nor by an explicit nuclear guarantee.''

OMB allegation: DOD is acquiring dedicated ships because of limited utility of commercial vessels. As a result of the limited utility of the commercial fleet for quick supply, the Department of Defense is currently acquiring sealift assets to supplement U.S. commercial ships.

Response: DOD's acquisition of dedicated sealift assets has nothing to do with the utility of merchant marine vessels. The acquisition of sealift assets such as the fast deployment ships (SL-7s) and the maritime prepositioned ships (TAKX) is to provide the rapid response capability of sealift to move forces to the scene of operations at the initial outbreak of hostilities or in the first days of a crisis. This is a role for which the U.S.-flag operating merchant marine has never been intended. Commander of the Military Sealift Command has explained that, ''The SL-7 program concept is to acquire high capacity, fast sealift ships, ready to load and go when a contingency requires.'' The maritime prepositioned ships store all of the equipment and supplies required by a marine amphibious brigade, maintained in dehumidified stowage and the ships prepositioned near potential crisis or contingency sites. The fast sealift ships are owned by the government, manned with civilian union crews, and home ported in the vicinity of the bases of those ground forces which are to be part of the RDF. They are maintained available in U.S. ports ready for rapid loading. The maritime prepositioned ships (either owned or on long-term charter to the U.S. government) will be positioned around the world and loaded with military supplies. They are not part of the operating U.S.-flag commercial fleet, as they must be on station in potential crises and cannot be diverted to trade routes. It is not for reasons of limited usefulness of the design of the commercial fleet that the Department of Defense is currently acquiring sealift assets to supplement U.S. commercial ships, but it is because our strategic mobility plans require dedicated ships. Therefore, those involved in ongoing commercial operations cannot be committed for this purpose.

OMB allegation: Long-term conflicts do not justify a merchant marine because actual requirements are impossible to foresee. In light of the limited short-term impact of the U.S. merchant marine, the major argument used to justify assistance to the U.S.-flag fleet has been based on the fleet's usefulness and availability in long-term conflicts, and the belief that other sources of sealift would not be reliable in time of war. A number of factors complicate attempts to examine the validity of this justification. First, it is not possible to obtain accurate assessments of sealift demand in a long-term conflict.

Reponse: The difficulty in foreseeing future contingencies precisely does not relieve the United States of being adequately prepared for events that may threaten its interests. The review demonstrates a basic lack of understanding of military planning. Military plans for an extended major conflict cannot be precise. One never knows what the requirements will be as the events unfold. In World War II, for example, who would have thought we would lose the Philippines and Guam and have to fight our way across the Pacific island by island. The military can and does plan with a fairly high degree of definition for the initial phases of a conflict, where the opening moves are relatively predictable, at least on our side.

Although a general war with the Soviet Union remains first in importance in terms of national survival, more attention is now being directed to lesser contingencies which, if left unresolved, could lead to general war, such as a limited conflict involving the deployment of the Rapid Deployment Force to Southwest Asia, a far more probable contingency than general war with the USSR. We have been involved in two of these limited wars in the past three decades.

In the opening phase of such a conflict, the earmarked elements of the RDF would be immediately loaded aboard the Rapid Deployment ships and gotten underway for Southwest Asia. It is anticipated that a Marine amphibious group would have moved ashore in assault craft, established a beachhead, and secured the necessary airfield and port facilities. This initial Marine assault force would be quickly augmented by a Marine brigade flown into the theater and married up with the equipment and supplies contained in the ships of the prepositioned force based in the vicinity of Diego Garcia. These marine forces would then be reinforced by the balance of the RDF which would arrive in the SL-7s with their heavy combat and support equipment.

Here is where the requirement for the U.S.-flag liner fleet becomes critical. The Commander of the Military Sealift Command has stated that in a contingency operation in Southwest Asia involving major elements of the RDF, about 350 dry cargo ships would be required to sustain that force in overseas operations. These ships will have to come from the operating liner fleet of the U.S.-flag merchant marine. There are six dry cargo ships in the Military Sealift Command Control Fleet (MSC). There are today 29 ships in the Ready Reserve Force of the NDRF. (That number will grow to 44 by 1987.) It is doubtful that more than 100 additional ships in the NDRF would be suitable to be put into an operating status. This total amounts to a maximum of about 150 ships from U.S.

government assets. For a unilateral U.S. military contingency operation, we cannot plan upon the use of cargo ships of any of our allies. Only a small number of the U.S.-owned foreign registry ships are suitable for this dry cargo lift purpose. That means that 200 or more dry cargo ships will have to be provided by the operating liner fleet of the U.S.-flag merchant marine. This requirement for 200 to 250 equivalent dry cargo ships can only be met by the requisitioning of the entire privately owned operating liner fleet.

OMB allegation: U.S.-flag merchant vessels have limited usefulness in military support. The utility of the U.S. merchant fleet should not be overemphasized since even in a long war a portion of the fleet is not well suited for military purposes. As noted above, public assistance has not been focused primarily on increasing the usefulness of the merchant marine for military purposes. Rather, the thrust has been on commercial viability. Those factors which improve the utility of certain types of ships for commercial purposes often limit their suitability for transporting military supplies.

The primary constraints limiting use of the fleet would be the speed of the vessels and the inability of many commercial vessels to carry outsized military equipment.

Response: The facts do not support this allegation. There are today approximately 250 [dry cargo] ships, operating under the U.S. flag. They consist of breakbulk freighters, container ships, barge carriers, and roll on-roll off vessels. All of these ships are useful for sealift, according to the Military Sealift Command. The highly automated container ships are most useful under circumstances when they can use the highly mechanized container port facilities that are available in certain modern port areas. Military cargo packaged in containers and shipped through highly automated handling facilities is by far the most expeditious way of moving war material quickly and efficiently. Roll on-Roll off ships (Ro/Ro) are ideally suited for the movement and delivery of the organic equipment of modern ground forces such as tanks, artillery, armored fighting vehicles, trucks, trailers, bulldozers, and even helicopters and light aircraft, which can be towed on and off these ships. The barge carriers discharge their cargo in handy sized barges which can be handled by virtually any kind of port facility or further distributed through waterways to more remote inland sites for unloading closer to the installations of the military users. Finally, there is the breakbulk freighter which discharges cargo from capacious holds through ship-installed cargo booms to piers or lighters for further movement. This is the slowest system of cargo delivery, but the breakbulk freighter is capable of delivering its cargo under the most primitive of conditions.

The inability of many commercial vessels to carry out-sized military equipment is not a primary constraint on the use of the commercial liner fleet for sealift purposes. The Military Sealift Command considers all breakbulk, Ro/Ro, and barge ships capable of handling out-sized cargo. There are 144 of these kinds of ships in the operating commercial liner fleet, 60 percent of the total.

OMB allegation: Availability of non-U.S.-flag assets decreases the need for a merchant marine. The U.S. merchant marine, while an important source of sealift in a long war, should be viewed as only one of a number of available resources. Government-owned reserve ships and other sources of sealift, such as the Effective U.S. Controlled Fleet and the fleets of other nations, should be viewed as important providers of sealift in time of war. Agreements and tradition argue strongly that the controlled fleet—U.S. citizen-owned vessels registered under the flags of Panama, Liberia, and Honduras—would be available when needed. Similarly, the nations which own and operate most free world shipping are our allies. This fact strongly strengthens the likelihood that this source of sealift will also be available in times of war.

Response: In the most probable contingencies requiring sealift, both the suitability and availability of foreign-flag assets is highly questionable. For unilateral U.S. military operations, such as the movement of the RDF to the Persian Gulf area, our allies cannot be counted upon for sealift support, both for political reasons and the understandable reluctance to take the war risk in a conflict in which they are not involved militarily. Recent history has demonstrated that our allies, both European and Japanese, will simply not participate or support a U.S. effort, particularly when it involves Arab interests or the Middle East. The threat of the oil weapon against their economies is simply too great.

The usefulness of the American owned ships of foreign registry (flags of convenience) does not rest upon the responsiveness of these vessels to the U.S. government. Requisitioning is not an issue, even though the availability of these foreign-flag, alien-crewed vessels is questionable, based upon the 1973 Yom Kippur War. The real issue is that all but a handful of these U.S.-owned, foreign-registered ships are extra large crude carriers and cannot fulfill the stated requirements of the Commander of the Military Sealift Command for dry cargo ships.

G

United States Seaports

State	Port
North Atlantic	
Maine	Searsport
	Portland
New Hampshire	Portsmouth
Massachusetts	Boston
	Fall River
	New Bedford
Rhode Island	Providence
Connecticut	New London
	New Haven
	Bridgeport
New York	Albany
New York/New Jersey	New York
New Jersey	Camden
	Paulsboro
Pennsylvania	Philadelphia
	Marcus Hook
Delaware	Wilmington
	Delaware City
Maryland	Baltimore
	Cambridge
Virginia	Alexandria
	Hopewell
	Richmond
	Newport News
	Norfolk
	Portsmouth
South Atlantic	
North Carolina	Morehead City
	Wilmington
South Carolina	Georgetown
	Charleston
	Port Royal

State	Port
Georgia	Savannah
	Brunswick
Florida	Jacksonville
	Port Canaveral
	Palm Beach
	Port Everglades
	Miami
Puerto Rico	San Juan
	Ponce
	Mayaguez
	Jobos
	Guayanilla
	Guanica
	Yabucoa
	Las Mareas
Virgin Islands	Charlotte Amalie
	Frederiksted
	Alucroix
	Limetree Bay
Gulf Coast	
Florida	Tampa
	Port Manatee
	Port St. Joe
	Panama City
	Pensacola
Alabama	Mobile
Mississippi	Pascagoula
	Gulfport
Louisiana	New Orleans
	Pilottown
	Venice
	Ostrica
	Port Sulphur
	Taft
	Reserve
	Gramercy
	St. Amelia
	Uncle Sam
	Baton Rouge
	Lake Charles
Texas	Beaumont
	Port Neches
	Port Arthur
	Orange
	Houston

State	Port
	Texas City
	Galveston
	Freeport
	Corpus Christi
	Brownsville
South Pacific	
California	San Diego
	Carlsbad
	Huntington Beach
	Long Beach
	Los Angeles
	El Segundo
	Port Hueneme
	Madalay Beach
	Ventura
	Carpinteria
	Gaviota
	Port San Luis
	Estero Bay
	Moss Landing
	Redwood City
	San Francisco
	Alameda
	Oakland
	Richmond
	Crockett
	Port Costa
	Vallejo
	Benicia
	Pittsburg
	Antioch
	Stockton
	Sacramento
	Eureka
	Crescent City
Hawaii	Hilo
	Kawaihae
	Kahului
	Kaunakakai
	Honolulu
	Barbers Point
	Nawiliwili
	Port Allen

State	Port
North Pacific	
Oregon	Coos Bay
	Newport
	Reedsport
	Astoria
	Portland
Washington	Longview
	Kalama
	Vancouver
	Raymond
	Willapa Harbor
	Grays Harbor
	Everett
	Port Angeles
	Port Townsend
	Winslow
	Portage
	Olympia
	Tacoma
	Seattle
	Point Wells
	Edmonds (Edwards Point)
	Anacortes
	Friday Harbor
	Bellingham
	Ferndale
Alaska	Ketchikan
	Wrangell
	Petersburg
	Sitka
	Juneau
	Haines
	Skagway
	Cordova
	Valdez
	Whittier
	Seward
	Homer
	Nikiski
	Kenai
	Anchorage
	Kodiak
	Iliuliuk
	Drift River

State	Port
Great Lakes	
Minnesota	Duluth
Wisconsin	Superior
	Kenosha
	Green Bay
	Manitowoc
	Milwaukee
	Sheboygan
Michigan	Marine City
	Muskegon
	Essexville
	Bay City
	Saginaw
	Detroit
Illinois	Chicago
Indiana	Burns Harbor
Ohio	Toledo
	Sandusky
	Huron
	Lorain
	Cleveland
	Fairport
	Ashtabula
	Conneut
Pennsylvania	Erie
New York	Buffalo
	Rochester
	Oswego
	Odgensburg

SOURCE: U.S., Maritime Administration, *National Port Assessment 1980/1990*, pp. 123–27.

H

Statement of George J. Nichols of the Georgia Ports Authority to the House Committee on Public Works and Transportation, Subcommittee on Water Resources, 23 March 1982

Honorable Chairman and Members: I am George J. Nichols, Executive Director of the Georgia Ports Authority, headquartered in Savannah, Georgia, and on the Steering Committee of the U.S. Port System Advocates.

Georgia Ports Authority, as a State authority, operates terminals at Georgia's two deep draft ports at Savannah and Brunswick. At Brunswick, in addition to bulk and general cargo facilities in use, we just opened bids for digging a channel extension to serve a projected public multi-purpose bulk cargo terminal. At Savannah, we have developed a major containerport complex of four berths with plans, in this decade, for two more berths. We handle grain, petroleum and other bulk products, as well as significant breakbulk cargoes. There are a number of thriving private terminals and industries associated with the harbor. In calendar year 1980, the last year for which official Federal figures are available, the

Port of Savannah ranked number one among the ten mainland South Atlantic ports in import and export tonnage handled. This was an increase of 32.9 percent in foreign commerce over 1978 which in turn increased 24 percent over 1977. In CY '81, U.S. Customs revenues collected at the Port of Savannah exceeded $133.7 million, whereas, fiscal year '81 Corps of Engineers allowance for maintaining Savannah Harbor totaled $7.59 million. The Port of Savannah has been a very good investment for the Federal government under the current traditional system of partnership between the Federal government and local ports. Georgia Ports Authority has invested in the past ten years more than $150 million in capital to build and equip our shoreside facilities at cargo terminals. Substantial private investments also were made.

Our bond program for major capital improvements at our two deep draft ports this year and next totals almost $108 million. In the next five years we plan to invest more than $200 million.

Georgia's ports have developed dramatically through the Federal government working in partnership with State and local governments and private industry. Federal costs have returned benefits many-fold to the Nation, as well as to the region and State. Recent data established that Savannah significantly serves shippers in more than 25 states. We support fiscal responsibility and some form of cost sharing with the Federal government where appropriate. However, it is essential to recognize that Georgia's deep draft ports are already an excellent Federal investment, and the same is true of the other ports serving the South Atlantic. We need a guaranteed source of funding for maintaining and improving our ports. This is especially important in that local assurors already are paying substantial sums for essential elements of Federal projects such as relocations and disposal areas. For Savannah Harbor the local assuror costs to support operation and maintenance are running five to six percent of actual Federal costs. An improvement project to enlarge a turning basin almost completed has cost the local assuror 29 percent of the total project cost of $5.49 million, and a new proposed widening of the inner harbor will impose 36 percent local cost of the total project cost of $14.6 million. States, counties and local port authorities have assumed a substantial cost burden for Federal channels that may not be appreciated by those calling for local participation.

In addition, we need a responsive, expeditious Federal procedure for authorization and funding of navigation improvement projects, and for permitting non-federally developed facilities. It has been more than 15 years since a study of widening Savannah Harbor was authorized. It was recommended by the District Engineer in 1976.

A 1981 Corps of Engineers Stage 1 report for the ongoing comprehensive study of Savannah Harbor reconfirmed that this widening of the inner harbor by 100 feet has a strong benefit to cost ratio, and is needed to decrease vessel delays and increase safety.

Georgia's ports have been long established. Industries and shippers, as well as the entire State, region and multi-state hinterland our ports serve has prospered under the long standing partnership whereby the Federal government provides the channels and private and public local interests provide the extensive shoreside facilities to handle the cargo.

If the Federal government removes itself partially or completely from the funding picture and Georgia's ports are required to recover dredging costs for each port through fees or taxes at that port, considerable differential cost per ton of cargo handled will be created between ports. This will economically harm Georgia and other South Atlantic ports by creating a downward spiral effect as more and more cargoes are diverted but channel costs remain the same or increase. The additional imposed cost differentials would motivate ocean carriers to concentrate their services in the lower cost ports.

Various estimates by the Federal government as well as others show, for example, that a difference of .65¢ or more per ton of cargo would be created between Savannah and the Port of New York. Commerce at smaller ports would tend to dry up and repayment of bond issues would be difficult. Industry that has located nearby would face increased inland transportation costs. New industries planning to locate nearby would have to re-evaluate their plans. Throwing open the national port system to funding by port specific fees also would be inequitable to ports such as Savannah that do not have naval installations, but are designated for use by rapid deployment forces. These effects have not been adequately and realistically analyzed by the Federal Administration. The statements we have heard that the effects of cargo diversions on ports, regions served, and foreign trade would be insignificant are simply not in accordance with the realities of the transportation industry.

The realities of port competitiveness leave open two reasonable options to preserve considerable local, shoreside facility investment and to foster continued maritime cargo growth.

The present system of no fees could continue only with a dependable commitment by the Federal government to adequately fund maintenance and improvements for our ports. Alternatively, a uniform, nationwide, federally administered fee or tax system on commodities can be used to partially or fully fund operations and maintenance, as well as improvements with any balance coming from Federal revenues.

As some form of user fees or taxes appears inevitable, we support HR 5897 just introduced on March 18th, and companion to Senate Bill S 2217, introduced March 16th. These provide for nationwide, uniform, federally administered fees or taxes on commodities that would provide a dependable source of funds for operations and maintenance of existing channels 45 feet deep and shallower, as well as pay for 90 percent of improvements not more than 45 feet deep.

The vast majority of the Nation's ports, including Georgia's, have and need channels shallower than 45 feet. A dependable source of funds, and expedited approval, will enable these ports of general maritime utility to prosper and grow. This requires continued Federal interest in a national port system and a commitment by the Administration not to cast aside the economically viable medium sized and smaller ports that comprise most of the Nation's system. Georgia's ports have and will continue to make a significant contribution to the foreign trade and economic well-being of this Nation. We ask that this contribution be recognized and nurtured.

AUTHOR'S NOTE: Congress did not pass a port improvement bill in 1982. However, two major port bills with multiple sponsors were introduced in Congress in March 1983. House and Senate hearings were scheduled for April and June 1983, respectively. Key provisions of these bills are as follows:

S. 865 imposes a national uniform vessel cargo tax designed to recover 40 percent of port operation and maintenance (O&M) expenses. The tax is on vessels with drafts over 24 feet and applies to cargo destined to a port outside the United States or coming into the United States.

Local entities would finance on a sliding scale between 20 and 75 percent of deep draft improvements. A trust fund would be established. The nonfederal share of O&M costs would begin at 20 percent in FY 1984 and rise to 40 percent by FY 1986.

H.R. 2406 is similar to S. 865 except that a part of the vessel cargo tax would be used for local improvements by those ports paying fees that exceeded their O&M costs. A portion of customs revenues (2.2 percent) would be used to cover the federal share of new port improvements. The nonfederal share would be determined on a sliding scale on a basis of channel depth. Ports would have the option of imposing port specific fees.

Notes

Chapter 1

1. "U.S. Merchant Shipbuilding: 1607–1976," *Marine Engineering/Log* 81 (August 1976): 65.

2. John G. B. Hutchins, *The American Maritime Industries and Public Policy, 1789–1914: An Economic History* (New York: Russell and Russell, 1969), p. 153.

3. *An Act Imposing Duties on Tonnage*, 1st Cong., 1st sess., 20 July 1789, ch. 3, sec. 1; *An Act Imposing Duties on the Tonnage of Ships or Vessels*, 1st Cong., 2d sess., 30 July 1790, ch. 30.

4. *An Act Concerning the Navigation of the United States*, 14th Cong., 2d sess., 1 March 1817, ch. 31.

5. The requirement that U.S.-registered ships be American built was repealed by the Panama Canal Act of 1912.

6. Samuel E. Morison, *The Maritime History of Massachusetts: 1783–1860*, p. 319.

7. J. T. Jenkins, *A History of the Whale Fisheries*, p. 238.

8. Frances Diane Robbotti, *Whaling and Old Salem*, p. 211.

9. Jenkins, *Whale Fisheries*, pp. 234–35.

10. Robbotti, *Whaling and Old Salem*, p. 215.

11. In 1980 the U.S. gross national product was $2,626 million. The value of exports moved in vessels of all flags was $120.9 billion (4.6 percent). The value of imports moved in these vessels was $165.1 billion (6.2 percent). U.S. receipts from ocean transportation, including port expenditures, was $7.7 billion (0.003 percent of GNP). Source: U.S. Bureau of the Census, *Statistical Abstract of the United States 1981*, 102d ed. (1981), tables 1135, 1136.

Chapter 2

1. "The Forbes Assets 500," *Forbes*, 10 May 1982, p. 228.

2. "The Fifty Largest Transportation Companies," *Fortune,* 12 July 1982, p. 142.

3. Some commentators have urged that whaling vessels were the first special purpose carriers to be developed after the War of 1812. However, the noted historian, Samuel E. Morison concludes that while "the barque rig became popular . . . little if any improvement was made in the model. . . . Capacity, not speed, was the desired quality; hence many ships which had outlived their usefulness in the merchant service were converted into whalers." See S. E. Morison, *The Maritime History of Massachusetts*, p. 318.

4. See note 2 of Chapter 7.

5. U.S., Maritime Administration, *Domestic Ocean Trade Area—Final Report*, p. I-A-11.

6. See Chapter 17 for detailed descriptions of general cargo vessels.

7. On 1 January 1959, fourteen companies operated forty passenger and combination passenger-cargo vessels under the American flag. In 1982, in addition to the four Delta Line combination cargo-passenger ships and the two cruise ships operated by American-Hawaii Cruises, six U.S.-flag companies offered accommodations for twelve passengers on their cargo ships: Farrell Lines, Moore-McCormack, Lykes, Prudential, American-President, and Delta Lines.

As a matter of interest, in 1978 the then laid up (government owned) SS *United States*, one-time flag ship of the American passenger fleet, was sold to be refurbished and used as a cruise ship. As of 1 July 1982 it was not in service.

8. Texaco's worldwide fleet operations are organized by functions. Its Marine Department handles operations of both its U.S. and international (foreign flag) ships.

9. A letter to C. H. Whitehurst, Jr., dated 23 June 1982 from J. William Charrier, Jr., Washington, D.C., representative of Delta Steamship Lines, contained Delta Lines' organizational chart.

10. At one time, Bethlehem Steel met a part of its ore shipment requirements with U.S.-flag vessels.

11. For a more detailed description of marine operations management in a liner company, see Lane C. Kendall, *The Business of Shipping*, particularly chapter V.

12. In 1979, at the request of Congress, the General Accounting Office (GAO) reviewed the relationship between the Maritime Administration and the National Maritime Council (NMC). The GAO report raised a number of questions; the result was that in 1983 the Maritime Administration no longer supports the NMC administratively. See U.S., General Accounting Office, *The Maritime Administration and the National Maritime Council—Was Their Relationship Appropriate?*

Chapter 3

1. *An Act to Provide for the Transportation of Mail between the U.S. and Foreign Countries and for Other Purposes*, 28th Cong., 2d sess., 3 March 1845, ch. 69; *An Act Authorizing the Establishment of Ocean Mail Steamship Service between U.S. and Brazil*, 38th Cong., 1st sess., 28 May 1864, ch. 98; *An Act to Provide for Ocean Mail Service between U.S. and Foreign Ports and to Promote Commerce*, 51st Cong., 2d sess., 3 March 1891, ch. 519.

2. Edmund A. Walsh, *Ships and National Safety: The Role of the Merchant Marine in a Balanced Economy* (Washington, D.C.: Georgetown University Press, 1934), p. 8.

3. *An Act to Require the Employment of Vessels of the U.S. for Public Purposes*, 58th Cong., 2d sess., 28 April 1904, ch. 1766.

4. *The Cargo Preference Act of August 26, 1954*, P. L. 664, 68 Stat. 832, as amended.

5. U.S., Maritime Administration, *Annual Report*, FY 1981, table 19.

6. Letter to the chairman of the House Merchant Marine and Fisheries Committee from President Jimmy Carter, 20 July 1979.

7. "A Program for the Development of an Effective Maritime Strategy," press release, Reagan and Bush Headquarters, Arlington, Va., 22 September 1980.

8. The use of tax legislation in support of shipping and shipbuilding dates from the acts of 1789 and 1790, which imposed tonnage taxes on non-U.S.-registered and non-U.S.-built vessels engaged in the coastwise trade: *An Act Imposing Duties on Tonnage*, 1st Cong., 1st sess., 20 July 1789, ch. 3, sec. 1; *An Act Imposing Duties on the Tonnage of Ships or Vessels*, 1st Cong., 2nd sess., 20 July 1790, ch. 30.

9. No new construction differential subsidies (CDS) were requested in the 1983 and 1984 budgets by the Reagan administration.

10. Land grant legislation required railroads to carry passengers and freight at 50 percent of established rates, and mail at 80 percent. By government estimates, savings to the federal government were ten times the original value of the land.

11. In testifying on the Omnibus Maritime Bill (1980), the subsidized liner operators, in fact, favored retaining the essential trade route concept, i.e., limiting the number of U.S. firms on a particular trade route. See Chapter 5 for a more detailed discussion of the Omnibus Maritime Bill.

12. As of 30 September 1981, twenty-one ODS agreements were in place (with eight liner and thirteen bulk companies). The notable liner company exception was Sea-Land Services, Inc. However, several of the eight liner companies do not receive a subsidy on every route they serve, e.g., U.S. Lines.

13. U.S., Maritime Commission, *Economic Survey of the American Merchant Marine*, pp. 70–75.

14. For a somewhat different and more detailed approach to government support for liners, see Chapter 9.

15. A philosophic rule laid down by William of Occam in the fourteenth century, which stated that entities should not be multiplied unnecessarily.

Chapter 4

1. Since foreign trade ocean shipping is an international business, American firms are also directly or indirectly affected by the national laws of their trading partners, either singly or collectively, e.g., as a member of a shipping conference.

2. A shipping conference consists of two or more steamship companies operating on one or more trade routes, usually in a defined geographic area of the world, e.g., U.S. East Coast–North Europe. By mutual agreement, the conference sets rates as well as the amount of service. If a conference is closed, membership is limited by conference rules. An open conference would be one that could not deny membership to any shipping line seeking it. In economic terms, conferences are oligopolies not monopolies, since there is always the possibility of outside competition.

3. *Shipping Act*, P.L. 260, 64th Cong., 1916, preamble.

4. With the ratification in 1980 by Colombia and Yugoslavia of SOLAS 1974, sixteen nations, representing over 50 percent of the world's tonnage, had ratified the convention.

5. Seaman's Act of 1915, in U.S., *Statutes at Large*, vol. 38, part 1, p. 1164.

6. U.S., Congress, House, Committee on Merchant Marine and Fisheries, *Safety of Life at Sea*, 84th Cong., 2d sess., 1956, H. Rept. 2969, p. 8.

In a hearing a year later, the question of substandard (foreign-built) ships engaging in U.S. trades was put to Admiral Jewell of the U.S. Coast Guard. In response to the question, "In other words, a foreign-flag cargo vessel then could be substandard as to construction or manning and come into our ports and take cargo," Admiral Jewell replied, "It could, yes sir." U.S., Congress, House, Committee on Merchant Marine and Fisheries, *Safety of Life at Sea*, 85th Cong., 1st sess., 1957, p. 22.

Identical questions were raised in 1976–77 when several Liberian-registered ships met disaster at sea, e.g., the grounding and breakup of the *Argo Merchant* in December 1976 off the Massachusetts coast.

7. Roy L. Nersesian, *Ships and Shipping*, p. 91.

8. Ibid.

9. In a laissez-faire economy, the "opportunity cost" of capital determines the extent of shipping investment. That is, if shipping offers the best return, investment will take place until returns in shipping are equal to returns on other investments. American investment in

shipping during the 1820–40 period is a case in point. Returns were so great that scarcely forty years after independence from Great Britain, the United States was one of the leading maritime powers.

10. With A as a conference member, the power of the oligopoly to set rates by limiting service is strengthened. In this case, an efficient producer of shipping services might earn a 20 percent return on an investment, while the less efficient member might earn only 10 percent. A classic argument against conferences is that in attempting to gain as much monopoly power as possible, conference rates will be set high enough to accommodate the least efficient member.

11. Some shipping is probably insured, since there is no real alternative to ocean transportation over great distances for many types of cargo, e.g., U.S. mainland to Hawaii. The model does not consider the possibility of a shipbuilding industry's being entirely sustained by a naval building program.

12. For example, domestic coastwise shipping cannot ignore the fact that the creation of "super railroads" (like Norfolk-Southern and CSX) stretching from Canada to the Gulf of Mexico will make these companies more competitive with shipping in the Gulf–East Coast trade.

13. Clinton H. Whitehurst, Jr., *Safety of Life at Sea: A Review of Passenger Vessel Certification Requirements* (Clemson, S.C.: Department of Industrial Management, Clemson University, 1979) and a summary of this study, Clinton H. Whitehurst, Jr., "Is the Legal Definition of a Passenger Ship Obsolete," *Journal of Maritime Law and Commerce*, July 1980.

14. Letter from Al May, executive vice-president, Council of American-Flag Ship Operators, to Clinton H. Whitehurst, Jr., 10 October 1978.

15. Whitehurst, "Is the Legal Definition of a Passenger Ship Obsolete," p. 533.

Chapter 5

1. Remarks by Conrad H. C. Everhard, President, Dart Container Line, 1979.

2. In vetoing the original Anti-Rebating Bill in late 1978, President Carter promised that a study would be conducted by an interagency task force. The task force completed its work in June 1979.

Chapter 6

1. Under Section 21 of the Merchant Marine Act of 1920, the president may permit foreign-flag vessels to operate in the Virgin Islands trade if such is necessary to insure adequate shipping service. From 1922 to 1936, successive presidents reissued proclamations with respect to this trade. In 1936 Congress amended the law to exempt the Virgin Islands from the Jones Act (the Merchant Marine Act of 1920, Section 27) until the president, by proclamation, determines otherwise. In the case of the Philippines, the issue became moot when the Philippines became independent in 1946.

2. U.S., Maritime Administration, *Domestic Waterborne Trade of the United States, 1975–1979*, p. 34.

3. Carl E. McDowell and Helen M. Gibbs, *Ocean Transportation*, pp. 95–98.

4. U.S., Maritime Administration, *Domestic Waterborne Trade*, pp. 19, 21.

5. As a general rule, domestic tonnage must be U.S. built without construction differential subsidy. This shipping, however, is eligible to participate in the Title XI ship financing guarantee program, which allows the Maritime Administration to issue mortgage insurance and allows carriers in noncontiguous trade to accumulate vessel replacement dollars in a tax-free fund.

6. In 1950 an amendment to the Jones Act allowed the secretary of the treasury to grant waivers to foreign-flag vessels when the secretary of defense certifies that such action is in the interest of national defense. Some maritime authorities see a parallel between legislation passed in 1981 that allowed operators of foreign trade vessels receiving ODS to build overseas and legislation that would permit foreign construction of ships in protected trades, and ultimately allow foreign-flag vessels access to these trades.

7. Presumably, the president can allow foreign-flag ships to enter the Virgin Islands trade by executive order. Periodically, bills have been introduced in Congress to make the Jones Act completely applicable to this trade and remove presidential discretion in the matter.

8. "Free the Alaska 600,000," *The Wall Street Journal*, 19 August 1981, p. 28.

9. A State Department–sponsored conference on "Future Trans-Isthmian Transportation Alternatives" was held in October 1982.

10. One bill that cleared committee in 1982 is S. 1692. Under this proposal local interests would pay the full cost of improvements, e.g., channel deepening, while operating costs would be shared, 75% federal, 25% state/local.

11. Before deciding that passenger ships have no defense use, one might remember the role of the *QE-2* and *Canberra* in transporting troops in the 1982 Falkland Islands conflict between Great Britain and Argentina.

12. The firms and the number of RO/ROs they operated were Coordinated Caribbean Transport (2), Matson Navigation Company (2), and Navieras de Puerto Rico (5).

13. It has long been recognized that high shipping costs in the offshore trade are a severe burden to both imports and exports—unlike the contiguous trade, where land transportation is an alternative. Thus any policy that will lower offshore shipping costs benefits not only defense, but also, and equally important, the economies of the noncontiguous states and territories.

14. The very high costs imposed on the economies of noncontiguous states and territories when maritime unions (longshore and seagoing) have struck the offshore trade illustrate better than any theory the importance of certainty of shipping service on these routes. As economically harmful as strikes by American seagoing labor might be, such strikes can still be disciplined under American law, an alternative not available for strikers on foreign-flag vessels.

15. Presumably, Congress would specify some level of U.S. investment to insure "effective management control" of this shipping. However, the question of equity with respect to owners of U.S.-built tonnage employed in the contiguous trade must also be considered. In the worst case, useful, i.e., relatively new ships, could be purchased by the government and retained in the National Defense Reserve Fleet if they could not be employed in other trade. Given the age of this fleet, the option would not be as expensive as it might first seem.

16. Where inland waterways exist, including the intercoastal waterway, modal competition obviously would be improved. However, in the Gulf–East Coast liquid-bulk movement, barge tows are too slow.

17. One option would be for Congress to allow U.S.-owned, foreign-flag tonnage into the coastwise and intercoastal trade on a trial basis, say for a period of five or ten years.

Chapter 7

1. Evidence that Congress supported a bulk and tanker fleet was not lacking. In 1974 both houses of Congress passed cargo preference legislation specifying that 30 percent of U.S. foreign oil imports ultimately be carried by U.S.-flag ships. (The bill was pocket-vetoed by President Gerald Ford.) Between 1978 and 1980, bills supporting U.S. bulk and tanker shipping were introduced in both the House and Senate. In 1982 hearings were held on the latest bill, H.R. 4627, a strongly backed bill that would require that 40 percent of all

U.S. dry bulk imports and exports over a ten-year period be carried in U.S.-built and -registered ships.

2. U.S., Maritime Commission, *Economic Survey of the American Merchant Marine*, p. 19.

3. U.S., Congress, House, Committee on the Interior and Insular Affairs, Subcommittee on Mines and Mining, *Hearings on Global Mineral Resources*, 96th Cong., 1980, p. 5.

4. Suggested readings, listed in the bibliography, are James T. Bennett and Walter E. Williams, *Strategic Minerals: The Economic Impact of Supply Disruptions*; James Arnold Miller, Daniel L. Fine, and R. Daniel McMichael, eds., *The Resource War in 3-D—Dependency, Diplomacy, Defense*; and William C. Mott, *Strategic Minerals: A Resource Crisis*.

5. U.S., Congress, House, Committee on Armed Services, *Capability of U.S. Defense Industrial Base*, 96th Cong., 2d sess., 1980, p. 455.

6. Major U.S. mineral imports from South Africa in 1980 included chrome, ferrochrome manganese, palladium, and platinum. Other imports were lead, mica, nickel, and zinc.

7. House, *Capability of U.S. Defense Industrial Base*, p. 1057.

8. Maxwell D. Taylor, "Changing Military Priorities," *Foreign Policy and Defense Review* 1 (1979): 5.

9. U.S., Maritime Administration, *Merchant Marine Data Sheet*, as of 1 March 1982. An additional eleven tankers were engaged in foreign-to-foreign trade. It might be fairly asked whether domestic trade tankers could replace foreign-owned tankers as carriers of foreign oil imports should the latter become unavailable (for whatever reason). Undoubtedly some could. If the Alaska-U.S. requirements for crude oil carriers and those of offshore states and territories (Hawaii and Puerto Rico) are subtracted, American-flag tankers could at best fill only 25 percent of the remaining needs.

10. The world's largest LNG is the Belgium-built *Methania* (1978) with a capacity of 131,500 cubic meters.

11. The most modern ULCC (ultra large crude carrier) is the Japanese-built *ESSO Atlantic*. Its engine room can be operated unmanned twenty-four hours a day. The largest ULCCs are French-built ones of 550,000 dwt.

12. House, *Hearings on Global Mineral Resources*, p. 23.

13. In a 1979 letter to the chairman of the House Merchant Marine and Fisheries Committee, President Jimmy Carter noted the lack of a U.S. bulk carrier fleet and proposed several amendments in U.S. shipping laws to encourage the rebuilding of this fleet.

14. In 1977 the Maritime Administration awarded a $281,000 contract for the design of a standardized dry bulk carrier. A brief discussion and a sketch of a proposed medium-sized dry bulk carrier with national defense features is found in the work of L. A. Wheeler and B. M. Collins, "Building a Fleet to Suit the Market and Military," *U.S. Naval Institute Proceedings* 107 (April 1981): 59.

15. According to assumptions made by the National Coal Association, a 12 percent share of the American coal export trade for U.S. ships in 1985 would cost an additional $409 million in shipping charges. Source: "U.S. and World Shipping," p. 88.

Chapter 8

1. U.S., Maritime Commission, *Economic Survey of the American Merchant Marine*, p. 27.

2. As of 1 July 1982 the Military Sealift Command listed 245 general cargo vessels of which 202 were in the foreign trade liner fleet. As of 1 June 1982 the authoritative *Marine Engineering/Log* estimated this fleet to number 200.

3. U.S., Maritime Administration, *U.S. Merchant Marine Data Sheet*, as of 1 September 1982, p. 3.

4. In 1982 plans were announced by Crowley Marine International to acquire Delta Lines and for LTV to sell Lykes Lines to the Interocean Steamship Corporation.

5. U.S., Maritime Commission, *Economic Survey*, pp. 28–29.

6. Approximately 80 percent of military resupply cargo can be containerized. When flat racks are available, up to half of a unit's equipment can be moved in container ships. A relatively new concept, Sea Shed, should further increase the military usefulness of container ships. Sea Shed is a cargo module that fits into a container ship's cell guides, converting the ship into a break-bulk ship. Sea Shed can also be used on bulk carriers.

7. The military usefulness of merchant ships can be enhanced by adding national defense features (NDF) during vessel construction. This government option was provided for in Sections 501(b) and 502(b) of the Merchant Marine Act of 1936. If there is any criticism of the NDF concept, it is that it has been too little used in the past.

8. No attempt was made to estimate the indirect costs of supporting a liner merchant fleet, e.g., military and government cargo preference programs. However, neither were the taxes paid by shipping companies and the indirect employment benefits considered.

9. National Academy of Sciences, *The Sealift Readiness Program*.

Chapter 9

1. U.S., General Accounting Office, *Changes in Federal Maritime Regulation Can Increase Efficiency and Reduce Costs in the Ocean Liner Shipping Industry*, pp. vi, 16.

Chapter 10

1. The Maritime Administration considers the Title XI program to be "one of the most successful under the Merchant Marine Act of 1936. Its total costs, including salaries of the MarAd staff employed in the merchant ship financing program, are underwritten by fees which are paid by users. The insurance premiums and guarantee fees go into the Federal Ship Financing Fund, a revolving fund which may be used for payment of any defaults. Since the inception of the Title XI program, only 11 companies have defaulted." U.S., Maritime Administration, *Annual Report*, FY 1980, p. 3.

2. The secretary of transportation has been designated as the chief Reagan administration spokesman on maritime matters. On 5 August 1982, Secretary Lewis, in unveiling additional elements of administration maritime policy, announced that the FY 1983 ceiling on Title XI commitments would be raised to $900 million. However, $300 million of this amount would be held in reserve to be used in the interest of national security.

3. *Merchant Marine Act*, P.L. 205, 66th Cong., 1920. This act, in particular Section 27, is often referred to as the "Jones Act."

4. "Interim Report on Maritime Policy," *American Shipper*, July 1982, p. 32.

5. Ibid. The traditional maritime countries, which supply most of the world's shipping tonnage, are members of OECD. Lesser developed countries (LDCs), however, are attempting to build up their merchant marines. As a rule, their crew costs are much lower than those of the traditional shipping nations.

6. *Economic Recovery Tax Act*, P. L. 97-34, 97th Cong., 31 August 1981.

7. As a basic proposition, equity and debt are the chief sources available to pay for new vessels. Equity capital is that accumulated from a vessel's operations, vessel sales, and the sale of stock. Debt is capital acquired from sources other than the shipowner such as from banks, governments, shipyards, and insurance companies.

An excellent textbook treatment of capital needs of shipping, sources of capital, and return to capital, is the work of Roy L. Nersesian, *Ships and Shipping*, ch. 11, 12, 13.

8. The safe harbor leasing provisions of the Economic Recovery Tax Act of 1981 (Title II, Subtitles A and B) allow the transfer of tax benefits from firms that cannot profitably use

them at a particular time to firms that can. A shipping company, for example, as a seller of its tax benefits, would be able to "benefit" from its existing tax benefits (tax credits, deductions) sooner than would otherwise be the case. For a good treatment of this topic see Emil M. Sunley, "Safe Harbor Leasing," *Tax Review*, April 1982, pp. 17–20.

9. *Tax Equity and Fiscal Responsibility Act*, P.L. 97–248, 97th Cong., 3 September 1982. For specific changes in the safe harbor provisions of the 1981 tax law see Ernst and Whinney, *The Tax Equity and Fiscal Responsibility Act of 1982* (Cleveland, Ohio: Ernst and Whinney, 1982), p. 11.

Chapter 11

1. Edmund A. Walsh, *Ships and National Safety: The Role of the Merchant Marine in a Balanced Economy* (Washington, D.C.: Georgetown University Press, 1934), p. 17.

2. *Shipping Act of 1916*, P.L. 260, 64th Cong., sect. 11.

3. Cited by Carl E. McDowell and Helen M. Gibbs, *Ocean Transportation*, p. 254.

4. In 1937 there were seven government-owned lines—America-France Line, American Hampton Roads–Yankee Line, Oriole Lines, American Republic Line, American Pioneer–Australia Line, American Pioneer–India Line, and American Pioneer–Orient Line. In FY 1937 these companies in total lost $1.9 million.

5. U.S., General Accounting Office, *The National Defense Reserve Fleet—Can It Respond to Future Contingencies?*, 1976.

6. U.S., Congress, House, Committee on Merchant Marine and Fisheries, *Hearings, Cargo for American Ships, Part 1*, 92d Cong., 1st sess., 1971, p. 472.

7. U.S., Congress, Senate, Committee on Interstate and Foreign Commerce, *Hearings, Merchant Marine Study and Investigation (Transportation of Cargoes by the Military)*, 81st Cong., 2d sess., 1950, p. 1071.

8. U.S., General Accounting Office, *A Time to Consider Alternative Sources of Quick-Response Sealift Capability*, 1979, p. 1.

9. *Merchant Marine Act*, P.L. 205, 66th Cong., 1920, sect. 1.

10. U.S., Maritime Administration, *Annual Report*, FY 1972, p. 15.

11. In testifying on the FY 1974 DOD budget, Secretary of the Navy John Warner estimated annual savings as $760,000 for fleet oiler, $820,000 for fleet ocean tugs, and $1,700,000 for store ships. See U.S., Congress, Senate, Committee on Appropriations, *Hearings, Department of Defense Appropriations FY 1974, Part 3*, 93d Cong., 1st sess., p. 41.

12. *Investigation of the Potential for Increased Civilian Manning on Fleet Support Ships*, draft final report, Vol. 1, prepared by Information Spectrum, Inc., for the Systems Analysis Division, Office of Chief of Naval Operations (Washington, D.C.: Information Spectrum, Inc., 1978), p. III-5.

13. *Civilianization of Navy Fleet Support Ships*, draft report, prepared by Ruttenberg, Friedman, Kilgallon, Gutchess & Associates, Inc., for the Joint Maritime Congress (Washington, D.C.: Ruttenberg et al., 1980), pp. vii, viii.

14. *Analysis of a Study Entitled Civilianization of Navy Fleet Support Ships Prepared for the Joint Maritime Congress*, prepared by Information Spectrum, Inc., for the Systems Analysis Division, Office of Chief of Naval Operations (Washington, D.C.: Information Spectrum, Inc., 1980), p. 4.

15. Ibid., table 37, p. 62.

16. U.S., Department of Defense, *Annual Report to Congress*, FY 1981, p. 116.

17. In 1980 the original request for fourteen ships was scaled back to twelve. It was also decided to modify existing ships rather than build new ones. With respect to the SL-7s, while the government has acquired all the ships, Congress has funded only four conversions, with fewer modifications than were originally requested by the navy.

18. U.S., Military Sealift Command, *Ship Register*, January 1982, p. 9.

19. To be eligible to bid on carriage of peacetime DOD cargoes, U.S. liner operators must commit a specified percentage of their fleet to call-up in a contingency. If operators do not make such a commitment, their bid is considered nonresponsive and they cannot be awarded a shipping contract. Over the years, this Sealift Readiness Program (SRP) has generated much controversy with respect to how agreements are implemented and the amount of compensation due the owner of a requisitioned vessel. (See Chapter 8 for a description of the SRP program.)

20. In 1975, as a part of its ongoing effort in the general area of sealift readiness, the U.S. General Accounting Office evaluated the Department of Defense Sealift Readiness Program. As a part of its evaluation, GAO auditors located at a particular time the ships of each company that had pledged vessels under an SRP agreement. For GAO comments on the SRP see U.S., General Accounting Office, Letter Report to Secretary of Defense, B-181714, 19 March 1976.

21. In 1983, plans to merge the Military Sealift Command and the Military Traffic Management Command are actively being considered in the Department of Defense.

22. "A Program for the Development of an Effective Maritime Strategy," press release, Reagan and Bush Headquarters, Arlington, Va., 22 September 1980.

23. U.S., Military Sealift Command, *Ship Register*, pp. 3–6. For a statement on how MSC views its future see "An Expanding MSC Needs More People," *Sealift: Magazine of the Military Sealift Command* 29 (No. 2): 1.

Chapter 12

1. Thomas B. Hayward, *Hearings before the Committee on Armed Services, U.S. Senate, Part 3*, 96th Cong., 1st sess., 1979, p. 1252. Admiral Hayward's statement was delivered 28 March 1979.

2. *Report of Secretary of Defense Caspar W. Weinberger to the Congress on the FY 1983 Budget, FY 1984 Authorization Request and FY 1983–1987 Defense Programs*, 8 February 1982, p. III-91.

3. Daniel Gans, "Fight Outnumbered and Win," *Military Review* 60 (December 1980): 42.

4. Jack Dorsey, "US Merchant Fleet Improvement Urged," *The Ledger Star* (Norfolk, Va.), 12 September 1980, p. C-4, reporting on a speech by Vice Admiral Sir Cameron Rusby, deputy supreme allied commander Atlantic (DEPSACLANT).

5. Data are based on Fearnleys, *World Bulk Trades 1980* (Oslo, Norway, 1981) tables 4, 10, 15, 19, 23, 26. The estimates are assessed as conservative because of the many commodities and manufactured products that are not included.

6. Dorsey, "Fleet Improvement Urged."

7. a. To determine shipping capacity, i.e., the total deadweight tonnage of shipping needed to sustain the transport of a given amount of cargo over a given route at a given speed (15 knots has been assumed), the following calculations have been used:

(1) 15 knots $\times$ 24 hours = 360 miles per day

(2) $\dfrac{\text{distance of route in miles}}{360}$ = days in route

(3) days in route + 4 days unload time in port $\times$ 2 = round trip days

(4) $\dfrac{365}{\text{round trip days}}$ = trips per ship per year

(5) deadweight tonnage shipping capacity required = $\dfrac{\text{annual tonnage}}{\text{trips per year}}$

b. To determine the number of ships required, the deadweight tonnage capacity is divided by the tonnage of a representative or notional ship selected for each given route.

c. Although it is appreciated that in some cases certain ships will embark return cargoes on certain routes, in most circumstances this will not be the case. Consequently, calculations have been made on the basis that ships will normally make their return trips without cargoes.

8. This ratio is based on information made available by NATO, staff of the supreme allied commander Atlantic. This same ratio is reflected in the calculations summarized by Paul H. Nitze and Leonard Sullivan, Jr., *Securing the Seas—The Soviet Naval Challenge and Western Alliance Options* (Boulder, Colo.: Westview Press, 1979) p. 163, table 6.1.

9. Numbers are based on *Jane's Fighting Ships 1949–1950* (New York: McGraw-Hill, 1949) and John Moore, ed., *Jane's Fighting Ships 1981–1982* (New York: Jane's Publishing, 1981), and include active and reserve battleships, aircraft carriers, cruisers, destroyers, frigates, escorts of 1,000 tons or greater, and submarines. The numbers do not include amphibious vessels. For NATO and Warsaw Pact countries, the comparison is as follows:

	1949	1981
NATO	1,662	773
Warsaw Pact	395	821

10. Samuel E. Morison, *Oxford History of the American People* (New York: Oxford University Press, 1965), p. 850. For example, just before war broke out in early August 1914, the German Imperial Chancellor Bethman Hollweg told former Chancellor Bulow "that he was reckoning with 'a war lasting three, or at the most, four months . . . a violent, but short storm'." Fritz Fischer, *Germany's Aims in the First World War* (New York: W. W. Norton, 1967), p. 92.

11. Alan Moorehead, *The Russian Revolution* (New York: Bantam Books, 1959), p. 98.

12. Chester Cooper, *The Lost Crusade: America in Vietnam* (New York: Dodd, Mead and Co., 1970), pp. 215–16.

13. Fred C. Ikle, "The Reagan Defense Program: A Focus on the Strategic Imperatives," *Strategic Review*, Spring 1982, p. 16.

14. See Stephen Barlas, "Huge Losses in Ammunition Attributed to Disrepair of Depots," *Los Angeles Times*, 17 June 1982, p. 1A, for reference to NATO niggardliness and the sorry state of overseas storage facilities and stocks.

15. This system of classification is taken from U.S., Maritime Administration, *A Statistical Analysis of the World's Merchant Fleets*, 31 December 1979, p. iii.

16. Numbers are as of 1 July 1981 and are taken from a computer printout processed 15 July 1982 and supplied on request by the Maritime Administration. Note that the numbers include all sizes of tankers, and bulk carriers, above 1000 dwt but do not include combinations and freighters of less than 10,000 dwt, since these are not considered suitable for the reinforcement and resupply tasks.

17. Calculations for 1950 are based on those in *The World Almanac and Book of Facts for 1952*, New York, 1952, p. 640. Those for mid-1981 are based on the Maritime Administration computer printout.

18. U.S., Maritime Administration, *Statistical Analysis; World Almanac 1952*.

19. Ernest Holsendolph, "Shipping Industry in U.S. Is Not in Trouble, GAO Says," *Virginia Pilot/Ledger Star*, 7 July 1982, pp. A1–A2.

20. U.S., Maritime Administration, *Statistical Analysis*, p. vi. The average age of the 569

privately owned vessels in this fleet is given as seventeen years; for the 296 government-owned ships it is thirty-three years. The world fleet average age is twelve, and that of the USSR is thirteen.

21. Bill Paul, "Shipbuilding Industry in U.S. Flounders as Federal Aid Ebbs and Navy Orders Lag," *Wall Street Journal*, 25 May 1982, p. 54.

22. U.S., Maritime Administration, *Foreign Flag Merchant Ships Owned by U.S. Parent Companies as of January 1, 1981*, shows a total of 639 such ships.

23. Jack Anderson, *Washington Post*, 12 June 1982, p. F27, quotes classified Pentagon documents indicating that as much as 15 percent of U.S. and allied reinforcement and resupply shipping would be lost. General John Hackett, Vice Admiral Sir Ian McGeoch, and others, *The Third World War–August 1985* (New York: Macmillan, 1978), p. 173, use a figure of nearly 20 percent.

24. Bruce Ingersoll, "Could U.S. Match the British Sealift? Probably Not," *Chicago Sun-Times*, 30 May 1982, p. 6, reporting on an interview with Vice Admiral Kent J. Carrol, USN, commander of the Military Sealift Command.

25. Ibid.

26. U.S., Maritime Administration, *United States Oceanborne Foreign Trade Routes*, November 1980, appendix D, table 1, p. 348.

Chapter 13

1. Samuel Eliot Morison and Henry Steel Commager, *The Growth of the American Republic* (New York: Oxford University Press, 1950), pp. 615–16.

2. Other famous clipper ships were the *Lightning, James Baines, Young America, Red Jacket, Westward Ho*, and *Witch of the Wave*. See Morison and Commager, *American Republic*, p. 617.

3. The NS *Savannah* was 595 feet long with a 78-foot beam and had a design speed of 21 knots. She had a gross tonnage of 15,500 tons and could carry 8,500 tons of cargo in approximately 652,000 cubic feet of cargo space. In addition, she could accommodate sixty passengers.

4. U.S., General Accounting Office, *Costs of Operating the Nuclear Merchant Ship Savannah* (1970), p. 12. The charter rate paid by First Atomic Ship Transport to the Maritime Administration was $1 per year.

5. Container ships were first introduced into the U.S. domestic trades by Sea-Land (1957–58), followed by the Matson Navigation Company in 1960, when its first container ship, the *Hawaiian Citizen*, went into service. The first large-scale container effort in foreign trade was made by Grace Line in 1961 with the introduction of two converted C-2 vessels in their Caribbean service,

6. Morison and Commager, *American Republic*, pp. 617–18.

7. In a comparative study of U.S. and foreign shipbuilding technology, American yards were found to lag behind their foreign counterparts in fifty-one out of seventy areas examined. See the paper by Robert Lowry and William L. Stevens presented at the 1980 meeting of the Society of Naval Architects and Marine Engineers as reported in *Marine Engineering/Log* 86 (February 1981): 18.

8. Donald H. Kern, "History and Current State of Shipboard Automation," in *Innovations in the Maritime Industry* (Washington, D.C.: National Academy of Sciences, 1979), appendix, pp. 139–40.

9. Ibid., pp. 136–37. An in-depth review of Scandinavian maritime industries found that in Denmark, Norway, Sweden, and Finland, the emphasis was on a "high value, high technology approach" (see Gene D. Heil, "Scandinavian Maritime Industries," *Marine Engineering/Log* 87 (October 1982): 71–92).

10. Three excellent summary articles on surface effect ship technology are Robert J. Johnson, "Hydrofoils in the U.S. Maritime Industry," in *Innovations in the Maritime Industry* (Washington, D.C.: National Academy of Sciences, 1979), appendix, p. 173; Greg Ovechka, "Hydrofoil, AVC Roundup," *Marine Engineering/Log* 84 (May 1979): 53; and E. G. Tattersall, "History and Future of the SES in the United Kingdom," *Naval Engineers Journal* 94 (April 1982): 267.

11. Tattersall, "Future of the SES," pp. 268, 274.

12. The various trade-offs in the performance characteristics of SES vessels are discussed by George C. Halvorson, "The Role of High-Speed Ships in the U.S. Navy," *U.S. Naval Institute Proceedings* 105 (January 1979): 33.

13. See "The Return of Sail Power: *Shin Aitoku Maru*," *Marine Engineering/Log* 85 (December 1980): 65; and Greg Ovechka, "Sail Cargo Ships to Arrive in the 1980s?" *Marine Engineering/Log* 85 (February 1980): 50.

14. The technical argument as to whether the medium-speed, four-stroke diesel plant is superior to the slow-speed, two-stroke plant or vice versa is not considered. Each has certain advantages. The medium-speed plant is more compact, and therefore more suitable for general cargo vessels; the slow-speed plant is more fuel efficient.

15. The Maritime Administration is devoting much research effort to the question of whether, and to what extent, blended or heavy diesel (more contaminated) fuel can be used in present marine diesel plants. It sponsored a seminar on "Heavy and Alternative Fuels Utilization in Diesels" in Pittsburgh, Pa., on 27 October 1982.

16. Coverage from transmitting stations is about 1,200 nautical miles by day (using ground waves) and about 2,000 nautical miles by night (using sky waves).

17. U.S., General Accounting Office, *Maritime Subsidy Requirements Hinder U.S.-Flag Operators' Competitive Position*, p. 32.

18. Kern, "State of Shipboard Automation," p. 144.

19. "Norwegian Bulk Carrier Has 13 Man Crew," *Marine Engineering/Log* 83 (December 1978): 27.

20. In a detailed and well-researched paper by James G. Mellis, Artis I. Plato, and Robert J. Rein, "Is Automation the Magic Potion for Manning Problems?" *Naval Engineers Journal* 94 (April 1982): 127, the authors conclude that on navy ships, "Automation may or may not reduce manning requirements. It definitely requires, however, higher skill demands for the new systems."

21. The 37,000-gross-ton, Japanese-built *Nichigoh Maru* is a fully automated container ship which carries a crew of eighteen.

22. Rachelle Delaney, "Coal-Fired Ships," *Marine Engineering/Log* 86 (September 1981): 38.

23. "Back to Coal for Power," *Marine Engineering/Log* 85 (July 1980): 35.

Chapter 14

1. U.S., Maritime Administration, *U.S. Merchant Marine Data Sheet*, as of 1 September 1982.

2. Ibid.

3. Those unions are American Radio Association; Associated Marine Officers; Brotherhood of Marine Officers; Marine Engineers Beneficial Association (MEBA); Marine Firemen's Union; Marine Staff Officers; Masters, Mates, and Pilots; National Maritime Union; Radio Officers Union; Sailors Union of the Pacific; Seafarers International Union; and Staff Officers Association.

4. Those unions are American Tanker Officers Association, Atlantic Maritime Officers Association, Atlantic Maritime Employees Union, Jersey Standard Tanker Officers Association, Exxon Radio Officers Association, Exxon Stewards Organization, Exxon Seamen's

Association, Mobil Tankermen's Association, Mobil Tanker Officers Association, Sabine Independent Officers Association, Sabine Independent Seamen's Association, Sun Marine Licensed Officers Association, Sun Marine Employees Association, Texaco Tanker Officers Association, Texaco Radio Officers Association, Getty Tanker Officers Association, Getty Tankermen's Association, and Gulf Oil Marine Department Association.

5. The U.S. Coast Guard establishes and enforces professional qualifications for seagoing employment as specified in U.S. statutes and international treaties that have been ratified by the United States.

6. The Lundeberg School is named for the late Harry Lundeberg, longtime head of the Sailors Union of the Pacific and first president of the Seafarers International Union. Lundeberg founded the Andrew Furuseth School of Seamanship in 1940 at the union's hiring hall in San Francisco, the first of the joint labor/management seamanship training programs.

7. One critically important job of the Lundeberg and other nautical training schools would be to provide refresher courses for the personnel who would be assigned to the World War II–built Victory ships should these ships be called into service. At present, 130 of these vessels are retained in the National Defense Reserve Fleet for national defense purposes. One, the *Catawba Victory*, is a part of the Ready Reserve Force, a select group of ships that are maintained in a high state of readiness, that is, can be broken out and on berth in five to ten days.

8. The concept that the Harry Lundeberg School should give its students more than just vocational training was largely due to Paul Hall, who was always aware of his own lack of formal education. He strongly favored academic courses along with vocational training to insure that SIU members became better-educated men and women and better citizens.

9. The 1981 Kings Point graduating class of 266 included 12 women. At the beginning of the 1981–82 school year there were 94 women in the Kings Point Midshipman Regiment. Women are also enrolled in all six state maritime colleges.

10. Flogging and corporal punishment were abolished by Congress in 1850 (46 U.S.C.A. 712) and crimping in 1862 (46 U.S.C.A. 708).

11. *Brown* v. *Lull*, Federal Case No. 2,018.

12. *Seaman's Act*, 63d Cong., 3d sess., 4 March 1915, ch. 153.

13. Maritime unions, for example, were instrumental in getting legislation through Congress in 1974 that mandated that U.S.-flag vessels carry 30 percent of the nation's imported oil. The bill was pocket-vetoed by President Gerald Ford.

14. The problem of keeping qualified men in seagoing positions is not unique to the merchant marine. In recent times, the retention rate in navy seagoing billets has suffered because of prolonged tours of sea duty, particularly among married men.

15. Not only must the maritime unions compete with foreign-flag shipping, but also they must compete with government-owned merchant shipping, that is, with ships operated by the Military Sealift Command with civil service crews. In this respect, the more efficient union-manned ships become, the stronger the union's case that more military and naval noncombatant transportation tasks be turned over to the privately operated fleet.

16. Over a twelve-month period, 171 ships were broken out of the NDRF and returned to service.

17. U.S., Maritime Administration, *Civilian Seafaring Manpower Requirements in Peace and War: 1978–84*.

18. Ibid., p. 10.

19. Ibid., p. 26. The Maritime Administration has estimated the following man-per-billet ratios, i.e., the number of seamen needed in peacetime to fill one job aboard a commercial ship for one year. For deck officers, the number is 1.91; engine officers, 1.89; radio officers, 1.86; staff officers, 1.74; and unlicensed deck, steward, and engine personnel, 1.61. The required workforce is estimated by multiplying the number of shipboard billets in

a particular job by the respective ratios; e.g., if there are 1,000 deck officer jobs to be filled, 1,910 deck officers are needed.

20. Ibid., p. 27.

21. Ibid., p. 17.

22. The Eightieth Congress, however, did not hold the World War II merchant seaman in particularly high regard. The Selective Service Act of 1948 (P.L. 759, 24 June 1948) did not give credit for wartime merchant marine service, and many seamen were later drafted during the Korean War on the rationale that they had not fulfilled their service obligation to their country. The best explanation for this behavior was that Congress was intent on indicating its displeasure at the lengthy seamen and longshoremen strikes that took place immediately after the war.

23. U.S., Maritime Administration, *Civilian Seafaring Manpower Requirements*, p. 11.

24. Ibid., p. 12.

25. A fair question to ask here is whether foreign seamen on U.S.-owned ships would support a major U.S. military commitment in an area where ship losses were all but certain. It might be noted that there were at least twelve instances between 1965 and 1968 when foreign crews refused to sail American cargo to Vietnam. See Bennet Caplan and Joseph E. Ryan, "A Critique of Flags of Convenience," *U.S. Naval Institute Proceedings* 107 (October 1981): 80.

Chapter 15

1. *Merchant Marine Act*, as amended, P.L. 835, 74th Cong., 1936, sect. 603(b).

2. U.S., Congress, House, Committee on Merchant Marine and Fisheries, *Labor-Management Problems of the American Merchant Marine*, 84th Cong., 2d sess., 1956, p. 28.

3. Ibid., p. 31.

4. U.S., General Accounting Office, *Maritime Subsidy Requirements Hinder U.S.-Flag Operators' Competitive Position*, p. 30.

5. Ibid., p. 32.

6. Ibid., p. 29.

7. Moore-McCormack Resources, *Annual Report* (Washington, D.C., 1981), p. 31.

8. The reader is cautioned that $47,368 is an average figure. Costs for specific ships and particular crew positions will differ markedly from an average obtained across a diversified fleet.

In testimony before Congress in 1981, the executive director of the Federation of American Controlled Shipping estimated the annual subsidy per billet on a forty-member-crew U.S.-flag ship was $65,000.

9. *Marine Engineering/Log* 85 (No. 4): 125–26.

10. Ernst and Whinney, *Cost Impact of U.S. Government Regulations on U.S.-Flag Ocean Carriers—Final Report* (Washington, D.C.: Ernst and Whinney, 1979), pp. 5–10, 11. The U.S. Coast Guard is the regulatory agency that determines minimum crew manning and crew technical qualifications, primarily for deck and engine room personnel.

11. Ibid., pp. 5–11, 12.

12. A shipping company's yearly contribution to social security for a second engineer in 1982 would be 6.7 percent of $31,800, or $2,130.60. The yearly contribution for unemployment insurance would be 3.4 percent of $6,000, or $204.

13. U.S., Department of Labor, Bureau of Labor Statistics, *Union Wages and Benefits: Building Trades July 3, 1978* (1979), p. 106.

14. U.S., Chamber of Commerce, Economic Policy Division, *Employee Benefits 1980* (1981), p. 30.

Chapter 16

1. Waterborne cargo movement in the United States in 1982 exceeded 2 billion tons, about half being in foreign trade. A 1978 Maritime Administration study, *What U.S. Ports Mean to the Economy*, determined that the port industry in 1970 was directly or indirectly responsible for gross sales of $28 billion within the economy, contributed $15 billion to the gross national product, and provided 1,046,800 jobs.

2. Marvin L. Fair and Ernest W. Williams, Jr., *Economics of Transportation* (New York: Harper and Brothers, 1959), pp. 57–59.

3. Under Section 15 of the Shipping Act of 1916, ports may form port associations and set charges. In this respect, they are exempt from the antitrust statutes.

4. Total transportation costs of ports in close proximity tend to be very close. In 1981 the total transportation charges for a container shipment from a common inland point to a foreign destination were Baltimore, $199.86; Norfolk, $199.47; Charleston, $199.65; Savannah, $199.65. Source: U.S., Congress, Senate, *Report on National Harbors Improvements and Maintenance Act of 1981*, 97th Cong., 1st sess., 1981, S. Rept. 97–301.

5. In the first half of the nineteenth century, the issue of whether, and to what extent, the federal government should participate in funding internal improvements was continuously debated in the Congress. Monies were suspended for harbor improvements between 1840 and 1844 and between 1845 and 1852. Water projects were not alone in this respect. Federal funds for building/maintaining the National Road linking Cumberland, Maryland, and the Ohio River were also suspended from time to time, and ultimately responsibility was turned over to the states.

6. U.S., Maritime Administration, *National Port Assessment 1980/1990*, p. 12.

7. Tangier, Safi, Agadir, Dakhia, Nouakchott, Dakar, Bissau, Freetown, Monrovia, Sassandra, Takoradi, Lome, Lagos, Port Harcourt, Douala, Port Gentil, Pointe Noire, Matadi, Cabinda, Luanda, Lobito, Walvis Bay, Port Nolloth, and Cape Town.

8. The only port area in the United States that can handle supertankers of the order of 200,000 dwt is Puget Sound.

9. U.S., Maritime Administration, *National Port Assessment 1980/1990*, pp. 16–17.

10. This is one of the most complex pieces of legislation ever passed by Congress. The act provides for consultation with "all interested Federal agencies . . . , any potentially affected state, and any interested members of the general public." Adjacent states have the right to veto a deep-water port. Provision is made for environmental and antitrust review. In addition, deep-water ports are considered common carriers and as such must be open to general use.

11. U.S., Maritime Administration, *National Port Assessment 1980/1990*, pp. 16–17.

12. Container ships are now being built in the 30,000-deadweight-ton class, and fully loaded they will draw over 40 feet of water.

13. U.S., General Accounting Office, *American Seaports—Changes Affecting Operations and Development*, p. 11.

14. Ibid.

15. Ibid.

16. Unless otherwise noted, statistics in this section of the chapter are all from U.S., Maritime Administration, *National Port Assessment 1980/1990*.

17. U.S., Maritime Administration, *The Effect of Federal Standards on U.S. Public Port Development*, pp. 1, 35.

18. U.S., Maritime Administration, *Planning Criteria for U.S. Port Development*, p. 4.

19. See note 4.

20. For general cargo commodities, the shipper is charged for (1) inland transportation, (2) wharfage at port (on East Coast vessel pays), (3) receipt and delivery cost at port, (4)

applicable seaway tolls on cargo, if any, and (5) ocean transportation. The ship operator pays for (1) dockage at port, (2) stevedoring at port, (3) pilots and tugs, and (4) vessel seaway tolls, if any. Source: U.S., Congress, S. Rept. 97–301.

21. U.S., Maritime Administration, *Planning Criteria for U.S. Port Development*, p. 5. Much of this port improvement opportunity would be found in the world's underdeveloped countries.

22. Ibid., p. 16.

23. National Academy of Sciences, Maritime Transportation Review Board, *Innovations in the Maritime Industry* (Washington, D.C.: National Academy of Sciences, 1979), appendix, p. 89.

24. U.S., General Accounting Office, *Longshoremen's and Harbor Workers' Compensation Act Needs Amending*, p. 1.

25. James A. Huston, *The Sinews of War*, p. 281.

26. Ibid., p. 343.

27. U.S., Department of the Army, Military Traffic Management Command, *An Analysis of Ports for National Defense U.S. Army Unit Deployment*, pp. 2–7. The Department of Defense has identified twenty-seven U.S. ports that would be used in any major deployment.

28. H.R. 4267 was combined with H.R. 4519. The latter was a bill mandating that a percentage share of U.S. bulk cargoes be reserved for U.S.-flag ships.

29. U.S., Congress, S. Rept. 97–301, pp. 28–33.

30. Another issue of concern to port authorities is the expeditious handling of the many federal laws and regulations that govern port development. Of particular importance is the time it takes to approve permits for specific projects, especially projects in which environmental concerns are raised.

31. In all cost recovery proposals, the federal government is responsible for a share of port costs in ports where naval (national defense) activities are located.

32. In a study by Donald L. Smith, "Southeastern Atlantic Ports under Crisis Demand," Master's thesis, Clemson University, 1980, Major Smith concluded that southeastern ports could increase their general cargo shipments from a present 14 million tons per year to 42 million using present port facilities. His figures indicate the potential of southeastern ports to handle additional shipments should capability be diminished at other East Coast ports and, by inference, make a strong national defense case for maintaining the viability of smaller and medium-sized ports.

Chapter 17

1. U.S., Maritime Administration, *Criteria and Requirements for Port Development and Operations*, p. 4.

2. A 40 × 8 × 8 foot dry van aluminum container weighs 6,200 lb; a 20 × 8 × 8 foot one weighs 3,200 lb. A 40 × 8 × 8 foot reinforced Fiberglas dry van container weighs 6,600 lb; a 20 × 8 × 8 foot one weighs 4,100 lb. A refrigerated aluminum 40 × 8 × 8 foot container weighs 9,900 lb.

3. A third reason inhibiting air shipments, particularly in containers, is the fact that to date no plane presently flying has been specifically designed for cargo. The loss of cube when rectangular containers are put into modified passenger-designed aircraft is considerable. The loss of cube earning capacity must be made up in higher freight rates.

4. The exception is ocean-air passenger movements. Cruise lines use joint air-ocean fares (routes) extensively, as does Cunard Lines with its *QE-2* during the scheduled summer sailings on the North Atlantic.

5. Association of American Railroads, *Yearbook of Railroad Facts,* pp. 9 and 43.

6. Ibid., p. 27.

7. An excellent discussion of land bridge movement is found in the work of David L. Gorman, "Innovations in the Maritime Industry: Land Bridge Services," in *Innovations in the Maritime Industry* (Washington, D.C.: National Academy of Sciences, 1979), appendix.

8. Donald F. Wood and James C. Johnson, *Contemporary Transportation* (Tulsa, Okla.: Petroleum Publishing Co., 1980), p. 129.

9. The main components of the inland waterway system are (1) the Mississippi River system and its tributaries (3,772 miles); (2) the Gulf intracoastal waterway—Florida to Texas (1,138 miles); (3) the Atlantic intracoastal waterway (1,129 miles); (4) the New York State Barge Canal (524 miles); (5) the Great Lakes—Duluth to Montreal (1,340 miles); and (6) the Columbia River, state of Washington (324 miles).

10. Rodney E. Eyster, "Federal Rules on Intermodal Ownership of Common Carriers," in *Forming Multimodal Transportation Companies: Barriers, Benefits and Problems*, ed. Clinton H. Whitehurst (Washington, D.C.: American Enterprise Institute, 1978), p. 13.

11. Ibid., p. 15.

12. William T. Coleman, Jr., *A Statement of National Transportation Policy* (Washington, D.C.: U.S. Government Printing Office, 1975), p. 21.

13. Whitehurst, *Forming Multimodal Transportation Companies*, p. 124.

14. "The Specter of Intermodal," *Forbes*, 12 April 1982, p. 42.

15. Robert C. Lieb, "Intermodal Ownership," p. 70. In January 1983 the ICC eliminated regulations that made it difficult for railroads to provide motor freight service. The commission defended its action by noting that rail affiliated motor carriers can now offer a full range of services rather than service limited to that provided as an auxiliary to rail service. The American Trucking Association indicated it will ask the ICC to reconsider its action or, failing that, go the U.S. Court of Appeals.

16. Whitehurst, *Forming Multimodal Transportation Companies*, p. 84.

17. Ibid., p. 85.

18. Emory R. Johnson, *Elements of Transportation*, p. 285. Johnson was professor of transportation and commerce at the University of Pennsylvania and was a member of the Isthmian Canal Commission, 1899–1904.

19. Clinton H. Whitehurst, Jr., "Multimodal Transportation Companies," p. 10.

20. "3 Railroads Given Approval by ICC to Merge in West," *The New York Times*, 13 September 1982, p. 32.

21. *Merchant Marine Act*, P.L. 835, 74th Cong., 1936, sect. 212(b).

22. Letter to Clinton H. Whitehurst, Jr., from Thomas H. Gunter, Jr., dean and professor of Marketing, School of Business, University of South Carolina at Spartanburg, 21 September 1982.

23. A strategic railroad corridor network (STRACNET) links 216 military and defense support installations with major U.S. cities and ports. This 32,000-mile rail network is the main-line U.S. rail system.

24. A transfer of some Military Sealift Command functions to the Military Traffic Management Command was proposed by DOD in September 1981. Secretary of Defense Caspar W. Weinberger in testifying before Congress estimated the transfer would save $2.6 million annually. Ultimately, it was planned to consolidate the two agencies. The transfers and consolidation were opposed by the navy and were not acted upon in the Ninety-seventh Congress.

25. Address by Major General H. R. Del Mar (Ret.) to the Tulsa Rotary Club, Tulsa, Oklahoma, 22 September 1982.

Chapter 18

1. Three Confederate raiders were built at Laird's shipyard in Liverpool, England: CSS *Alabama*, CSS *Florida*, and CSS *Georgia*. The commerce-raiding tactics of Raphael Semmes, captain of the *Alabama*, were acknowledged half a century later by the commander of the German Fleet in World War I when he said: "I reverence the name of Semmes. In my opinion he was the greatest admiral of the Nineteenth Century. At every conference with my admirals I counsel them to read and study closely Semmes' *Memoirs of Service Afloat*." Quoted by Edward Boykin, *Ghost Ship of the Confederacy* (New York: Funk and Wagnalls, 1957), p. 36.

2. Boykin, *Ghost Ship of the Confederacy*, pp. 389–90.

3. Rodney P. Carlisle, *Sovereignty for Sale*, p. 83. This book is highly recommended as a complete and authoritative history of flag-of-convenience shipping.

4. A not insignificant consideration for flag-of-convenience nations is ship registry revenue. In 1978, Liberian registry revenues totalled $11 million. See Rodney Carlisle, "Liberia's Flag of Convenience: Rough Water Ahead," *ORBIS: A Journal of World Affairs*, Winter 1981, p. 887.

5. Carlisle, *Sovereignty for Sale*, p. 54. Other nations registering vessels in Panama in the 1930s included Britain, Greece, France, Norway, the Netherlands, and Germany.

6. U.S., Maritime Administration, *Effective United States Control of Merchant Ships: A Statistical Analysis 1970* (Washington, D.C.: U.S. Government Printing Office, 1970), p. 9.

7. Ibid.

8. This estimate assumes that, in terms of numbers and tonnage, the relation in 1975 between Liberian, Panamanian, and Honduran U.S.-owned tonnage and other U.S.-owned foreign tonnage was the same in 1981. As of 1 January 1975 the number of U.S.-owned ships registered in Panama, Honduras, and Liberia was 455 out of a total of 706 U.S.-owned, foreign-flag vessels. The deadweight U.S.-owned tonnage of Panama, Liberia, and Honduras in 1975 was 36.5 million out of 52.7 million dwt of U.S. foreign-flag shipping.

9. U.S., Maritime Administration, *Foreign Flag Merchant Ships Owned by U.S. Parent Companies* (Washington, D.C.: U.S. Government Printing Office, 1975), p. 8.

10. Appendix E lists the parent companies of U.S.-owned, foreign-flag shipping.

11. For a brief history of the code and its implications for U.S. shipping policy, see Clinton H. Whitehurst, Jr., "Convention on a Code of Conduct for Liner Conferences."

12. See Exxon Corporation, Public Affairs Department, *Tankers and the Flags They Fly*.

13. Letter to chairman, House Merchant Marine and Fisheries Committee, from President Jimmy Carter, 20 July 1979.

14. Letters to Chairman C. L. Zablocki, House Committee on Foreign Affairs, dated 19 and 20 April 1982.

15. Specific criteria are listed in the section "Effective Control?" of this chapter.

16. U.S., Congress, House, Committee on Merchant Marine and Fisheries, *Strategic Implications of the Omnibus Maritime Bill, H.R. 6899: A White Paper*, p. 11.

17. A brief history of the effective control issue is found in the work of John G. Kilgour, "Effective United States Control?" *Journal of Maritime Law and Commerce* 8 (No. 3): 337.

18. Even if Liberia or Panama could take control of EUSC ships in a Liberian or Panamanian port, very few U.S.-owned, foreign-flag ships ever call at their home ports. The vast majority of Liberian-registered ships, for example, are launched, serve out their normal life, and are scrapped without ever putting into the Liberian port of Monrovia.

19. Norman Polmar, *Soviet Naval Challenge for the 1970s* (New York: Crane, Russak & Co., 1974), p. 78. The difficulty of exercising effective control of American-owned (or licensed) assets within the jurisdiction of another nation was amply demonstrated in 1982 when President Reagan attempted to impose an embargo against shipping to the Soviet Union American-licensed, high-technology products that were manufactured in Europe.

While the European governments sympathized with the American purpose of penalizing the Soviets for their support of military rule in Poland, their economic self-interest carried the day. There is no reason to expect other nations to behave otherwise in the case of American-owned, foreign-flag shipping.

20. Testimony (mimeographed) of John J. Bennet before the Merchant Marine Subcommittee of the House Committee on Merchant Marine and Fisheries, 5 June 1975, p. 11.

21. Testimony of Admiral Isaac C. Kidd, Jr., before the House Committee on Merchant Marine and Fisheries, 20 September 1978, quoted by Irwin M. Heine, *The U.S. Maritime Industry in the National Interest* (Washington, D.C.: Acropolis Books, 1980), p. 69.

22. A possibility that cannot be ignored is a limited or general naval war between the Soviet Union and the United States/NATO, a war fought entirely at sea, most probably having its origins in a perceived threat to Western imports of fuel/minerals.

23. In 1965 there were 492,000 production workers in the U.S. mining industry. Work-related deaths were estimated at 1,000, giving a rate of 1 death for every 492 persons employed. In August 1966 the *Baton Rouge Victory* was mined in the Saigon River. Seven crew members were lost, the only reported merchant marine casualties of the Vietnam War. In that year there were an average of 54,790 shipboard jobs in the American merchant marine. Sources: U.S., Maritime Administration, *Annual Report*, 1967; U.S., Bureau of Census, *Statistical Abstract of the U.S.*, 1966, tables 315, 343.

24. In the event of a war between the United States/NATO and the Soviet Union, Soviet submarine commanders will hardly respect the neutrality of a Liberian- or Panamanian-registered ship. They will be as adept at recognizing foreign-flag Western tonnage as they are in identifying the various types of ships in the U.S.- and NATO-registered fleets.

25. No responsible authority has yet suggested that any meaningful number of American crews could be assembled and transported to ports where U.S.-owned ships have been "abandoned" by their foreign crews.

26. Interview with Steven M. Moodie, Washington, D.C., representative of the Federation of American Controlled Shipping, 14 May 1982.

27. See Chapter 15 for an analysis and discussion of U.S. seagoing wages.

28. Of most concern to the foreign-flag shipowner is not the salary differential of two or three officers, but the possibility that once any American officers are employed on their vessels, maritime unions will use them as an excuse to insist on further hirings, e.g., Why only the chief engineer and not the first assistant, and if the first assistant, why not the second assistant?

Chapter 19

1. U.S., Maritime Administration, *Merchant Fleets of the World: September 1, 1939–December 31, 1951*, pp. 48, 49.

2. See Chapter 18 for a discussion of flag-of-convenience shipping.

3. U.S., Maritime Administration, *Annual Report*, FY 1981, table 11.

4. In 1982 the United States with one fourth the number of ships approximately equalled the deadweight tonnage of the Soviet merchant fleet.

5. U.S., Congress, Senate, Committee on the Judiciary, Subcommittee to Investigate the Administration of the Internal Security Act and Other Internal Security Laws, *Russia's Burgeoning Maritime Strength*, 88th Cong., 1st sess., 1963, p. 6.

6. Norman Polmar, *Soviet Naval Power: Challenge for the 1970s* (New York: Crane, Russak and Co., 1972), pp. 105–6. For a more detailed analysis on the integration of the Soviet merchant marine and navy, see U.S., Congress, House, Committee on Merchant Marine and Fisheries, *Hearings on Merchant Marine*, 95th Cong., 2d sess., 27 October 1977.

7. U.S., Congress, House, Committee on Armed Services, *Capability of U.S. Defense Industrial Base*, 96th Cong., 2d sess., p. 458.

8. U.S., Maritime Administration, *A Statistical Analysis of the World's Merchant Fleets*, p. vi.

9. U.S., Maritime Administration, *New Ship Construction 1980*, p. 1.

10. U.S., Maritime Administration, *Expansion of the Soviet Merchant Marine into the U.S. Maritime Trades*, p. 59.

11. U.S., Maritime Administration, *The Soviet Merchant Marine* (1967), p. 3.

12. U.S., Maritime Administration, *Expansion of Soviet Merchant Marine*, p. 27.

13. *Ocean Shipping Act*, P.L. 95-483, 94th Cong., 1978.

14. *Shipping Act Amendments*, P.L. 96-25, 94th Cong., 1979.

15. Richard Bell, "European Shipowners Demand Action against Trans-Siberian Box Line, *Container News*, April 1981, p. 12.

16. Quoted in "Soviet Merchant Fleet," *Defense Transportation Journal* 34 (No. 2): 6.

17. U.S., Maritime Administration, *Expansion of Soviet Merchant Marine*, pp. 6-8.

18. Ghana, India, Nigeria, Pakistan, Republic of China (Taiwan), Colombia, Indonesia, South Korea, Lebanon, Morocco, the Philippines, Saudi Arabia, and Israel.

19. M. J. Shah, "The Dispute Settlement Machinery in the Convention on a Code of Conduct for Liner Conferences," *Journal of Maritime Law and Commerce* 7 (No. 1): 131.

20. The Code of Conduct for Liner Conferences is discussed in Chapter 3.

21. U.S., Maritime Administration, *United States Oceanborne Foreign Trade Routes*, p. 2.

22. U.S., Maritime Administration, *Merchant Fleets of the World*, p. 48.

23. U.S., Maritime Administration, *Annual Report*, FY 1981, table 11.

24. Irwin M. Heine, "Red China: The New Maritime Superpower," *Seapower* 18 (No. 2): 14-18.

25. For a discussion on selling U.S.-built warships abroad see Norman Polmar, "The U.S. Navy: Selling (and Buying) Abroad," *U.S. Naval Institute Proceedings* 108 (May 1982): 213.

Chapter 20

1. The average foreign able seaman wage is $2,719 compared to an American wage cost of $3,301. If the same ratio was applied to an American second engineer wage cost, it would yield $2,719 × $8,212/$3,301 = $6,764.

2. The assumption made is that the difference in wages between the American merchant seaman and his foreign counterpart is an approximate measure of any justifiable difference between U.S. and foreign shoreside wages.

3. If Sea Shed (see note 6 to Chapter 8) can be easily adapted to bulk ships, then such U.S.-owned, foreign-flag ships become more militarily useful.

4. Alfred Thayer Mahan, *The Influence of Seapower upon History: 1660-1783* (New York: Sagamore Press, 1957), p. 75.

5. New and more stringent rules to prevent pollution from ships go into effect on 2 October 1983. Any oceangoing ship of 400 gross tons or more will be required to install a filtering system for the treatment of engine room bilge water. Records noting the time, location, and method of discharge of oily water must be maintained.

6. *Marine Engineering/Log*, September 1981, p. 37.

7. Norman Polmar, "The U.S. Navy: Selling (and Buying) Abroad," *U.S. Naval Institute Proceedings* 108 (May 1982): 214.

8. A proposal made by W. J. Amoss, president of Lykes Brothers Steamship Company and chairman of the National Maritime Council, would maintain a defense shipyard capability by providing CDS funds for merchant ship construction whenever naval construction and repair work fell off to a point where the U.S. shipyard mobilization base was threatened. Otherwise, U.S.-flag operators would have the option of building in lower cost foreign yards.

9. U.S., Maritime Commission, *Economic Survey of the American Merchant Marine*, p. 85.

Bibliography

Primary Sources

U.S. Maritime Administration

Documents include not only those cited specifically in footnotes or as secondary bibliographic sources, but also all reports and studies dating from the passage of the Merchant Marine Act of 1936 and the creation of the then U.S. Maritime Commission. Of invaluable assistance were the agency's annual reports, 1937–81. These materials are found in the Maritime Administration section of the main library of the Department of Transportation.

Maritime Administration officials have also been most cooperative in granting interviews, answering questions, and obtaining needed reports and must be rightly noted as primary research sources. Of particular assistance was the Director, Office of Ship Operations, and the Deputy Director, Office of Maritime Labor and Training.

For the serious student/researcher of maritime affairs, the Maritime Administration must be considered as the premier source of information.

U.S. General Accounting Office

Primary research sources are the various reports to the Congress on the merchant marine during the period 1972–82. These reports generally originated in the Logistics and Communications Division (now the Procurement, Logistics and Readiness Division) of the General Accounting Office (GAO) and the General Government Division (now the Community and Economic Development Division). GAO auditors in the Procurement, Logistics and Readiness Division were extremely knowledgeable and helpful in the writing of this book and are acknowledged as primary research sources.

Secondary Sources

Abrahamsson, Bernhard J. *International Ocean Shipping: Current Concepts and Principles*. Boulder, Colo.: Westview Press, 1980.

Ackley, Richard T. "The Soviet Merchant Fleet." *U.S. Naval Institute Proceedings* 102 (February 1976): 27.

Allen, Thomas B. "Rebuilding the Infrastructure." *Seapower* 25 (July 1982): 32.

Association of American Railroads. *Year Book of Railroad Facts*. Washington, D.C.: Association of American Railroads, 1982.

Baker, Warren P. "Next: A Resource War." *Seapower* 23 (October 1980): 55.

Barnett, Frank R. "Conflict Chess in a Global Mode." Paper read for the Pepperdine University Great Issues Series. January 1980.

Bennathan, Esra, and Walters, A. A. *Port Pricing and Investment Policy for Developing Countries*. New York: Oxford University Press, 1979.

Bennett, James T., and Williams, Walter E. *Strategic Minerals: The Economic Impact of Supply Disruptions*. Washington, D.C.: The Heritage Foundation, 1981.

Bess, David. "An Act of Faith and Hope Revisited." *U.S. Naval Institute Proceedings* 107 (October 1981): 70.

Bess, David, and Farris, Martin T. "U.S. Maritime Policy: A Time for Reassessment." *Transportation Journal* 21 (Summer 1982): 4.

Blenkey, Nicholas. "Living with the Law." *Marine Engineering/Log* 86 (February 1981): 34.

Caplan, Bennett, and Ryan, Joseph E. "A Critique of Flags of Convenience." *U.S. Naval Institute Proceedings* 107 (October 1981): 78.

Carlisle, Rodney P. *Sovereignty for Sale*. Annapolis, Md.: Naval Institute Press, 1981.

Clark, J. W. "U.S. Regulation of Ocean Commerce—Help or Hindrance." *Defense Transportation Journal* 34 (June 1978): 40.

Council of American-Flag Ship Operators. *The U.S. Merchant Marine and Our National Security*. Washington, D.C.: Council of American-Flag Ship Operators, 1981.

Council on Economics and National Security. *The Resource War and the U.S. Business Community: The Case for a Council on Economics and National Security*. Washington, D.C.: Council on Economics and National Security, October 1980.

Cunningham, James H. "Third World Seeks Control of World Merchant Shipping." *U.S. Naval Institute Proceedings* 107 (October 1981): 131.

Del Mar, H. R. "PBEIST—Making Sure Transportation Systems Work in Wartime." *Defense Transportation Journal* 34 (April 1978): 12.

Exxon Corporation, Public Affairs Department. *Tankers and the Flags They Fly*. New York: Exxon Corporation, 1979.

Fingleton, Eamonn. "The Specter of Intermodal." *Forbes*, 12 April 1982, p. 42.

Heine, Irwin M. *The U.S. Maritime Industry: In the National Interest*. Washington, D.C.: National Maritime Council, 1980.

Hiltzheimer, Charles I. "Entering the Intermodal Age." *Defense Transportation Journal* 34 (June 1978): 18.

Hull, William J., and Hull, Robert W. *The Origin and Development of the Waterway Policy of the United States*. Washington, D.C.: National Waterways Conference, 1967.

Huston, James A. *The Sinews of War: Army Logistics 1775–1953*. Washington, D.C.: U.S. Army, Office of Chief of Military History, 1966.

Hutchins, John G. B. *The American Maritime Industries and Public Policy, 1878–1914: An Economic History*. Cambridge, Mass.: Harvard University Press, 1941.

Jantscher, Gerald R. *Bread upon the Waters: Federal Aids to the Maritime Industries*. Washington, D.C.: The Brookings Institution, 1975.

Jenkins, J. T. *A History of the Whale Fisheries*. Port Washington, N.Y.: Kennikat Press, 1971.

Johnson, Emory R. *Elements of Transportation*. New York: D. Appleton and Co., 1909.

Kendall, Lane C. *The Business of Shipping*. 3rd ed. Centreville, Md.: Cornell Maritime Press, 1979.

Lieb, Robert C. "Intermodal Ownership: The Perspective of Railroad Chief Executives." *Transportation Journal* 21 (Spring 1982): 70.

Marcus, Henry S.; Short, James E.; Kuypers, James E.; Kuypers, John C.; and Roberts, Paul O. *Federal Port Policy in the United States*. Cambridge, Mass.: MIT Press, 1976.

McDowell, Carl E., and Gibbs, Helen M. *Ocean Transportation*. New York: McGraw-Hill, 1954.

Middendorf, William J., II. "Strategy for the Coming Resource War." An address to the Leeds Castle Conference, Maidstone, Kent, England. 26 July 1980.

Miller, James Arnold; Fine, Daniel L.; and McMichael, R. Daniel, eds. *The Resource War in 3-D—Dependency, Diplomacy, Defense*. Pittsburgh, Pa.: World Affairs Council of Pittsburgh, 1980.

Morison, Samuel E. *The Maritime History of Massachusetts: 1783–1860*. Boston: Houghton Mifflin, 1921.

Mott, William C. *Strategic Minerals: A Resource Crisis*. Washington, D.C.: Council on Economics and National Security, 1981.

Nagorski, Boudan. *Port Problems in Developing Countries*. Tokyo, Japan: International Association of Ports and Harbors, 1972.

National Academy of Sciences. *Innovations in the Maritime Industry*. Washington, D.C.: National Academy of Sciences, 1979.

———. *Innovations in the Maritime Industry*. Washington, D.C.: National Academy of Sciences, 1979, appendix.

———. *The Impact of Overseas Troop Reductions on the U.S.-Flag Merchant Marine*. Washington, D.C.: National Academy of Sciences, 1980.

———. *The Sealift Readiness Program: The Commercial Implications of a Military Contingency Call-up*. Washington, D.C.: National Academy of Sciences, June 1975.

Naval Education and Training Command. *Naval Science for the Merchant Marine Officer*. Washington, D.C.: Naval Education and Training Program Development Center, 1981.

Nersesian, Roy L. *Ships and Shipping: A Comprehensive Guide.* Tulsa, Okla.: Penn Well Publishing Co., 1981.

Ovechka, Greg. "Canal's Container Traffic Shifts; Panama's Loss; U.S.'s Gain." *Marine Engineering/Log* 86 (June 1981): 16.

———. "The Omnibus Maritime Bill: Maximum Flexibility to Shipbuilders and Ship Owners." *Marine Engineering/Log* 85 (January 1980): 75.

Prina, Edgar L. "Soviet Merchant Marine Takes a Great Leap Forward." *Seapower* 20 (December 1977): 9.

Robbotti, Frances Diane. *Whaling and Old Salem.* New York: Fountainhead Publishers, 1962.

Sansone, Wallace T. "Domestic Shipping and American Maritime Policy." *U.S. Naval Institute Proceedings* 100 (May 1974): 40.

Schmeltzer, Edward, and Weiner, George J. "Liner Shipping in the 1980's: Competitive Patterns and Legislative Initiatives in the 96th Congress. *Journal of Maritime Law and Commerce* 12 (1980): 25.

Smith, Donald L. "Southeastern Atlantic Ports under Crisis Demand." Master's thesis, Clemson University, 1980.

Taylor, Maxwell; Norman, Lloyd; and Canby, Steven L. "Priorities in the U.S. Defense Policy." *Foreign Policy and Defense Review* 1 (1979): 2.

Thomas, Vincent C., Jr. "Navies for Sale." *Seapower* 26 (January 1983): 40.

Thoyer, Michael E. "Legal Aspects of Current Financing Techniques under Title XI of the Merchant Marine Act, 1936, as Amended." *Journal of Maritime Law and Commerce* 12 (1981): 197.

Transportation Institute. *Analysis of the Direct Impact of the Merchant Marine on National Security.* Washington, D.C.: Transportation Institute, May 1976.

"U.S. and World Shipping." *Marine Engineering/Log* 87 (June 1982): 85.

United States, Congress, House, Committee on Armed Services. *Capability of U.S. Defense Industrial Base.* 96th Cong., 2d sess., 1980.

United States, Congress, House, Committee on the Interior and Insular Affairs, Subcommittee on Mines and Mining. *Hearings on Global Mineral Resources.* 96th Cong., 1st sess., 1980.

United States, Congress, House, Committee on Merchant Marine and Fisheries. *Omnibus Maritime Regulatory Reform, Revitalization and Reorganization Act of 1979, H.R. 4769.* 96th Cong., 1979.

———. *Providing an Adequate and Well-Balanced Merchant Fleet.* 95th Cong., 1978, H. Rept. 95-1524.

———. *Strategic Implications of the Omnibus Maritime Bill, H.R. 6899: A White Paper.* 96th Cong., 2d sess., 1980.

United States, Congress, House, Committee on Merchant Marine and Fisheries, Subcommittee on the Merchant Marine. *Hearings on UN Conference on Trade and Development (UNCTAD) Oversight.* 96th Cong., 1979.

United States, Congress, Senate, Committee on Commerce, Science and Transportation. *Ocean Shipping Act of 1980.* 96th Cong., 1980, S. Rept. 96-956.

United States, Department of the Army, Military Traffic Management Command. *An Analysis of Ports for National Defense U.S. Army Unit Deployments.* June 1978.

United States, Department of Commerce, Maritime Administration. *Bulk Carriers in the World Fleet*. January 1981.

————. *Civilian Seafaring Manpower Requirements in Peace and War, 1978–1984*. November 1978.

————. *The Competitive Position of Domestic Shipping in the U.S. Transportation Market*. July 1980.

————. *Criteria and Requirements for Port Development and Operation*. September 1977.

————. *Current Trends in Port Pricing*. August 1978.

————. *Domestic Ocean Trade Area—Final Report*. February 1974.

————. *Domestic Waterborne Trade of the United States, 1975–1979*. December 1981.

————. *The Effect of Federal Standards on U.S. Public Port Development*. April 1978.

————. *Expansion of the Soviet Merchant Marine into the U.S. Maritime Trades*. August 1977.

————. *Maritime Subsidies*. January 1981.

————. *Merchant Fleets of the World: September 1, 1939–December 31, 1951*. November 1952.

————. *National Port Assessment 1980/1990*. June 1980.

————. *Ocean Trade Study Virgin Islands to U.S. Mainland*. April 1974.

————. *Planning Criteria for U.S. Port Development*. December 1977.

————. *Public Port Financing in the United States*. June 1974.

————. *Seafaring Guide and Directory of Labor Management Affiliations*. 1980.

————. *A Statistical Analysis of the World's Merchant Fleets*. 31 December 1979.

————. *United States Oceanborne Foreign Trade Routes*. August 1981.

————. *United States Port Development Expenditure Survey*. January 1980.

————. *What U.S. Ports Mean to the Economy*. September 1978.

United States, Department of the Navy, Military Sealift Command. *Ship Register*. January 1982.

————. *Ship Register*. July 1982.

United States, Department of Transportation. *An Analysis of Financing Public Ports*. Prepared by Theresa Hughes and Associates, September 1981.

————. *A Prospectus for Change in the Freight Railroad Industry*. October 1978.

United States, Department of Transportation, Coast Guard. *Rules and Regulations for Cargo and Miscellaneous Vessels*. September 1977.

United States, Department of Transportation, Maritime Administration. *Effective U.S. Control (EUSC) as of June 30, 1981*. November 1981.

————. *Estimated Vessel Operating Expenses*. 1981.

————. *Foreign Flag Merchant Ships Owned by U.S. Parent Companies as of January 1, 1981*. November 1981.

————. *New Ship Construction 1980*. 1981.

————. *Relative Costs of Shipbuilding*. 1981.

United States, General Accounting Office, *American Seaports—Changes Affecting Operations and Development*. 1979.

————. *Cargo Preference Programs for Government-Financed Ocean Shipments Could Be Improved*. 1978.

——. *Changes in Federal Maritime Regulation Can Increase Efficiency and Reduce Costs in the Ocean Liner Shipping Industry.* 1982.

——. *Cost of Cargo Preference.* 1977.

——. *Essential Management Functions at the Federal Maritime Commission Are Not Being Performed.* 1980.

——. *The Federal Role in Merchant Marine Officer Education.* 1977.

——. *Longshoremen's and Harbor Workers' Compensation Act Needs Amending.* 1982.

——. *The Maritime Administration and the National Maritime Council—Was Their Relationship Appropriate?* 1979.

——. *Maritime Subsidy Requirements Hinder U.S.-Flag Operators' Competitive Position.* 1981.

——. *Transportation: Evolving Issues for Analysis.* 1982.

United States, Interstate Commerce Commission. *Rail Merger Study.* April 1977.

United States, Maritime Commission. *Economic Survey of the American Merchant Marine.* November 1937.

United States, Office of Management and Budget. *U.S. Maritime Programs and Policy.* 1982.

Whitehurst, Clinton H., Jr. "Convention on a Code of Conduct for Liner Conferences." *Marine Policy Reports* 3 (1980): 1.

——. *The Defense Transportation System: Competitor or Complement to the Private Sector?* Washington, D.C.: American Enterprise Institute for Public Policy Research, 1976.

——. "Multimodal Transportation Companies: The Case for Rail-Ocean Shipping Combinations." *Defense Transportation Journal* 53 (June 1979): 5.

——. "The Multimodal Transportation Company: An Idea Whose Time Has Come?" *Review of Industrial Management and Textile Science* 19 (Spring 1980): 9.

Whitehurst, Clinton H., Jr., ed. *Forming Multimodal Transportation Companies: Barriers, Benefits and Problems.* Washington, D.C.: American Enterprise Institute for Public Policy Research, 1978.

World Affairs Council of Pittsburgh. *Seapower: The Nation's Lifeline Today and Tomorrow.* Pittsburgh, Pa.: World Affairs Council of Pittsburgh, 1981.

Glossary

Bareboat Charter   An arrangement under which a shipper contracts for the exclusive use of a vessel for a defined (usually long) period of time. The contractee is responsible for crewing, supplying, and servicing the vessel during the contract period.

Break-Bulk Cargo   Various kinds of general cargo, ranging from pallet-size lots of canned fruits to bales of cotton to outsize types of cargo such as earth-moving machinery and diesel locomotives.

Break-Bulk Ship   A ship designed to carry break-bulk cargo. The cargo is loaded through four to six hatches. The ship's booms (cargo gear) are capable of loading or unloading the ship without using shoreside facilities.

Capital Construction Fund (CCF)   A government-administered account into which ship operator earnings can be deposited on a tax-deferred basis for the ultimate purpose of building or acquiring U.S.-flag, U.S.-built, vessels.

Construction, Alteration, and Repair (CAR)   The types of shipyard work performed on naval vessels.

Construction Differential Subsidy (CDS)   A subsidy paid to U.S. shipyards by the federal government. The amount of the subsidy equals the difference in dollar cost between building a vessel in the United States and building it overseas. Payments historically have had an upper limit of 50 percent, i.e., the government paid 50 percent of the U.S. shipyard price.

Contingency   A military term usually denoting a quick-breaking situation in which national interests are threatened but not so threatened that a national mobilization is declared.

Cross Trade   A trade route between two foreign countries served by a vessel flying the flag of a third country.

C-Type Ship   A Maritime Administration–designed break-bulk vessel. The C-1 is a ship of about 4,500 gross tons; the C-2 about 8,200 gross tons; the C-3 about 9,200 gross tons; and the C-4 about 11,500 gross tons.

Deadweight Tons (dwt)   A vessel's carrying capacity in tons of 2,240 pounds each.

Effective U.S. Control (Shipping) (EUSC)   U.S.-owned ships registered under the flags of Liberia, Honduras, and Panama.

Flag-of-Convenience Shipping   Shipping owned by nationals of one country that flies the flag of another. U.S.-owned, foreign-flag shipping is registered primarily, but not only, under the flags of Liberia, Honduras, and Panama.

Gross Tons (GT)   The internal cubic capacity of a vessel's cargo space expressed in tons of 100 cubic feet each.

Joint Maritime Congress (JMC)   A research and promotional organization sponsored by the maritime industry and maritime unions and located in Washington, D.C.

Jones Act   Legislation that prohibits foreign-flag shipping from engaging in U.S. domestic ocean trades. Specifically, Section 27 of the Merchant Marine Act of 1920.

Land Bridge   A container freight movement originating in Europe destined for the Far East (or vice-versa) in which the container is unloaded at a U.S. port, transits the United States by rail, and is loaded on a ship for the final leg of the movement. Essentially, the continental United States is a "bridge" between the Atlantic and Pacific oceans.

Lesser Developed Countries (LDC)   Third World or underdeveloped nations.

Lighter aboard Ship (LASH)   A general cargo vessel that carries barges loaded with cargo. Barges are floated to and from the ship and loaded or unloaded by an elevator crane on the ship's stern.

Liquid Natural Gas Carrier (LNG)   A vessel specifically designed to transport liquid natural gas.

Logistics over the Shore (LOTS)   A military term used to describe the supply and resupply of military forces from ships in areas where there are no pier/dock facilities.

Long Range Navigation (LORAN)   An electronic navigation system by which a ship's position is fixed by use of signals transmitted from shore stations. LORAN A was the initial system; LORAN C is the most advanced.

Microbridge   A container freight movement originating in (or destined for) an inland U.S. location. The container moves from the inland point by rail to a seaport where it is loaded aboard ship for the final leg of its journey to either Europe or the Far East.

Minibridge   A container freight movement originating in Europe and destined for a U.S. West Coast city or originating in the Far East and destined for a U.S. East Coast city. The container is unloaded at a U.S. port and crosses the United States by rail to its final destination.

National Defense Feature (NDF)   An addition to a merchant vessel that enhances its usefulness as a naval or military auxiliary, e.g., radio equipment capable of communicating with naval ships.

Operating Differential Subsidy (ODS)   A subsidy paid by the federal government to U.S.-flag operators meeting specific criteria. The amount of the subsidy equals the difference between operating a vessel under the U.S. flag and operating it under competing foreign flags on a particular trade route. ODS is paid in a number of categories; wages account for the largest amount.

Organization for Economic Cooperation and Development (OECD)   An organization of economically (industrialized) Western nations.

Rapid Deployment Force (RDF)   Ships loaded with military supplies and located at likely world trouble spots, e.g., ships, including loaded tankers and general cargo ships, based at Diego Garcia in the Indian Ocean. Also, government-owned or -controlled cargo ships that are kept in a high state of readiness in the United States and that could be rapidly deployed worldwide if the need arose.

Ready Reserve Force (RRF)   A part of the National Defense Reserve Fleet that can be broken out and on berth in five to ten days.

Roll-on/Roll-Off (RO/RO)   A type of general cargo vessel that primarily carries highway trailers/trucks. Vehicles drive on and off ship.

Seabee   A type of LASH vessel developed by Lykes Brothers' Steamship Company. Barges carried on Seabees are somewhat larger than those carried on typical LASH vessels.

Sealift Readiness Program (SRP)   A program under which private U.S.-flag shipping companies that wish to bid on Department of Defense shipments pledge a part of their fleet and support equipment to DOD for use in a nonmobilization emergency.

Sea Shed   A cargo module that fits into a container ship's cell guides. Essentially, the module converts a container ship into a break-bulk ship. It can also be used on bulk carriers.

SL-7   A high-speed (33 knot), steam-turbine-powered container ship built for Sea-Land Services in the early 1970s.

Strategic Railroad Corridor Network (STRACNET)   A 32,000-mile rail network linking 216 military and defense support installations with major U.S. cities and ports.

T-AKRX   A Military Sealift Command program to convert eight former Sea-Land Service SL-7 (33 knot) container ships to fast logistic support vessels. Ships are to be converted to a RO/RO configuration.

T-AKX   A maritime prepositioned ship program. Under this Military

Sealift Command program, loaded cargo vessels and tankers are geo-graphically prepositioned at likely world trouble spots.

Twenty-Foot Container Equivalent Unit (TEU)   A standard measure of container ship capacity. For example, a ship that carried ten 40-foot containers and eight 20-foot containers would have a 28-TEU carrying capacity.

Ultra Large Crude Carrier (ULCC)   A tanker ranging in size from 250,000 to 500,000 deadweight tons.

Underway Replenishment (UNREP)   At sea replenishment (with stores, fuel, ammunition, etc.) of combatant naval vessels by noncom-batant naval or civilian-manned ships.

Very Large Bulk Carrier (VLBC)   A vessel ranging in size from 100,000 to 200,000 deadweight tons.

Very Large Crude Carrier (VLCC)   A tanker ranging in size from 100,000 to 250,000 deadweight tons.

Index